Cracking the
AP Computer Science
A & AB Exams

The Princeton Review

Cracking the
AP Computer Science
A & AB Exams

Mehran Habibi, Michael Fritz, and Robb Cutler

2006–2007 Edition

Random House, Inc.
New York

www.PrincetonReview.com

The Princeton Review, Inc.
2315 Broadway
New York, NY 10024
E-mail: booksupport@review.com

ISBN-10: 0-375-76528-X
ISBN-13: 978-0-375-76528-5
ISSN: 1546-9069

AP and Advanced Placement are registered trademarks of the College Entrance Examination Board, which was not involved in the production of, and does not endorse, this book.

The source code for the AP® Computer Science Marine Biology Simulation, which appears on pages 257–318 of this book and is quoted throughout this book, is copyright © 2002 College Entrance Examination Board (www.collegeboard.com). Individual author information and version numbers are printed with relevant portions of the source code.

The source code for the simulation is free software; you can redistribute it and/or modify it under the terms of the GNU General Public License, which is reprinted in the Appendix to this book.

The source code for the simulation is distributed in the hope that it will be useful, but WITHOUT ANY WARRANTY; without even the implied warranty of MERCHANTABILITY or FITNESS FOR A PARTICULAR PURPOSE. See the GNU General Public License for more details.

Editor: Ruth Mills
Production Editor: Katie O'Neill
Production Coordinator: Jennifer Arias

Manufactured in the United States of America.

9 8 7 6 5 4 3 2 1

2006–2007 Edition

ACKNOWLEDGMENTS

MEHRAN HABIBI

I'd like to thank my co-author Michael Fritz and the staff of The Princeton Review. This book is dedicated to my wife, Dr. Angela Young.

MICHAEL FRITZ

Thank you to my co-authors and the staff of the Princeton Review for all their hard work. Special thanks and my love to my family for their support.

ROBB CUTLER

A big thank you to David Gillespie of Hawken School and Bekki George of James E. Taylor High School for their thoughtful and insightful comments on the practice tests and exam tips, to Ellen and Tim for their editorial prowess, and especially to my wife and best friend, Heather Blair and my children Elizabeth, Andrew, David, Ethan, and Katharine for their love, encouragement, support, and, most of all, for putting up with me.

Additional thanks go to Monty Armstrong, Katie O'Neill, Stephen White, Jennifer Arias, Jeff Rubinstein, Tom Russell, Patricia Dublin, and Leanne Coupe.

CONTENTS

Introduction

WHAT IS THE PRINCETON REVIEW?

The Princeton Review is an international test-preparation company with branches in all the major U.S. cities and many abroad. In 1981, John Katzman started teaching an SAT course in his parents' living room. Within five years, The Princeton Review had become the largest SAT coaching program in the country.

The Princeton Review's phenomenal success in improving students' scores on standardized tests was (and continues to be) the result of a simple, innovative, and radically effective approach: Study the test, not what the test *claims* to test. This approach has led to the development of techniques for taking standardized tests based on the principles the test-writers themselves use to write the tests.

The Princeton Review has found that its methods work not only for cracking the SAT, but also for any standardized test. We've already successfully applied our system to the GMAT, LSAT, MCAT, and GRE, just to name a few. Although in some ways the AP Computer Science exams are very different from the exams mentioned above, a standardized test is still a standardized test. This book uses our time-tested principle: Crack the system based on how the test is written.

We offer courses, books, and online services on an enormous variety of education and career-related topics. If you're interested, check out our website at http://www.PrincetonReview.com.

1

About the AP Computer Science A and AB Exams

WHAT IS THE ADVANCED PLACEMENT PROGRAM?

The Advanced Placement (AP) program allows high school students to take college-level courses and get college course credit. Approximately 15,000 schools worldwide offer AP courses to their students. In 2004, almost two million AP exams were taken by students worldwide. There are currently 34 different AP courses in 19 subject areas and plans to develop more.

The AP program is coordinated by an organization called The College Board. For each AP subject, The College Board appoints a Test Development Committee consisting of six teachers of the subject, three from colleges or universities and three from high schools. The Test Development Committee is responsible for developing the curriculum for the AP course and writing the AP exams. Once the exam is developed, The College Board hands it over to Educational Testing Services (ETS), which prints and administers it. ETS also plays a role in developing the exam. ETS is the same organization that produces and administers the SAT and many other admissions exams.

Athough most students who take the AP Computer Science exam take an AP-level course in high school beforehand, this is not required. You are allowed to register for and take the exam without having taken a class in high school that covers the material on the exam.

The AP exams are given each May. AP grades are reported to students, their schools, and their designated colleges in July.

SHOULD I TAKE AP CLASSES? SHOULD I TAKE AP EXAMS?

There's an obvious downside to taking AP classes: They're more difficult than regular classes. Compared with regular classes, AP classes mean more detailed lectures, more homework, more research papers, more tests, and, possibly, a lower grade. So why take an AP course?

First, if you're looking to go to college, you want as many AP courses on your transcript as you can handle. These classes indicate to your prospective schools that you're serious about studying. Many admissions offices will give your AP grade a one-level "bump": that is, they will consider your "C" a "B." (That's how some high school students end up with GPAs above 4.0: they get almost all As, including their AP courses.) College admissions officers are more favorably disposed to students who take AP courses.

Second, AP courses help you develop skills you will need in college. A good AP teacher will assign research papers and essay tests; require you to study primary source material; and lecture in such a way that you have to take good notes to pass the course. All of these aspects of AP courses will help prepare you for your college courses.

Third, AP courses are supposed to prepare you for AP exams, which can be quite helpful in getting your college degree. Many schools award college credit for good grades on the AP. Because college credits cost money, success on AP exams could save you or your parents a lot of money. Some schools will admit you as a sophomore if you get high enough marks on three (or in some schools more) AP exams. In a best-case scenario, then, the APs can help you skip a year of college (and save a year's tuition). It is important to know that it is the individual college, and not The College Board, that decides whether to grant advanced placement for AP scores. The schools themselves also determine what is considered a satisfactory grade. (AP exams are graded on a scale of 1–5, with 5 being the highest possible score.) Before committing to an AP exam, contact your prospective schools and find out their AP policies. You could also check the school's course catalog: Almost all schools print their AP policies in their catalogs, which are often available at local libraries. Ask the reference librarian for assistance.

Taking AP tests can help your college application in other ways as well. The College Board confers a number of awards to students who excel on three or more AP exams. The **AP Scholar Awards** are given to students who exceed an average grade of 3 on three or more exams; more prestigious awards are given to students who take more tests and receive higher grades. These awards are noted on the score reports that are sent to your prospective colleges.

So remember: *You do not have to take an AP course* to take an AP exam. If you feel that you are up to speed in a subject, you should take the AP exam regardless of the course you took.

HOW YOUR EXAM RESULTS ARE USED BY COLLEGES

The AP grade scale ranges from 1 (lowest) to 5 (highest). Following is the meaning of each grade according to The College Board:

Grade	Meaning
5	Extremely well qualified
4	Well qualified
3	Qualified
2	Possibly qualified
1	No recommendation

Although The College Board is responsible for writing and grading the exam, each individual college and university determines how it will use your grade. Generally, schools will give college credit for scores of 4 and 5 and will not give college credit for scores of 1 and 2. Scores of 3 are on the border, and whether or not you receive credit depends on the school. Check with the schools to which you are applying to find out how they use exam results. The school's catalog is a good place to start.

REGISTERING FOR THE EXAM

The AP Coordinator for your school can assist you in registering for the exam. The AP Coordinator is usually a teacher or counselor at your school. Your guidance counselor should be able to direct you to the appropriate person.

As of May 2005, the registration fee for AP Exams was $82 per exam. The College Board also offers a fee-reduction program for qualifying students who can demonstrate financial need. Please visit The College Board's website (http://www.collegeboard.com) or speak with your AP Coordinator for more information.

STUDENTS WITH DISABILITIES

The College Board offers a variety of accommodations for students with disabilities: tests are available in Braille, in enlarged text, and on audiocassette. Students must submit an eligibility form to request these services or for more time to take the exam. Contact your AP Coordinator well in advance of the actual test to make any necessary arrangements.

WHAT TO BRING TO THE EXAM

- Your secondary-school code number.
- A watch to pace yourself. On each exam, there are 75 minutes allotted for 40 multiple-choice questions and 105 minutes allotted for 4 free-response questions.
- One black or dark blue ballpoint pen for signing your name on the exam.

- Several number 2 pencils with erasers.
- Optional: Your social security number *if* you want it used for identification and printed on your AP grade reports.

WHAT NOT TO BRING

- Textbooks, notebooks, a dictionary, or a pocket encyclopedia. In short, no books!
- A laptop computer.
- A camera (to prevent you from photographing the exam and giving the pictures to someone writing a test prep book, like us).
- A portable stereo or radio.

CHEATERS NEVER PROSPER

This book describes a number of desirable strategies for test taking; cheating is not one of them. Years of experience have led to a series of effective policies against cheating on the exam. Don't bother trying anything that's against the rules. You'll always lose.

HOW TO GET MORE INFORMATION

Additional information on AP policies and the AP Computer Science exam is available on The College Board's website at http://www.collegeboard.com or by contacting:

The AP Program
PO Box 6671
Princeton, NJ 08541-6671
609-771-7300 or toll free in the United States and Canada 877-274-6474
Fax: 609-530-0482
TTY: 609-882-4118
E-mail: apexams@info.collegeboard.com

WHAT IS COVERED ON THE AP COMPUTER SCIENCE A AND AB EXAMS? WHAT'S THE DIFFERENCE?

Although the programming language for the exam is Java™, the exam is meant to test programming and computer concepts, not just the Java language. Many of the topics that are covered in a typical first-year programming course are not covered on the exam. For example, you will not need to know how to build a graphical user interface or read data from a file.

Among the topics that are emphasized on the exam are: loops, object-oriented design and programming, arrays and collection classes, algorithms, and fundamental Java library classes such as String and Math. In addition, the AB exam places a strong emphasis on data structures and more advanced algorithms.

COMPUTER SCIENCE A VS. COMPUTER SCIENCE AB

The material covered on the A version of the exam is meant to be equivalent to that covered in a one-semester introductory college course in programming. The AB exam is meant to be equivalent to a full-year course. All of the topics that are covered on the A exam are also covered on the AB exam. In addition, the AB exam covers a few more advanced topics, most notably: Big-Oh notation, advanced data structures, collection classes, and algorithms. Object-oriented design and programming are covered on both exams, though the AB exam covers object-oriented concepts in more depth. On the A exam, you may need to modify existing classes. On the AB exam, you will need to design classes based on criteria given on the exam.

THE MARINE BIOLOGY SIMULATION CASE STUDY

A case study is one way to apply the principles learned throughout the AP Computer Science course to a real-world programming problem. The College Board has prepared the Marine Biology Simulation (MBS) as one example of such a case study. The MBS attempts to model fish interacting in a marine environment. The problem statement, Java source code, documentation, and a narrative that describes the case study and explains the design decisions made throughout are all part of the case study.

Approximately 20 percent of the AP Computer Science exam (at least 5 out of 40 multiple-choice questions and 1 out of 4 free-response questions) requires knowledge of the Marine Biology Simulation Case Study. Questions on the exam will involve analysis of the code, explanation of design decisions, understanding the results of running the program, developing test cases, and making modifications and enhancements to the source code.

If you have taken a high school AP Computer Science course, you most likely used the case study in your class. If you are not familiar with the case study, The College Board provides all of the related files on their website at http://apcentral.collegeboard.com. A useful overview of the MBS is provided in Chapter 12.

THE STRUCTURE OF THE EXAM

Both the A and AB version of the AP Computer Science Exam consist of 40 multiple-choice questions and 4 free-response questions. You are given 3 hours to complete the exam: 1 hour and 15 minutes for the multiple-choice section and 1 hour and 45 minutes for the free-response section. You will be given a 5- to 10-minute break between the multiple-choice and free-response section. If you finish with the multiple-choice question section early, you will NOT be allowed to start the free-response section, nor will you be able to use any of the time allotted for the free-response section to work on the multiple-choice section.

MULTIPLE-CHOICE QUESTIONS

The exam contains 40 multiple-choice questions. Each question has 5 answer choices to choose from. For each question you get right, you are given 1 raw point. For each question you get wrong, you lose 1/4 a point.

How To Score Your Best

To score your best on the multiple-choice portion of this test, you need to remember these three rules:

1. There is no such thing as a "guessing penalty"; rather, there is a guessing *reward*.

2. Finishing is not the goal; *accuracy* is.

3. Four out of every five answer choices you read are *wrong*.

Guessing Reward

Think about it. There are 5 answer choices for each multiple-choice question. If you were to select (C) as your answer to every question in the section, how many questions would you get right? 1/5 of them or 8 questions. That gives you 8 points. You would lose 1/4 of a point for each of the remaining 32 questions. 1/4 of 32 is 8, so you would lose 8 points. In other words, if you were to randomly guess throughout the entire test, you would end up at zero—8 points earned, 8 points lost. Doesn't sound like much of a penalty, does it?

Now let's say that instead of randomly guessing, you were able to eliminate one wrong answer for each question on the entire multiple-choice section. That would mean you would be choosing from among 4 answer choices each time, so random odds say you would get 1/4 of the questions correct. That's 10 questions or points. If you got the remaining 30 questions wrong and lost 1/4 of a point for each, you would lose 7.5 points, leaving you with a gain of 2.5 points.

Now 2.5 points is not going to get you to your ultimate goal of a grade 3 or above, but you won't be randomly guessing on the entire test. The point is that there really is no guessing penalty on the exam. If you guess randomly on the entire test, you lose nothing. If you get rid of even one wrong answer on each question throughout the test, you begin to gain points.

So does this mean you should guess randomly? Of course not. What it does mean is that if you can get rid of even one answer choice, you should take a guess. *Be aggressive!*

Order of Difficulty

There is a rough order of difficulty to the multiple-choice portion of the exam, so a higher percentage of students get early questions rather than later questions correct. The order of difficulty is not purely incremental, however. Expect a few difficult questions at the beginning of the exam. In addition, there may be some easier questions throughout the exam. The order of difficulty is also subjective. There will be questions that many people get wrong but that you may find easy simply because you understand the subject that the question is testing.

Believe it or not, you are more likely to score a 4 or 5 on the test if you go in not expecting to get every multiple-choice question right! Don't get bogged down in a difficult question. Eliminate any answers that you can and then take a guess. If you have time, you can come back to it.

FREE-RESPONSE QUESTIONS

In addition to the multiple-choice questions, the exam also has 4 free-response questions. Each free-response question will contain two to four parts. One of the free-response questions will have to do with the Marine Biology Simulation Case Study. You will most likely see at least one question that has to do with object-oriented design and, if you are taking the AB version of the exam, at least one question that involves data structures such as binary trees or linked lists. The free-response section and multiple-choice section are given equal weight in determining your score.

Free-response questions are generally scored by high school teachers who teach AP computer science courses or introductory computer science courses at the college level.

You will not be penalized for small errors that do not affect the overall logic of the code you write. For example, although all statements in Java should end in a semicolon, you won't be penalized if you forget a semicolon. (As a programmer, however, this could cost you many hours of frustration!) In fact, there's a 9-point rubric for each question that is used to assess a student's answers, which means that there are some parts of a problem for which you can be awarded points even if you don't know how to answer the overall problem. Beware, though: There's also—separate from the rubric—a list of usage points that can be deducted from the final score on the question. Syntax and logical errors, for instance, fall into three groups:

1. Not Penalized (e.g., accidental omission of a semicolon)

2. Minor Usage Errors (e.g., use of the wrong method name, like getLocation() rather than location())

3. Major Usage Errors (e.g., using private data or a private method when not accessible)

Detailed score guidelines are published every year on The College Board's website (http://www.collegeboard.com).

You can earn up to 9 points for each of the 4 multiple-choice questions. Points are awarded for answering each question completely and accurately. You won't earn extra points for providing a clever or original answer, however. In fact, any nonstandard answer will take longer for a reader to grade and therefore be subject to more scrutiny than a standard answer would be. The AP exam is not a place to show off!

HOW THE EXAM IS SCORED

The multiple-choice and free-response questions are weighted equally in determining your score. The process that The College Board uses to determine your score can seem a bit convoluted. Here's how it works.

The College Board takes your raw score for the multiple-choice section and multiplies it by a constant. Your raw score for the free-response section is multiplied by another constant. These scores are then added together and your grade is determined by a matrix developed by The College Board.

Here is a typical formula The College Board would use to grade the exam. Although grade calculations may differ a bit from year to year, you can apply these formulas to your scores on the practice exams in this book to get a rough idea of your standing.

$$\text{MultipleChoiceRawScore} \times 1.0 + 1.1111 \times \text{FreeResponseRawScore}$$

MultipleChoiceRawScore is calculated by adding 1 point for each multiple-choice question you get right and subtracting 1/4 point for each question you get wrong. Because there are 40 multiple-choice questions, you can earn a maximum of 40 points for this section.

The free-response section consists of 4 multipart questions that are worth a maximum of 9 points each, for a total maximum of 36 points. Note that in the formula, the FreeResponseScore is multiplied by 1.1111, which curves the maximum number of points for this section to 40, the same as the multiple-choice section.

Here is a scoring grid similar to those used in the past for grading the exam.

Composite Score Range	AP Grade
60–80	5
45–59	4
33–44	3
25–32	2
0–24	1

Using this hypothetical grid, let's take a look at a specific scenario.

Suppose you answer 35 of the 40 multiple-choice questions and get 27 right and 8 wrong. Because you lose 1/4 point for each incorrect answer, your raw score will be $27 - .25(8) = 25$. What if you then get 25 of the 36 available points on the free-response section? Your score of 25 will be multiplied by 1.1111 to give you 27.77. This is added to the 25 points you earned for the multiple-choice section to give you 52.77 points. This is then rounded to the nearest whole number to give you a composite score of 53. This composite score will easily give you an AP grade of 4.

Take another look at the number of questions you got right in the example above. For the multiple-choice section, it was 27 out of 40. On the free-response section, it was 25 out of 36. In other words, you got less than 70 percent of the questions right on both parts of the exam. On a typical noncurved exam in school, a score slightly less than 70 percent is a D, nothing to be proud of. But on the AP exam, slightly less than 70 percent earns you a score of 4, which will get you course credit at most colleges.

Although you certainly don't need to answer all of the questions to get a good score, you will typically need to answer a minimum of 18 multiple-choice questions correctly to get a 3, 24 questions correctly to get a 4, and 30 questions correctly to get a 5. Similarly on the free-response section, you'll need to answer about 45 percent of the section correctly for a 3, 60 percent for a 4, and 75 percent for a 5.

Please note that the score ranges for the exam that you take will most likely be slightly different from those listed above. However, the logic illustrated above will still apply: You don't need to get all of the questions correct, or even most of the questions correct, to get a great score.

TEST-TAKING STRATEGIES

The key to doing well on the AP Computer Science exam (and standardized exams in general) is not just knowing the material tested on the exam. You also need to know *how to take the exam.*

The AP exam is not like a test that you take in school. Typically, to get a good grade on an exam in school, you need to get a high percentage of the questions correct. As we saw in the example above, this isn't the case on the AP exam.

The following test-taking strategies will help you get the best mark possible on your exam. Note that some of the strategies are specific to technical elements of the Java language—don't forget to return to this section and reread them after you've finished this book. You may also want to review this chapter before trying the practice exams at the back of this book.

MULTIPLE-CHOICE STRATEGIES

Process of Elimination (POE)

As you work through the multiple-choice section, always keep in mind that you are not graded on your thinking process or scratchwork. All that ultimately matters is that you indicate the correct answer. Even if you aren't sure how to answer a question in a methodically "correct" way, see if you can eliminate any answers based on common sense and then take a guess.

Throughout the book, we will point out areas where you can use common sense to eliminate answers.

Although we all like to be able to solve problems the "correct" way, using a Process of Elimination (POE) and guessing aggressively can help earn you a few more points. And it may be these points that make the difference between a 3 and a 4 or push you from a 4 to a 5.

If you don't know the answer but can eliminate an answer choice, guess!

Eliminating just one of the answer choices from consideration means that it is worth your while to guess if you don't know the answer to any given problem. Obviously, the more incorrect answers you can eliminate, the better your odds of guessing the correct answer.

Know the Marine Biology Simulation Case Study

Five questions in the multiple-choice section are guaranteed to involve the Marine Biology Simulation Case Study. This is 12.5 percent of the multiple-choice section or 6.25 percent of the entire exam. Although the Case Study seems imposing, the questions about it on the exam are usually quite simple—as long as you have some knowledge of the code. Learn the Case Study and don't let easy points go to waste.

Skip long or time-consuming multiple-choice questions

Some multiple-choice questions require a page or two of reading to answer the question. Skip any questions that will either take a long time to read or a long time to calculate. Circle the questions and come back to them after you've completed the rest of the section.

Don't turn a question into a crusade!

Most people don't run out of time on standardized tests because they work too slowly. Instead, they run out of time because they spend half the test wrestling with two or three particular questions.

You should never spend more than a minute or two on any question. If a question doesn't involve calculation, then you know the answer, you can take an educated guess at the answer, or you don't know the answer. Figure out where you stand on a question, make a decision, and move on.

Any question that requires more than two minutes worth of calculations probably isn't worth doing. Remember, skipping a question early in the section is a good thing if it means that you'll have time to get two right later on.

Watch for special cases in algorithm descriptions

On the AB exam, you may know that the average runtime for finding an element in a binary search tree is $O(n \log n)$. Watch out if the question casually mentions that the data is inserted in the tree in sorted order. Now the runtime deteriorates into the worst case, $O(n)$. Similar special cases occur on the A exam.

Remember the base case in recursive algorithms

Recursive methods without a base case run forever. Be sure that a base case exists and is the correct base case. For example, a factorial function whose base case is

```
if (n == 1)
    return 0;
```

is incorrect because 1! = 1.

Watch for < vs. <= and > vs. >=

Especially in loops, the difference between < and <= or between > and >= can be huge.

Know how to use the Java library classes

This chapter offers strategies that will help make you a better test taker and, hopefully, a better scorer on the AP Computer Science exam. However, there are some things you just have to know. Although you'll have a Quick Reference for the AP Java Classes as part of the exam, review the AP Java library classes beforehand and know what methods are available, what they do, and how to use them. The Quick Reference will help, but it won't substitute for knowing the classes.

Preconditions and postconditions

Read these carefully when given. They may provide the clue needed to answer the question. For instance, a precondition may state that the array passed to a method is in sorted order.

Parameter passing

Remember that arguments passed to methods do not keep changes made to them inside the method. For instance, it is impossible to write a method that swaps the value of two integer primitives. Don't confuse this, however, with changing the contents (attributes) of an object that is passed to a method.

Client program vs. method

There is likely to be at least one question that defines a class and asks you to choose among different implementations for a method. Pay close attention to whether the method is a "client program" or a method of the class. If it's a client program, the implementation of the method may not access any private data fields or private methods of the class directly. If it's a method of the class, the implementation is free to access both private data fields and private methods.

Boolean short-circuiting

Conditionals in if statements and while statements "short-circuit". For example

```
if ((a != 0) && (b / a == 5))
```

is *not* the same as

```
if ((b / a == 5) && (a != 0))
```

Memorize DeMorgan's Laws

There will be at least one question on the exam where they will be useful.

```
!(p || q) is equivalent to !p && !q
!(p && q) is equivalent to !p || !q
```

Final data in a class

Watch out for answer choices that have code segments that attempt to change a data field declared final. This is illegal code.

Mixing double and int in an expression

In operations that have both an int variable and a double variable, unless explicitly cast otherwise, the int is converted to a double and the result of the operation is a double.

FREE-RESPONSE STRATEGIES

Write Java code, not pseudocode

Only Java code is graded; pseudocode is *not* graded. Don't waste time writing pseudocode if you don't know how to code the solution to a problem. (On the other hand, write pseudocode as a starting point to writing your Java code if it helps you to do so.)

Don't comment your code

Unless you write some code that is extremely tricky (and see below for whether you should do that!), there's no need to write comments. It just takes time (that you don't have a lot of) and the comments will be largely ignored by the graders anyway (you won't get points if your comment is correct but your code is wrong). You also run the risk of misleading the grader if your code is correct but your comments are incorrect.

Write legibly

This seems obvious, but if a grader can't read your code, you won't get any points.

Don't erase large chunks of code

If you make extensive changes to the code you're writing, it's better to put a big "X" through the bad code rather than erase it. It saves you time and is easier for the graders to read.

Don't write more than one solution to a problem

Graders will grade the first solution they see. If you rewrite a solution, be sure to cross out the old one.

Don't leave any problem blank

You don't get any points if you don't write anything down. Even if you're unsure how to answer a particular problem (or part of a problem), analyze the problem and code the method's "infrastructure." For instance, if the method signature indicates that it creates and returns an ArrayList, writing

```
ArrayList returnedList = new ArrayList();
return returnedList;
```

is likely to get you at least partial credit—even if you don't know how to fill the ArrayList with the correct objects.

KISS (Keep It Simple, Student)

The problems are designed to make the solutions relatively straightforward. If your solution is getting complicated, there's probably an easier or better way to solve the problem. At the same time, don't try for seemingly elegant but unreadable code. Remember that graders must read hundreds of exams in a week—they may not be able to figure out all of the nuances of your code. KEEP IT SIMPLE!

Write standard solutions

Use AP-style variable, class, and method names and follow the indentation style of the AP sample code (even if you don't like their style!). Although graders always try to be fair and accurate, they are human and do make mistakes. The closer your answer adheres to the sample solution given to the graders, the easier it will be for them to grade.

Wherever possible, use clear and intuitive nomenclature. For example, use r and c or row and col for looping through the rows and columns of a two-dimensional array; don't use x and y or a and b or jack and jill. This ensures that graders can easily follow the flow of your code.

If the pseudocode for an algorithm is given, use it!

Sometimes you will have to create your own algorithm for a method. Often though, the pseudocode for the algorithm or method is given to you as part of the problem; all you need to do is implement the algorithm. In that case, use pseudocode that's given to you! Don't make it harder on yourself by trying to re-create the algorithm or by trying to implement your own special version. Futhermore, you can often write the code for a method based on given pseudocode even if you don't understand the underlying algorithm.

Answer part (c) to a problem even if you couldn't do parts (a) and (b)

Many parts of free-response problems build on previous parts. For example, the question in part (c) may use the methods you wrote in parts (a) and (b). However, you do not need to have answered parts (a) and (b) correctly in order to get full credit for part (c). In fact, part (c) is sometimes easier than either part (a) or (b).

If part (c) states that you should use parts (a) and (b), use them!

Often part (c) of a free-response problem will state that you can or should use the methods you wrote in the earlier parts of the problem. If the problem makes that statement, be sure to call those methods; otherwise you will not receive full credit for the problem.

Don't make easy-to-avoid mistakes

Students often lose points on the free-response section because they make common errors. Here are some things you can do to avoid these mistakes.

- Unless the problem *explicitly* asks you to output something (using System.out.print), *never* output anything in a method you write.

- Watch method signatures. Be sure to call methods with the correct name and correct number and type of parameters. If the method is nonvoid, be sure that the method you write returns a value with the correct type as specified in the signature.

- Use the objectName.methodName() syntax when calling methods of a given object; use the ClassName.methodName() syntax when calling static methods such as the getInstance method of the RandNumGenerator class in the Case Study.

- Be sure to declare any variables you use (and give them descriptive names).

- Don't create objects when you don't need to. For instance, if a method you call returns an ArrayList, declare it as

```
ArrayList returnedList;
returnedList = obj.getList();
```

not

```
ArrayList returnedList = new ArrayList();
returnedList = obj.getList();
```

- Use proper indentation. Even if you use curly braces for all of your conditionals and loops, the indentation will demonstrate your intent even if you forget, for example, a closing curly brace.

Once again—know the case study

One problem in the free-response section is guaranteed to involve the Marine Biology Simulation Case Study. This is 25 percent of the free-response section or 12.5 percent of the entire exam. Although the case study seems imposing, the questions about it on the exam are usually quite simple—as long as you have some knowledge of the code. Learn the case study and don't let easy points go to waste.

Design question

One problem in the free-response section is likely to be a design problem where you will be given a description of a class and asked to write an interface for it. You may also be asked to implement selected methods in your class. Be sure to use appropriate class, method, and private data field names. For example, "method1" is not likely to be a good name for a method that returns the total price of an object; "totalPrice" is a more appropriate name. Be sure to include all methods, private data fields, and *all* of the constructors (including the default constructor) asked for in the problem. If you are asked to implement a method, be sure to use the correct class, method, and private data field names *as you defined them* in the design part.

Arrays and ArrayLists

One problem on the exam (much more probable on the A than on the AB exam) is likely to involve walking through arrays and/or ArrayLists. Know the differences between the two types of structures and how to loop through elements in the array or an ArrayList. For the AB exam, know how to use iterators and how to work with two-dimensional arrays.

Trees (AB only)

One problem in the free-response section of the AB exam is highly likely to be a problem involving trees. Remember that trees and recursion go hand-in-hand; the solution to a tree problem is often most easily solved using recursion.

Linked Lists (AB only)

One problem in the free-response section of the AB exam is likely to be a problem involving linked lists. Be sure you know the standard ways of manipulating linked lists, and watch out for typical linked list errors such as walking off the end of a list and inadvertently throwing a NullPointerException.

GENERAL STRATEGIES

The following strategies apply to both the multiple-choice and free-response sections of the exam.

Pace yourself and keep track of time

On the multiple-choice section, you should take an *average* of about 1 minute 40 seconds per problem. This will give you 2 minutes to look over the test at the beginning and 6 minutes for a final check at the end. As a comparison, if you take 3 minutes per problem, you're only going to answer 25 questions; if you take 5 minutes per problem, you're only going to answer 15 questions.

On the free-response section, you should pace yourself at a rate of 20 minutes per complete problem. This will give you 6 minutes per problem to check your answer and 1 minute at the beginning to look over the problems.

Write in the test booklet

Don't try to do the questions in your head. Write things down! Take notes on the question. In addition to making the problem easier to solve, having notes in the test booklet will make it easier to come back and check your work if you have time at the end of the test.

Underline key words in questions

Words like *client program*, *sorted*, *ordered*, *constant*, *positive*, *never*, *always*, and *must* all specify conditions to a problem. On both the multiple-choice and free-response sections, underline these key words as you read the question to reinforce their importance to the problem.

Don't do more work than you need to

You are not graded for your work at all on the multiple-choice section, and you are not given extra credit for clever or well-documented answers on the free-response section. Keep it simple and strive to get the answer right rather than impress the graders.

Look through the exam first—use the Two-Pass System

Keep in mind that all of the multiple-choice questions are worth the same number of points, and each free-response question is worth the same number of points as the other free-response questions. There is no need to do them in order. Instead use a two-pass system.

Go through each section twice. The first time, do all the questions that you can get answers to immediately. That is, the questions with little or no analysis or the questions on computer science topics in which you are well versed.

The first time through, skip the questions in the topics that make you uncomfortable. Also, you might want to skip the ones that look like number crunchers (even without a calculator, you might still be expected to crunch a few numbers). Circle the questions that you skip in your test booklet so you can find them easily during the second pass.

Once you've done all the questions that come easily to you, go back and pick out the tough ones that you have the best shot at.

That's why the two-pass system is so handy. By using it, you make sure that you get to see all the questions that you can get right, instead of running out of time because you got bogged down on questions you couldn't do earlier in the test.

A word of caution though: If you skip a multiple-choice question, be sure that you take extra care in marking your answer sheet. Always be sure that the answer you bubble in on the answer sheet is for the correct question number. In addition, don't forget to circle the skipped question in the multiple-choice booklet so that you remember to come back to it if you have time at the end of the test.

FINALLY...

Don't panic. If you've prepared, the test is easier than it looks at first glance. Take your time, approach each question calmly and logically, remember the tips in this chapter, and you'll be fine.

GET READY TO MOVE ON...

Now that you have the hints, strategies, and background information locked in, it's time to move on to the serious business at hand…the subject review. Read over the following chapters, take notes, and compare them to your textbook and class notes as preparation to take The Princeton Review sample tests in the back of the book. Once you've mastered what's in this book and learned from your mistakes on the practice tests, you'll be ready to ace the real AP exam.

Java Fundamentals

INTRODUCTION

In this chapter, we will review the basic Java concepts that are tested on the AP Computer Science Exam. Java is an extensive language, but only a small subset of the language is tested on the AP exam. For example, you'll be expected to know the most common primitive variable types (int, double, and boolean), but not other primitives like short, long, byte, char, and float.

Although this book will give you a good overview of the material and principles needed to pass the AP Computer Science Exam, it's no substitute for studying the material you learned in class. Because this is undoubtedly not the first time you have been introduced to the Java language, we've chosen to present this material as a review rather than an introduction. If you encounter areas that remain unclear, we recommend you flag them for future reference; you may find, upon completing this book, that concepts that initially seemed difficult or abstract suddenly make much more sense within the overall context of the Java language.

Good luck!

GETTING STARTED

This book covers several complex concepts you'll need to know when taking the AP Computer Science Exam, as well as a few concepts you may wish to know for your own curiosity. We'll attempt to clearly distinguish each type of material throughout this book; if it's not something you absolutely need to know for the exam, we'll tell you that.

To begin, let's start with a few of the most basic programming concepts every Java programmer must understand.

CODE FORMAT

You'll notice throughout this book that the code segments provided are indented in several places, most often between parentheses or within conditional loops. Although the Java compiler doesn't care whether certain lines are indented or not, it's easier for programmers to read source code that clearly demarcates structure. We've therefore employed a common programmer's practice of structurally indenting lines, and we encourage you to follow the same practice in your own programs.

COMMENTS

Comments are used to provide extra information in your code for yourself or other programmers and are ignored by the computer. There are two types of comments that you are expected to understand for the exam: single-line comments and multi-line comments.

Single-line comments begin with a double forwards-slash (//).

```
// This is a single-line comment
int x = 10; // This is a comment on the same line as some code
```

In the second example above, the computer will process the beginning of the line (int x = 10;) but will ignore everything after the two forward slashes.

Multi-line comments begin with a slash-asterisk pair (/*) and end with the reverse (*/).

```
/* This is a
   multi-line comment */
```

You'll notice that throughout this book, we use comments to communicate information to the reader within code segments. For instance, a poorly written piece of code might end with "// Error!" as a way of letting you know that the line in question would generate an error if compiled.

BRACES FOR METHODS AND CONDITIONAL STATEMENTS

Although it's acceptable to place the opening curly brace of a method or conditional statement at the end of the same line where the statement appears, many programmers prefer to place opening braces at the beginning of the following line. Because this is the convention you're most likely to see on the exam, we've adopted the second approach.

```
public myMethod(int x)
{
if (x == 1)
   {
      return true;
   }
```

```
        else
        {
            return false;
        }
    }
```

INPUT AND OUTPUT

On the exam, you will not be expected to know how to get input from or write output to files, databases, or Graphical User Interfaces (GUIs). All input to a program will be indicated in the following manner:

```
String s = /* call to a method that reads a string */ ;
```

or:

```
String s = IO.readString();
```

In the example above, IO.readString() is a method called to read user input.
For output, you are only expected to understand how to use

```
System.out.print();
```

and

```
System.out.println();
```

Both of these statements print information to the console. The second statement adds a line break at the end of the output, so any subsequent output will be printed on a new line.

VARIABLES

A variable is used to store information. All variables must have a type that specifies what kind of information the variable can store. Every variable must be either a primitive type or a reference type.

PRIMITIVE TYPES (INT, DOUBLE, AND BOOLEAN)

Primitive variables store simple data such as numbers. The only primitive types you will be expected to use and understand on the AP exam are int, double, and boolean.

int

An **int** variable holds a 4-byte (32 bit) integer value. The value it holds can range from -2^{31} to $2^{31} - 1$ (or –2,147,483,648 to 2,147,483,647).

The following example shows a legal variable declaration:

```
int i = 10;
```

This next expression, however, is not legal, because 10.0 has a decimal point.

```
int i = 10.0; // Error!
```

double

A **double** variable holds an 8-byte (64 bit) floating point number. A floating point number is simply a number that is allowed a decimal point.

```
double a = 22.345;
double b = -3652.34;
```

The number that is assigned to a double variable does not need to have a decimal point for it to be legal, however. The following expressions are all legal:

```
double a = 10;
int b = 10;
double c = b;
```

boolean

A **boolean** variable's value must be either true or false.

```
boolean b = true;
boolean c = false;
```

Note that the values true and false are not enclosed in quotes because they're not String values. The following statements will cause errors when compiled:

```
boolean b = "true"; // Error!
boolean b = "false"; //Error!
```

In all of the examples above, we assigned a value to each primitive variable on the same line that the variable was declared. It is also possible to declare a variable and not initially assign a value to it. A value can then be assigned later in your program.

```
int i;
i = 10;
```

In the first line above, the int variable *i* is declared but a value is not explicitly assigned to it until the second line. In the second line, we skip the int keyword in front of the variable, because we already declared *i* to be of type int in the first line.

In the following example, the second line will cause an error because we have already defined *i* as an int in the first line:

```
int i;
int i = 10; //Error!
```

CASTING PRIMITIVE VALUES

As we saw in the section above, the value of an int variable can be assigned to a double variable.

```
int a = 20;
double b = a;
```

But what happens if we try to assign the value of a double variable to an int variable?

```
double a = 20.7;
int b = a; // Error!
```

The code above will cause a compile-time error. The compiler alerts us because when we assign a double to an int variable, it's possible that we may lose some precision. Remember that doubles can hold numbers with decimal points as well as much larger numbers than integer variables can hold.

The compiler will balk even if our double variable holds an integer literal.

```
double a = 10;
int b = a;  // Error!
```

So how do we fix the problem? We have to explicitly tell the compiler that we want to put a double value in an int variable. We do this with a **cast**.

```
double a = 20.7;
int b = (int) a;
```

When a double is cast to an int, the decimal portion of the double is dropped. In the example above, the variable b will hold the value 20.

REFERENCE TYPES

Variables can hold primitive values, such as int, double, and boolean. Variables can also hold references to objects. A reference is like a handle that points to an object.

The following line declares a variable s that can hold a reference to a String object:

```
String s;
```

Note that we didn't actually create an object in the line above. We simply declared a variable that can hold a reference to an object.

The following line creates a String object and assigns it to the variable s that we declared above:

```
s = new String("Mayonnaise");
```

Graphically, this process resembles the following:

A String reference

s

A String object

"Mayonnaise"

The next line of code creates another String variable named x and points it to the same object as s. It does not make a copy of the String object.

```
String x = s;
```

We can therefore visualize this process as

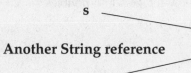

A String reference

s

A String object

"Mayonnaise"

Another String reference

x

OPERATORS

Operators are simply symbols that act on one or more values or expressions. The values or expressions that operators act on are called **operands**. In the second statement below, the plus sign (+) is an operator and its operands are the variable *a* and the integer literal 10. The equal sign (=) is also an operator in the second statement and its operands are the variable b and the integer 15 (which is the result of *a* + 10).

```
int a = 5;
int b = a + 10;
```

INCREMENT AND DECREMENT OPERATORS

The **increment operator** (++) is used to increase the value of a number by one. For example, if the value of a variable *x* is 3, then x++ will increment the value of *x* to 4. This has the exact same effect as writing $x = x + 1$, and is nothing more than convenient shorthand.

Conversely, the **decrement operator** (−−) is used to quickly decrease the value of a number by one. For example, if the value of a variable named *x* is 3, then x−− decreases the value of *x* to 2. This has the exact same effect as writing $x = x - 1$.

ASSIGNMENT OPERATOR

The **assignment operator** (=) is used to assign a value to a variable, as in the following examples:

```
int i = 10;
boolean b = true;
String s = "A String";
```

ARITHMETIC OPERATORS

The following arithmetic operators are tested on the exam: plus (+), minus (−), multiplication (*), division (/), and modulus (%).

The **plus operator** (+) is used to add together integers or doubles.

```
int i = 5 + 12 + 32;
double d = 10.4 + 34.43;
```

It can also be used to concatenate strings.

```
String s = "This is " + "a String";
```

The **minus operator** (−) is used to subtract integers and doubles. The minus operator *cannot* be used with strings.

```
int i = 20 - 10;
double d = 20.5 - 10.43
```

The **multiplication operator** (*) is used to multiply integers and doubles.

```
int i = 20 * 10;
double d = 20.5 * 10.43;    // double d = 20.5 * (double) i; ?    //Casting
```

The **division operator** (/) is used to divide integers and doubles.

```
int x = 20 / 10;
double d = 20.5 / 10.43
```

> When the division operator is used with integer operands, the result is truncated such that the remainder is chopped off and only the integer portion remains. For example, 13 / 5 returns a value of 2, not 2.6.

```
int x = 18 / 5;
```

In the example above, the result of 18 divided by 5 is assigned to the variable *x*. Because both 18 and 5 are integers, 18 / 5 is 3, not 3.6.

```
double x = 18 / 5;
```

This time, *x* is declared to be a double rather than an int. However, the result of the right side of the equation is still truncated to 3 because the operands, 18 and 5, are not themselves doubles.

```
double x  = (double) 18 / 5;
```

In the final example above, the integer 18 is cast to a double, and then this double is divided by the integer 5. When an arithmetic operator acts on two operands one of which is a double and the other an integer, the integer operand is automatically promoted to a double. Because 18 has been cast to a double in our example, 5 is also cast to a double before it is divided into 18. Because both operands are doubles, the result of the division is also a double: 3.6.

The **modulus operator** (%) gives the remainder when the number before the operator is divided by the number after the operator.

```
int x = 10 % 3;
```

[handwritten annotation: 10%3 is 10/3 with remainder 1, 3·3 = 9, 10-9 = 1]

In the example above, the value of *x* will be the remainder when 10 is divided by 3. The result is 1 because 3 goes into 10 evenly 3 times and leaves a remainder of 1.

A useful property of the modulus operator is that it returns 0 if the left-hand operand is a multiple of the operand on the right. The following examples all assign a value of 0 to *x* because each of the numbers on the left of the modulus operator is evenly divisible by the number on the right:

```
int x = 3 % 3;
int x = 6 % 2;
int x = 10 % 5;
int x = 12 % 4;
```

The following method determines if the value passed to the parameter is even. An even number is one that is divisible by 2; in other words, the remainder when dividing the number by 2 is 0.

```
public static boolean isEven(int x)
{
  if (x % 2 == 0)
  {
    return true;
  }
  else
  {
    return false;
  }
}
```

RELATIONAL OPERATORS

Relational operators are used to compare the values held by two variables. The following relational operators are on the exam: equal to (==), not equal to (!=), less than (<), less than or equal to (<=), greater than (>), greater than or equal to (>=). All relational operators evaluate to a boolean value of true or false.

When used with primitive variables, the **equality operator** (==) is used to test if the values held by two variables are equal.

```
int i = 10;
int j = 20;
boolean b = (i == j);
System.out.println(b);
```

When executing the above code segment, "false" will be printed because 10 is not equal to 20.

When used with reference variables, the equality operator (==) only evaluates to true if the variables hold references to the same object. We'll have more to say about this when we discuss object-oriented programming in Chapter 4.

With primitive values, the **not equal operator** (!=) returns true if the left and right operands are not equal in value. With reference variables, the != operator returns false if the references refer to different objects.

The four remaining relational operators are greater than (>), less than (<), greater than or equal to (>=), and less than or equal to (<=). These four operators can only be used with primitive values. Attempting to use these operators with object references will cause a compile-time error.

COMBINED OPERATORS

The following **combined assignment/arithmetic operators** are in the AP Java subset: +=, −=, *=, /=, %=. These operators are simply shorthand for the arithmetic operators that we reviewed above.

> i += 10 is equivalent to i = i + 10
>
> j -= 23 is equivalent to j = j - 23
>
> k *= 4.6 is equivalent to k = k * 4.6
>
> m /= -2 is equivalent to m = m / -2
>
> n %= 4 is equivalent to n = n % 4

LOGICAL OPERATORS

The following logical operators are in the AP Java subset: and (&&), or (||), and not (!). These logical operators return a boolean value of true or false.

The **and operator** (&&) returns true if the operands on both sides of the operator are true. For example, the following statement will evaluate to true if x is greater than 0 and less than 10; otherwise, it will return a value of false:

```
x > 0 && x < 10
```

The **or operator** (||) returns true if either one of the operands is true. For example, the following statement will evaluate to true if x is less than 0 or greater than 10:

```
x < 0 || x > 10
```

The **not operator** (!) switches the value of a boolean. Thus, if a value of a boolean variable named *b* is true, then !b will change the value to false. Similarly, if *b* is false, then !b will change the value to true.

[handwritten: new boolean b= true;]

Short-Circuit Evaluation

[handwritten: b= !b ?]

On the exam, you will need to understand the concept of **short-circuit evaluation**.

Consider the statement "2 plus 2 is 5, *and* there are exactly 145 Italian restaurants in Chicago."

For this statement to be true as a whole, both things that are asserted in the statement need to be true. It must be true that 2 plus 2 is 5 and it also must be true that there are exactly 145 Italian restaurants in Chicago. If either one is false, the statement as a whole is false, regardless of the veracity of the other statement.

So what's the best way to evaluate this statement? Well we know that "2 plus 2 is 5" is false. So there's no point in wasting time finding out if there are exactly 145 Italian restaurants in Chicago. We can stop, or "short-circuit," our evaluation of the sentence. It must be false because the first part is false.

Now consider the sentence "2 plus 2 is 4 *or* there are exactly 98 Japanese restaurants in Chicago."

This time, there is an "or" between the two parts of the statement. For this statement to be true as a whole, we only need one part to be true. Because 2 plus 2 does equal 4, the statement as a whole is true, and there is no point in evaluating the second part.

Now let's take a look at what this has to do with Java and programming. If a conditional statement uses an and operator (&&), both operands must be true for the statement to be true. If one of the operands is false, the condition as a whole is false regardless of the value of the other operand.

In the case of the or operator (||), the statement will be true if either one of the operands is true regardless of the value of the other condition.

Consider the following if statement:

```java
if (x > 10 && x < 100) {
   // code to be executed if above condition is true
}
```

For the condition in the if statement to be true, *x* must be both greater than 10 and less than 100. Suppose that *x* is 5. The first part of the condition is false, so there is no need to evaluate the second part (*x* < 100). Even if the second part is true, the statement as a whole will be false.

Now consider a different example.

```java
int x = 6;
int y = 10;
int z = 0;
if (z != 0   && x < y/z)
{
   System.out.println("true");
}
else
{
   System.out.println("false");
}
```

Take a look at the condition in the if statement. There's a problem with the part in bold; we are trying to divide a number by 0. If this part of the condition were evaluated, an error would occur. The code runs without a problem, though, because the operand to the left of the and operator (&&) is false and thus the code to the right is never evaluated; the error never has a chance to occur, and the output is "false."

EVALUATING BOOLEAN EXPRESSIONS

Some questions on the exam may ask you to evaluate boolean expressions, possibly in the context of while or for statements.

EXAMPLE 1

Consider the following question:

Which of the expressions below is equivalent to !(a > b)?

    I. b < a
   II. a < b
  III. a <= b

(A) I only
(B) II only
(C) III only
(D) I and II
(E) I and III

The expression !(a > b) can be translated as "it's not true that a is greater than b" or, equivalently, "a is not greater than b." If *a* is not greater than *b*, it must be true that *a* is less than or equal to *b*. This is what expression III states. The correct answer, therefore, is (C).

Now take a look at the following chart:

The expression	Is equivalent to
!(a <= b)	a > b
!(a < b)	a >= b
!(a >= b)	a < b
!(a > b)	a <= b

As you can see, to invert an inequality all you have to do is follow these two steps:

1. Flip the inequality sign around.

2. If the original expression had an equal sign (=), an equivalent expression without the not (!) symbol will not have an equal sign. If the original expression did not have an equal sign, an equivalent expression without the not (!) symbol will have an equal sign.

EXAMPLE 2

Consider another question.

If a and b are boolean variables, the expression ! (a || b) is equivalent to which of the following expressions?

     I.   !a || !b
    II.   !(a && b)
   III.   !a && !b

(A) I
(B) II
(C) III
(D) I and II
(E) I and III

The expression a || b is only false if both *a* and *b* are false; it is true otherwise. The operator ! inverts expressions that it comes before, so ! (a || b) will be true if both *a* or *b* are false, and false otherwise.

One way to solve this problem is to plug values in for *a* and *b*. For example, we know that if *a* is true and *b* is false, then !(a || b) is false. The equivalent expression should also be false for the same values of *a* and *b*.

Let's start with !a || !b. If *a* is true, then !a is false, and if *b* is false then !b is true. So the expression becomes false || true, which is true. Therefore, expression I is not correct, and we can get rid of answer choices (A), (D), and (E).

If *a* is true and *b* is false, then a && b is false, so !(a && b) is true. We can therefore get rid of expression II and answer choice (B). The only remaining answer choice is (C).

Here's another way to solve this. If you have a compound boolean expression with a not (!) operator in front of it that applies to the whole expression, such as !(a || b), you can distribute the not operator into the expression. The trick is that if the boolean expression has an or (||) operator, you need to switch it to an && (and). Conversely, if it has an && (and) operator, you must switch it to an or (||). These rules of logic, which are known as DeMorgan's laws, can be summarized as

> **!(a && b) is equivalent to !a || !b**
>
> **!(a || b) is equivalent to !a && !b**

OPERATOR PRECEDENCE

Expressions can contain more than one operator. When they do, they are evaluated according to **operator precedence**.

Consider the following example:

```
int i = 2 + 3 * 5;
System.out.println(i);
```

In the example above, the expression 2 + 3 * 5 is not evaluated from left to right. Instead, 3 and 5 are first multiplied together to get 15, and then 2 is added to the result to get a final result of 17. This is because multiplication has a higher precedence than addition.

The following table lists from highest to lowest the operators that you can expect to see on the exam:

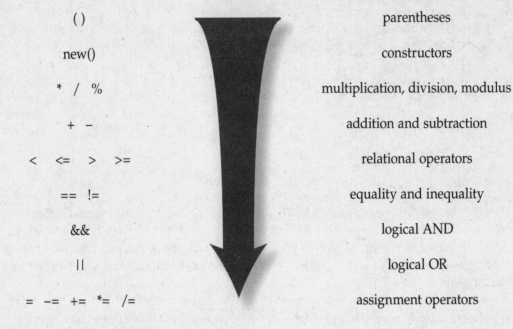

( )	parentheses
new()	constructors
* / %	multiplication, division, modulus
+ –	addition and subtraction
< <= > >=	relational operators
== !=	equality and inequality
&&	logical AND
||	logical OR
= –= += *= /=	assignment operators

CONTROL STRUCTURES

Control structures allow a program to proceed in a non-sequential fashion. The following control structures are tested on the AP exam: if, if/else, while, for, and return.

IF STATEMENTS

Sometimes in a program, you will want a statement or group of statements to be evaluated only if a certain condition is true. **If statements** are used to isolate code and allow it to run only if a condition is met.

The general form of an if statement is

```
if (boolean-expression)
{
    // statements
}
```

For example

```
int x = 10;
int y = 20;
if (x < y)
{
    System.out.println("x is less than y");
}
```

In the example above, the if statement has a condition that x < y. If this condition is met, then the code within the if block is run. In our example, because the condition x < y is true for x = 10 and y = 20, "x is less than y" is printed to the screen.

The condition in an if statement must evaluate to either true or false; in other words, it must be a boolean. The following example will cause a compile-time error because the condition doesn't evaluate to true or false:

```java
int i = 1;
if (i)
{
    System.out.println("Hello");
}
```

In the prior two examples, we used braces to surround the code that is executed if the condition in the if statement is true. The braces are optional if there is only one statement in the if block. The following two code examples are therefore equivalent:

```java
int i = 10;
if (i == 10)
{
    System.out.println("The condition is true");
}
```

```java
int i = 10;
if (i == 10)
System.out.println("The condition is true");
```

We recommend, however, that you always use braces for clarity.

If statements can be nested within other if statements, as in the following example:

```java
int x = 10;
if (x >= 0)
{
    System.out.println("x is greater than zero");
    if (x < 100)
    {
        System.out.println("x is less than 100");
    }
}
```

Because both conditions return true, this would generate the output

```
x is greater than zero
x is less than 100
```

What would happen if we changed the first line in the example above to int x = 200?

```
int x = 200;
if (x >= 0)
{
   System.out.println("x is greater than zero");
   if (x < 100)
   {
      System.out.println("x is less than 100");
   }
}
```

This would generate the following output, because the second conditional is no longer true:

```
x is greater than zero
```

Finally, if we changed *x* to a negative number, there would not be any output because x >= 0 is false, and therefore the second if statement is never evaluated.

IF/ELSE STATEMENTS

If/else statements allow your program to perform one action if a condition is met, or a different action if the condition is not met.

The general form of an if/else statement is

```
if (boolean expression)
{
   // code to run if expression is true
}
else
{
   // code to run if the expression is not true
}
```

Here's an example.

```
int x = 30;
int y = 5;
if (x < y)
{
   System.out.println("x is less than y");
}
else
{
   System.out.println("x is NOT less than y");
}
```

In this program, the condition of the if statement is false. Therefore, the code within the if block is skipped and instead the code within the else block is run, generating the output "*x* is NOT less than *y*."

You will also be expected to understand if/else statements on the exam. Consider the following example:

```
01:   int x = /* call to a method that returns an integer */
02:   if (x < 10)
03:   {
04:      System.out.println("x is less than 10");
05:   }
06:   else if (x < 20)
07:   {
08:      System.out.println("x is less than 20");
09:   }
10:   else if (x < 30)
11:   {
12:     System.out.println("x is less than 30");
13:   }
14:   else {
15:     System.out.println("x is greater than or equal to  30");
16:   }
```

In the code sample above, if x is 15, then the conditional on line 6 will evaluate to true and "x is less than 20" will be printed. At this point, the rest of the code is not evaluated due to the else statements and nothing else is printed. Note that the else statement on line 14 is optional and provides default behavior if none of the conditional statements above it are true.

Contrast the example above with the following:

```
01:   int x = /* call to a method that returns an integer */
02:   if (x < 10)
03:   {
04:      System.out.println("x is less than 10");
05:   }
06:   if (x < 20)
07:   {
08:      System.out.println("x is less than 20");
09:   }
10:   if (x < 30)
11:   {
12:      System.out.println("x is less than 30");
13:   }
14:   else {
15:      System.out.println("x is greater than or equal to  30");
16:   }
```

In this example, lines 6 and 10 contain if statements rather than if/else statements. If x is once again equal to 15, line 6 will be true and "x is less than 20" will be printed. In contrast to the previous example, line 10 will also be evaluated, and because its condition is true, "x is less than 30" will also be printed.

WHILE STATEMENTS

While statements are used to evaluate a block of code more than once.

```
int x = 5;
while (x > 0)
{
   System.out.print(x);
   x = x - 1;
}
```

In the example above, the variable x is assigned the value 5. Next, the condition in the while statement ($x > 0$) is evaluated. Because this condition is true ($5 > 0$), the code within the while block is executed: the value of x is printed to the screen and then decreased by 1 so that its value becomes 4. Control then passes back to the while statement and the condition is evaluated again. Because the condition is still true ($4 > 0$), the code inside the while block is executed again and the current value of x is printed to the screen. The looping continues until x becomes 0 and the condition in the while statement becomes false. At the end of the program, the console will read 54321, each digit having been printed every time the program looped.

FOR STATEMENTS

For statements are similar to while statements; they allow the program to execute a block of code a certain number of times.

The general form of a for statement is

```
for (initialization; condition; updateincrement)
{
   //code to execute
}
```

Now let's take a look at an example.

```
for (int k = 0; k < 5; k++)
{
   System.out.print(k);
}
```

This would generate the following output:

```
01234
```

For statements can be nested inside other for statements. Consider the following code segment, which contains nested for statements. What will be the output when the following code is evaluated?

```
for (int k = 0; k < 3; k++)
{
  for (int j = 1; j < 4; j++)
  {
    System.out.print(j + " ");
  }
  System.out.println("");
}
```

(A) 1 2 3 4
     1 2 3 4
     1 2 3 4

(B) 0 1 2
     0 1 2
     0 1 2
     0 1 2

(C) 1 2 3
     1 2 3
     1 2 3

(D) 1 2 3
     1 2 3
     1 2 3
     1 2 3

(E) 1 2 3 4
     1 2 3 4
     1 2 3 4
     1 2 3 4

The answer is (C). The inner loop starts at 1, and it ends when *j* is equal to 4. Therefore only 1, 2, and 3 will be printed by the statement in the body of the inner loop. We can eliminate answers (A), (B), and (E) because they contain numbers other than 1, 2, and 3. The outer loop will run 3 times, so three rows will be printed to the console.

Contrast the example above with the following:

```
for (int k = 1; k < 5; k++)
{
  for (int j = 0; j < k; j++)
  {
    System.out.print(j + " ");
  }
  System.out.println("");
}
```

Note the part in bold. This time, the statement in the inner loop is dependent on the condition of the outer loop.

Here's what we'll get when the code above is evaluated.

```
0
0 1
0 1 2
0 1 2 3
```

The results look like a triangle rather than a rectangle. This is often the case when the condition in the inner loop is dependent on that of the outer loop.

WHILE VS. FOR STATEMENTS

Note that although **while** loops and **for** loops look different, they accomplish the same purpose—namely, to execute a block of code multiple times.

A good rule of thumb is to use a **for** loop when you know exactly how many times you wish to perform the same set of instructions. Use a **while** loop when it's not obvious how many times the set of instructions needs to be performed.

Remember that any **for** loop can easily be converted into a **while** loop. For example

```
for (int j = 0 ; j < 10 ; j++)
{
   // body of loop
}
```

can be rewritten as

```
int j = 0;
while (j < 10)
{
   // body of loop
   j++;
}
```

RETURN STATEMENTS

A **return statement** is used to return a primitive or object reference from a non-void method or to immediately return execution to the caller from a void method. Methods and return statements are covered in depth in Chapter 4.

HARDWARE AND SOFTWARE

The official AP Computer Science Course Description lists hardware and software topics as one of the requirements of an AP Computer Science course. It is very unlikely that you will see questions about these topics on the exam, but you should at least be familiar with the following:

Processor: Also known as a CPU or Central Processing Unit. This is the brain of the computer, where the processing takes place.

Random Access Memory: Also known as RAM, or simply "memory." This is where programs and the data that they use are kept. RAM is volatile: When a computer is turned off, anything stored in RAM disappears.

Peripherals:	Extra devices that you use with a computer, such as a mouse or printer.
Source Code:	This is the code that you write, which is readable by humans. In Java, source code files end in .java.
Compiler:	A program that reads source code and translates it into a set of low-level instructions that the computer understands. In Java, the compiler translates source code to bytecode—an intermediate level of instructions that can be understood by many different types of computers. A compiler also detects errors in code. For example, if you forget to include a semicolon at the end of a statement, the compiler will give you an error message. Files of compiled code in Java end with a .class extension.
Bytecode:	An intermediate step between source code, which is readable by humans, and machine code, which is very low-level code read by the hardware. A Java compiler produces bytecode.
Java Virtual Machine (JVM):	A piece of software that reads the bytecode produced by the compiler and runs the program. Different JVMs exist for different types of computer operating systems (such as Windows, Unix, or Macintosh). Each JVM can take the same bytecode and run it on the particular operating system for which the JVM is designed.

RESPONSIBLE USE OF COMPUTER SYSTEMS

The College Board also lists "Responsible Use of Computer Systems" as a requirement of an AP Course. This is another topic that you are unlikely to actually see on the exam, however.

In the unlikely event that you do see a question related to this topic, just use common sense. Obviously, computer professionals should respect the privacy of the people who use their software, and they should strive to produce software that is useful and error free. Now that software is in many of the things that we use every day, such as cars, phones, and airplanes, whether or not software is reliable and well designed can quite literally be a matter of life or death.

SYNOPSIS

Here's a quick synopsis of which concepts from this chapter you can expect to find on the exam, and which you won't.

	Concepts Covered on the AP Computer Science Exam	Concepts *Not* Covered on the AP Computer Science Exam
Primitives	• int • double • boolean	• short • long • byte • char • float
Increment / Decrement Operators	• x++ • x--	• ++x • --x
Logical Operators	• == • != • < • <= • > • >= • && • || • !	• & • | • ^ • << • >> • >>>
Conditional Statements	• if/else • for • while	• do/while • switch • plain and labeled break • continue
Miscellaneous		• ?: (ternary operator) • User input • JavaDoc comments

REVIEW QUESTIONS

Answers to the review questions can be found in Chapter 11.

1. Consider the following code segment:

```
01: int a = 10;
02: double b = 10.7;
03: double c = a + b;
04: int d = a + c;
05: System.out.println(c + " " + d);
```

What will be output as a result of executing the code segment?

(A) 20 20
(B) 20.0 20
(C) 20.7 20
(D) 20.7 21
(E) Nothing will be printed because of a compile-time error.

2. Consider the following code segment:

```
01: int a = 10;
02: double b = 10.7;
03: int d = a + b;
```

Line 3 will not compile in the code segment above. With which of the following statements could we replace this line so that it compiles?

```
  I. int d = (int) a + b;
 II. int d = (int) (a + b);
III. int d =  a + (int) b;
```

(A) I
(B) II
(C) III
(D) I and III
(E) II and III

3. Consider the following code segment.

```
01: int a = 11;
02: int b = 4;
03: double x = 11;
04: double y = 4;
05: System.out.print(a / b);
06: System.out.print(", ");
07: System.out.print(x / y);
08: System.out.print(", ");
09: System.out.print(a / y);
```

What is printed as a result of executing the code segment?

(A) 3, 2.75, 3
(B) 3, 2.75, 2.75
(C) 2, 3, 2
(D) 2, 2.75, 2.75
(E) Nothing will be printed because of a compile-time error.

4. Consider the following code segments:

```
I.  int x = 10;
    int y = 20;
    int z = 0;
    if (x < y && 10 < y / z)
        System.out.println("Homer");
    else
        System.out.println("Bart");
```

```
II.  int x = 10;
     int y = 20;
     int z = 0;
     if (x > y && 10 < y / z)
         System.out.println("Homer");
     else
         System.out.println("Bart");
```

```
III.  int x = 10;
      int y = 20;
      int z = 0;
      if (x < y || 10 < y / z)
          System.out.println("Homer");
      else
          System.out.println("Bart");
```

Which of the code segments above will run without error?

(A) I only
(B) II only
(C) III only
(D) II and III
(E) I, II, and III

5. Consider the following code segment:

```java
for (int i = 1; i < 100; i = i * 2)
{
   if (i / 50 == 0)
      System.out.print(i + " ");
}
```

What is printed as a result of executing the code segment?

(A) 1 2 4 8 16 32 64
(B) 1 2 4 8 16 32
(C) 2 4 8 16 32 64
(D) 2 4 8 16 32
(E) 4 8 16 32 64

6. Consider the following code segment:

```java
for (int i = 200; i > 0; i /= 3)
{
   if (i % 2 == 0)
      System.out.print(i + " ");
}
```

What is output as a result of executing the code segment?

(A) 200 66 22 7 2
(B) 66 22 7 2
(C) 200 66 22 2
(D) 200 66 22
(E) 7

7. Consider the following output:

```
0 1
0 2 4
0 3 6 9
0 4 8 12 16
```

Which of the following code segments will produce this output?

(A)
```
for (int x = 1; x < 5; x++)
{
   for (int z = 0; z <= x; z++)
   {
      System.out.print(x * z + " ");
   }
   System.out.println("");
}
```
(B)
```
for (int x = 1; x <= 5; x++)
{
   for (int z = 0; z < x; z++)
   {
      System.out.print(x * z + " ");
   }
   System.out.println("");
}
```

(C)
```
for (int x = 1; x < 5; x++)
{
   for (int z = 0; z <= 4; z++)
   {
      System.out.print(x * z + " ");
   }
   System.out.println("");
}
```

(D)
```
for (int x = 1; x < 5; x++)
{
   for (int z = 0; z <= 4; z += 2)
   {
      System.out.print(x * z + " ");
   }
   System.out.println("");
}
```

(E)
```
for (int x = 1; x <= 5; x++)
{
   for (int z = 0; z <= x; z++)
   {
      System.out.print(x * z + " ");
   }
   System.out.println("");
}
```

8. Consider the following statement:

```
int i = x % 50;
```

If x is a positive integer, which of the following could NOT be the value of i after the statement above executes?

(A) 0
(B) 10
(C) 25
(D) 40
(E) 50

9. The speed limit of a stretch of highway is 55 miles per hour (mph). The highway patrol issues speeding tickets to anyone caught going faster than 55 miles per hour. The fine for speeding is based on the following scale:

Speed	Fine
greater than 55 mph but less than 65 mph	$100
greater than or equal to 65 mph but less than 75 mph	$150
greater than or equal to 75 mph	$300

If the value of the int variable speed is the speed of a driver who was pulled over for going faster than 55 mph, which of the following code segments will assign the correct value to the int variable fine?

```
I.   if (speed >= 75)
       fine = 300;
     if (speed >= 65 && speed < 75)
       fine = 150;
     if (speed > 55 && speed < 65)
       fine = 100;

II.  if (speed >= 75)
       fine = 300;
     if (65 <= speed < 75)
       fine = 150;
     if (55 < speed < 65)
       fine = 100;

III. if (speed >= 75)
       fine = 300;
     if (speed >= 65)
       fine = 150;
     if (speed > 55)
       fine = 100;
```

(A) I only
(B) II only
(C) III only
(D) I and II
(E) I and III

10. Consider the following code segment:

```
int x = 10;
int y = 3;
boolean b = true;
for (int i = 0; i < 15; i += 5)
{
    x = x + y;
    b = (x % y == 2);
    if (!b)
    {
        y++;
        i += 5;
    }
}
```

What is the value of x after the code segment executes?

(A) 10
(B) 15
(C) 17
(D) 22
(E) 25

11. In the following statement, a and b are boolean variables:

```
boolean c = (a && b) || !(a || b);
```

Under what conditions will the value of c be true?

(A) Only when the value of a is different than the value of b.
(B) Only when the value of a is the same as the value of b.
(C) Only when a and b are both true.
(D) Only when a and b are both false.
(E) The value of c will be true for all values of a and b.

12. Consider the following code segment:

```
while ((x > y) || y >= z)
{
    System.out.print("*");
}
```

In the code segment above, x, y, and z are variables of type int. Which of the following must be true after the code segment has executed?

(A) x > y || y >= z
(B) x <= y || y > z
(C) x > y && y >= z
(D) x < y && y <= z
(E) x <= y && y < z

13. Consider the following code segment:

```java
int a = 0;
for (int i = 0; i < 10; i ++)
{
   for (int k = 0; k <= 5; k++)
   {
      for (int z = 1; z <= 16; z = z * 2)
      {
         a++;
      }
   }
}
```

What is the value of a after the code segment executes?

(A) 31
(B) 180
(C) 200
(D) 300
(E) 400

14. Consider the following code segment:

```java
int x = 10;
int y = x / 3;
int z = x % 2;
x++;
System.out.println(x)
```

What is printed as a result of executing the code segment above?

(A) 2
(B) 4
(C) 10
(D) 11
(E) 15

15. Consider the following code segment:

```java
int a = 10;
double b = 3.7;
int c = 4;
int x = (int) (a + b);
double y = (double) a / c;
double z = (double) (a / c);
double w = x + y + z;
System.out.println(w);
```

What is printed as a result of evaluating the code above?

(A) 10
(B) 15
(C) 15.5
(D) 17
(E) 17.5

16. Consider the following code segment:

```
int i = 1;
int k = 1;
while (i < 5)
{
    k *= i;
    k++;
}
System.out.print(k);
```

What is printed as a result of executing the code above?

(A)   6
(B)   10
(C)   24
(D) 120
(E)   Nothing is printed.

Designing, Testing, and Performance

INTRODUCTION

The AP exam requires that you demonstrate mastery of testing and design issues, including specific evaluation techniques. Accordingly, we'll discuss object-oriented design, top-down analysis, implementation, testing, types of errors, assertions, preconditions, postconditions, boundary tests, integration tests, and Big-Oh techniques in this chapter by providing both explanations and examples.

DESIGNING A PROGRAM

The goal of any computer program is to solve a given problem in the correct way. This requires certain best practices and professional techniques on the part of the programmer. These practices allow your program to adapt to changing environments while remaining reusable. The goal of this section is to define and explain how this is done.

As with most things, the first step toward writing a good software solution is defining the problem carefully. Next, you want to design a solution that meets those stated needs. Finally, you need to provide an implementation that meets your design. The next three subsections will discuss how to formally identify a problem, how to design a solution, and how to begin your implementation.

PROBLEM IDENTIFICATION

The process of defining your software problem can be broken down into three simple steps. These are:

1. specification of purpose and goals

2. identification of objects and classes (abstract data types)

3. identification of class responsibilities (operations on abstract data types)

A formal written description of what your program is trying to achieve is referred to as the **specification**.

In Java, interfaces are used to define the **role** being served, rather than providing an implementation of that role. One real-world metaphor might be a car. Although the Car role might be fulfilled by several different companies in several different ways, the role itself is consistent, and defines a predictable set of behaviors; for instance, if you know how to drive, you already know which pedal provides acceleration, regardless of which company makes your particular vehicle. In Java, this consistent behavior is specified by providing empty method signatures in an interface file, or by declaring a primitive. An interface is most often used.

A Class encompasses the methods and data that logically define a functional unit. A good real-world metaphor might be a RacingCar class which implements the basic Car interface in its own unique way. This means that the RacingCar class provides a working version of each method defined in the Car interface.

For the interface Car, we might have the following code:

```
public interface Car
{
   public boolean speed(int mph);
}
```

Correspondingly, for the class RacingCar, which implements Car, we might have the class definition below. The intention of the speed method is to return true if the requested speed does not exceed the MAX_SPEED. If it does not, then true is returned. If it does, then false is returned. The getColor method simply returns the color of the car.

```
public class RacingCar implements Car
{
   private int MAX_SPEED = 200;
   private String color = "Red";
   //precondition
   public boolean speed(int mph)
```

```
        {
          boolean retval = false;
          if (mph <= MAX_SPEED)
          {
            retval = true;
          }
          return retval;
        }
        public String getColor()
        {
          return color;
        }
      }
```

Example

Say you need a program that will add two numbers together and return the result; perhaps you're building a primitive calculator. The first step is to define the problem carefully. For example, do we need to be able to add any two numbers together, or just ints? How about complex numbers, or numbers that are not base 10? What if one number is an int, and the other is a float? Do we return a rounded int, or a float value? Do we need to deal with negative numbers? These are all important questions for your program. For the sake of simplicity, we'll assume that we only need to deal with ints. However, we want an adaptable design that will accommodate other requirements, just in case we are asked to implement them. Our specification of purpose and goals therefore becomes "Provide a program that will add two ints together, and return their sum as an int." So far, so good.

Next, we need to define our program's necessary Class. Our program is providing a service, so how should users take advantage of that service? Because we have not been given any explicit directions, we are going to assume that the simplest design possible is sufficient: We'll use int primitives to pass in the two numbers that need to be added together, and use an int primitive to return the result. The goal of the add method will be to add two values together and return the resulting sum. Our specification will therefore read as follows:

1. Provide a program that will add two numbers together and return the result.

2. The program will add two ints together, and return their sum as an int.

3. This program is a simple adding mechanism. It will not be expected to deal with overflow, underflow, or exception cases. Its return type will be primitive ints, both for input and for output.

TOP-DOWN DESIGN

Once a specification has been created, we need to design a solution. In object-oriented programming, we engage in **top-down design**. In other words, we specify what our program actually needs to do, and then break that solution down into smaller and smaller steps until those steps don't need further explanation.

You're already familiar with top-down-design-based problem solving: you've been doing it your whole life. For example, when you walk to the kitchen and grab a bite to eat, you're engaging in top-down-design problem solving. You have designed a solution ("walk to the kitchen and get food") based on the process of breaking the problem down into smaller and smaller steps. The process works something like the following:

- get out of your chair
- determine which direction the kitchen is in
- walk toward kitchen
- open the door to the refrigerator
- and so on…

Of course, any one of these steps can be decomposed into smaller steps still. For example, the step "Walk toward kitchen" can be broken down into several smaller steps.

- brace leading leg
- push off with trailing leg
- take an 18-inch step
- and so on…

In software design, the top-down approach is a design technique that aims to describe functionality at a very general level, and then partitions it repeatedly into more detailed levels, one level at a time, until the detail is sufficient to allow coding.

Most software top-down design starts at the design of the client interface. In general, the steps are the following:

- top-down design of user/client interface
- choice of data structures and algorithms
- function decomposition
- identification of reusable components from existing code

As you'll see, top-down design and object-oriented design work well together. In the next section, we'll discuss how object-oriented design can be used in conjunction with top-down design to provide solid software development techniques.

Object-Oriented Design

Object-oriented design, or OOD, is a methodology in which a software system is modeled as cooperating objects. It is generally performed in the following distinct stages:

- identification of classes and objects
- identification of class attributes
- identification of the relationships of the classes to each other

To create a simple calculator, we might model our program as an interface (say, the Calculator Interface) that offers an add(int, int) method. Building methods that represent discrete elements of functionality is the essence of object-oriented programming, because it makes the code conceptually easy to understand. For more details on object-oriented concepts, please see Chapter 4.

Thus, our OOD becomes

- The Client will interact with the Calculator interface by using the public add(int val1, int val2) method.

- The Calculator interface will offer a public int add(int val1, int val2) method, which will sum val1 and val2 and then return the result. The interface, of course, will only define the role; the implementing class will provide actual logic.

- The Calculator interface will not need any other objects at this time.

Our design leads to the following interface:

```
public interface Calculator
{
    public int add(int val1, int val2);
}
```

As you can see, in addition to object-oriented design, we also used top-down design here, because we broke the class down from a high specification to interface-level method signatures.

IMPLEMENTATION

The next step is to actually write the implementing code. Once again, top-down design principles can help us. Of course, Calculator is a trivial example, but the process is the same regardless of the specific application. This same approach will allow you to write complicated programs that play chess, surf the Web, and control satellites and cars.

General Implementation Process:

1. Implement the Interface that was generated by the OOD phase.

2. Choose your data structures and algorithms.

3. Refine methods step-by-step as necessary.

4. Identify reusable components from existing code.

For the Calculator example, we have the following Calculator implementation process:

1. Implement the Calculator interface.

2. No data structures other than the ones indicated by the Interface are necessary. Also, no complicated algorithm is necessary; a simple arithmetic add will do.

3. Refine methods step-by-step as necessary.

4. There are no existing components that can be reused.

The following example adds two ints together, and returns the resulting int value:

```
public class CalculatorImpl implements Calculator
{
    public int add(int val1, int val2)
    {
        int retval = val1 + val2;
        return retval;
    }
}
```

So now our example works perfectly. Or does it? How do we know, one way or the other? That's where testing comes in.

TESTING A PROGRAM

Testing is a method of measuring programming correctness and robustness. **Programming correctness** is the ability of a program to do what it was designed to do, whereas **robustness** is the general ability to deal with "out of bounds" situations. For example, a robust program won't give inaccurate data for some inputs, won't crash if the data is invalid, and won't give a wrong answer if invalid data is entered. The following sections provide some general information about testing and errors that you need to know.

TYPES OF ERRORS

The types of errors you need to be aware of for the exam are

Compile-time errors: These are the errors that can occur when attempting to compile a program. They generally point to a syntax or usage problem. For example, using a "string" with a lowercase "s" instead of a "String" with an uppercase "S," or forgetting to put a semicolon in place will generate compile-time errors.

Logical errors: These occur when your program fails to meet the defined specifications. For example, if you meant to add two numbers together but subtracted them instead, or if your loop iterated one too few times, you would have a logical error. In this case, your program will run, but it will not work as specified.

Run-time errors: These occur when your program encounters a problem while executing. If you've ever used a program and had it unexpectedly crash, then you've experienced a run-time error. Errors such as these can occur for any number of reasons, including attempting to access a null object, dividing by zero, running out of memory, indexing a nonexistent element in an array, or situations that cause exceptions (like NullPointerException, ArrayIndexOutOfBoundsException, ArithmeticException, and ClassCastException) to be thrown. Any uncaught exception can lead to a run-time error.

ASSERTIONS

An **assertion** is a precise statement about the state of code at a given time, which proves that the program is working correctly up to that point.

For instance, in our Calculator example, we might assert that the first number is always larger than the second number, so that our answers will be positive.

```
public int add(int val1, int val2)
{
    // assert that ( val1 >= val2 );
    int retval = val1 + val2;
    return retval;
}
```

PRECONDITIONS

Preconditions are assertions that must be true before your code starts to execute. For example, if you are going to divide *x* by *y*, then a reasonable precondition might be that *y* is not equal to 0. Alternately, you may wish to use the precondition that *x* be greater than *y*, so that your answer will always be greater than 1. Generally speaking, preconditions are checked at the beginning of your code, before execution begins in proper. If your preconditions are not satisfied, then the program should not execute; an exception or an error code would be in order.

For example, if your code needs to search a given String for a given character, it's a reasonable precondition that the string not be null. Of course, preconditions need to be checked by the programmer. They are not automatically checked just because they are stated. For example

```
// precondition: phrase != null
public String search(String phrase, char c)
{
   //search for the character
}
```

The search method given above expects that the phrase is not null before proceeding to the rest of the logic.

POSTCONDITIONS

Postconditions are assertions that must be true after your code executes. For example, if you are going to multiply two positive numbers, then a reasonable postcondition might be that the result be positive, as this can help guard against overflow and underflow. Or if your program is transferring money from one account to another, a reasonable postcondition would be to make sure that the target has more funds after you are finished than when you started. If a method returns a value, the postcondition will also specify what the nature of the value is. If your method doesn't return a value, then a postcondition is a description of what the method does. For example

```
// postcondition: Returns a positive number
public double multiplyPositive(double arg1, double arg2)
{
   double retval = arg1 * arg2;
   return retval;
}
```

In the example above, the method multiplyPositive() has a postcondition that the returned value be positive.

BOUNDARY TEST

Boundary conditions occur in situations in which your methods can accept a range of values as input. For instance, the Calculator example was open to boundary testing because the inputs to the add method are ints, and ints can have a range of values.

A boundary test should validate data that is in the legal range, as well as input that is above and below the boundary. For example, the range of an int is -2^{31} to $2^{31} - 1$. Thus, it's important to see what happens when both of the arguments to the Calculator program are inside that range: when one is above that range and another is not, when one is an extremely big negative number, and so on. Even if you don't decide to change the program, it's important to know how tolerant your code is.

```
01:    public void testAddBelowRange()
02:    {
03:       Calculator calc = new CalculatorImpl();
04:       //just outside the lower range of an integer
05:       double arg1 = -2147483649.0;
06:       int result = calc.add((int)arg1,0);
07:       //verify that arg1 != result
08:    }
```

This first test, testAddBelowRange, examines what happens when we undershoot the int boundary range. As you can see on lines 4 and 5, we deliberately step outside the boundary by casting down a double that is too large to be an int, and we verify that the output is not equal to itself when added to 0 on line 7.

This next test, testAddAboveRange, examines what happens when we overshoot the int boundary range. We deliberately step outside the boundary by casting down a double that is too large to be an int, and we verify that the output is not equal to itself when added to 0.

```
01:    public void testAddAboveRange()
02:    {
03:       Calculator calc = new CalculatorImpl();
04:       //just outside the upper range of an integer
05:       double arg1 = 2147483648.0;
06:       int result = calc.add((int)arg1,0);
07:       //verify arg1 != result
08:    }
```

Finally, we test legal but extreme boundary conditions with the method below.

```
01:    public void testAddBoundryCase()
02:    {
03:       Calculator calc = new CalculatorImpl();
04:       //check the strictest legal limits
05:       int arg1 = -2147483648;
06:       int arg2 = 2147483647;
07:       int result = calc.add(arg1,arg2);
08:       //assert result == -1;
09:    }
```

DEBUGGING TECHNIQUES

Debugging is the process of looking through code for errors in an attempt to identify and fix problems. To that end, assertions can be an invaluable resource. Here are a few good suggestions for debugging.

- Make sure you know exactly what you're looking for and only deal with one bug at a time. If you find another bug along the way, make a note of it, prioritize it, and go forward.

- Check boundary conditions. Make sure you have tests both inside it and outside it.

- Check preconditions and postconditions. They can help you narrow down approximately where the code is failing.

- Consider using a debugging tool, or an Integrated Development Environment, IDE, like JBuilder or a free one like GEL, BlueJ, or JCreator.

UNIT TESTING

Unit testing is the process of testing all of the methods in your class. It is referred to as unit testing because you are only testing a single unit of code in isolation. Generally, programmers will write a "driver" program, which is specifically designed to test a given class in isolation. Thus, calling a single method on your UnitTestDriver might run any number of tests on your class's methods.

Although it's impossible to compute and test every possible scenario, you should endeavor to test the most likely ones. The goal of unit testing is to see what your methods do with the type of data expected, as well as how they perform with the most common types of data not expected.

The three tests given above (testAddBelowRange, testAddAboveRange, testAddBoundryCase) are minimally sufficient to serve as a unit test of the Calculator interface.

INTEGRATION TESTING

Unit testing shows you how your class works in isolation. **Integration testing** is a complement to unit testing, and it shows you how your class works with other classes. For example, your add method may work perfectly with positive numbers when unit tested, but it may never have come across the unique combination of challenges that actually running it in the real world can offer, which integration testing can simulate.

Integration testing is intended to remedy this scenario by examining how various classes within your program work together. At the same time, integration testing can help isolate the number of participating classes, so that if there's a problem, the suspected classes can be quickly isolated.

MEASURING PERFORMANCE

Program performance can be measured by gauging efficiency. Efficiency, in turn, has two dimensions. The first is the amount of CPU time it takes to execute a program. This is referred to as Running Time, and can be measured algorithmically by using Big-Oh analysis. The second dimension is the amount of memory a program uses.

BIG-OH NOTATION (AB ONLY)

Suppose that your teacher has a pile of exams, which she has graded, and that you would like to get your exam from her to see what your grade is. Suppose also that the exams are not in any order, so she will need to start at the top of the stack and look at each exam one by one until she finds yours.

On average, the time it takes her to find your exam will be proportional to the number of exams in the pile. You would expect that on average, it will take her twice as long to find your exam if there are 20 exams in the stack than it would to find your exam if there are only 10.

Big-Oh notation is used to indicate how the time to complete a task or algorithm changes as the amount of data changes. In the example above, you can think of the data as the stack of exams and the task as finding one particular exam in the pile. Because the time it takes to find the correct exam is proportional to the overall number of exams, we say that the task is $O(n)$; think of the n as standing for the number of data items. $O(n)$ means that the amount of time it takes to complete the task is linearly proportional to n.

Now consider another case. Suppose that your teacher keeps the exams in alphabetical order, beginning with A, and your last name is first alphabetically in the entire school. No matter how many exams there are in the pile, yours will always be on top, so no matter how many exams are in the pile, it will always take a constant time to find your exam. In this case, we would say that the time to find your exam is constant, or $O(1)$ in Big-Oh notation. The "1" indicates that the execution time is not dependent on the number of data items.

Here's an example of a method that is $O(n)$.

```
01:  public int find(char[] elements, char ch)
02:  {
03:    int position = -1;
04:    for (int i=0; i < elements.length; i++)
05:    {
06:      if (elements[i] == ch)
07:      {
08:        position = i;
09:      }
10:    }
11:    return position;
12:  }
```

This implementation will take, at most, $O(n)$ time as the size of the elements array grows. Here's why.

The first assignment, on line 3, will take a constant amount of time, say T1. Next, the program will enter the loop on line 4. The number of times this loop runs varies, depending on the size of the elements array. The number of iterations is some function of n, where n is the size of the array.

Of course, it's possible that the element will be found right away, in which case the search will be very fast. However, that's a best-case scenario and can't be a basis for our analysis. Thus, we have to assume that the search will take n time.

Some common algorithmic runtimes are listed below, in order of their efficiency.

Description	Type
$O(1)$	Constant time
$O(\log n)$	Logarithmic
$O(n)$	Linear
$O(n^2)$	Quadratic
$O(n^3)$	Cubic
$O(2^n)$	Exponential

We have already seen examples of $O(1)$ and $O(n)$ above. $O(\log n)$ is often seen with searches of ordered data. For example, the binary search discussed in Chapter 10 runs in $O(\log n)$ time on average. $O(n^2)$ is often associated with nested loops when accessing elements of a two-dimensional array. We'll see an example of this in the practice questions in Chapters 13 and 15.

Worst-case Analysis

A **worst-case scenario** analysis occurs when your program takes as long as theoretically possible to complete. Say your program is designed to look through a group of football players and find the one whose uniform bears a given number (an example of this is provided in Chapter 6). If the number you're looking for happens to be at the end of the line, then you've hit your worst-case scenario.

Average-case Analysis

An **average-case scenario** analysis occurs when you configure your program to run under the conditions that it is most likely to encounter. For example, in the football program mentioned above, the player you're looking for will probably be somewhere in the middle of the group. Thus, on average, you'll have to look through half of the football players to find the one you need. This is your average-case scenario.

Best-case Analysis

The **best-case scenario** analysis occurs when your program operates as fast as theoretically possible. For example, say your program again tries to find a given football player from a group of football players. If the player you're looking for happens to be the first one in line, then you have a best-case scenario, because your program only had to look at a single player.

Deciding Which Case Applies

It's important to be aware that your scenario analysis should be based on empirical evidence, and not on what you expect to happen. For example, you might find that you're always looking for the hardest-working players, and that they finish practice last, and so always end up at the back of the line. In this scenario, your average-case is also your worst-case, because on average, you have to step through the entire line. Thus, although it's usually easy to define a best-case and a worst-case scenario, the average-case really depends on usage.

REVIEW QUESTIONS (AB ONLY)

Answers to the review questions can be found in Chapter 11.

1. Suppose that a stack of books is on a table. There are n books in the stack, where n is a positive integer. Suppose that you want to look for a specific book that is in the stack, and to do this you remove books one by one from the top of the stack until you find the book that you are looking for. Which of the following best characterizes the average time it will take to find the book in the stack?

   (A) $O(1)$
   (B) $O(n)$
   (C) $O(\log n)$
   (D) $O(n^2)$
   (E) $O(n!)$

2. Consider the stack of randomly ordered books described in question 1. Suppose you are given the task of selecting the book that is on top of the stack. Which of the following best characterizes the average time it will take to find the book in the stack?

   (A) $O(1)$
   (B) $O(n)$
   (C) $O(\log n)$
   (D) $O(n^2)$
   (E) $O(n!)$

3. Consider the following code segment:

```
for (int x = 0; x < n; x = x + 2)
{
    //a call to a method that runs in O(1) time
}
```

   Of the following, which best characterizes the running time of the code segment?

   (A) $O(\log n)$
   (B) $O(n)$
   (C) $O(n \log n)$
   (D) $O(n^2)$
   (E) $O(n!)$

4. Consider the following code segment:

```
for (int i = 0; i < n; i++)
{
   for (int x = 0; x < n; x++)
   {
     //a call to a method that runs in O(1) time
   }
}
```

Of the following, which best characterizes the running time of the code segment?

(A) $O(\log n)$
(B) $O(n)$
(C) $O(n \log n)$
(D) $O(n^2)$
(E) $O(n!)$

5. Consider the following code segment:

```
for (int x = 1; x <= n; x = x * 2)
{
   //a call to a method that runs in O(1) time
}
```

Of the following, which best characterizes the running time of the code segment?

(A) $O(\log n)$
(B) $O(n)$
(C) $O(n \log n)$
(D) $O(n^2)$
(E) $O(n!)$

6. Consider the following code segment:

```
for (int i = 0; i < n; i++)
{
   for (int x = 0; x < n; x = x * 2)
   {
     //a call to a method that runs in O(1) time
   }
}
```

Of the following, which best characterizes the running time of the code segment?

(A) $O(\log n)$
(B) $O(n)$
(C) $O(n \log n)$
(D) $O(n^2)$
(E) $O(n!)$

Object-Oriented Design and Programming

INTRODUCTION

In the programming world, experience has shown that software engineers work best when they are able to model the procedures and data they need to work with as interacting objects. The practice of doing so is a foundation of object-oriented programming, which is the focus of this chapter. We'll discuss classes, inheritance, attributes, methods, overloading, overriding, static methods, exceptions, constructors, encapsulation, abstract classes, interfaces, IS-A versus HAS-A relationships, and polymorphism. It's important to study this material carefully, as concepts explained here are the cornerstones of understanding Java.

CLASSES

Just as most objects in the real world need a template that defines how they should be built, objects in the software world need **classes**. A class is simply a template that defines the features of one or more objects. Conceptually, you're already aware of classes, which can be thought of as categories used to define groups of things.

OBJECTS

An **object** is simply an instance of a class, a specific case based on the structure of the overall class. For example, every student in a classroom might be an American (that is, a member of the class American), but John Smith is an instance of that class and therefore an object. In Java, to create an instance of a class you would write the following code:

```
American johnSmith = new American();
```

Remember that objects of a class are distinct from each other. In other words, just because the American John Smith is able to drive does not mean that the American Jill Johnson is also able to drive. Each is a separate entity that happens to belong to the same classification as the other.

ATTRIBUTES AND METHODS

In the example above, we have created a class to define an American. Let's specify that each object of the American class has three defining attributes: life, liberty, and pursuitOfHappiness

An **attribute** is a characteristic of an object. Attributes describe the values that objects of a given class have. Similarly, we can define certain things that objects of this class can do. These are called **methods**. Methods describe all the operations that an object within a given class can perform. For example, if a student were modeled as an object, studentName would be an attribute (because it's a characteristic of the student), whereas studyJava() would be a method (because it's something a student does). Likewise, the car sitting in your driveway has attributes such as a horn, windshield wipers, and a radio, and it also performs certain operations (methods) such as honkHorn(), playRadio(), and driveFast().

You might also want to think of it this way: A class is simply a piece of code that describes the attributes and methods that an object, as an instance of this class, will have.

To model a method for our American class above, we might choose an activity such as voting, which is something that all Americans are able to do.

```
public void vote()
{
   // body of the method vote()
}
```

Our overall model of an American therefore becomes

```
public class American
{
   public void vote()
   {
      System.out.println("My candidate");
   }
```

```
    private Object life = new Object();
    private Object liberty = new Object();
    private Object pursuitOfHappiness = new Object();
}
```

When introducing a new method, it's important to provide a **method signature**. In Java, method signatures tell the computer what to expect from your method. They define any modifiers the method can have, the type of object it returns, the name of the method, the parameters it accepts, and the exceptions it might throw. Exceptions will be explained later in this section, but for now you can think of them as a list of things that might go wrong in your program. Note that the throw clause, which is not tested on the exam, simply shows which checked exceptions can be thrown by the method. As far as the AP exam is concerned, don't worry about checked exceptions at all.

A methods signature must have a specific format.

```
Modifiers returnValue methodName(params) throwClause
```

In public void vote(), our modifier is public, our return value is void, our methodName is vote, we have no parameters, and we have no throw clause because the method does not throw an exception.

ACCESS MODIFIERS

Attributes and methods can be assigned different levels of access, depending on whether or not you want other parts of your program to use them. These levels of accessibility, known as **access modifiers**, include public, private, protected, static, final, and abstract.

PUBLIC AND PRIVATE

A **public** attribute or method is freely available to any object, whereas a **private** attribute or method is restricted to the use of the object in which it is defined. Consider your own name, for instance. Although it belongs to you, it is freely accessible to anyone. Alternately, your money is private and isn't readily accessible to anyone but you. For the purposes of the AP Java subset, all classes are public, all instance variables are private, and all methods, constructors, and constants (static final variables) can be either public or private. *As far as the AP exam is concerned, attributes should be private.*

STATIC

A **static** final attribute or static method is accessible by the entire class. For example, in the class American, Mount Rushmore might be modeled as a static final attribute. It is a single instance, yet it is shared by every American, and it is unchanging. The code for doing so might look something like the following:

```
public class American
{
    static final String mountRushmore = "Mount Rushmore";
    private Object life = new Object();
    private Object liberty = new Object();
    private Object pursuitOfHappiness = new Object();
}
```

Another example might help. Say you and your friends all own cell phones made by the same manufacturer. If one of you figures out a way to push a sequence of buttons and ring everyone else's cell phone, then that person is executing a static method—one that immediately affects every object of the class cellPhone. Alternatively, if one of you breaks your phone, that is an instance method—it doesn't affect anyone else. In the following example, object_1 uses a static method to set an attribute. We are then able to extract that value from object_2.

```
public class staticMethodExample
{
   private static String staticName ="";
     public static void main(String args[])
     {
       /* create one instance of
          staticMethodExample */
       staticMethodExample object_1 = new staticMethodExample();
       /* create another instance of
          staticMethodExample */
       staticMethodExample object_2 = new staticMethodExample();
       /* set the static name on
          object_1 */
       object_1.setStaticName("object_1");
       /* now print the static value of
          the second object, even though
          we've never modified object_2 */
       System.out.println(object_2.staticName);
     }
     public static void setStaticName(String newName)
     {
       staticName = newName;
     }
}
```

FINAL

When used with a variable, **final** indicates that the value assigned to that variable cannot be changed. The following example would generate an error:

```
final int i = 10;
i = 20;
```

In the example above, we assigned the value 10 to *i*, and then tried to change its value to 20. This causes a compile-time error because *i* is declared as final on the previous line.

ABSTRACT

Abstract methods will be defined in the "Abstract Classes" section later in this chapter. For now, think of them as a way to force an obligation on child classes. In other words, if a class has an abstract method, then any child classes that derive from it must implement abstract methods.

METHOD OVERLOADING

Java provides a mechanism that allows methods with the same name to behave differently depending on the type and number of input parameters that are passed to them. This is referred to as **overloading**. In the following example, we provide three "add" methods that are overloaded. Note that all of the methods share the same name, even as they accept different parameters.

```java
public void add(int i)
{
   System.out.println("add(int)");
}
public void add(String input)
{
   System.out.println("add(String)");
}
public int add(int in, String input)
{
   System.out.println("add(int, String)");
   return 0;
}
```

Note that changing only the return type of a method does not constitute an overloaded method: In fact, that could not even be a legal method. Thus, the following would be illegal, because it is identical to the public void add(int i) method, except for the return type:

```java
//this is an illegal overload of the add method
public int add(int i)
{
   System.out.println("add(int) return i");
   return i;
}
```

EXCEPTIONS (AB ONLY)

Exceptions are Java objects that provide a programmer with information about a problem that has occurred during compilation or execution of the code. Exceptions are an extremely valuable part of well-structured code, as they can unambiguously indicate where a problem occurred, what the nature of the problem is, and exactly which method is generating the problem.

Unchecked exceptions are the only type of exceptions that you need to be concerned with for the exam. They're thrown by the JVM when something unexpected happens and the JVM does not know how to deal with the situation. As a programmer, you are not required to catch unchecked exceptions. For the exam, however, you need to be concerned with NullPointerException, IndexOutOfBoundsException, ClassCastException, and ArithmeticException.

The following example illustrates one of the situations in which these sorts of exceptions might be thrown. The first method, throwNullPointerException, throws an exception when we attempt to call a method (tmp.toString();) on an object that is null.

```
01:    public void throwNullPointerException()
02:    {
03:       // calling a method on a null object
04:       // throws a NullPointerException
05:       String tmp = null;
06:       tmp.toString();
07:    }
```

The next example, throwIndexOutOfBoundsException, throws an exception on line 9 when we try to refer to an index that does not exist (int tmp = myArray[1];). The array that we define only contains a single element, and that element exists at index 0 not 1.

```
01:    public void throwIndexOutOfBoundsException()
02:    {
03:       //Attemping to reach into an array at an
04:       //index that does not exist causes an
05:       //IndexOutOfboundsException to occur.
06:       //There is no index 1 to this array,
07:       //only index 0.
08:       int[] myArray = new int[1];
09:       int tmp = myArray[1];
10:    }
```

(Arrays will be covered in greater depth in Chapter 7.)

The following example, throwClassCastException, causes an exception to be thrown when we attempt to cast an object of type Object to an object of type String. Because an object is not a string, this results in a ClassCastException.

```
01:    public void throwClassCastException()
02:    {
03:       // attempting to cast an Object to a
04:       // string causes a ClassCastException,
05:       // because an Object is not a String.
06:       Object obj = new Object();
07:       String string = (String)obj;
08:    }
```

The following method causes an exception to be thrown on line 5 when we attempt to divide 5 by 0, which is not a legal operation between two integers:

```
01:    public void throwArithmeticException()
02:    {
03:       // attempting to divide by zero causes a
04:       //ArithmeticException to be thrown
05:       int t = 5/0;
06:    }
```

THROWING EXCEPTIONS (AB ONLY)

Your own programs can be written to easily throw exceptions for dealing with any number of error conditions that might occur. For example, if you want to indicate that a method should not be called at the current time, you might instantiate an IllegalStateException and then throw it using the throw keyword. Recall that instantiation is merely the process of creating an object based on a given class. In the following example, lines 4 and 5 instantiate an "ise" object based on the IllegalStateException class. Note that the exception is explicitly instantiated on line 5 and explicitly thrown on line 8.

```
01:   public void throwIllegalStateException()
02:   {
03:      //create an object of type
04:      //IllegalStateException
05:      IllegalStateException ise =
06:      new IllegalStateException("not right now");
07:      //now throw the IllegalStateException
08:      throw ise;
09:   }
```

If you wanted to indicate that your method did not have access to a requested element, you might instantiate a NoSuchElementException and then throw it using the throw keyword. Note that the exception is explicitly instantiated on lines 7 and 8 and explicitly thrown on line 10.

```
01:   public void throwNoSuchElementException()
02:   {
03:      //create the error message
04:      String msg = "That element doesn't exist";
05:      //create an object of type
06:      //NoSuchElementException
07:      java.util.NoSuchElementException nse =
08:      new java.util.NoSuchElementException(msg);
09:      //now throw the NoSuchElementException
10:      throw nse;
11:   }
```

Finally, note that you do not need to explicitly create an exception object to throw an exception. A call to the throwIllegalStateException() method illustrated above could more concisely be replaced by one line of code.

```
throw(new IllegalStateException("not right now"));
```

CONSTRUCTORS

Constructors are specialized methods in Java that have exactly the same name as the class to which they belong but never return a value. They are executed when a new instance of the class is created using the new command. In the following example, a default constructor is used to create a new String object:

```
String tmp = new String();
```

The default constructor is, by definition, the constructor that takes no parameters.

We are *not* calling the default constructor in the following example because we're passing the string "Hello World" as a parameter:

```
String tmp = new String("hello World");
```

When we want to define a constructor in a class, the process is very similar to the way we create normal methods in a class. However, there are a few things to keep in mind:

1. **A constructor must have the same name as the class it is in.** Thus, in a class named Citizen, all of the constructors are named Citizen. If they take different parameters, they become overloaded, as explained earlier in this chapter. In the following example, the class Citizen has two constructors, one that takes no parameters, and another that takes a string as a parameter:

```
01:   public class Citizen
02:   {
03:      private String name=null;
04:      public Citizen(){ }
05:      public Citizen(String in)
06:      {
07:        name = in;
08:      }0
09:   }
```

The first constructor on line 4 takes no parameters, so calling new Citizen() executes the code beginning on line 4. Similarly, the constructor on line 5 takes a String as a parameter, so calling new Citizen("Jim") executes the code that begins on line 5.

2. **Constructors do not have a return type.**

3. **Every class has a default "invisible" constructor that does absolutely nothing.** This is why you have been able to instantiate objects of classes in the past for which you have not provided an explicit constructor. It's important to note, however, that you lose access to this "invisible" constructor if you implement any constructors of your own, as in the example below.

```
public class catfish
{
  private String name=null;
  public catfish(String in)
  {
    name = in;
  }
}
```

As you can see, you cannot compile code that tries to create a catfish object by using the default constructor. Thus, catfish ct = new catfish(); will not compile. The point is that if you provide any constructors at all, you must provide all of your own constructors.

4. **Constructors are not inherited.** This will be explained in more detail later in this chapter when we discuss inheritance. However, it's important to understand at this point that a constructor in a class can call the constructor of the **super class**. A super class is the class that your class is based on. When it does so, that call must be the first line of code in the constructor. This means that a given constructor can call its peer constructors or the constructor of its base class; it cannot, however, do both.

For example, in the code below, the Cat class derives from the Animal class. Also, the Cat class constructor calls the Animal class constructor. That is, when line 14 executes, it automatically calls to line 4.

```
01: public class Animal
02: {
03:    //..other methods
04:    public Animal(String sound)
05:    {
06:       System.out.println(sound);
07:    }
08: }
09: public class Cat extends Animal
10: {
11:    private String tail = "red tail";
12:    public Cat()
13:    {
14:       super("meow");
15:    //optionally execute other code
16:    }
17: }
```

Again, if Cat had attempted to call other methods or execute other statements before calling the constructor of its superclass, the code would have failed to compile. If your constructor is going to make a call to a constructor of its superclass, that call must be the first statement executed by your method.

ENCAPSULATION AND INFORMATION HIDING

Encapsulation is the tendency of classes to restrict access to their private member variables. Member variables should all be private, and that access should only be granted through the use of methods.

Imagine that you are modeling a Person class, and that one of the attributes of a Person is an integer that represents this person's money. If you made this member variable public, other objects could go and take the money, thereby reducing the person to bankruptcy. However, if you provided a mechanism where other objects had to ask to receive money, then you could control the amount of money given out. In this fashion, you could always guarantee that a Person retained at least five dollars, as shown in the following example:

```
01: public int borrowMoney(int amount)
02: {
03:    int retval =0;
04:    if (money - amount >= 5)
05:    {
06:       money = money - amount;
07:       retval = amount;
```

```
08:      }
09:    else
10:       retval = money - 5;
11:    return retval;
12: }
```

The example above assumes that the member variable money is a private one. Thus, line 4 checks to make sure that the person has more then five dollars before lending out any money.

INFORMATION HIDING

Along the same lines, most object-oriented languages advocate a sense of privacy for classes. Modifiers should therefore be as restrictive as possible. Don't make a method public when it is intended for internal use by the class. The same is true for member variables.

For example, returning to the Person class example, an appropriate private method might be to breathe. It is something that Person objects must do, yet not something that others need access.

```
private void breathe()
{
   // inhale, exhale, etc.
}
```

ABSTRACT CLASSES

An **abstract class** cannot be instantiated. Rather, it's meant to provide a base class from which other classes extend. Abstract classes can, and often do, provide some implemented methods that their child classes can take advantage of, while providing other *abstract* methods that those child classes are required to implement. Because an abstract method is implemented in a subclass, it does not need to have a body. Abstract methods are a way for an abstract class to require that the subclasses implement the abstract method.

For example, consider the abstract class waterCraft, as defined below. It provides a navigate() method which any of its child classes can take advantage of. However, it also imposes a requirement on all of its child classes that they provide some implementation of the go() method.

```
public abstract class waterCraft
{
  public void navigate()
  {
    System.out.print("find north");
  }
  public abstract void go();
}
public class speedBoat extends waterCraft
{
  public abstract void go()
  {
    //go very, very fast
  }
}
```

In the example above, the speedBoat class extends the waterCraft class. Thus, speedBoat gets to have a navigate() method that works without having to write one. However, it is forced to define its own go() method.

INTERFACES

An **interface** is a Java construct, very much like a class, that helps define the various roles that an object can assume. It is intended to be implemented by a class or extended by another interface. For example, consider the following Student interface:

```
01: public interface Student
02: {
03:    public void study(String subject);
04: }
```

There are a few important things to notice here. On line 1, note that Student is defined as an interface, not as a class. Also, note that the study method defined on line 3 does not have a body. This simply means that any class that implements the interface Student *must* provide a method that implements the interface public void study(String).

For example, the Person object might choose to implement the Student interface. To do so, it must do two things: It must declare that it implements the Student interface, as it does in line 1 below, and it must implement the study method, which it does on lines 3–6.

```
01:    public class Person implements Student
02:    {
03:       public void study(String topic)
04:       {
05:          System.out.println("topic = " + topic);
06:       }
07:    }
```

A class can implement several interfaces: for example, a Person can implement a Brother interface, a Son interface, and an Athlete interface as in the example below.

```
public interface Athlete
{
    public void exercise(String game);
}
```

For the Person class to implement both the Student interface and the Athlete interface, you might write something like the following example:

```
public class Person implements Student, Athlete
{
   public void study(String topic)
   {
      System.out.println("topic = " + topic);
   }
   public void exercise (String game)
   {
      System.out.println("game = " + game);
   }
}
```

Finally, it's possible for one Interface to extend another. Thus, the BrainyStudent interface could extend the Student interface, as shown below.

```
public interface BrainyStudent extends Student
{
   public void setPocketProtector(String color);
}
```

Any class that wants to extend the BrainyStudent must implement both the setPocketProtector() method and the Study() method.

INHERITANCE

Inheritance is the ability of one class to assume the methods of another class without having to re-create those methods. This is a mechanism for code reusability that allows an extended class to take advantage of its parent. In Java vernacular, the parent class is referred to as the **super class**.

For example, imagine that you have a class named Animal and another class named Dog. Because there are certain behaviors that are general to all animals, like eat and speak, you might choose to put those behaviors in the parent class. Thus, the Animal class might look like the following example:

```
public class Animal
{
   public void eat(String food)
   {
      System.out.println("eating " + food);
   }
   public void speak()
   {
      System.out.println("animal sound ");
   }
}
```

The Dog class, because it inherits from the Animal class, might look like the example below.

```
public class Dog extends Animal
{
   public void speak()
   {
      System.out.println("bark ");
   }
}
```


EXTENDING A CLASS

Because the Dog class extends the Animal class, instances of the class Dog inherit the eat() and speak() methods: in a sense, they get them for "free." You'll note the Dog class does provide a speak() method. Why would it do so if a speak() method has already been inherited from the Animal class?

The speak() method in Dog overrides the speak() method in Animal, allowing objects of type Dog to do something that is different from normal animals when told to speak. In this case, we want Dogs to "bark"; in all other ways, however, Dogs are just like Animals.

In Java, objects can only directly extend from a single class. In this case, Dog extends from Animal, and Animal extends from Object, because all Java objects extend from the Object class by definition. In other words, a Dog is a Dog, a Dog is an Animal, and a Dog is also an Object.

HAS-A AND IS-A RELATIONSHIPS

In the Java literature, a great deal is made of the distinction between the **IS-A** relationship and the **HAS-A** relationship. In actuality, these are very straightforward ideas and you should refuse to be intimidated by them.

An IS-A relationship refers to the type of extended relationship that Dogs and Animals have. When one class extends another, it has an IS-A relationship with that class. As we saw above, a Dog IS-A Animal, because a Dog extends that class. The same is true for any interface an object implements. For example, if we had had a Pet interface which was implemented by the Dog class, then it would be appropriate to say that a Dog IS-A pet.

A HAS-A relationship, on the other hand, refers to the member variables of the class in question. Thus, a Dog object might have a tail as a member variable; this is a HAS-A relationship. For example, given the class Animal above, you might be required to design a "class Cat which is an Animal and has a Tail." By looking for key words like IS-A and HAS-A, you would know that the following is the expected result:

```
public class Cat extends Animal
{
   private String tail = "red tail";
}
```

The Cat class IS-A Animal, because it extends the Animal class. It also HAS-A tail.

METHOD OVERRIDING

A method that is inherited from a super class, yet still explicitly appears in the extended (or child) class, is considered to be overridden. Thus, in the Dog example above, the speak() method was overridden because it explicitly appeared in the Dog class and had the same signature as the speak() method in the Animal class. In contrast, the eat() method is not overridden because it does not explicitly appear in the Dog class and does appear in the Animal class. The following is an example of overriding because the speak() method (which takes no parameters) overrides the speak() method in the Animal class:

```
public class Dog extends Animal
{
   public void speak()
   {
      System.out.println("bark ");
   }
}
```

In contrast, the following is an example of overloading because all of the method names are "speak," but they take different types of parameters:

```
public void speak(String msg)
{
   System.out.println(msg);
}
public void speak(int count)
{
   for (int i=0; i < count; i++)
   {
      System.out.println(i);
   }
}
```

POLYMORPHISM

Polymorphism refers to the ability of an object to act like one of its ancestors, while still remembering its own type. For example, in the following code, we refer to an object of type Dog with a reference of type Animal:

```
01: Animal pet = new Dog();
02: pet.eat();
03: pet.speak();
```

The variable pet is a reference, which points to an object. The call to the eat() method in line 2 invokes pet to act like one of its ancestors because while a Dog doesn't have its own eat() method, it inherits from the Animal class, which does. The call to the speak() method on line 3, however, demonstrates that the object to which pet refers knows that it's a Dog and an Animal because the output is "bark" and not "animal sound."

CASTING

When two objects have an IS-A relationship, the super class can be **cast** to the child class. Thus, when Dog extends Animal, the following is perfectly legal code:

```
Dog spot = new Dog();
Animal tmp = new Dog();
```

However, this can lead to some complicated behavior. Imagine that the Dog class has a method that the Animal class does not—say wagTail().

```
public class Animal
{
  public void speak()
  {
    System.out.println("animal sound ");
  }
}
public class Dog extends Animal
{
  public void wagTail()
  {
    System.out.println("wag wag wag");
  }
}
```

In this scenario, it would be perfectly legal to execute a call to spot.wagTail(). However, the call to tmp.wagTail() would cause a compile-time error. Why? Because when we write Animal tmp = new Dog(), we're telling the JVM that we want to treat this Dog as an Animal. This being the case, we are not allowed to treat it like a Dog until we make a special effort to do so. That special effort is referred to as **casting**. We can cast the Animal object tmp to a Dog reference (Dog myDog = (Dog)tmp;) and then call Dog specific methods on it, like wagTail().

This brings up an interesting case, where it's possible to cast a reference to an object to which it is *not* a type. For example, we could, in theory, try to cast a Dog to a String, as shown below.

```
String someString = (String)tmp;
```

The reference tmp is not of type String, but the compiler won't know this at compile time. Thus, the compiler will allow us to compile this code. However, when it actually tries to execute the code, we get a ClassCastException. In effect, the JVM is telling us "Hey, a Dog isn't a String; I'd better stop you right now." The point here is that it's possible to cause these sorts of errors when you're casting. However, it's impossible to cause these problems when there is no casting. Thus, keep a sharp eye for questions that bring up ClassCastException as an option when there's no casting going on. Doing so will help you eliminate impossible alternatives on the test.

REVIEW QUESTIONS

Answers to the review questions can be found in Chapter 11.

1. A development team is building an online bookstore that customers can use to order books. Information about inventory and customer orders is kept in a database. Code must be developed that will store and retrieve data from the database. The development team decides to put the database code in separate classes from the rest of the program. Which of the following would be an advantage of this plan?

   I. The database access code could be reused in other applications that also need to access the database.
   II. The database access code can be tested independently. It will be possible to test the database access code before the interface is developed.
   III. A team of programmers can be assigned to work just on the code that is used to access the database. The programmers can work independently from other programmers, such as those who develop the user interface.

   (A) I only
   (B) II only
   (C) III only
   (D) I and II only
   (E) I, II, and III

2. In Java, data fields and methods can be designated public or private. Which of the following best characterizes the designation that should be used?

   (A) Data fields and methods should always be public. This makes it easier for client programs to access data fields and use the methods of the class.
   (B) Data fields should be either public or private, depending on whether or not it is beneficial for client programs to access them directly. All methods should be public. A private method is useless because a client program can't access it.
   (C) Keep all methods and data fields private. This enforces encapsulation.
   (D) Data fields should always be private so that clients can't directly access them. Methods can be either public or private.
   (E) All data fields should be public so client programs can access them, and all methods should be private.

3. Which of the following are signs of a well-designed program?

   I. Clients know how data is stored in the class.
   II. Classes and methods can be tested independently.
   III. The implementation of a method can be changed without changing the programs that use the method.

   (A) I only
   (B) II only
   (C) II and III
   (D) I and II
   (E) I, II, and III

4. Consider the following classes:

```java
public class Sample
{
    public void writeMe(Object obj)
    {
        System.out.println("object");
    }
    public void writeMe(String s)
    {
        System.out.println("string");
    }
}
```

What will be the result of executing the following?

```java
Sample s = new Sample();
String tmp = new String("hi");
s.writeMe(tmp);
```

(A) Compile-time error
(B) "hi"
(C) "object"
(D) "string"
(E) Run-time error

5. Consider the following class:

```java
public class Sample
{
    public void writeMe(Object obj)
    {
        System.out.println("object");
    }
    public void writeMe(String s)
    {
        System.out.println("string");
    }
}
```

What will be the result of executing the following?

```java
Sample s = new Sample();
Object tmp = new Object();
s.writeMe(tmp);
```

(A) Compile-time error
(B) "string"
(C) "object"
(D) "hi"
(E) Run-time error

6. Consider the following class:

```
public class Sample
{
    public void writeMe(Object obj)
    {
        System.out.println("object");
    }
    public void writeMe(String s)
    {
        System.out.println("string");
    }
}
```

What will be the result of executing the following?

```
Sample s = new Sample();
Object tmp = new String("hi");
s.writeMe(tmp);
```

(A) Compile-time error
(B) "hi"
(C) "object"
(D) "string"
(E) Run-time error

7. Consider the following class:

```
public class Sample
{
    public void writeMe(Object obj)
    {
        System.out.println("object");
    }
    public void writeMe(String s)
    {
        System.out.println("string");
    }
}
```

What will be the result of executing the following?

```
Sample s = new Sample();
String tmp = new Object();
s.writeMe(tmp);
```

(A) Compile-time error
(B) "hi"
(C) "object"
(D) "string"
(E) Run-time error

8. Consider the following class:

```
public class Sample
{
    int val = 0;
}
```

Is val an attribute or a method?

(A) Neither: a compile-time error occurs when we try to execute this code.
(B) val is an attribute.
(C) val is a method.
(D) val is both an attribute and a method.
(E) Neither, val is a primitive.

9. Consider the following class:

```
public class Sample
{
    public String writeMe(String s)
    {
        System.out.println("object");
    }
    public void writeMe(String s)
    {
        System.out.println("string");
    }
}
```

What will be the result of executing the following?

```
Sample s = new Sample();
Object tmp = new Object()
s.writeMe(tmp);
```

(A) Compile-time error
(B) "hi"
(C) "object"
(D) "string"
(E) Run-time error

10. Consider the following two classes:

```
public class Parent
{
    public void writeMe(String s)
    {
        System.out.println("object");
    }
}
public class Child extends Parent
{
    public void writeMe(String s)
    {
        System.out.println("object");
    }
}
```

Which of the following best describes the writeMe method of the Child class?

(A) An inherited method
(B) An overridden method
(C) An overloaded method
(D) An interface method
(E) An abstract method

11. Create two classes, Jaguar and Car, where a Car has a public wheel, and a Jaguar is a Car. Assume wheel is a String.

12. Given the following Class, create an interface for it, named Sample:

```
public class SampleImpl
{
    public String writeMe(String s)
    {
        System.out.println("object");
    }
}
```

13. How many classes can a given class extend?

(A) None
(B) 1
(C) 2
(D) As many as it needs to

14. How many interfaces can a given class implement?

(A) None
(B) 1
(C) 2
(D) As many as it needs to

15. How many other interfaces can a given interface extend?

    (A) None
    (B) 1
    (C) 2
    (D) As many as it needs to

16. How many classes can a given interface implement?

    (A) None
    (B) 1
    (C) 2
    (D) As many as it needs to

17. Consider the following class:

```
public class Sample
{
    int var =0;
    public static void writeMe(String string)
    {
        System.out.println("string");
    }
}
```

What is the result of executing the following?

```
Sample.writeMe("hello");
```

    (A) This is not a legal call because there is no instance variable.
    (B) "hello"
    (C) "null"
    (D) "string"
    (E) Run-time error

18. Consider the following class:

```
public class Sample
{
    int static final var =0;
}
```

What is the result of executing the following?

```
System.out.println(Sample.var);
```

    (A) This is not a legal call because there is no instance variable.
    (B) −1
    (C) 0
    (D) The value is unknowable.
    (E) This is not a legal call because var is final.

For questions 19–20, consider the following class:

```
public class Sample
{
  String name;
  public Sample (String in)
  {
    name = in;
  }
  public void writeMe(String s)
  {
    String val = null;
    if (val.equals(s))
    {
      System.out.println("me");
    }
    else
    {
      System.out.println("you");
    }
  }
}
```

19. What will be the result of executing the following?

```
Sample s = new Sample();
String tmp = new String("hi");
s.writeMe(tmp);
```

(A) Compile-time error
(B) Run-time error
(C) "hi"
(D) "string"
(E) "Sample"

20. What will be the result of executing the following?

```
Sample s = new Sample("sample");
String tmp = new String("hi");
s.writeMe(tmp);
```

(A) "hi"
(B) Run-time error
(C) "me"
(D) "sample"
(E) "you"

Questions 21–22 refer to the following information:

Consider the following declaration for a class that will be used to represent a rectangle:

```
public class Rectangle
{
  private double width;
  private double height;
  public Rectangle()
  {
    width = 0;
    height = 0;
  }
  public Rectangle(double w, double h)
  {
    width = w;
    height = h;
  }

  // postcondition: returns the height
  public double height()
  {
    return height;
  }
  // postcondition: returns the width
  public double width()
  {
    return width;
  }
}
```

The following incomplete class declaration is intended to extend the above class so the rectangles can be filled with a color when displayed:

```
public class FilledRectangle extends Rectangle
{
  private String color;
  // constructors go here
  public String getColor()
  {
    return color;
  }
}
```

21. Consider the following proposed constructors for this class:

```
I.  public FilledRectangle()
    {
      color = "red";
    }

II. public FilledRectangle(double w, double h, String c)
    {
      super(w, h);
      color = c;
    }

III. public FilledRectangle(double w, double h, String c)
     {
       width = w;
       height = h;
       color = c;
     }
```

Which of these constructors would be legal for the FilledRectangle class?

(A) I only
(B) II only
(C) III only
(D) I and II
(E) I and III

22. Based on the class declarations for Rectangle and FilledRectangle given above, which of the following code segments would be legal in a client class? Assume that the constructor that takes no arguments has been implemented for FilledRectangle.

```
I.   FilledRectangle r1 = new  Rectangle();
     double height = r1.getHeight();

II.  Rectangle r2 = new FilledRectangle();
     double height = r2.getHeight();

III. Rectangle r3 = new FilledRectangle();
     r3.getColor();
```

Which of the code segments above are legal?

(A) I only
(B) II only
(C) III only
(D) I and II
(E) II and III

23. An apartment rental company has asked you to write a program to store information about the apartments that it has available for rent. For each apartment, they want to keep track of the following information: number of rooms, whether or not the apartment has a dishwasher, and whether or not pets are allowed. Which of the following is the best design?

(A) Use four unrelated classes: `Apartment`, `Rooms`, `Dishwasher`, and `Pets`.

(B) Use one class, `Apartment` which has three subclasses: `Room`, `Dishwasher`, and `Pet`.

(C) Use one class, `Apartment`, which has three data fields: int `rooms`, boolean `hasDishwasher`, boolean `allowsPets`.

(D) Use three classes `Pets`, `Rooms`, and `Dishwasher`, each with a subclass `Apartment`.

(E) Use four classes: `Apartment`, `Pets`, `Dishwasher`, and `Rooms`. The class `Apartment` contains instances of the other classes as attributes.

24. Consider the following class declaration:

```
public interface Inter
{
    int inter1();
}
```

Which of the following classes will compile without error?

```
I.  public class A implements Inter
    {
        private int inter1()
        {
            return 7;
        }
    }
II. public abstract class B implements Inter
    {
    }
III. public class C implements Inter
    {
        public double inter1()
        {
            return 7;
        }
    }
```

(A) None of the above
(B) I only
(C) II only
(D) III only
(E) I and III

25. Consider the following class declarations:

```
public class Vehicle
{
  private int maxPassengers;
  public Vehicle()
  {
    maxPassengers = 1;
  }
  public Vehicle(int x)
  {
    maxPassengers = x;
  }
  public int maxPassengers()
  {
    return maxPassengers;
  }
}
public class Motorcycle extends Vehicle
{
  public Motorcycle()
  {
    super(2);
  }
}
```

Which of the following code segments will NOT cause a compilation error?

(A) `Motorcycle m1 = new Motorcycle(3);`
(B) `Vehicle v1 = new Motorcycle(4);`
(C) `Motorcycle  m2 = new Vehicle();`
(D) `Vehicle v2 = new Motorcycle();`
(E) `Vehicle v3 = new Vehicle();`
    `    int max = v3.maxPassengers;`

26. Consider the following two classes:

```java
public class SuperClass
{
  public int A()
  {
    return A() + 3;
  }
  public int B()
  {
    return 7;
  }
}
public class SubClass extends SuperClass
{
  public int A()
  {
    return super.B() + 2;
  }
  public int B()
  {
    return super.A() + 5;
  }
  public int C()
  {
    return super.A();
  }
}
```

Assume the following declaration appears in a client program:

```java
SuperClass x = new SubClass();
```

What is printed as a result of the call System.out.print(x.B())?

(A) 8
(B) 12
(C) 15
(D) 17
(E) Nothing is printed because of infinite recursion.

27. Assume the following declaration appears in a client program:

```java
SuperClass y = new SuperClass();
```

What is printed as a result of a call to System.out.print(y.A())?

(A) 8
(B) 12
(C) 15
(D) 17
(E) Nothing is printed because of infinite recursion.

28. Consider the following two classes:

```
public class A
{
   public int method1(int x)
   {
      return 2;
   }
}
public class B extends A
{
}
```

Which of the following could be the signature of a method in class A that correctly overloads method1() in class A?

(A) public int method1(String x)
(B) public int method1(int y)
(C) private int method1(int x)
(D) public int method2(String x)
(E) public int method1(int y)

Java Library Classes

INTRODUCTION

In the previous chapter, we reviewed how to define custom classes and interfaces in Java. On the AP exam, you will also be expected to know how to use some of the prewritten classes and interfaces that come with Java. The standard edition of Java comes with hundreds of prewritten classes and interfaces that you can use in the applications that you build. Fortunately, only a small subset of the library classes is covered on the AP exam.

In this chapter, we will review the following classes and interfaces: Object, String, Math, Random, Comparable, Integer, and Double. In the standard version of Java, each of these classes and interfaces contains many methods; you will only be expected to know some of these methods for the AP exam. We cover the methods that you should know in detail below.

To completely understand the material in this chapter, you will need to be comfortable with inheritance and method overriding. These topics are reviewed in Chapter 4.

THE OBJECT CLASS

The **Object class** is at the top of the Java class hierarchy. Every class in Java extends the Object class, either directly or indirectly.

Usually, if a class extends another class, it is necessary to use the extends keyword to indicate this. However, it is not necessary to use extends to indicate that a class extends the Object class; this relationship is implied even if a class does not explicitly declare that it extends Object.

In other words, the two class declarations below are equivalent.

```
public class Animal
{
   //code
}
public class Animal extends Object
{
   //code
}
```

What if we were to have a class that extended Animal? Would this class also extend the Object class? Consider the following example:

```
public class Dog extends Animal
{
   // code
}
```

Because the Dog class extends the Animal class, and the Animal class extends the Object class, the Dog class also extends the Object class and inherits all of its methods. The following diagram illustrates the class hierarchy:

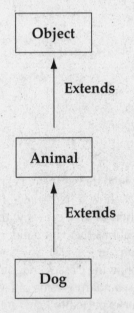

Consider the following example, which creates a Dog object and assigns it to the reference myDog:

```
Dog myDog = new Dog();
```

In the example above, the object that myDog references is a Dog because it is an instance of the Dog class. It is also an Animal, because the Dog class extends Animal. Finally, it is an Object because the Animal class extends the Object class.

Note that we can say that myDog is an object (with a lowercase o) because it is an instance of a class. We can also say it is an Object (with an uppercase O) because it is an instance of a class that extends the Object class.

So why have an Object class? The Object class provides methods that all classes in Java need. For example, any object should be able to give a String representation of itself, so the Object class provides a toString() method that does this. And because we sometimes need to know if two objects are equal, the Object class provides an equals() method. Because all classes extend the Object class, all classes inherit the methods defined in the Object class definition.

As we saw in Chapter 4, some methods can accept object references as arguments. Sometimes it is useful to have the parameter type in a method be Object. This way, the method can accept objects of any type, because any object in Java is an Object. For example, we saw above that a Dog object is an Object because the Dog class extends the Animal class which extends the Object class. We'll see how this is useful when we cover collection classes in Chapter 8.

OBJECT METHODS

Listed below are the methods of the Object class that are tested on the exam. Note that hashCode() is only tested on the AB version of the exam.

- `class java.lang.Object`
- `boolean equals(Object other)`
- `String toString()`
- `int hashcode()` *(AB only)*

String toString()

This method returns a String representation of an object. We'll use the following class to take a look at how this works:

```
public class Student
{
  private double gradePtAvg;
  private String lastName;

  public Student(double gpa, String ln)
  {
    gradePtAvg = gpa;
    lastName = ln;
  }

  public double getGradePtAvg()
  {
    return gradePtAvg;
  }
```

```
    public String getLastName()
    {
      return lastName;
    }
}
```

Let's create a Student object, call the toString() method on it, and then print out the results.

```
Student student1 = new Student(4.0, "Fritz");
String student1AsString = s1.toString();
System.out.println(student1AsString);
```

Here is the output.

```
Student@cac268
```

Even though we did not define a toString() method in the Student class, we can still call the toString() method on a Student object. Why is this? Like all classes, the Student class implicitly extends the Object class. Because it extends the Object class, it will inherit the Object class's implementation of the toString() method.

The other thing to note is that the implementation of the toString() method provided by the Object class is not very useful. It simply returns the name of the class, followed by the @ sign, followed by the memory address of the object (and no, you don't need to know this detail for the exam).

What if we would like the toString() method to return something more useful, like the student's last name and grade-point average? All we need to do is provide an implementation of the toString() method in the Student class. This will override the toString() implementation provided by the Object class.

Let's add the following method to the Student class defined above, and then instantiate a new Student object and call its toString() method:

```
 public String toString()
 {
   return "The GPA for " + lastName + " is " + gradePtAvg;
 }
Student student2 = new Student(4.0, "Fritz");
String student2AsString = student2.toString();
System.out.println(student2AsString);
```

Here is the output after overriding toString().

```
The GPA for Fritz is 4.0
```

boolean equals(Object other)

This method provided by the Object class determines whether two object references refer to the same object.

The code below uses the Student class defined above.

```
Student student1 = new Student(3.5, "Smith");
Student student2 = new Student(3.5, "Smith");
boolean areTheyEqual = student1.equals(student2);
System.out.println(areTheyEqual);
```

This produces the output

```
false
```

In the example above, areTheyEqual would be false, even though the two objects we created contain the same data. The Student class does not have an equals() method, so it inherits the equals() method that is provided by the Object class. Even though student1 and student2 refer to objects with the same data, they refer to different objects, and because the equals() method provided by the Object class only returns true if they refer to the same object, the method returns false.

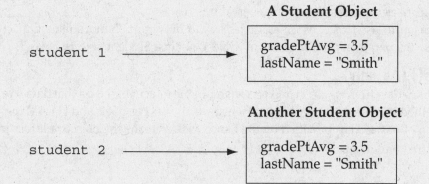

Much of the time, the behavior of the equals() method that is provided by the Object class is not very useful. What if, for example, you want your program to consider two different Student objects to be equal if they have the same gradePtAvg? In this case, you will need to add an equals() method to the Student class that overrides the equals() method provided by the Object class.

The following equals() method could be added to the Student class so that two different Students with the same gradePtAvg are equal:

```
01:   public boolean equals(Object o)
02:   {
03:       Student student = (Student) o;
04:       if (getGradePtAvg() == student.getGradePtAvg())
05:       {
06:           return true;
07:       }
08:       else
09:       {
10:           return false;
11:       }
12:   }
```

On line 3 above, we cast "o" to a Student object, because we will be calling a method of the Student class (getGradePtAvg()) later in the code. What happens if we try to pass an object that is not a Student to this method? In this case, a ClassCastException will be thrown on line 3 and the rest of the code won't execute. This is desired behavior because we only want to be able to compare a Student object to other Student objects. It would not make sense to compare a Student instance to, for example, a Dog instance.

Why don't we just make the parameter of the equals() method a Student rather than an Object like so?

```
public boolean equals(Student s)
{
    //Error!
}
```

If we did this, the problem is that the equals() method defined in the Student class would no longer override the equals() method defined in the Object class. An overriding method must have exactly the same signature as the method that it is overriding.

Another reason to use Object as a parameter has to do with polymorphism. Our code is more general because the parameter can refer to any Object, not just Student objects.

int hashcode() (AB only)

This method takes data from an object and returns a unique integer based on that data. We'll cover the hashcode() method in more detail in Chapter 9 when we discuss HashSets and HashMaps. The default implementation of hashCode() provided by the Object class returns the objects address in memory.

THE STRING CLASS

WHAT IS THE STRING CLASS?

The **String class** is used to represent character strings such as "This is a sentence", "4 is a number", or "" (the empty string).

CREATING A STRING OBJECT

You can create a String using a constructor, which you should recall is simply a command for creating an object.

```
String s1 = new String("This is a String");
```

For convenience, Java also provides a way to create a String instance without using a constructor. Simply set a String reference equal to a string of characters in quotation marks. Note that string values must be delimited using double quotation marks (" "). Single quotation marks (' ') will not work.

```
String s2 = "This is another String";
```

STRING IMMUTABILITY

String objects are immutable, which means that they can't be changed once they are created. This does not mean, however, that a String reference can't be changed to point to a different String object. For example, the following is perfectly legal:

```
String s1 = "A String";
s1 = "Another String";
```

In the example above, we are not changing the string "A String". Instead we are creating a new String object that represents "Another String" and assigning it to s1 in place of "A String ". "A String" is no longer referenced by a variable, and it will be discarded from memory by the JVM.

The important distinction here is between an object and a variable that holds a reference to that object. A reference is just a pointer or handle to an object. In the example above, s1 is a variable that holds a reference to a String object with the value "A String ". This looks like the following:

After the second line (s1 = "Another String") executes above, s1 references a different String object; it no longer references the object with the value "A String ". This looks like.

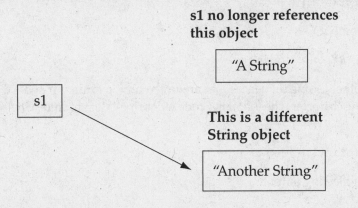

The String object that contains the value "A String" is no longer referenced by a variable, so the JVM will remove it from memory.

So at this point, we have a variable called s1 that holds a reference to a String object with the value "Another String". What if we want to change the name of the variable to s2 but don't want to change the object itself? We could do the following:

```
s2 = s1;
```

The line above will create another variable that holds a reference to the same String object as s1. Here's what this looks like.

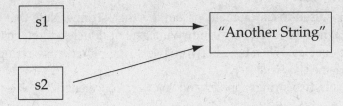

If we now want to get rid of the s1 reference (but not the object that it refers to) we could do this

```
s1 = null;
```

Now s1 refers to nothing.

ESCAPE SEQUENCES

The beginning and end of a string must be delimited with quotation marks. This can cause a problem if the string you are trying to create contains a quotation mark, because the compiler will assume that the second quotation mark indicates the end of the string. The following example will cause a compile-time error because of the enclosed quotation mark:

```
String s = "This is a "String" object"; // Error!
```

If you want to include a quotation mark in a string, you must put the escape character \ in front of the quotation mark.

```
String s = "This is a \"String\" object";
System.out.println(s);
```

This produces the output

```
This is a "String" object
```

There are two other escape sequences that are tested on the exam: \n and \\.

\n is the new line character. The following code will print "Megan" and "Chelsea" on two separate lines:

```
System.out.println("Megan\nChelsea");
```

This produces the following output:

```
Megan
Chelsea
```

\\ adds a backslash to the string.

```
System.out.println("Megan\\Chelsea");
```

This produces the output

```
Megan\Chelsea
```

STRING CONCATENATION

The plus operator (+) is used to **concatenate**, or join together, strings. Note that the + operator is an overridden operator. When it is used between two integers or doubles, it returns the arithmetic sum of the two integers or doubles. When used between two strings, it returns a string that represents the two strings joined together.

In the example below, two strings "apple" and "pie" are concatenated.

```
String s1 = "apple" + "pie";
System.out.println(s1);
```

This produces the output

```
applepie
```

What happens if you try to concatenate an object with a string? The concatenation operator will automatically call the toString() method on the object. All classes have a toString() method, even if they don't explicitly implement one. Why is this? Recall that all classes extend the Object class, and thus can inherit the toString() method defined in Object.

Consider the following class, which has a toString() method that returns the name of the student:

```
public class Student
{
  private String name;

  public Student(String n)
  {
    name = n;
  }

  public String toString()
  {
    return name;
  }
}
```

The following code makes use of the Student class above:

```
Student s = new Student("Mike");
String myString = s + " is a student.";
System.out.println(myString);
```

This produces the output

```
Mike is a student.
```

When a number and a string are joined together, the number is converted to a string.

```
int a = 101;
String b = " Dalmatians";
String s = a + b;
System.out.println(s);
```

This produces the output

```
101 Dalmatians
```

Note that the output is one complete string, not an integer followed by a string. In other words, "101" is three characters in the string "101 Dalmatians".

What happens if we concatenate more than one number with a string?

```
String s = 3 + 4 + " Samurai";
System.out.println(s);
```

This produces the output

```
7 Samurai
```

In the code above, 3 + 4 + " Samurai" is evaluated from left to right. Because 3 and 4 are integers, integer addition is performed, resulting in the integer 7. Next, the integer 7 and the string " Samurai" are joined together. Because " Samurai" is a string, 7 is converted to a string and concatenated with " Samurai", producing the string "7 Samurai".

Contrast the example above with the following:

```
String s = "Magnificent " + 3 + 4;
System.out.println(s);
```

This produces the output

```
Magnificent 34
```

This time, the 3 and 4 weren't added together to produce 7. Why not? In the code above, "Magnificent " + 3 + 4 is evaluated from left to right. First, "Magnificent " is concatenated with the integer 3 to produce the string "Magnificent 3". The 3 is no longer an integer; it is just another character in the string. Then, the string "Magnificent 3" is concatenated with the integer 4 to produce the string "Magnificent 34".

Now, let's look at the methods of the String class.

STRING METHODS

Below are the methods of the String class that are tested on the exam. The String class is in the java.lang package and implements the Comparable interface.

```
class java.lang.String implements java.lang.Comparable
```

- int compareTo(Object other)
- boolean equals(Object other)
- int length()
- String substring(int from, int to)
- String substring(int from)
- int indexOf(String s)

int compareTo(Object other)

This method is used to compare two String objects based on alphabetical order. If the String that this method is called on would be alphabetically sorted *before* the String that is passed as an argument, then a negative integer is returned. If the String that this method is called on would be alphabetically sorted *after* the String that is passed as an argument, then a positive integer is returned. If the two Strings are equal, 0 is returned.

Note that any capital letter comes before all lowercase letters alphabetically. For example, "B" comes before "a".

The following code compares two String instances:

```
String s1 = new String("cat");
String s2 = new String("dog");
int i = s1.compareTo(s2);
System.out.println(i);
```

This produces the output

```
-1
```

In the example above, the compareTo() method is called on String s1 ("cat"), whereas s2 ("dog") is passed as an argument. Because "cat" comes before "dog" alphabetically, a negative number is returned.

Contrast the example above with the following:

```
String s1 = new String("cat");
String s2 = new String("dog");
int i = s2.compareTo(s1);
System.out.println(i);
```

This produces the output

```
1
```

In this example, we are using the same character strings that we used in example 1. This time, however, we call the compareTo() method on s2 ("dog") and pass s1 ("cat") as an argument to the method. Because "dog" comes after "cat" alphabetically, a positive number is returned.

The following example uses a capital letter in one of the strings:

```
String s1 = new String("dog");
String s2 = new String("Cat");
int i = s1.compareTo(s2);
System.out.println(i);
```

This produces the output

```
31
```

Note here that s2 ("Cat") begins with an uppercase C. Because lowercase letters come after uppercase letters, "dog" comes after "Cat". Therefore, a positive number is returned. The actual number that is returned is unimportant. What is important is the sign of the number.

Let's take a look at one more example.

```
String s1 = new String("dog");
String s2 = new String("doghouse");
int i = s1.compareTo(s2);
System.out.println(i);
```

This produces the output

```
-5
```

In the example above, one of the words "dog" is the same as the beginning of the other word "doghouse". In a case like this, the shorter word comes before the longer word, so a negative number is returned.

boolean equals(Object o)

This method returns true if the String object that is passed as an argument to the method represents the same character string as the object that this method is called on.

```
String s1 = "cat";
String s2 = "cat";
String s3 = "Cat";
boolean a = s1.equals(s2); // a is true
boolean b = s1.equals(s3); // b is false
boolean c = "dog".equals("cat"); // c is false
```

int length()

This method returns the length of the string as an integer.

```
String s = "a string";
int i = s.length(); // i is equal to 8
String s = "";
int i = s.length(); // i is equal to 0
```

A string with a length of zero is also known as an "empty string".

> Watch out for strings that have escape sequences. An escape sequence such as \\
> increases the length of a string by only one because it will only output a single char-
> acter:
>
> ```
> String s = "A\\B";
> int i = s.length(); //i is equal to 3
> ```

String substring(int from)

This method returns the remainder of a string beginning at the position that is passed as an argument. The underlying string is not modified. The argument must be greater than or equal to 0 and less than or equal to the length of the string. Strings are **zero-indexed,** meaning that the first character in a string is at position 0, not position 1.

Consider the string "computer". The graphic below shows the position of each character in the string.

```
0 1 2 3 4 5 6 7
c o m p u t e r
```

The table below shows the results of calling the substring(int) method with different argument values on the string "computer".

substring() call	return value
"computer".substring(0);	"computer"
"computer".substring(2);	"mputer"
"computer".substring(7);	"r"
"computer".substring(8);	""
"computer".substring(9);	An IndexOutOfBoundsException is thrown.

String substring(int from, int to)

Like the substring() method above, this method returns a portion of a string. This method does not modify the underlying string. The substring that is returned starts at the "from" parameter and ends at the position immediately before the "to" parameter.

The table below shows the results of calling the substring(int, int) method with different argument values on the string "computer".

substring() call	return value
"computer".substring(2, 3);	"m"
"computer".substring(3, 7);	"pute"
"computer".substring(0, 7);	"compute"
"computer".substring(0, 8);	"computer"
"computer".substring(3, 3);	""
"computer".substring(0, 9);	An IndexOutOfBoundsException is thrown.

The fact that the character at the position indicated by the "to" argument is not included in the returned substring, but the character at the position indicated by the "from" argument is included in the returned substring, often trips up programmers. Something to note is that the length of the string that is returned by the substring(int, int) method is always the difference between the second and first index.

Example

Try the following example question:

What is the value of s after the following statement is executed?

```
String s = "computer".substring(4, 6);
```

(A) pu
(B) put
(C) ut
(D) ute
(E) u

Because the difference between the two arguments 4 and 6 is 2, the correct answer choice must be two characters long. This lets us eliminate answer choices (B), (D), and (E) immediately. The first character of s will be the character at position 4 in "computer". Because this character is "u", we can get rid of answer choice (A). Therefore, the correct answer must be (C).

int indexOf(String s)

This method determines if a string contains another string. The value returned by this method is the starting position of the sought-after substring, which is passed as an argument, or –1 if the string that is passed as an argument does not occur within the string that this method is called on.

In the following example, we look for the position of the string "cde" within the string "abcdefg":

```
String s = "abcdefg";
int i = s.indexOf("cde");
System.out.println(i);
```

This produces the following output:

```
2
```

In the example above, the string that we passed as an argument ("cde") matched a substring within string s "abcdefg". This match begins at position 2 in string s, so the indexOf() method returns a value of 2.

In the following example, the string we pass as an argument to the indexOf() method is not contained within the string that we call the method on:

```
String s = "abcdefg";
int i = s.indexOf("cdf");
System.out.println(i);
```

This produces the following output:

```
-1
```

This time, the string that we pass as an argument ("cdf") does not match a substring of "abcdefg". When there is no match, the indexOf() method returns –1.

What happens if the string that we pass as an argument matches in more than one position? In this case, the indexOf() method returns the starting position of the first occurrence of the substring.

Consider the following example:

```
String s = "xabcabd";
int i = s.indexOf("ab");
System.out.println(i);
```

This produces the following output:

```
1
```

Note in the example above that "ab" occurs at both position 1 and 4 in the string "xabcabd". The indexOf() method returns the starting position of the first occurrence of the substring, so 1 is returned.

THE MATH CLASS

WHAT IS THE MATH CLASS?

The **Math class** provides methods for performing mathematical functions. All of the methods of the Math class are static; you will never need to create an instance of the Math class. See Chapter 4 for more information on static methods.

MATH METHODS

Below are the methods of the Math class. The Math class is in the java.lang package.

```
class java.lang.Math
```

- `static int abs(int x)`
- `static double abs(double x)`
- `static double pow(double base, double exponent)`
- `static double sqrt(double x)`

static int abs(int x)

This method finds the absolute value of its argument. If the argument is positive or 0, the return value is the same as the argument. If the argument is negative, the return value is the negation of the argument.

```
int a = Math.abs(15);
int b = Math.abs(0);
int c = Math.abs(-7);
```

In the example above, *a* will be 15, *b* will be 0, and *c* will be 7.

static double abs(double x)

This method is the same as the one above, except the argument and return value are doubles.

```
double a = Math.abs(15.7);
double b = Math.abs(0.0);
double c = Math.abs(-6.3);
```

static double pow(double base, double exponent)

This method is used to calculate exponential functions. It raises the "base" argument to the "exponent" argument.

The following code calculates $2.0^{3.0}$:

```
double b = 2.0;
double c = 3.0;
double result = Math.pow(b, c);
System.out.println(result);
```

This produces the output

```
8.0
```

Both of the arguments of the pow() method are doubles. Because integers are automatically cast to doubles, we can also pass int variables to this method.

```
int a = 4;
int b = 3;
double result = Math.pow(a, b);
System.out.println(result);
```

This produces the following output:

```
64.0
```

Even though we passed ints to the pow() method, the output was still a double. If we want to work with the return value of this method as an integer, we'll need to use an explicit cast.

```
int result = (int) Math.pow(a, b);
```

double sqrt(double x)

This method returns the square root of the argument.

```
double result = sqrt(100);
System.out.println(result);
```

This produces the output

```
10.0
```

THE RANDOM CLASS

WHAT IS THE RANDOM CLASS?

The **Random class** is used to generate random numbers. For example, this class could be used in a program that needs to simulate the rolling of a die, in which each roll is a random number between 1 and 6. The Random class uses the clock of the computer to generate the random number. The numbers generated in this way are sometimes referred to as "pseudorandom" because they aren't truly random. They are, however, random enough for most purposes.

CREATING A RANDOM OBJECT

A constructor without any arguments is used to create an instance of the Random class.

```
Random r = new Random();
```

RANDOM METHODS

Below are the methods of the Random class that are tested on the exam. The Random class is in the java.util package.

- int nextInt(int n)

- double nextDouble()

int nextInt(int n)

This method returns a random number that is greater than or equal to zero and less than the integer that is passed as an argument.

The following code will create a random integer that is between 0 and 9 inclusive and assign it to *i*:

```
Random r = new Random();
int i = r.nextInt(10);
```

The following code simulates the roll of six-sided die. It generates a number between 1 and 6 inclusive:

```
Random r = new Random();
int roll = r.nextInt(6) + 1;
```

The random integer is assigned to the variable roll. In the second line, r.nextInt(6) will generate a number between 0 and 5 inclusive. We then need to add 1 to get a number between 1 and 6 for the roll of the die.

How would you generate a random int between 7 and 12 inclusive? First, note that we need to generate one of 6 random numbers: 7, 8, 9, 10, 11, and 12. We can generate a random number with a range of 6 numbers by doing the following:

```
Random r = new Random();
int i = r.nextInt(6);
```

Note that the random number will be between 0 and 5 inclusive. In other words, the numbers from which we'll be arbitrarily choosing are 0, 1, 2, 3, 4, and 5.

The next step is to figure out how much we need to "bump up" the lower end of the range. Right now, the low end is 0 and we want to change it to 7, so simply add 7 to the end of the second line above so that it becomes

```
int i = r.nextInt(6) + 7;
```

Note that this change will also bump up the upper range from 5 to 12, which is exactly what we want.

Try the following question:

The junior class of Jones High School has at least 150 students. The names of these students are stored in an array of length 150, one name to a cell, in ascending order based on the grade-point average of each student; so, for example, the index of the name of the student with the highest GPA is 149. The school administration would like to randomly select one of the top 10 students to represent the school at a leadership conference. Write a method called topTenStudent to accomplish this. The method should take an array of Strings with a length as a parameter and return a String randomly chosen from the last 10 positions in the array.

Here is one way to do this.

```
public String topTenStudent(String[] students)
{
    int end = students.length - 1;
    // end is the index of the last cell in the array
    int start = end - 10;
    /* start is the index of the 10th cell
       from the end of the array */
    Random r = new Random();
    int index = r.nextInt(10) + start;
    return students[index];
}
```

THE COMPARABLE INTERFACE

Sometimes you will need to compare two different instances of a class to see if one instance is less than, equal to, or greater than the other instance. The **Comparable interface** is implemented by the String, Integer, and Double class; this provides a convenient way to compare instances of these classes. You should also implement the Comparable interface in classes that you design if programs that use your classes will need to compare instances of them.

Consider the following class:

```
public class Student
{
    private double gradePtAvg;
    private String lastName;
    public Student(double gpa, String ln)
    {
        gradePtAvg = gpa;
        lastName = ln;
    }
    public int getGradePtAvg()
    {
        return gpa;
    }
    public String getLastName()
    {
        return lastName;
    }

}
```

First, let's create a Student with the last name "Adams" whose grade-point average is 3.5.

```
Student student1 = new Student(3.5, "Adams");
```

Now we'll create a Student with the last name "Zena" whose grade-point average is 2.0.

```
Student student2 = new Student(2.0, "Zena");
```

If we were to order the Student objects from least to greatest, which one would come first? We could argue that student1 should come first, because the last name "Adams" comes before "Zena" alphabetically. We could also argue that student2 should come first, because student2's grade-point average is lower than student1's.

The answer will depend on the needs of your application. If your program is going to print out a student roster alphabetically, then we will want to order the students based on their last names. On the other hand, a program that is used to figure out a student's class rank would need to order them based on their grade-point averages.

By implementing the Comparable interface, a class can specify how objects in that class should be ordered. Classes that implement the Comparable interface must provide the following method:

```
public int compareTo(Object obj)
```

This method returns a negative integer if the object that it is called on is less than the object that is passed as an argument. If the object that this method is called on is greater than the object that is passed as an argument, a positive number is returned. If the two objects are equal, 0 is returned.

Let's change the Student class so that it implements the Comparable interface such that Student objects are ordered from least to greatest according to their grade-point averages.

The first step is to change the class declaration.

```
public class Student implements Comparable
{
   //code goes here
}
```

Next, we need to implement a compareTo() method in the Student class. Here's one way that we could do this.

```
public int compareTo(Object obj)
{
   Student otherStudent = (Student) obj;
   double otherStudentsGPA = otherStudent.getGradePtAvg();

   if (gradePtAvg < otherStudentsGPA)
   {
      return -1;
   }
   else if (gradePtAvg > otherStudentsGPA)
   {
      return 1;
   }
   else
   {
      return 0;
   }
}
```

The student class now looks like the following:

```
public class Student
{
  private double gradePtAvg;
  private String lastName;
  public Student(double gpa, String ln)
  {
    gradePtAvg = gpa;
    lastName = ln;
  }
  public int getGradePtAvg()
  {
    return gpa;
  }

  public String getLastName()
  {
    return lastName;
  }

  public int compareTo(Object obj)
  {
    Student otherStudent = (Student) obj;
    double otherStudentsGPA = otherStudent.getGradePtAvg();
    if (gradePtAvg < otherStudentsGPA)
    {
      return -1;
    }
    else if (gradePtAvg > otherStudentsGPA)
    {
      return 1;
    }
    else
    {
      return 0;
    }
  }
}
```

The following code creates three new Student objects:

```
Student s1 = new Student(4.0, "Fritz");
Student s2 = new Student(1.5, "Habibi");
Student s3 = new Student(4.0, "Jones");
```

What happens if we now call the compareTo() method on s1?

```
int i = s1.compareTo(s2);
```

The value of the variable *i* will be 1. Let's walk through the compareTo() method that we wrote to see why.

The first thing to note is that we are calling the method on s1 and passing s2 as an argument to the compareTo() method. Because the parameter of compareTo() is defined as an Object, it is necessary to cast the object that is passed as an argument to a Student object. We do this on the first line of our compareTo() method.

```
Student otherStudent = (Student) obj;
```

Because we are going to compare students based on their grade-point averages, we then get the grade-point average of the student that was passed to the method.

```
double otherStudentsGPA = otherStudent.getGradePtAvg();
```

What about s1's grade-point average? Because this method was called on s1, we can refer to the variable that holds s1's grade-point average directly within the compareTo() method.

So, in our first if statement, gradePtAvg refers to s1's grade-point average.

```
if (gradePtAvg < otherStudentsGPA)
{
   return -1;
}
```

The if conditional above will return –1 if s1's grade-point average is less than s2's grade-point average, indicating that s1 is less than s2.

What happens if the condition in the first if loop evaluates to false? In that case, control falls to the following else conditional:

```
else if (gradePtAvg > otherStudentsGPA)
{
   return 1;
}
```

If s1's grade-point average is greater than s2's grade-point average, then a positive number is returned, indicating that s1 is greater than s2.

If the conditions in both of the if statements above are false, then s1's grade-point average is neither less than nor greater than s2's grade-point average, so it must be the case that the students' grade-point averages are equal. Therefore, we return 0 in the last else conditional. When 0 is returned by the compareTo() method, it indicates that the two objects that we are comparing are equal.

```
else
{
   return 0;
}
```

What if instead of sorting students based on their grade-point averages, we sort alphabetically based on last names? In this case, we'll need to replace the compareTo() method that we wrote above with something like the following:

```
public int compareTo(Object obj)
{
   Student otherStudent = (Student) obj;
   String otherStudentsLastName = otherStudent.getLastName();
   return lastName.compareTo(otherStudentsLastName);
}
```

This time, we are basing our comparison on the value of the students' last names. We take advantage of the fact that the String class implements its own compareTo() method that compares Strings alphabetically. Our method just returns the results of the String class's compareTo() method.

THE INTEGER CLASS

Generally when we deal with integers, we use the primitive int variable type. For example, the following code assigns 4 to a variable named *a* that is of type int:

```
int a = 4;
```

Sometimes, however, we will want to deal with integers as objects, not as primitives. The **Integer class** acts as a wrapper for integers. It allows us to take a primitive value and turn it into an object.

CREATING AN INTEGER

Here is the constructor for the Integer class.

```
Integer(int value);
```

An Integer object can be created by passing an integer literal to the constructor.

```
Integer a = new Integer(4);
```

Alternatively, an int variable can be passed as the argument.

```
int a = 4;
Integer a = new Integer(a);
```

INTEGER METHODS

Below are the methods of the Integer class that are tested on the exam. The Integer class is in the java.lang package and implements the Comparable interface.

```
class java.lang.Integer implements java.lang.Comparable
```

- int intValue()
- boolean equals(Object other)
- int compareTo(Object other)
- String toString()

int intValue()

Integer objects are used to wrap primitive int values. This method returns the value of the int primitive that the object is wrapping.

```
Integer a = new Integer(-10);
int b = a.intValue();
System.out.println(b);
```

This gives the following output:

```
-10
```

boolean equals(Object other)

This method returns true if the argument is an Integer object and wraps the same integer value as the object that this method is called on.

```
Integer l = new Integer(10);
Integer m = new Integer(20);
Integer n = new Integer(10);
boolean b = l equals(m); //b is false
boolean c = l equals(n); //c is true
```

Make sure that you always use the equals() method when you are trying to figure out if the values of two Integer objects are the same. A common mistake is to use == instead. If you use == to compare two Integer objects, the result of the comparison will tell you if they are the same objects, not if they have the same value. This rule applies to the Double class (discussed on the next page) as well.

int compareTo (Object other)

This method is used to compare the values of two Integer objects. It compares the integer value of the object that this method is called on to the integer value of the argument. If the value of the object that this method is called on is smaller than the value of the argument, an integer less than 0 is returned. If the value of the argument is greater, an integer greater than 0 is returned. If the two values are equal, 0 is returned.

Even though the argument is defined as an Object in the method definition, it is expected that the argument will be an instance of the Integer class. If it's not, this method throws a ClassCastException.

Here are a few examples of the compareTo() method.

```
Integer l = new Integer(10);
Integer m = new Integer(20);
Integer n = new Integer(30);
Integer o = new Integer(20);
String s = "20";
int a = m.compareTo(l); // a is greater than 0
int b = m.compareTo(n); // b is less than 0
int c = m.compareTo(o); // c equals 0
int d = m.compareTo(s); // a ClassCastException is thrown
```

String toString()

This method returns the Integer's value as a String object.

```
Integer i = new Integer(-10);
String s = i.toString();
System.out.println(s);
System.out.println(s.length());
```

Here is the output from the code above.
```
-10
3
```

WORKING WITH INTEGER OBJECTS

Consider the two Integer objects *a* and *b* below.

```
Integer a = new Integer(10);
Integer b = new Integer(25);
```

Suppose that we want to find the sum of *a* and *b*. Unfortunately, we can't do the following:

```
a + b; // Error!
```

This causes an error because the + operator can only be used to find the sum of two integer primitives, not two Integer objects.

The solution to this dilemma is to first get the primitive integer values from our Integer objects, and add the primitive values together. This is where the intValue() method comes in handy.

```
int sum = a.intValue() + b.intValue();
```

The same strategy applies with the other arithmetic operators: –, *, /, ++, -- , and %. These operators cannot be used directly on Integer objects. Instead, the primitive value that the Integer object holds must first be extracted using the intValue() method.

THE DOUBLE CLASS

The **Double class** acts as a wrapper for primitive double values. Its methods are very similar to those of the Integer class.

CREATING A DOUBLE

Here is the constructor for the Double class.

```
Double(double value);
```

A Double object can be created by passing a double literal to the constructor.

```
Double a = new Double(4);
```

Alternatively, a double variable can be passed as the argument.

```
double a = 2.71;
Double a = new Double(a);
```

DOUBLE METHODS

Below are the methods of the Double class that are tested on the exam. The Double class is in the java.lang package and implements the Comparable interface.

```
class java.lang.Double implements java.lang.Comparable
• double doubleValue()
• boolean equals(Object other)
• int compareTo(Object other)
• String toString()
```

double doubleValue()

Just as Integer objects are used to wrap primitive int values, Double objects are used to wrap primitive double values. This method returns the value of the double primitive that the object is wrapping.

```
Double a = new Double(-4.5);
double b = a.doubleValue();
System.out.println(b);
```

This gives the following output:

```
-4.5
```

boolean equals(Object other)

This method returns true if the argument is a Double object and wraps the same double value as the object that this method is called on.

```
Double l = new Double(10.2);
Double m = new Double(20.45);
Double n = new Double(10.2);
boolean b = l.equals(m); //b is false
boolean c = l.equals(n); //c is true
```

int compareTo(Object other)

This method is used to compare the values of two Double objects. It compares the value of the object that this method is called on to the value of the argument. If the value of the object that this method is called on is smaller than the value of the argument, an integer less than 0 is returned. If the value of the argument is greater, an integer greater than 0 is returned. If the two values are equal, 0 is returned.

Note that even though the argument is defined as an Object in the method definition, it is expected that the argument will be a Double. If it's not, this method throws a ClassCastException.

Here are a few examples of the compareTo() method.

```
Double l = new Double(10.5);
Double m = new Double(20.21);
Double n = new Double(30.8);
Double o = new Double(20.21);
Integer x = new Integer(20);
int a = m.compareTo(l); // a is greater than 0
int b = m.compareTo(n); // b is less than 0
int c = m.compareTo(o); // c equals 0
int d = m.compareTo(x); // a ClassCastException is thrown
```

String toString()

This method returns the Double's value as a String object.

```
Double d = new Double(-10.24);
String s = d.toString();
System.out.println(s);
System.out.println(s.length());
```

Here is the output from the code above.

```
-10.24
6
```

REVIEW QUESTIONS

Answers to the review questions can be found in Chapter 11.

1. What will be the value of the variable *i* when the code below is executed?

```
String s = "ab\n\\\"c";
int i = s.length();
```

(A) 5
(B) 6
(C) 7
(D) 8
(E) 9

2. If the string "computer science" is assigned to the variable *s*, which of the following will return the string "science"?

```
    I.  s.substring(9);
   II.  s.substring(9, 15);
  III.  s.substring(9, 16);
```

(A) I only
(B) II only
(C) III only
(D) I and II
(E) I and III

3. Consider the class Foo below.

```
public class Foo
{
   public static String concat(int a)
   {
     String s = "";
     for (int i = 0; i < a; i++)
     {
        for (int j = 0; j < a; j++)
        {
          s = s + i + j;
        }
     }
     return s;
   }
}
```

What will be the value of *s* after the following statement is executed?

```
String s = Foo.concat(2);
```

(A) 00011011
(B) 0112
(C) 01010101
(D) 02012012
(E) 012012

4. Which of the following correctly declare and initialize a variable of type String?

```
    I.  String s1 = new String("apple");
    II. String s2 = new String('banana');
    III. String s3 = "orange";
```

(A) I only
(B) II only
(C) I and II
(D) I and III
(E) I, II, and III

5. Consider the following statements:

```
String s1 = "One";
String s2 = "Two";
s2 = s1;
s1 = "Three";
```

After the code above executes, what will be the value of the object referenced by s2?

(A) "One"
(B) "Two"
(C) "Three"
(D) "" (the empty string)
(E) The object that s2 references will be null.

6. In which of the following code segments will myString be "Catch 22"?

```
    I.  String myString = "Catch " + 11 + 11;
    II. String myString = "Catch " + (11 + 11);
    III. String myString = "Catch " + 2 + 2;
```

(A) I only
(B) II only
(C) III only
(D) I and II only
(E) II and III only

Recursion

INTRODUCTION

Recursion is a way of getting repetitive behavior from a method. It is noteworthy for two reasons.

- The first is that recursion involves a method calling itself (or calling another method that ends up calling the original method).

- The second is that recursion must involve a base case, or a situation in which a method stops calling itself.

The AP exam requires that you understand how recursion works, what types of problems it can help you solve, and the performance penalties associated with it. To that end, this chapter will help you understand the underlying concepts, their place in your computer science toolset, and the pros and cons of using them.

UNDERSTANDING RECURSION

A **recursive** method is one that calls itself unless a certain condition is met. For example, the following method calculates the factorial of an integer. A factorial is a mathematical value calculated when a number is multiplied by its immediate predecessor, which in turn is multiplied by its own immediate predecessors until 0 is reached. Thus, 4! = 4 * 3 * 2 * 1 = 24. By definition, 0! = 1.

```
01:   public double fact(int arg)
02:   {
03:      //precondition: assert arg >= 0
04:      //postcondition: returns 0 if args == 0
05:      //otherwise, calls fact(arg -1)
06:      int retval = -1;
07:      // base case
08:      if (arg <= 0)
09:      {
10:         return 1;
11:      }
12:      // recursive case
13:      else
14:      {
15:         retval = arg * fact(arg -1);
16:      }
17:      return retval;
18:   }
```

What's going on here? As we can see, line 15 is calling the same method in which it resides. Why isn't a method that's calling itself getting stuck in an infinite loop? The secret is that there is an important loophole called the "base case." That loophole and its recursive counterpart are explored below.

EXAMPLE 1: THE BASE CASE

When working with recursive code, the terminating condition (the one that doesn't call the method recursively again) is called the **base case**. Thus, if we call the fact() method with the base case 0, we see that because 0 is equal to 0, we enter the code block defined by the bracket on line 9. That code block returns a 1, so we now know that fact(0) = 1.

EXAMPLE 2: THE RECURSIVE CASE

If we call the fact() method for the next larger number, 1, we see that we get past line 4 again, and find our way to the "else" condition starting on line 13 below.

```
13: if (arg == 0)
. . .
15: else // recursive case
16: {
17:    retval = arg * fact(arg -1);
18: }
```

Because 1 > 0, we enter the code block on line 14. This is where things get interesting. Line 15 defines the return value retval as being equal to 1 * fact(0), so the program withholds judgment until it can figure out what the value of fact(0) is. The program thus goes through the same calculations we just performed in the previous example and finds that fact(0) == 1. Once the program figures this out, it calculates the value of retval = 1 * 1 == 1. Thus, fact(1) == 1.

EXAMPLE 3: CALCULATING THE FACTORIAL OF 4

If we call the fact() method for the argument 4, we see that we eventually find our way to line 8.

```
08:    if (arg == 0)
. . .
13:  else // recursive case
14:  {
15:    retval = arg * fact(arg -1);
16:  }
```

Because 4 > 0, we enter the code block on line 14. Line 15 defines the return value retval as being equal to 4 * fact(3). The method is being called again, this time to figure out what the factorial of 3 is. We know that the factorial of 3 is 3 multiplied by the factorial of 2. And we know that the factorial of 2 is equal to 2 multiplied by the factorial of 1. Thus:

$$fact(4) = 4 * fact(3)$$
$$fact(3) = 3 * fact(2)$$
$$fact(2) = 2 * fact(1)$$
$$fact(1) = 1 * fact(0)$$
$$fact(0) = 1$$
$$fact(4) = 4 * fact(3)$$
$$fact(3) = 3 * fact(2)$$
$$fact(2) = 2 * fact(1)$$
$$fact(1) = 1 * 1 == 1$$
$$fact(4) = 4 * fact(3)$$
$$fact(3) = 3 * fact(2)$$
$$fact(2) = 2 * 1 == 2$$
$$fact(4) = 4 * fact(3)$$
$$fact(3) = 3 * 2 == 6$$
$$fact(4) = 4 * 3 == 24.$$

We therefore find that the factorial of 4 is 24.

WRITING A RECURSIVE METHOD

The general form of a recursive method is shown below.

```
returnType recursiveMethod(arg)
{
   if (//base case)
   {
      //do something and
   }
   // recursive case
   else
   {
      return recusiveMethod(...)
   }
}
```

The base case is the condition reached when no other recursive calls should be made. In the factorial example above, the base case was that arg was equal to 0. Often, it's the simplest possible condition.

The recursive case calls for the method to call itself. Of course, if the method does call itself, then something regarding the parameter must change; otherwise, you really will have an infinite loop. In the factorial example, this change was the decrementing of the parameter.

WHEN TO USE RECURSION

A problem is a candidate for a recursive solution if it can be framed as involving a simpler case of itself, and if it has a base case. For example, you need to write a program that reverses the characters in a String.

- If the string consists of a single character, then return that character.

- Else, take the last character and append it to the reverse of the remaining characters.

To write this as code, we start with a general outline.

```
01: recursiveMethod(arg)
02: {
03:    if (//base case)
04:    {
05:       //do something and
06:    }
07:    // recursive case
08:    else
09:    {
10:       return recursiveMethod(...)
11:    }
12: }
```

Then we add the base condition because it's generally the easiest part. This would be the code between lines 3 and 6.

```
01:  public String reverse(String arg)
02:  {
03:    if (arg.length() == 1)
04:    {
05:      return arg;
06:    }
07:    // recursive case
08:    else
09:    {
10:      return reverse(...)
11:    }
12:  }
```

Next, we define the functionality for the recursive section of the code in lines 8–19.

```
01:  public String reverse(String arg)
02:  {
03:    String retval = null;
04:    if (arg.length() == 1)
05:    {
06:      return arg;
07:    }
08:    // recursive case
09:    else
10:    {
11:    /* extract the last char
12:       from the arg
13:       extract remaining chars
14:       from the arg
15:       reverse the remaining strings
16:       and pre-pend the last char
17:       return the result */
18:    }
19:  }
```

Finally, we write the actual implementation.

```
public String reverse(String arg)
{
  String retval = null;
  if (arg.length() == 1)
  {
   return arg;
  }
  // recursive case
  else
  {
   //extract last char
   String lastChar =
       arg.substring(arg.length()-1,arg.length());
   //extract remaining chars
   String remainingString =
   arg.substring(0, arg.length() -1);
   //call recursive loop
   String tmp = lastChar + reverse(remainingString);
   //return the result
   return tmp;
  }
}
```

That was a fairly easy way to accomplish the task, all things considered. The code was more elegant than the corresponding iterative solution would have been, and it's easier to understand and maintain. So why not use recursive methods whenever possible? The answer is performance and memory usage. By their nature, recursive methods are very memory intensive; for example, the reverse number will make five different method calls for the string "Hello", because "Hello" has five characters. For "Mr. Johnson", it will have made 12 separate method calls. So when should you actually use recursion?

Generally speaking, recursion works best when you're parsing a tree-like structure like a directory. Otherwise, it's almost always more efficient to use an iterative solution.

TRACING A CALL TO A RECURSIVE METHOD

Many of the questions on the exam that involve recursion will require you to trace through a call to a recursive method and figure out what value will be returned. Let's look at an example.

EXAMPLE 1

Consider the following method:

```
public void mystery(int x)
{
  if (x <= 0)
  {
  }
  else
  {
    System.out.print(x + " ");
    mystery(x - 2);
  }
}
```

Which of the following will be printed as a result of the call `mystery(10)`?

(A) 10 8 6 4 2
(B) 2 4 6 8 10
(C) 10 9 8 7 6 5 4 3 1
(D) Nothing is printed due to a compile-time error.
(E) Nothing is printed due to infinite recursion.

When tracing a recursive method, you should always first determine the base case. Remember that the base case is the condition in which the method stops calling itself recursively. In the example above, the base case occurs when $x <= 0$. It may seem strange that the body of the base case is empty, but that's fine for this example because the return type for the method is void.

When mystery() is initially called with an argument of 10, 10 will be printed and mystery() will call itself again with an argument of 8. The second time through, 8 will be printed and mystery() will be called with an argument of 6.

At this point, we can get rid of answer choices (B) and (C). It looks like the answer will be (A), but we still need to make sure that a compile-time error doesn't occur and that the recursive calls eventually end.

Is it possible that this method won't compile? One concern is that the body of the base case does not contain any statements. Because the method doesn't return anything, however (it is void after all), this won't be a problem.

Will infinite recursion occur? Because our initial argument to the method is 10 and the method reduces that argument by 2 each time the method is called, eventually we will hit the base case where the argument is less than or equal to 0. Thus, infinite recursion won't occur.

The correct answer is (A).

EXAMPLE 2

Now let's look at another example. The method in this example is very similar to the one above, with one important difference. Make sure that you spot it.

Consider the following method:

```java
public void mystery(int x)
{
  if (x <= 0)
  {
  }
  else
  {
    mystery(x - 2);
    System.out.print(x + " ");
  }
}
```

Which of the following will be printed as a result of the call mystery(10)?

(A) 10 8 6 4 2
(B) 2 4 6 8 10
(C) 10 9 8 7 6 5 4 3 1
(D) Nothing is printed due to a compile-time error.
(E) Nothing is printed due to infinite recursion.

Did you notice the difference between this method and the one in the previous question? This time, the statement that prints the value comes *after* the recursive call, rather than before.

To understand what is happening here, let's look at a simpler example: mystery(4). If we call mystery(4), a recursive call is immediately made to mystery(2) before anything is printed. The method will eventually print out 4, but for now, the call to mystery(2) has top priority. Think of the method as adding "print out 4" to its to-do list.

So what happens when mystery(2) is called? The method makes a recursive call to mystery(0). Once again, the method will eventually need to print out 2, but for now it adds that task to the top of its to-do list also. What's important is that printing out 2 is now at the top of the to-do list, ahead of 4.

The base case is 0, so the call to mystery(0) returns immediately to the call to mystery(2). The next thing that we need to do in the call to mystery(2) is print out 2.

Now the call to mystery(2) is done, and we can return to the call to mystery(4). Remember the 4 that was waiting around? Now it gets printed.

So a call to mystery(4) prints out 2 4. Following the same logic, a call to mystery(10) will print out 2 4 6 8 10.

This method prints the numbers out in reverse order.

The correct answer is (B).

RECURSIVELY TRAVERSING ARRAYS

Although it is more common to use a for loop to step through an array, it is also possible to use a recursion. For example, say you have a lineup of football players, each of whom has a numbered helmet. You want to step through the lineup, and find the position of the person who has "9" written on his helmet:

A recursive solution for this problem is very easy to implement. You need to look through an array of int values and find the position of a specific value, if it's there.

First, we'll need describe the problem in recursive terms.

- If we've looked through every item, then return –1.

- If the current item in the array is a match, return its position.

- Else, restart the process with the next item in the array.

```
public int findPosition
(int nums[],int key,int currentIndex)
{
    //if we've already looked through
    //the entire array
    if (nums.length <= currentIndex)
      return -1;
    //if the next item in the array is match,
    //then return it
    if (nums[currentIndex] == key)
      return currentIndex;
    //else, step past the current item in the array,
    //and repeat the search on the next item
    return findPosition(nums,key,currentIndex + 1);
}
```

This example is slightly more subtle than the others because we're carrying information from one recursive call to the next. Specifically, we're using the currentIndex field to pass state information from one recursive call to another. Thus, the first recursive call starts looking at position 0, the next one at position 1, and so on.

Let's go back to our football-player example. You want to step through a lineup of football players and return the position of the player who has the helmet with "9" written on it. Your code would be of the form

```
int[] players = //represents the football players
int pos = findPosition(players,9,0);
```

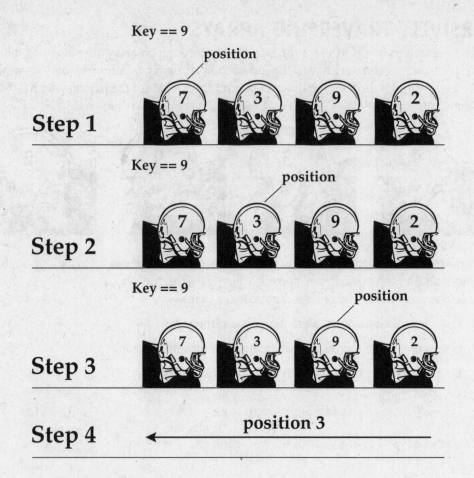

Key == 9

position

Step 1

Key == 9

position

Step 2

Key == 9

position

Step 3

Step 4   ← **position 3**

RECURSION AND PROGRAM PERFORMANCE

Although the exam will grade based on accuracy rather than efficiency, recursion and program performance are important concepts for programmers to understand.

Because recursive methods call themselves, they create a lot of overhead on the system. For example, every time a method is called, the system not only has to actually take the time to call it, but it must allocate space for all of its local variables and step through all of those loops. With recursive methods, this cost can grow prohibitively high very quickly.

Fortunately, every recursive method can be written as an iterative method. If performance is your overriding consideration, then you probably want an iterative method. However, if clarity and ease of development is your overriding concern, then you should consider a recursive method.

Let's try another example. This one revolves around the Fibonacci sequence from Mathematics. The Fibonacci sequence is 1, 1, 2, 3, 5, 8, 13, 21, 34… where the next number is the sum of the previous two digits; thus, 3 = 2 + 1, 34 = 21 + 13, and so on. Say we want to calculate the Fibonacci sequence for the Nth number in the sequence. A recursive solution for the code follows:

```
01:   public double fibonacci(int arg)
02:   {
03:      // check precondition
04:      // assert arg >= 0;
```

```
05:      // check   postcondition
06:      // assert retval > 0;
07:      double retval = -1;
08:      // test base case
09:      // the fib sequence for
10:      // 1 and 2 is 1
11:      if (arg < 3 )
12:      {
13:        return 1;
14:      }
15:      // recursive case
16:      else
17:      {
18:       retval = fibonacci(arg - 1)
19:        + fibonacci(arg - 2 );
20:      }
21:      return retval;
22: }
```

As you can see on lines 18 and 19, each recursive call makes two more recursive calls in turn. This indicates the underlying runtime of $O(2^n)$, which is exponential, and therefore exceptionally resource-intensive. For more about runtime analysis, please see Chapter 3.

REVIEW QUESTIONS

Answers to review questions can be found in Chapter 11.

1. Consider the following method:

```
// precondition: x >= 0
   public int mystery(int x)
   {
     if (x == 0)
     {
       return 0;
     }
     else {
       return ((x % 10) + mystery(x / 10));
     }
   }
```

Which of the following is returned as a result of the call mystery(3543)?

(A) 10
(B) 15
(C) 22
(D) 180
(E) Nothing is returned due to infinite recursion.

2. Consider the following recursive method:

```java
public int mystery(int x)
{
  if (x == 1)
    return 2;
  else
    return 2 * mystery(x - 1);
}
```

What value is returned as a result of the call mystery(6)?

(A) 2
(B) 12
(C) 32
(D) 64
(E) 128

3. Consider the following recursive method:

```java
public static int mystery(int x)
{
  if (x == 0)
  {
    return 0;
  }
  else
  {
    return (x + mystery(x / 2) + mystery(x / 4));
  }
}
```

What value is returned as a result of a call to mystery(10)?

(A) 10
(B) 12
(C) 20
(D) 22
(E) 35

4. Consider the following nonrecursive method:

```
//precondition: x >= 0
public static int mystery(int x)
{
    int sum = 0;
    while(x >= 0)
    {
        sum += x;
        x--;
    }
    return sum;
}
```

Which of the following recursive methods are equivalent to the method above?

```
 I. public static int mystery2(int x)
    {
        if (x == 0)
        {
            return 0;
        }
        return (x + mystery2(x - 1));
    }
```

```
II. public static int mystery3(int x)
    {
        if (x == 0)
            return 0;
        else
            return mystery3(x - 1);
    }
```

```
III. public static int mystery4(int x)

    {
        if (x == 1)
        {
            return 1;
        }
        return (x + mystery4(x - 1));
    }
```

(A) I only
(B) II only
(C) III only
(D) I and II
(E) II and III

5. Consider the following method:

```java
public int mystery(int x, int y)
{
   if (x >= 100 || y <= 0)
   {
      return 1;
   }
   else
   {
      return mystery(x + 10, y - 3);
   }
}
```

What value is returned by the call mystery(30, 18)?

(A) 0
(B) 1
(C) 6
(D) 7
(E) Nothing will be returned due to infinite recursion.

6. Consider the following incomplete method:

```java
public int mystery(int x)
{
   if (x <= 1)
   {
      return 1;
   }
   else
   {
      return (<missing code>);
   }
}
```

Which of the following could be used to replace *<missing code>* so that the value of mystery(10) is 32?

(A) mystery(x - 1) + mystery(x - 2)
(B) 2 * mystery(x - 2)
(C) 2 + mystery(x - 1)
(D) 4 * mystery(x - 4)
(E) 4 + mystery(x - 1)

Arrays and the ArrayList Class

INTRODUCTION

Up to now, we have been working with individual objects and primitives. There are times however, that we will want to work with groups of similar objects or primitives. For example, we may have a group of grades for an exam and want to find the highest score or the average, or we may have a group of String objects and want to find all those that begin with the substring "neo". An array or an ArrayList can be used to hold a group of similar elements.

ARRAYS

Consider a class that is designed to calculate statistics for a course's final exam. The statistics include the average, score range, highest score, and lowest score for the exam. The class will need to store 10 exam scores.

A naive way to attempt this would be to create an instance variable for each grade.

```
private int grade1;
private int grade2;
private int grade3;
private int grade4;
private int grade5;
private int grade6;
private int grade7;
private int grade8;
private int grade9;
private int grade10;
```

A better way would be to store the grades in an array. An array can be used to hold multiple values of the same type, much like an egg carton can be used to hold individual eggs. An array is a type of object that is able to store primitive values or references to other objects.

Shown below is an array that is able to store 10 items.

0	1	2	3	4	5	6	7	8	9

Note that the first item is stored at position 0. Unlike human beings, who generally begin counting at the number 1, arrays are said to be "zero-indexed," which means they begin counting at 0.

DECLARING AND CREATING AN ARRAY

The following statement declares a variable named grades that can hold an array of integers. The brackets after int indicate that grades will hold an array of ints, not just a single int.

```
int[] grades;
```

The brackets can be also be placed after the variable name (although this form is not used on the AP exam). The following statement is equivalent to that above:

```
int grades[];
```

At this point, we have not actually created the array; we've just declared a variable to hold it. The second statement below creates an array using the new operator and assigns it to the variable grades.

```
int[] grades;
grades = new int[10];
```

The array that we created above will hold 10 ints, as indicated by the integer in the brackets. An array must be given a size when it is created. The following statement will cause a compile-time error, because a size for the array is not indicated:

```
int[] grades[];
grades = new int; // Error!
```

An array can also be created and assigned to a variable in one statement.

```
int[] grades = new int[10];
```

More than one variable can reference the same array. For example, the following statement will create a variable called grades2 that refers to the same array as the variable grades:

```
int[] grades = new int[10];
int grades2 = grades;
```

When an array is first created, its members are assigned default values based on the type of array. In our example, the 10 positions in the array will each contain 0, the default value for ints. Our array looks like the following; The position, or "index," of each element in the array is shown above each cell of the array.

0	1	2	3	4	5	6	7	8	9
0	0	0	0	0	0	0	0	0	0

Now that we have created the array, we can store integers in it. The following will store the integer 85 in the first position of the array:

```
grades[0] = 85;
```

We could also have written the above as

```
int x = 85;
grades[0] = x;
```

or even

```
int x = 85;
int k = 0;
grades[k] = x;
```

Here is what our array now looks like.

0	1	2	3	4	5	6	7	8	9
85	0	0	0	0	0	0	0	0	0

We don't have to assign values to positions of the array in order. The following statement assigns the value 90 to the fifth position in the grades array:

```
grades[4] = 90;
```

Here is what the grades array looks like after the statement above is evaluated.

0	1	2	3	4	5	6	7	8	9
85	0	0	0	90	0	0	0	0	0

Although an array is often created and then populated with data one position at a time, this can be done in a single step.

```
int[] grades = {85, 71, 92, 100, 85, 68, 88, 85, 78, 60};
```

0	1	2	3	4	5	6	7	8	9
85	71	92	100	85	68	88	85	78	60

What would happen if we tried to add an integer to an index of the array that does not exist?

```
grades[12] = 94;
```

This would cause an ArrayIndexOutOfBoundsException to be thrown at runtime, because the highest index in the array is 9. Remember, the largest index in an array is one less than its length because the program starts its count at 0. Our array has a length of 10, so its largest index is 9.

FINDING THE LENGTH OF AN ARRAY

To find the length of an array, simply use the length attribute.

```
int[] grades = new int[10];
int theLength = grades.length;
System.out.print(theLength);
```

This will generate the following output:

```
10
```

Be aware that length is an attribute, not a method. In practice, all this means is that you do not use parentheses as you would with a method call. The value of the length attribute is the number of objects or primitives that the array can hold, not the number of objects or primitives that have actually been assigned to the array. Also, once an array has been created, its length cannot be changed.

LOOPING THROUGH AN ARRAY (TRAVERSAL)

Sometimes, you will want to access every element in an array. For example, if we want to find the average grade in our grades array, we will first need to find the sum of all the grades in the array. Likewise, finding the highest grade will entail looking at every grade in the array. A for loop can be used in both of these cases.

Consider the case in which we want to find the average (arithmetic mean) of an array of numbers. Here's one way that we could do this.

```
//precondition: g.length > 0
//postcondition: returns the average of the integers in
                        array g
public static int findAverageGrade(int[] g)
{
  int sumOfGrades = 0;
  for (int k = 0; k < g.length; k++)
  {
    sumOfGrades += g[k];
  }
  return sumOfGrades / g.length;
}
```

Pay special attention to the for statement in the code above—this is a common idiom for looping through an array.

The following method will find the highest grade in the array that is passed as an argument:

```
//precondition: g.length > 0
//postcondition: returns the largest integer in array g
public static int findHighestGrade(int[] g)
{
  int highestGrade = g[0];
  for (int k = 1; k < g.length; k++)
  {
    if (g[k] > highestGrade)
    {
      highestGrade = g[k];
    }
  }
  return highestGrade;
}
```

ARRAYS OF OBJECTS

In the examples so far, we have been storing primitive values in arrays. Arrays can also hold references to objects. These can include instances of Java library classes such as Strings, Integers, and Doubles, or instances of custom classes.

Consider the following class:

```
public class Person
{
    private String name;

    public Person(String s)
    {
        name = s;
    }
    public void setName(String s)
    {
        name = s;
    }
    public String getName()
    {
        return name;
    }
}
```

The following statement creates an array that can hold references to three Person objects and assigns it to the variable personArray:

```
Person[] personArray = new Person[3];
```

At this point, our array does not hold any references to Person objects. Instead, the array contains null references. Creating an array to hold objects does not create the objects themselves.

0	1	2
null	null	null

Now we'll add a few Person objects to the array.

```
Person p1 = new Person("Mike");
Person p2 = new Person("George");
personArray[0] = p1;
personArray[1] = p2;
```

The diagram on the next page shows what our array now looks like. The array contains references to Person objects in the first and second positions of the array. These are indicated by the arrows. The variables p1 and p2 also refer to these same objects. What this means is that when the objects were put in the array, copies were not made of the objects. Instead, a reference to the original object was added to the array.

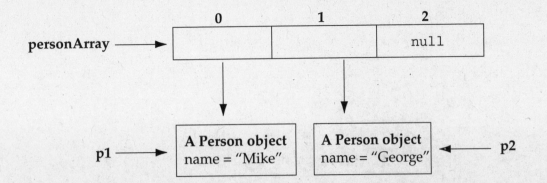

So how would we get the name of the Person object that is stored at the second position of the array? personArray[1] refers to this object, so the following statement will get the name of the Person and assign it to a variable called name:

```
String name = personArray[1].getName();
```

In the statement above, name will be assigned the string "George".

In our example, p2 and personArray[1] both refer to the same object. Therefore, any changes that we make to the object through p2 will be seen through personArray[1] and vice-versa. Consider the following two statements:

```
p2.setName("Joe");
String name = personArray[1].getName();
```

After the two statements above execute, the name will be assigned the string "Joe".

The same object can be referenced by two different cells of an array. For example, the following would be legal:

```
Person[] personArray = new Person[2];
Person p = new Person("Jon");
personArray[0] = p;
personArray[1] = p;
```

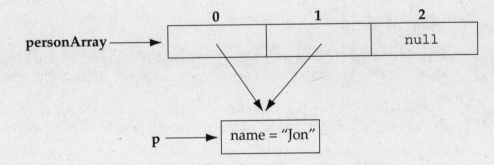

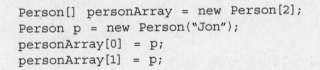

It's also possible for an object to be referenced in more than one array.

```
Person p = new Person("Liz");
Person[] a1 = new Person[2];
Person[] a2 = new Person[3];
a1[0] = p;
a2[1] = p;
```

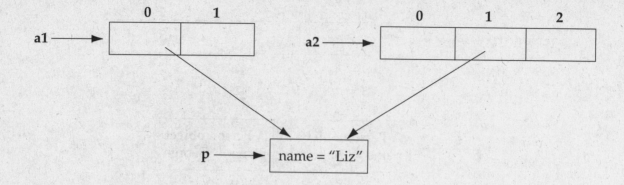

TWO-DIMENSIONAL ARRAYS (AB ONLY)

In our examples so far, we have been working with grades for one exam. What if we want to work with grades for multiple exams? Take, for example, a class in school with 4 students that has 3 exams. The table below shows the scores for each exam.

	student 1	student 2	student 3	student 4
exam 1	100	82	95	85
exam 2	87	88	72	98
exam 3	93	90	60	78

You can think of this table as a two-dimensional array with 3 rows and 4 columns. Here is how we would declare such a two-dimensional array.

```
int[][] grades;
```

Note that we use two pairs of brackets after the type of the array.
The following statement creates a 3-by-4 array of ints and assigns it to the grades variable:

```
grades = new int[3][4];
```

Once again, we use two pairs of brackets after the type. The number in the first pair of brackets indicates the number of rows, the number in the second pair of brackets indicates the number of columns.

Just like with one-dimensional arrays, the rows and columns of a two-dimensional array are zero-indexed. Here is how we would assign the grades for exam1-student1 (which is the first row and first column) to our array.

```
grades[0][0] = 100;
```

And here is how we would assign the grade for exam3-student2 (which is in the third row, second column) to our array.

```
grades[2][1] = 90;
```

To assign a value to a two-dimensional array of integers, use the following form:

```
grades[row][column] = an_integer
```

The table below shows how we would refer to each element in the array.

	student 1	student 2	student 3	student 4
exam 1	grades[0][0]	grades[0][1]	grades[0][2]	grades[0][3]
exam 2	grades[1][0]	grades[1][1]	grades[1][2]	grades[1][3]
exam 3	grades[2][0]	grades[2][1]	grades[2][2]	grades[2][3]

If g is a two-dimensional array:

g.length will give the number of rows in g

g[0].length will give the number of columns in g

Let's assume that we have entered all of the grades from our table into the grades array. What if we now want to find the average grade for exam 2? The first thing that we need to do is add all of the grades from the second row of our table together. We could use the following:

```
grades[1][0] + grades[1][1] + grades[1][2] + grades[1][3];
```

However, a better way is with a for loop.

```
int sumOfGrades = 0;
for (int k = 0; k < grades[0].length; k++)
{
   int grade = grades[1][k];
   sumOfGrades = sumOfGrades + grade;
}
```

What if we want to look at every cell in a two-dimensional array? In this case, use nested for loops.

```
int numRows = grades.length;
int numCols = grades[0].length;
for (int j = 0; j < numRows; j++)
{
   for (int k = 0; k < numCols; i++)
   {
      //do something with grades[j][k];
   }
}
```

The following code segment will calculate the average of all of the grades in the grades array:

```
int totalTestPoints = 0;
int numTests = 0;
int numRows = grades.length;
int numCols = grades[0].length;
for (int r = 0; r < ; r++)
{
  for (int c = 0; c < numCols; c++)
  {
    numTests++;
    totalTestPoints = totalTestPoints + grades[r][c];
  }
}
int averageTestScore = totalTestPoints / numTests;
```

THE ARRAYLIST CLASS

INTRODUCTION

One of the downsides to arrays is that they cannot be resized once they are created. This is not a problem if we know how many elements an array will need to hold when it is created, but it can cause a problem in cases where we may have an unknown number of elements in a group. Unfortunately, we often don't know how many members will be in the group that we are working with. For example, our program may let an instructor enter an unknown number of grades from the keyboard. The instructor may only enter two grades, but he may instead enter 100.

If we do not know how many elements will be in our group, it is often preferable to use an ArrayList rather than an array.

An ArrayList is much like an array in that it holds multiple elements in order. Unlike an array, however, an ArrayList does not have a fixed size. ArrayLists also differ from arrays in that ArrayLists can hold only object references, they cannot hold primitives. Also, an ArrayList instance can hold a heterogeneous group of items; in other words, all of the objects in an ArrayList do not need to be objects of the same class.

DECLARING AND CREATING AN ARRAYLIST

An instance of an ArrayList is created with the default constructor.

```
ArrayList myList = new ArrayList();
```

On the exam, you may also see something similar to the following:

```
ArrayList myArray = //call to a method that returns an
                    //ArrayList
```

ArrayList Methods

The following methods of ArrayList will be tested on the exam:

- `int size()`

- `boolean add(Object x)`

- `Object get(int index)`

- `Object set(int index, Object x)`

- `void add(int index, Object x)`

- `Object remove(int index)`

- `Iterator iterator()` *(AB only—discussed in Chapter 8)*

- `ListIterator()` *(AB only—discussed in Chapter 8)*

ArrayList: int size()

The size() method returns the number of elements that are in the ArrayList. If the ArrayList is empty, size() returns 0. Note the difference between getting the size of an ArrayList using the size() method and getting the length of an array using the length attribute.

```
List myList = //call to a method that returns an ArrayList
int listSize = myList.size();
```

The variable listSize will contain the number of objects in myList.

ArrayList: boolean add(Object x)

The add(Object x) method adds an object reference to the end of an ArrayList. The size of the list is increased by 1. Note that the argument that is passed to the method must be an object reference; passing a primitive will cause a compile-time error to occur. This method always returns true.

In the examples that follow, we'll create a roster for a class using an ArrayList. To keep things simple, the roster will only store the first names of students who are in the class. We will also show the String objects in the ArrayList, although technically ArrayLists store object references rather than the objects themselves, just like arrays do. And just like an array, an ArrayList can store a reference to the same object in multiple indices, and a reference to the same object can appear in multiple ArrayLists.

```
ArrayList roster = new ArrayList();
roster.add("Annie");
```

At this point, roster looks like the following:

If we then call the add() method again, the object that we pass to the method will be added to the end of the list.

```
roster.add("George");
```

Here is what roster now looks like.

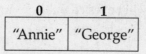

ArrayList: void add(int index, Object x)

The add method that we just looked at always adds the object that is passed as an argument to the end of the ArrayList. There are times, however, that we will want to add an object to the beginning or middle of a list. Say, for example, we have an ArrayList variable called roster that looks like the following:

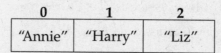

What if we want to add the name "George" to our list, but we also want to keep the list in alphabetical order? We can't use roster.add("George"), because this will add the string "George" after the string "Liz". What we want is a method that will insert "George" into the list before "Harry" and after "Annie".

In this case, we can use the add(int index, Object obj) method. The second parameter in this method is the object that is to be added to the list, the first parameter indicates the index in the ArrayList where the object should be inserted. Elements will be shifted one position to the right to make room for this new element.

```
roster.add(1, "George");
```

Roster now looks like the following:

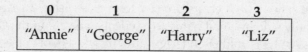

Note that the values that were at positions 1 and 2 ("Harry" and "Liz") were shifted to the right.

The integer that you pass as the first parameter to the add(int index, Object x) method cannot be greater than the size of the ArrayList. For example, the following will throw an IndexOutOfBounds-Exception because theList currently contains four elements:

```
Roster.add(5, "Fred"); //ERROR!
```

ArrayList: Object set(int index, Object x)

Sometimes, you will need to replace an object reference in a list with another one. For example, in our roster, "Harry" might want to be called "Harrison" instead, so we will need to replace the string "Harry" that is at index 2 with the string "Harrison".

The set(int index, Object x) method is used to replace the object at the parameter index with the object that is passed to the parameter x. This method removes and returns the object that is currently located at the indicated index.

Consider an ArrayList called roster that looks like the following:

	0	1	2	3
	"Annie"	"George"	"Harry"	"Liz"

The following statement will replace "Harry" with "Harrison":

```
String s = (String) roster.set(2, "Harrison");
```

Now roster looks like the following:

	0	1	2	3
	"Annie"	"George"	"Harrison"	"Liz"

The variable *s* above will contain "Harry", the value that was at index 2 in the ArrayList before the set() method was called. Note that the set() method returns the element that was replaced as type Object, even though it is really an instance of the String class. Because of this, we need to cast it back to a String before we assign it to variable *s*.

Even though the set() method returns an object reference, you do not have to assign the returned reference to a variable if you have no use for it. If we did not need to know what the value of the element in the array was before it was replaced, we could rewrite our call to the set() method above as the following:

```
roster.set(2, "Harrison");
```

The integer that you pass as the first parameter to the set(int index, Object x) method must be less than the size of the ArrayList. For example, the following will throw an IndexOutOfBoundsException because roster currently contains four elements:

```
roster.set(4, "Fred"); //Error!
```

ArrayList: Object remove(int index)

The remove(int index) method removes the element at the indicated index and shifts all elements to the right of the removed element one position to the left in the ArrayList, reducing the size of the ArrayList by one. This method also returns a reference to the removed element.

Consider an ArrayList called roster that looks like the following:

	0	1	2	3
	"Annie"	"George"	"Harrison"	"Liz"

Suppose that George decides to drop the class. We can remove his name from roster as follows:

```
String s = (String) roster.remove(1);
```

Now roster looks like the following:

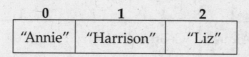

The variable *s* will now contain "George", the string that was located at index 1 before remove() was called.

Even though the remove() method returns an element, you do not have to assign the returned value to a reference if you have no use for it. If we did not need to know what the value of the element in the array was before it was removed, we could rewrite the statement above as the following:

```
roster.remove(1);
```

The integer that you pass as the first parameter to remove(int index) must be less than the size of the ArrayList. For example, the following will throw an IndexOutOfBoundsException because roster currently contains three elements:

```
roster.remove(3);
```

ArrayList: Object get(int index)

What if we want to take a look at an object that is located at a particular index without actually removing it from the ArrayList? The get(int index) method returns a reference to the element that is located at the position indicated by the value that is passed to the parameter index. Note that the type of the reference returned is Object. To work with the object, you will need to cast it to the appropriate type.

Consider our roster, which looks like the following:

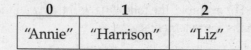

The following method call gets the String that is located at the second position of roster:

```
String name = (String) roster.get(1);
```

Note that the get() method does not modify the ArrayList. Our roster still looks like it did before the method was called.

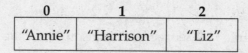

LOOPING THROUGH AN ARRAYLIST

A for loop can be used to loop through the elements of an ArrayList in much the same way that it is used to loop through the elements of an array. The only difference is that we use the size() method of ArrayList to get the number of elements in the ArrayList.

```
ArrayList myList = /* a call to a method that returns an
                       ArrayList instance of Strings */
for (int i = 0; i < myList.size(); i++)
{
   String s = (String) myList.get(i);
   // do something with s
}
```

Watch out for code within a loop that calls the remove() or add() method on an ArrayList. These methods change the size of the ArrayList instance.

Try the following question:

```
ArrayList letters = new ArrayList();
letters.add("A");
letters.add("B");
letters.add("C");
letters.add("D");
letters.add("E");
for (int i = 0; i < letters.size() - 1; i++)
{
   letters.remove(i);
   System.out.print(letters.get(i));
}
```

What is printed to the screen when the code above executes?

(A) ABCDE
(B) ACE
(C) BCD
(D) BD
(E) AE

The ArrayList letters initially contains "ABCDE". The first time through the for loop, i is equal to 0, so A is removed from letters. When get(0) is called on the next line, "B" is returned because it is now in position 0. On the next pass through the for loop, i equals 1, so we remove the element at position 1 in letters, and letters now contains "BDE". We then return the element that is at index 1; this is "D".

Next, we evaluate the for loop with i equal to 2. Because letters.size() is now 3, i is no longer less than letters.size() – 1 and control exits from the for loop.

The correct answer is (D).

ARRAYLISTS AND THE WRAPPER CLASSES

One difference between arrays and the ArrayList class is that an array can hold primitive values such as doubles or ints, but an ArrayList can hold only object references. What if we want to store primitives in an ArrayList? For example, how would we create a gradebook like the one from the arrays section using an ArrayList?

If we want to store integers in an ArrayList, we need to use the Integer wrapper class that was covered in Chapter 5.

In the following example, we store four Integers in an instance of an ArrayList called grades:

```
ArrayList grades = new ArrayList();
grades.add(new Integer(80));
grades.add(new Integer(75));
grades.add(new Integer(90));
grades.add(new Integer(100));
```

SUMMARY: ARRAYS VS. ARRAYLISTS

The following table recaps the differences between arrays and ArrayLists:

Arrays	ArrayList
After an array is created, it cannot be resized.	ArrayLists will automatically resize as new elements are added.
No import statement is needed to use an array, unless the array holds elements that require an import statement.	You must import java.util.ArrayList, or use the full package name whenever you use an ArrayList.
Elements are accessed using index notation (e.g., myArray[2]).	Elements are accessed using methods of the ArrayList class (e.g., myList.get(2), myList.add("George")).
Arrays can be constructed to hold either primitives or object references.	ArrayList instances can hold only object references, not primitives. The Integer and Double wrapper classes must be used to store integer and double primitives in an ArrayList.
Each array can be declared for only one type of element. For example, if an array is declared to hold Strings, you cannot store an Integer in it.	An ArrayList can hold a heterogeneous collection of objects. For example, the following is perfectly legal (though not recommended): ArrayList list = new ArrayList(); list.add(new String("A String")); list.add(new Integer(4));

REVIEW QUESTIONS

Answers to review questions can be found in Chapter 11.

1. Consider the following code segment:

```
String[] s = new String[2];
String[] t = {"Michael", "Megan", "Chelsea"};
s = t;
System.out.print(s.length);
```

What is printed as a result of executing the code segment?

(A) 1
(B) 2
(C) 3
(D) Nothing will be printed due to a compile-time error.
(E) Nothing will be printed due to a run-time error.

2. Consider the following code segment:

```
final int[] a1 = {1, 2};
int[] b1 = {3, 4};
a1 = b1;
System.out.print(a1[1]);
```

What is printed as a result of executing the code segment?

(A) 2
(B) 3
(C) 4
(D) Nothing is printed due to a compile-time error.
(E) Nothing is printed due to a run-time error.

3. Consider the following code segment:

```
final int[] myArray = {1, 2};
myArray[1] = 3;
System.out.print(myArray[1]);
```

What is printed as a result of executing the code segment?

(A) 1
(B) 2
(C) 3
(D) Nothing is printed due to a run-time error.
(E) Nothing is printed due to a compile-time error.

4. Consider the following incomplete method:

```
public static int Mod3(int[] numbers)
{
  int count = 0;
  for (int i = 0; i < a.length; i++)
  {
    // code not shown
  }
  return count;
}
```

Method Mod3 is intended to return the number of integers in the array numbers that are evenly divisible by 3. Which of the following code segments could be used to replace // code not shown so that Mod3 will work as intended?

```
  I. if (i % 3 == 0)
     {
       count++;
     }
```

```
 II. if (a[i] % 3 == 0)
     {
       count++;
     }
```

```
III. while (a[i] % 3 == 0)
     {
       count++;
     }
```

(A) I only
(B) II only
(C) III only
(D) I and II
(E) II and III

5. Consider the following code segment:

```
ArrayList list = new ArrayList();
list.add("A");
list.add("B");
list.add(0, "C");
list.add("D");
list.set(2, "E");
list.remove(1);
System.out.println(list);
```

What is printed as a result of executing the code segment?

(A) [A, B, C, D, E]
(B) [A, B, D, E]
(C) [C, E, D]
(D) [A, D, E]
(E) [A, C, D, E]

6. Consider the following data fields and method:

```
private ArrayList letters;
// precondition: letters.size() > 0
// letters contains String objects

public void letterRemover()
{
    int i = 0;
    while (i < letters.size())
    {
        if (letters.get(i).equals("A"))
            letters.remove(i);
        i++;
    }
}
```

Assume that ArrayList letters originally contains the following String values:

```
[A, B, A, A, C, D, B]
```

What will letters contain as a result of executing letterRemover()?

(A) [A, B, A, A, C, D, B]
(B) [B, C, D, B]
(C) [B, A, C, D, B]
(D) [A, B, A, C, D, B]
(E) [A, A, B, C, D, B, D]

7. Consider the following method:

```
private ArrayList myList;
// precondition: myList.size() > 0
// myListcontains String objects
public void myMethod()
{
    for (int i = 0; i < myList.size() - 1; i++)
    {
        myList.remove(i);
        System.out.print(myList.get(i) + " ");
    }
}
```

Assume that myList originally contains the following String values:

```
[A, B, C, D, E]
```

What will be printed when the method above executes?

(A) A B C D E
(B) A C E
(C) B D E
(D) B D
(E) Nothing will be printed due to an IndexOutOfBoundsException.

8. Consider the following code segment: *(AB Only)*

```
int[][] numbers = new int[4][4];
initializeIt(numbers);

int total = 0;
for (int z = 0; z < numbers.length; z++)
{
   total += numbers[z][numbers[0].length - 1 - z];
}
```

The call to `initializeIt()` on the second line initializes the array `numbers` so that it looks like the following:

```
1 2 5 3
7 9 4 0
3 3 2 5
4 5 8 1
```

What will be the value of `total` after the code has executed?

(A) 11
(B) 12
(C) 13
(D) 14
(E) 15

9. Consider the following code segment: *(AB only)*

```
int[][] numbers = new int[3][6];
initializeIt(numbers);

int total = 0;
for (int j = 0; j < numbers.length; j++)
{
   for (int k = 0; k < numbers[0].length; k += 2)
   {
      total += numbers[j][k];
   }
}
```

The call to `initializeIt()` on the second line initializes the array `numbers` so that it looks like the following:

```
2 4 6 3 2 1
5 6 7 4 2 9
4 0 5 6 4 2
```

What will be the value of `total` after the code has executed?

(A) 18
(B) 35
(C) 37
(D) 72
(E) 101

10. Consider the following code segment:

```
ArrayList list = new ArrayList();
for (int i = 1; i <= 8; i++)
{
   list.add(new Integer(i));
}
for (int j = 1; j < list.size(); j++)
{
   list.set(j / 2, list.get(j));
}
System.out.println(list);
```

What is printed as a result of executing the code segment?

(A) [2, 4, 6, 8, 5, 6, 7, 8]
(B) [1, 2, 3, 4, 5, 6, 7, 8]
(C) [1, 2, 3, 4]
(D) [1, 2, 3, 4, 1, 2, 3, 4]
(E) [2, 2, 4, 4, 6, 6, 8, 8]

11. Consider the following code segment: *(AB only)*

```
int[][] num = new int[4][4];

for (int i = 0; i < num.length; i++)
{
   for (int k = 0; k < num[0].length; k++)
   {
      num[i][k] = i * k;
   }
}
```

What are the contents of num after the code segment has executed?

(A) 0 0 0 0
     0 1 2 3
     0 2 4 6
     0 3 6 9

(B) 0 1 2 3
     1 2 3 4
     2 3 4 5
     3 4 5 6

(C) 0 3 6 9
     0 2 4 6
     0 1 2 3
     0 0 0 0

(D) 1 1 1 1
     2 2 2 2
     3 3 3 3
     4 4 4 4

(E) 0 0 0 0
     1 2 3 4
     2 4 6 8
     3 6 9 12

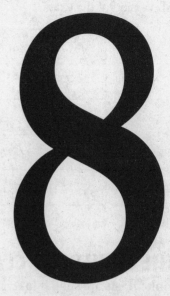

Advanced Collection Classes

(AB only)

INTRODUCTION

In the previous chapter, we reviewed arrays and the ArrayList class. Both arrays and ArrayLists are containers that are used to hold groups of similar elements. In this chapter, we will review other collection classes that are covered on the AB exam.

> The material in this chapter is tested only on the AB version of the exam. If you are taking the A version of the exam, you can skip this entire chapter.

You will be expected to understand the following interfaces and implementation classes for the AB version of the exam:

Interface	Implementation Classes
List	ArrayList, LinkedList
Set	HashSet, TreeSet
Map	HashMap, TreeMap
Iterator, ListIterator	Not Tested

THE LINKEDLIST CLASS

LinkedLists are similar to ArrayLists in that they are used to hold an ordered sequence of elements and can contain duplicates. So why bother to have another class? Depending on how they are used, one class can offer better performance than the other.

Because the ArrayList implementation actually uses an array to store elements, ArrayLists provide better performance for random access to the elements of the list, since elements of an array can be accessed by index. On the other hand, performance for ArrayLists suffers if you add or remove elements from the middle or beginning of the list. This is because the elements in the array must be shifted.

In Big-Oh notation, ArrayLists provides $O(1)$ performance for random access. Deletion and insertion at the end of the list are also $O(1)$. Deletion and insertion in the middle of the list are $O(n)$.

The LinkedList class is implemented with a doubly linked list (doubly linked lists are discussed in Chapter 9). LinkedLists provide constant time performance $O(1)$ for insertions and deletions from the beginning and end of the list. On the other hand, performance suffers if you are randomly accessing elements in a LinkedList.

The LinkedList class also provides different methods from those of the ArrayList class. The methods of the LinkedList class are discussed below.

LinkedList Methods

The following methods of the LinkedList class are tested in the AP Computer Science subset:

- `int size()`
- `boolean add(Object x)`
- `Object get(int index)`
- `Object set(int index, Object x)`
- `void addFirst(Object x)`
- `void addLast(Object x)`
- `Object getFirst()`
- `Object getLast()`
- `Object removeFirst()`
- `Iterator iterator()`
- `ListIterator listIterator()`

LinkedList: int size()

This method returns the number of elements in the LinkedList. It functions in exactly the same way as the size() method of the ArrayList class.

LinkedList: add(Object x)

The add(Object x) method adds an element to the end of a LinkedList. It functions in exactly the same way as the add(Object x) method of the ArrayList class. Please see the discussion of the add(Object x) method of the ArrayList class in Chapter 7 for a detailed explanation.

LinkedList: Object get(int index)

The get(int index) method gets an element from the indicated index in the LinkedList. It functions in exactly the same way as the get(int index) method of the ArrayList class.

LinkedList: Object set(int index, Object x)

The set(int index, Object x) method replaces the object that is currently at the indicated index in the LinkedList with the object that is passed as the second parameter. It returns the object that was replaced in the LinkedList. Note that unlike the set method of the ArrayList class which runs in constant, $O(1)$, time, the set method of the LinkedList class runs in linear, $O(n)$, time because it needs to iterate to the correct position from the beginning of its underlying linked list.

LinkedList: void addFirst(Object x)

The addFirst(Object x) method adds an element to the beginning of a LinkedList. If the list contains other elements, the index of each of these elements is increased by 1, shifting them to the right. Note that this method also increases the size of the list by 1.

LinkedList: void addLast(Object x)

The addLast(Object x) method adds an element to the end of a LinkedList. It has the same effect as the add(Object x) method.

LinkedList: Object getLast()

The getLast() method returns a reference to the last element in the LinkedList. If the list is empty, this method throws a NoSuchElementException. Note that the element is not removed from the LinkedList.

LinkedList: Object getFirst()

The getFirst() method returns a reference to the first element in the array. The element itself is *not* removed from the LinkedList, however. If the list is empty, this method throws a NoSuchElement-Exception.

LinkedList: Object removeFirst()

The removeFirst() method removes the first element in the LinkedList, shifting all elements to the left in the List. This method also returns a reference to the removed element. If the list is empty, this method throws a NoSuchElementException.

LinkedList: Iterator iterator() and ListIterator listIterator()

These methods return an Iterator and ListIterator respectively. Iterators and ListIterators can be used to visit every element in an ArrayList or LinkedList. We will discuss Iterators and ListIterators in detail below.

THE LIST INTERFACE

The ArrayList and LinkedList classes are implementations of the **List interface** that represents lists: data structures that hold a sequence of elements. Recall from our discussion in Chapter 4 that interfaces define the methods that implementing classes should have, but interfaces don't provide the code for those methods.

LIST METHODS

The List interface defines the following methods:

- `boolean add(Object x)`
- `int size()`
- `Object get(int index)`
- `Object set(int index, Object x)`
- `Iterator iterator()`
- `ListIterator listIterator()`

All classes that implement the List interface must implement these methods. As we've seen, both the ArrayList and LinkedList classes implement the List interface and its methods.

Example

Consider the following code:

```
List myList = /* a call to a method that
                  returns an ArrayList instance
                  that contains Strings */
String s = (String) myList.remove(1);
```

If myList looks like the following:

| "java" | "coffee" | "tea" |

What will be the result of executing the code above?

(A) s will contain the string "java".
(B) s will contain the string "coffee".
(C) s will contain the string "tea".
(D) A compile-time error will occur.
(E) A runtime error will occur.

Here's How to Crack It: The answer is (D). Even though the method call on the first line returned an ArrayList instance, the variable myList is of type List. Therefore, we can only call methods on myList that are defined in the List interface. Since remove() is not defined in the List interface, an error occurs when the code is compiled.

In order to call the remove() method on myList, we would need to first cast it to an ArrayList like the one below.

```
ArrayList myArrayList = (ArrayList) myList;
String s = (String) myArrayList.remove(1);
```

So if we have a variable of type List that holds a reference to a List object, how can we view objects in the List? As we'll see in the next section, we can use an Iterator.

THE ITERATOR INTERFACE

Suppose we have an ArrayList that contains String objects. How could we find out if the ArrayList contains the word "computer"?

One way is to use a for loop. The following method returns true if the array that is passed to the first parameter contains the string that is passed to the second parameter:

```
public static boolean containsWord(ArrayList theList,
                                      String word)
{
   for (int i = 0; i < theList.size(); i++)
   {
     String s = (String) theList.get(i);
     if (s.equals(word))
     {
       return true;
     }
   }
   return false;
}
```

What could we do in the following case, where a method returns a list as type List? As we saw in the previous section, we can't use the get() method, since get() isn't defined in the List interface.

```
List myList = // call to a method that returns a List
```

In this case, we can use an Iterator to examine every object in the List, much as we used a for loop above.

Here is what the code above would look like if we used an Iterator.

```
public static boolean containsWord2
(List theList, String word)
{
   Iterator iter = theList.iterator();
   while (iter.hasNext())
   {
     String s = (String) iter.next();
     if (s.equals(word))
     {
       return true;
     }
   }
   return false;
}
```

In the code above, we get an Iterator by calling the iterator() method on the List object theList. The line iter.hasNext() returns true if there are more elements in the List to examine, and false if we are at the end of the List. Inside the while loop, the call to i.next() returns the next object in theList. We can then check if the String that is returned by iter.next() matches the parameter word. The while loop will continue to execute until either a matching word is found or there are no more elements left to check in theList.

Since Iterator is an interface, you can't instantiate an Iterator using the new() operator. The following would cause an error:

```
Iterator i = new Iterator(); //Error!
```

So how do you get an Iterator? Call the iterator() method on an instance of either the ArrayList, LinkedList, HashSet, or TreeSet classes. We will discuss the HashSet and TreeSet classes later in this chapter.

ITERATOR METHODS

The following methods of the Iterator interface are tested in the AP Computer Science subset:

- `boolean hasNext()`
- `Object next()`
- `void remove()`

Iterator: Object next()

The next() method returns a reference to the next element in the Iterator.

```
01: ArrayList list = new ArrayList();
02: list.add("A String");
03: list.add("Another String");
04: Iterator i = list.iterator();
05: String s1 = (String) i.next();
06: System.out.println(s1);
07: String s2 = (String) i.next();
08: System.out.println(s2);
```

This would generate the following output:

```
A String
Another String
```

In the code above, we create an ArrayList and add two Strings to it in lines 1–3. We then get an Iterator for the list on line 4. On line 5 we call the next() method of the Iterator, which returns a reference to the first String in the underlying list ("A String"). In line 7, we call next() method again, which returns a reference to the second String in the ArrayList ("Another String").

What would happen if we were to append the following line to the example above?

```
09: String s3 = (String) i.next();
```

This would cause NoSuchElementException to be thrown at runtime since there are no more elements in the Iterator to visit. How can you prevent such an error from occurring? Use the hasNext() method before calling next().

Iterator: boolean hasNext()

The hasNext() method returns true if the Iterator has another element and false if it does not.

```
ArrayList list = new ArrayList();
list.add("A String");
Iterator i = list.iterator();
boolean b1 = i.hasNext();
System.out.println(b1);
```

```
i.next();
boolean b2 = i.hasNext();
System.out.println(b2);
```

This would generate the output true followed by false.

The hasNext() method is often used in conjunction with the next() method to loop through the elements of an Iterator.

```
ArrayList list = new ArrayList();
list.add("A String");
list.add("Another String");
Iterator i = list.iterator();
while (i.hasNext())
{
   System.out.println(i.next());
}
```

This would generate the output "A String" followed by "Another String".

Iterator: void remove()

This method removes from the list the most recent object accessed by the next() method. You must call the next() method before using this method.

```
01: ArrayList list = new ArrayList();
02: list.add("A String");
03: list.add("Another String");
04: Iterator i = list.iterator();
05: i.next();
06: i.remove();
07: int listSize = list.size();
08: System.out.println("The list size is: " + listSize);
09: String s = (String) list.get(0);
10: System.out.println("The only String is: " + s);
```

This would generate the output

```
The list size is 1
The only String is: Another String
```

It's important that you call the next() method before every call to remove(). If we were to add another call to i.remove() immediately after line 6 in the code above, an IllegalStateException would be thrown at runtime when the second remove() call was reached.

How could we alter the code above to remove the second element of the list rather than the first? Simply add another call to i.next() between lines 5 and 6. This second call will return the second String in the array, and it is this String that will be removed from the list when i.remove() is subsequently called.

THE LISTITERATOR INTERFACE

The **ListIterator interface** extends the Iterator interface. In addition to the methods contained in the Iterator interface, the ListIterator interface defines two new methods: add(Object obj) and set(Object obj).

LISTITERATOR METHODS

The following methods of the ListIterator interface are tested in the AP Computer Science subset:

- `boolean hasNext()`
- `Object next()`
- `void remove()`
- `void add(Object obj)`
- `void set(Object obj)`

Please see the Iterator section above for an explanation of the first three methods (hasNext(), next(), and remove()).

ListIterator: void add(Object obj)

The add(Object obj) method of ListIterator adds an object to the underlying List. The object is added immediately before the object that would be returned by a call to next().

```
01: Student s1 = new Student("Mike", 32);
02: Student s2 = new Student("Mehran", 31);
03: List myList = new ArrayList();
04: myList.add(s1);
05: myList.add(s2);
06: System.out.println("Size before: " + myList.size());
07: ListIterator myListIterator = myList.listIterator();
08: Student aNewStudent = new Student("Megan", 27);
09: myListIterator.add(aNewStudent);
10: System.out.println("Size after: " + myList.size());
```

This would generate the following output:

```
Size before: 2
Size after: 3
```

In lines 1–5 above, we create an ArrayList and add two Student objects to it. On line 6, we print out the size of the ArrayList, which is 2. Line 7 uses the listIterator method of myList to get a ListIterator, and then lines 8–9 add a new Student object to the ArrayList *using the ListIterator that we got on line 7.* On line 10, we print out the size of the ArrayList, which is now 3.

What would happen if we now use the ListIterator to traverse through the List?

```
11: while (myListIterator.hasNext())
12: {
13:    Student s = (Student) myListIterator.next();
14:    System.out.println(s.getName());
15: }
```

This would generate the following output:

```
Mike
Mehran
```

Surprisingly, "Megan" was not printed to the screen, even though we added her to our ArrayList using the ListIterator. If we get a new ListIterator from our ArrayList, "Megan" will now be in it.

```
16: ListIterator myListIterator2 = myList.listIterator();
17: while (myListIterator2.hasNext())
18: {
19:    Student s = (Student) myListIterator2.next();
20:    System.out.println(s.getName());
21: }
```

This will generate the output

```
Megan
Mike
Mehran
```

ListIterator: void set(Object obj)

The set(Object obj) method will replace the last object that was returned by next() with the object that is passed as an argument to the set(Object obj) method.

THE SET INTERFACE

A **Set** is a collection of objects that cannot contain duplicates. Two objects, for example object1 and object2, are considered duplicates if object1.equals(object2). Because Set is an interface, it cannot be instantiated directly. The following would cause an error:

```
Set s = new Set(); // Error!
```

Logically, a Set can contain only one null element, since two nulls would constitute duplicates.

METHODS OF THE SET INTERFACE

The following methods of the Set interface are tested in the AP Computer Science subset:

- `int size()`
- `boolean add(Object x)`
- `boolean contains(Object x)`
- `boolean remove(Object x)`
- `Iterator iterator()`

Set: int size()

This method returns the number of elements in the Set.

Set: boolean add(Object x)

This method will add x to the set if it is not already present, and return true. If x is already in the Set, it will not be added and false will be returned. How the Set determines if an object is already present depends on the implementation. A HashSet uses the object equals() method. Since methods that are added to a TreeSet must implement the Comparable interface, a TreeSet will use an objects compareTo() method.

Set: boolean contains(Object x)

This method returns true if object x is already in the Set and false otherwise.

Set: boolean remove(Object x)

If the Set contains object x, it will be removed from the Set and true will be returned. If object x is not in the Set, false is returned.

Set: Iterator iterator()

Returns an Iterator that can be used to visit all the elements in the Set.

HASHSET AND TREESET CLASSES

The **HashSet** and **TreeSet** classes both implement the Set interface. Neither of these classes adds any additional methods.

HashSet	TreeSet
The elements in a HashSet are unordered. If you use an Iterator to visit the elements of a HashSet, do not expect them to be returned in the same order in which they were added.	The elements of a TreeSet are ordered. This order is *not* based on the order that elements are added to a TreeSet. Instead, elements that are added to a TreeSet must implement the Comparable interface; i.e., they must have a compareTo(Object obj) method. The TreeSet uses this method internally to order the elements. See Chapter 5 for more information on the Comparable interface.
A HashSet is backed by a hash table.	A TreeSet is backed by a balanced binary tree.
The methods add(), remove(), contains(), and size() offer constant time performance. In Big-Oh notation, this is $O(1)$. This means that the number of elements in the HashSet won't affect the time it takes to search for, add, or remove elements.	A TreeSet provides $O(\log n)$ performance for add(), remove(), and contains(). This means as we add more elements, it will take longer to search for, add, or remove elements.

In other words, if you need to keep the elements of the Set ordered, use a TreeSet. Otherwise, use a HashSet as it offers better performance.

THE MAP INTERFACE

WHAT IS A MAP?

Imagine that you want to write a program that can be used as a phone book. In your program, you will need to associate each person's name with a phone number. For example, the name "Bert" would be associated with the phone number "614-555-1234" and the name "Cookie Monster" would need to be associated with another phone number, "212-555-4321". A Map can be used to logically associate names with phone numbers in your program.

A **Map** is a Collection object that associates keys with values. In our phone book example, each name is a key, and the phone number is its value.

The keys within a Map must be unique. For example, our phone book cannot use "Bert" twice as a key. Values, on the other hand, do not need to be unique. In our phonebook example, two different names could have the same phone number.

Note that Map is an interface. Therefore, you can't directly instantiate an instance of the Map interface. The following will cause an error:

```
Map m = new Map(); // Error!
```

Instead, you need to instantiate one of the classes that implements the Map interface, either Hash-Map or TreeMap. For example

```
Map m1 = new HashMap();
Map m2 = new TreeMap();
```

METHODS OF THE MAP INTERFACE

The following methods of the Map interface are tested in the AP Computer Science subset:

- `int size()`
- `Object put(Object key, Object value)`
- `Object get(Object key)`
- `Object remove(Object key)`
- `boolean containsKey(Object key)`
- `Set keySet()`

Map: int size()

The size() method returns the number of key-value pairs contained in the Map. This method returns 0 if the Map is empty.

In the following example, we get a Map from a call to a prewritten method. We then use the size() method to find out how many key value pairs are in the Map.

```
Map myMap = //a call to some method that returns a map
int mapSize = myMap.size();
```

Map: Object put(Object key, Object value);

The put() method is used to store a key and its value in a Map. Note that both the key and the value must be objects.

```
Map myMap = new HashMap();
myMap.put("Bert", "614-555-1234");
myMap.put("Cookie Monster", "212-555-4321");
int mapSize = myMap.size();
System.out.println(mapSize);
```

This would generate the following output:

```
2
```

In the example above, we create a HashMap and add two key-value pairs to it. We then print out the size of the Map, which is 2.

Now let's try adding another key-value pair to the example above, using a key that is already in the Map.

```
myMap.put("Cookie Monster", "203-555-5555");
mapSize = myMap.size();
System.out.println(mapSize);
```

This would generate the following output:

```
2
```

Note that the size of the Map didn't change, since the key we are adding ("Cookie Monster") already exists in the Map. Instead, the phone number that was associated with "Cookie Monster" will be changed from "212-555-4321" to "203-555-5555".

What happens if we add a key-value pair that contains a *value* that is already in the Map? Continuing our example

```
myMap.put("Ernie", "614-555-1234");
mapSize = myMap.size();
System.out.println(mapSize);
```

This would generate the following output:

```
3
```

Notice that the Map now contains an additional entry. As we've seen, Maps are allowed to have multiple entries with the same values.

Map: Object get(Object key)

The get() method returns a value for a given key. Note that the value is returned as type Object. In your code, you will need to cast it to the appropriate type.

Continuing our example above, the following line would return the phone number we have stored for "Bert":

```
String bertsNumber = (String) myMap.get("Bert");
```

The variable bertsNumber will now reference the value that is associated with "Bert" in the Map: "614-555-1234".

Map: Object remove(Object key)

Like the get() method, the remove() method returns a value for a given key. But whereas get() leaves the key-value pair in the Map, the remove() method removes the pair from the Map, as the name of the method implies. If the key is not in the Map, this method returns null.

Map: boolean containsKey(Object key)

This method returns true if the Map contains the key that is passed as a parameter, and false otherwise.

Map: Set keySet()

The keySet() method returns a Set that contains all of the keys in a Map. This method is useful for looking at all of the key-value pairs in a Map.

Consider the following code segment:

```
Map myMap = new HashMap();
myMap.put("Bert", "614-555-1234");
myMap.put("Cookie Monster", "212-555-4321");
myMap.put("Ernie", "614-555-1234");
myMap.put("Big Bird", "203-555-4321");
```

Suppose that we would like to print out all of the names in the phone book, along with their phone numbers. Here's how we might do this.

```
01: Set myKeys = myMap.keySet();
02: Iterator iter = myKeys.iterator();
03: while (iter.hasNext())
04: {
05:    Object key = iter.next();
06:    Object value = myMap.get(key);
07:    System.out.println(key + " -- " + value);
08: }
```

Line 1 gets a Set of the keys using the keySet method. Once we have the Set myKeys, we can call any of the methods defined in the Set interface on it. On line 2, we get an Iterator. We can use this Iterator to look at each key in the Set. Line 3 uses the standard interface to loop through the values in the Iterator.

On line 5, we get the next key from the Iterator, and then on line 6 we get the corresponding value for the key from the Map. Finally, we print out each key-value pair on line 7.

HASHMAP AND TREEMAP CLASSES

The **HashMap** and **TreeMap** classes both implement the Map interface. Neither of these classes adds any additional methods.

HashMap	TreeMap
The elements in a HashMap are unordered.	The keys of a TreeMap are ordered. This order is *not* based on the order in which elements are added to a TreeMap. Instead, elements that are added to a TreeMap must implement the Comparable interface; i.e., they must have a compareTo(Object obj) method. The TreeMap uses this method internally to order the elements. See Chapter 5 for more information on the Comparable interface.
A HashMap is backed by a hash table.	A TreeMap is backed by a balanced binary tree.
The methods put(), get(), containsKey(), and size() offer constant time performance. In Big-Oh notation, this is $O(1)$. This means that the number of elements in the HashMap won't affect the time it takes to search for, add, or remove elements.	A TreeMap provides $O(\log n)$ performance for add(), remove(), and containsKey(). This means that as we add more elements, it will take longer to search for, add, or remove elements.

If you need to keep the elements of the Map ordered, use a TreeMap. Otherwise, use a HashMap as it offers better performance.

REVIEW QUESTIONS

Answers to review questions can be found in Chapter 11.

1. Consider the following class and code segment:

```
public class Person
{
  private String name;
  private int age;

  public Person(String n, int a)
  {
    name = n;
    age = a;
  }
  public String name()
  {
    return name;
  }

  public int age()
  {
    return age;
  }
}
```

```
01: Person p1 = new Person("Mike", 32);
02: Person p2 = new Person("Mike", 32);
03: Set s = new HashSet();
04: s.add(p1);
05: s.add(p2);
06: int theSize = s.size();
07: System.out.print(theSize);
```

What will be printed as a result of executing the code segment?

(A) 0
(B) 1
(C) 2
(D) 3
(E) 4

2. Consider the following code segment:

```
List myList = new ArrayList();
myList.add("A");
myList.add("B");
myList.add("C");
myList.add("D");
ListIterator iter = myList.listIterator();
System.out.println(iter.next());
iter.add("E");
System.out.println(iter.next());
iter.remove();
System.out.println(iter.next());
```

What will be printed as a result of executing the code segment?

(A) ABC
(B) AEB
(C) ABD
(D) BCD
(E) Nothing will be printed due to a run-time error.

3. You have been given the task of writing a program for a school. It will be used to keep track of the clubs to which students belong. The program should allow users to enter the name of a club, and the program should print the names of all students that are members of the club in alphabetical order. There is no need to print the names of the clubs in order.

Which of the following would be the best choice of data structures to use for this program?

(A) Store the names of clubs in an ArrayList and store the names of students in a separate ArrayList.
(B) Store the information in a TreeMap. The names of the clubs should be the keys of the TreeMap and the values should be TreeSets that contain the names of the students in each club.
(C) Store the information in a HashMap. The names of the clubs should be the keys of the HashMap and the values should be TreeSets that contain the names of the students in each club.
(D) Store the information in a TreeMap. The names of the students should be the keys of the TreeMap and the values should be HashSets that contain the names of the clubs to which the student belongs.
(E) Store the information in a HashMap. The names of the clubs should be the keys of the HashMap and the values should be HashSets that contain the names of the students in each club.

Data Structures
(AB Only)

INTRODUCTION

This chapter examines linked lists, stacks, queues, priority queues, binary trees, heaps, and hashtables. You're already familiar with many of the concepts discussed in this section, and you use them in your everyday life. By and large, the trick in this chapter is going to be linking the computer science terminology to already familiar concepts. For example, the phonebook you have at home is a Map, with names as *keys* and phone numbers as *values*.

The members of your family form a tree, with your grandparents at the top, and yourself at the bottom. Your name is a pointer, which directs people to the unique being you are. As you read through this chapter, it's important that you refuse to let yourself be intimidated by complex software engineering jargon. For the most part, you probably already understood most of the concepts being discussed before you ever opened a computer book.

LINKED LISTS

WHAT IS A LINKED LIST?

Imagine that you're standing at the top of a cliff, you have five dollars in your pocket, and there is a rope tied around your waist. Dangling from that rope is your best friend, who has two dollars in her pocket. Your best friend, in turn, has a rope tied around her waist. Dangling from that rope is your favorite teacher, who has six dollars in his pocket.

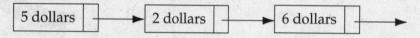

Believe it or not, you've just formed a **linked list**. You're the head ListNode, and your teacher, way at the bottom, is the tail ListNode.

As we go through the rest of this chapter, we will sometimes build our own data structure, or describe how to build our own data structure, instead of using the default Java classes such as array, ArrayLists, LinkedLists, and Maps. The point of doing so is to understand the efficiency costs in using these data structures so you can make informed decisions about performance. It's fine to understand what collections are, but it's also very important to understand how they actually work.

THE LISTNODE CLASS

In Java terms, a linked list consists of **ListNodes**. Each ListNode, in turn, has two member variables: one holds the value that the ListNode is carrying, and the other points to another ListNode (or null, if it's the tail ListNode, and there is no other). In other words, it points to the memory location of the next ListNode. In the metaphor above, you, your best friend, and your favorite teacher are ListNodes. Each ListNode, in turn, carries a value (in this case, the money) and a reference to the next ListNode (in this case, the rope).

Here is the ListNode class that will be provided on the AP Computer Science Exam.

```
public class ListNode
{
  private Object value;
  private ListNode next;
  public ListNode(Object initValue, ListNode initNext)
  {
    value = initValue;
    next = initNext;
  }
  public Object getValue()
  {
    return value;
  }
  public ListNode getNext()
  {
    return next;
  }
  public void setValue(Object theNewValue)
  {
    value = theNewValue;
  }
  public void setNext(ListNode theNewNext)
  {
    next = theNewNext;
  }
}
```

A CustomLinkedList Class

Correspondingly, the linked list that holds these ListNodes might look like the following. Notice that the CustomLinkedList class is really just a data structure that keeps track of ListNodes and controls their relationship to each other. Please take a minute and look over the code below. In particular, try to identify the places where the methods might incur overhead in terms of Big-Oh performance, and where they are avoiding such overhead.

Note that unlike the ListNode class above, the CustomLinkedList class will not be provided on the exam. Instead, you may be asked to implement part of a CustomLinkedList class yourself. By studying and understanding the following, you will be prepared if you see a question that asks you to do so:

```java
public class CustomLinkedList
{
  private ListNode headNode;
  private ListNode tailNode;
  public void addFirst(Object item)
  {
    ListNode newNode = new ListNode(item);
    if (headNode == null)
    {
      headNode = newNode;
      tailNode = newNode;
    }
    else
    {
      newNode.setNext(headNode);
      headNode = newNode;
    }
  }

  public void addLast(Object item)
  {
    if (tailNode == null)
    {
      addFirst(item);
    }
    else
    {
      ListNode newNode = new ListNode(item);
      tailNode.setNext(newNode);
      tailNode = newNode;
    }
  }
  public Object getFirst()
  {
    Object retval = null;
    if (headNode != null)
    {
      retval = headNode.getValue();
    }
    return retval;
  }
  public Object getLast()
  {
    Object retval = null;
    if (tailNode != null)
    {
      retval = tailNode.getValue();
    }
```

```
          return retval;
      }
      public Object removeFirst()
      {
        Object retval = getFirst();
        if (retval != null)
        {
          headNode = headNode.getNext();
        }
        return retval;
      }
      public Object removeLast()
      {
        Object retval = null;
        if (headNode == tailNode)
        {
          retval = removeFirst();
        }
        else
        {
          retval = tailNode.getValue();
          ListNode currentNode = headNode;
          while (currentNode.getNext() != tailNode)
          {
            currentNode = currentNode.getNext();
          }
          tailNode = currentNode;
          tailNode.setNext(null);
        }
        return retval;
      }
  }
```

Note that the first ListNode points to the next ListNode, which in turn points to the next ListNode, and so on, and the CustomLinkedList class keeps track of the entire structure by tracking the first node and the last.

INSERTING A LISTNODE INTO A LINKED LIST

To create the data structure that represents you and your friends hanging off the cliff, we might write the following code:

```
01: CustomLinkedList linkedList = new CustomLinkedList();
02: linkedList.addFirst("5 dollars");
03: linkedList.addLast("2 dollars");
04: linkedList.addLast("6 dollars");
```

What we've done here is create a **Data Structure:** We wrote Java code that represents the ListNodes we want. Data structures are the means by which information is represented within a program. Thus, if you were writing a program to track a group of people hanging off a cliff, you could use the CustomLinkedList class.

In the code segment above, line 2 indirectly creates the ListNode that represents you, with five dollars in your pocket. Line 3 indirectly creates the ListNode that represents your best friend, with two dollars in her pocket, and line 3 represents your favorite teacher, with six dollars in his pocket. Visually, the data structure can be thought of in the following way:

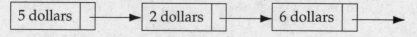

We use the term *indirectly*, because a client program using the CustomLinkedList class never actually sees that ListNodes are being created. That process is encapsulated in the addFirst() and addLast() methods of the CustomLinkedList class.

This practice of complexity hiding, or **encapsulation**, is discussed in detail in Chapter 4. The client program (that is, the program that will be using your class) knows as little as possible about the inner functionality of how specific services are provided. This way, the client can focus on its needs without having to worry about how those needs are met. This is conceptually similar to how you interact with a car: You don't need to know the car actually works beyond the bare minimum of putting gas in it and so on. You are therefore free to concentrate on using the car to get your various tasks done.

This example uses the term "CustomLinkedList" to avoid confusion with the java.util.LinkedList class, but the concept is the same.

CREATING A LISTNODE

The above notwithstanding, as the person designing the CustomLinkedList class you need to know how to create and manipulate ListNodes. So let's take a closer look at the addFirst() method.

```
01:  public void addFirst(Object item)
02:  {
03:    ListNode newNode = new ListNode(item);
04:    if (headNode == null)
05:    {
06:      headNode = newNode;
07:      tailNode = newNode;
08:    }
09:    else
10:    {
11:      newNode.setNext(headNode);
12:      headNode = newNode;
13:    }
14:  }
```

The actual algorithm for inserting a new item is fairly simple, and it is based on how real life objects interact. The first step, shown on line 3 above, is to put the item into a ListNode node. The next step, shown on line 4, is to see if this is the first node we're inserting into the CustomLinkedList. If so, then it is both the head (first) node and the last node, as shown on lines 6 and 7. If it is not the first node, then the new node points to the current head of the list, as shown on line 11 and is made the new head node, as shown on line 12.

DELETING A LISTNODE FROM A LINKED LIST

The process of deleting a ListNode from the list is very similar to the process of inserting a ListNode, in terms of activity. You still have to find the ListNode that needs to be removed, and then you need to make sure that you don't lose references further down the chain from the targeted ListNode.

For example, imagine that your mother is holding your sister's hand, and that your sister is holding your hand, so you're at the end. Now imagine that your sister needs to leave, but you don't want to break the chain. The process is the following: Your mother should let go of your sister's hand, and grab the hand of whoever is down the line, if there actually is anyone down the line. Then your sister is free to leave at her leisure without jeopardizing the chain. Please take a moment to study the removeLast() method, and look over this process.

There is one subtle point. If you are trying to remove the last item in the linked list, your code will have to start at the first node in the list and iterate through every element in the list until the position of the next-to-last ListNode is found. Even though the CustomLinkedList class maintains a reference to the last ListNode in the list, we can't simply remove the last node using this reference, since we also need to have the lastNode reference point to the new last node. Thus, the process of deleting a ListNode can be a performance-intensive operation, depending on how many elements are in your list. If you need to remove the last item in the CustomLinkedList class, you'll have to iterate through the entire list.

DOUBLY LINKED LISTS

The linked list we introduced above is technically referred to as a **singly linked list** because each ListNode maintains a reference to only the next ListNode, and not to the previous ListNode. A **doubly linked list** is a slight variation on a linked list in that it allows ListNodes to know not only what they are holding onto, but also to know what is holding onto them. Doubly linked lists therefore require more memory because they are keeping more information. However, they require less processing because you don't have to iterate from the beginning to get to a node anywhere else in the list.

Doubly linked lists are ideal when you want to be able to traverse a list forward and backward. To change our singly linked list to a doubly linked list, we need to make a few very minor changes. First, we need to add a **previous** member variable to the ListNode class that points to the previous ListNode, just as the **next** member variable points to the next ListNode. Second, we need to keep the previous member variable current when we insert or delete a ListNode. Conceptually, a doubly linked list looks like the following, in which the gray indicates the previous reference:

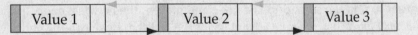

Let's take a look at how the addFirst() and removeLast() methods of our CustomLinkedList class would change if the class implemented a doubly linked list. We assume in the examples below that we have added the methods setPrevious() and getPrevious() to the ListNode class; these methods are used to set and get a reference to the previous node in the linked list.

```
01:  public void addFirst(Object item)
02:  {
03:    ListNode newNode = new ListNode(item);
04:    if (headNode == null)
05:    {
06:      headNode = newNode;
07:      tailNode = newNode;
08:    }
09:    else
10:    {
11:      newNode.setNext(headNode);
12:      headNode.setPrevious(newNode);
13:      headNode = newNode;
14:    }
15:  }
```

The only change we need to make to the addFirst() method is to set the reference to the previous node in the current headNode so that it points to the new node.

Here is what the removeLast() method looks like for a doubly linked list.

```
01:  public Object removeLast()
02:  {
03:    Object retval = null;
04:    if (headNode == tailNode)
05:    {
06:      retval = removeFirst();
07:    }
08:    else
09:    {
10:      retval = tailNode.getValue();
11:      tailNode = tailNode.getPrevious();
12:      tailNode.setNext(null);
13:      return retval;
14:    }
15:  }
```

Recall that in the removeLast() method for a *singly linked* list, we needed to iterate from the start of the list in order to find the second-to-last node and make it the new last node. In the removeLast() method for a *doubly linked* list, we take advantage of the fact that if we call the getPrevious() method on the last node, it returns a reference to the second-to-last node. This is shown on line 11 above.

CIRCULAR LINKED LISTS

A **circular linked list** is very similar to a singly linked list, except that the tail ListNode points back to the head ListNode. Conceptually, this is similar to a group of children forming a circle by holding hands: there is no head or tail, and the last element points back to the first. Let's consider this visually.

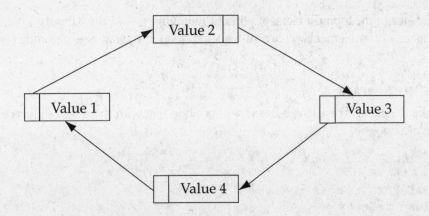

Performance Analysis of Linked Lists

The best-case scenario for searching a list is $O(1)$; this occurs when the element you are looking for is the first element in the LinkedList. The worst-case scenario and the average-case scenario for a linked list is $O(n)$ because the search time is directly proportional to the number of elements in the list.

Adding an element to the beginning of the list takes constant time, $O(1)$, whereas adding an element to the end of the list takes $O(n)$ time for a linked list that only maintains a reference to the head node. This is because you have to iterate through every element in the list to get to the last element. If the list maintains a reference to the tail node, then adding a node to the end of the list is $O(1)$.

For both doubly and singly linked lists, removing the first element is $O(1)$. Removing the last node from a doubly linked list that maintains a reference to the tail node is $O(1)$, whereas removing the last node from a singly linked list is $O(n)$ since, as we saw above, it is necessary to iterate through the list from the beginning.

Inserting and removing elements from the middle of a linked list are $O(n)$ operations because it is necessary to iterate to the middle of the list, which takes $O(n)$ time. Once the position of the insertion or deletion is reached, the actual act of inserting or deleting is $O(1)$.

STACKS

What Is a Stack?

A **stack** is what you would get if you put all of your books on top of each other. Take a minute and put a few books on top of each other, as it will help illustrate some of the concepts we are about to discuss.

The first thing you will notice is that the stack is **Last In First Out**, or LIFO. That is, the first element that you will remove from the stack will be the topmost book, which also happens to be the last element you put on. This is the distinctive feature of stacks. For example, if you want a program that keeps track of how many people can enter a phone booth, a stack might be the best implementation, since the last person in is also the first person out.

The Stack Interface

The stack interface has four operations. You can push items onto the stack, you can pop items off the stack, you can examine the stack's first element without actually removing it, and you can see if the stack is empty. Imagine that you have a stack of four books. The push() method puts a fifth book on the stack. The pop() method removes the topmost book, leaving the rest. The peekTop() method returns a reference to the topmost element without removing it, and the isEmpty() method tells you if the stack has any more elements. That's all well and good, but what does the code for a stack look like?

IMPLEMENTING A STACK

When you take the exam, The College Board will provide you with the interface for a Stack. Here is what the interface looks like.

```
public interface Stack
{
   // returns true if the stack is empty
   boolean isEmpty();
   // adds x to the top of the stack
   void push(Object x);
   // removes the top element from the stack
   // and returns it
   Object pop();
   // returns the top element of the stack, but
   // does not actually remove it from the stack
   Object peekTop();
}
```

It's possible that you will be asked on the exam to write code that implements one or more of the methods above. Let's examine how this could be done.

The following code uses the LinkedList class from the Java class library to implement the Stack interface:

```
01: public class ListStack implements Stack
02: {
03:    private LinkedList myList
04:       = new LinkedList();
05:    public void push(Object item)
06:    {
07:       myList.addFirst(item);
08:    }
09:    public Object pop()
10:    {
11:       return myList.removeFirst();
12:    }
13:    public boolean isEmpty()
14:    {
15:       boolean retval = false;
16:       if (peekTop() == null)
17:       {
18:          retval = true;
19:       }
20:       return retval;
21:    }
22:    public Object peekTop()
23:    {
24:       return myList.getFirst();
25:    }
26: }
```

A LinkedList instance is used "under the hood" to store the values that are pushed when the push() method of the ListStack class is called. Note that the push(), pop() and peekTop() methods all delegate to the LinkedList instance. The isEmpty() method works by calling the peekTop() method. If peekTop() returns an object, then we know the Stack is not empty and isEmpty() will return false; otherwise it will return true.

How else could we have implemented the isEmpty() method? Recall that LinkedList class has a size() method that returns 0 if there are no elements in the instance. So isEmpty() could also be written as

```
public boolean isEmpty()
{
  if (myList.size() == 0)
     return true;
  else
    return false;
}
```

Or, keeping in mind that the equality operator returns a boolean value itself, we could trim this down to

```
public boolean isEmpty()
{
  return (myList.size() == 0);
}
```

Changing the implementation will not change the behavior that the client will see.

Note that the relationship between the ListStack class and the LinkedList class is one of *composition*. The ListStack class contains a LinkedList instance as a private data variable that it uses to store data. This illustrates the concepts of encapsulation and information hiding. We've encapsulated the LinkedList instance within our ListStack class; by making it private, we hide it from clients who use the class.

PUSHING AN OBJECT ONTO A STACK

To insert an element onto the stack, all you have to do is call the push() method. This places the new element on top of every other element already there. The code for doing this follows:

```
Stack myStack = new ListStack();
// ListStack implements Stack
myStack.push("Item 1");
myStack.push("Item 2");
myStack.push("Item 3");
```

Visually, the stack might look like the following. Note that the first item that was pushed onto the stack is on the bottom.

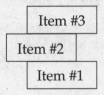

REMOVING AN OBJECT FROM A STACK

To remove an element from the stack, all you have to do is call the pop() method. This removes and returns the topmost element from the stack. Using the myStack instance defined above, the code for doing this follows:

```
Object obj = myStack.pop();
```

In the example above, this operation results in the following data structure:

SEARCHING A STACK

Imagine that you've stacked all of your CDs on your desk, but the CD cases aren't labeled. How would you go about finding a particular CD? You would probably start removing CDs from the top of the stack, examine each one, and then pull out the one you need. A computer's stack is searched in the same way.

```
//myCDs is an instance of a class that implements the Stack
   interface.
while (! myCDs.isEmpty())
{
   if ("Elvis".equals(stack.pop()))
   {
      //play cd
   }
}
```

Note, however, that once you've found Elvis's CD, you have lost all of the CDs that were on the stack above Elvis. Stacks are typically not used for searching; use a List or Tree structure instead.

PERFORMANCE ANALYSIS OF STACKS

Since Stack is an interface, its performance will depend on how it is implemented. In our implementation above, we delegated calls to the stack's methods to the underlying LinkedList instance. In order to analyze the performance of our ListStack class, we need to look at the performance of the methods that we call on the LinkedList instance. The LinkedList library class is implemented with a doubly linked list that has references to both the head and tail. Therefore the calls to addFirst() and removeFirst() will occur in constant time, or $O(1)$.

Regardless of how large the stack becomes, the performance associated with pushing elements onto the stack and popping the topmost element off the stack is very efficient: It is $O(1)$. That is, it's just as easy to remove the topmost item from a stack of one million items as it is to remove the topmost item from a stack of two items.

This provides optimal performance for the best-case, the average-case, and the worst-case scenarios. Thus, although using a more flexible structure to store your data can be most adaptable, using a task-specific data structure like a stack can boost performance; it's really a matter of what your program needs to do. Are you going to be storing several items and removing only the last one you added at any given time? If so, then you want a stack as your data structure. Understanding concepts like this gives you the information you will need to balance the benefits of flexibility in your project against the benefits of performance.

QUEUES

WHAT IS A QUEUE?

A **queue** represents a line, like you might find at the grocery store. Although it is similar to a stack, it differs in one important way: a queue is **First In First Out**, or FIFO. The first element added to a queue is the first element that is removed from it. Thus, the first person in line is also the first person out of line.

THE QUEUE INTERFACE

The standard interface for a Queue used on the AP exam is the following:

```
public interface Queue
{
    //adds the item to the end of the queue
    void enqueue(Object item);
    //removes and returns the item at the
    //front of the queue
    Object dequeue();
    //returns true if the queue is empty
    boolean isEmpty();
    //returns but does NOT remove the item at the
    //front of the queue
    Object peekFront();
}
```

IMPLEMENTING A QUEUE

On the exam, you will *not* be provided with a class that implements the Queue interface shown above. You may be expected to implement some or all of the methods yourself. Let's take a look at how you can do this.

To implement the Queue interface, we will need to create a data structure in which to store values. Note that when we enqueue() an element into a queue, it will be stored at the back of the Queue. When we dequeue() an element, it will be taken from the front of the queue. The LinkedList class that comes in the Java library will provide what we are looking for, because it comes with addLast() and remove-First() methods that we can use to implement the queue's enqueue() and dequeue() methods.

A sample implementation of a queue, using the LinkedList class, is given below. Please take a moment to look over the code and see where performance bottlenecks might be.

```
public class ListQueue implements Queue
{
  private LinkedList myList =
  new LinkedList();

  public void enqueue(Object item)
  {
    myList.addLast(item);
  }

  public Object dequeue()
  {
    return myList.removeFirst();
  }

  public boolean isEmpty()
  {
    boolean retval = false;
    if (peekFront() == null)
    {
      retval = true;
    }
    return retval;
  }

  public Object peekFront()
  {
    return myList.getFirst();
  }
}
```

PERFORMANCE ANALYSIS OF QUEUES

As with the ListStack class, our ListQueue class has constant runtimes for the operations it supports. Enqueuing or dequeuing items from the queue, looking at the front-most item in the queue, and checking to see if the queue is empty all take $O(1)$ runtime.

PRIORITY QUEUES

WHAT IS A PRIORITY QUEUE?

Not all queues are created equal. For example, although the line at the emergency room needs to be orderly, it also needs to take priority into account. A person having a heart attack should get treated first, regardless of the order of the patients in the line.

To solve this problem in general terms, we need to define what we mean by "higher priority." What, exactly, are we comparing? In the example above, priority is determined by the potential impact of the patient's condition. But what about, say, the various programs running on your computer?

These also constitute a list of items. How do we know which one of these gets a higher priority? Does your Web browser get priority over your printer? What about a system shutdown command: does that get priority over everything else? Your computer needs some way to track its internal list of tasks.

So the answer, in general, is that we have to decide on some criteria. In Java, this means that we expect our objects to implement the Comparable interface. This way, the objects in the queue can be ranked by priority.

THE PRIORITY QUEUE INTERFACE

The **PriorityQueue** interface defines the methods shown below. It's important to notice that the method uses the term "Min" to refer to the object with the highest priority. This can be a little confusing, but it makes sense when you think it through. For example, your number 1 priority is your highest priority. It beats out priority number 10. This is also the case with PriorityQueues.

```
public interface PriorityQueue
{
   //adds an item to the priority queue
   public void add(Object item);
   //removes and returns the object
   //with the highest priority
   public Object removeMin();
   //is the priority queue empty?
   public boolean isEmpty();
   //returns the highest priority
   //item without removing
   public Object peekMin();
}
```

IMPLEMENTING

A priority queue will generally use a **binary tree** or a **min-heap** to store its internal state, both of which are discussed below. This is because a priority queue forces us to make a difficult decision. In order to insert an item in the "correct" place, we need to be able to find that place. Thus, we have to search the entire list to insert items. With an array or linked list, that could take up to $O(n)$. With trees and min-heaps, we can reduce that time to $O(\log n)$. To understand why, please read the following sections.

TREES

WHAT IS A TREE?

A **tree**, in computer science terms, is a structure that consists of **nodes** that hold values and edges that connect the nodes. In a tree, each node can have multiple "children," but each child can have at most one "parent." In the example below, the children of the "Grandfather" node are "Aunt," "Uncle," and "Father." Your family ancestry might be thought of as a tree, with the criterion being seniority. Thus, your family tree might look something like the following:

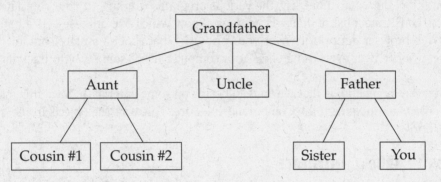

TREE TERMINOLOGY

There is a unique vocabulary that goes along with trees. Here are the terms that you should be familiar with in order to do well on the exam.

Nodes

Every element in a tree is stored in a **node**. Nodes also keep track of the child nodes that are connected to them. In the example above, the node labeled "Aunt" stores the value "Aunt" and also keeps track of the "Cousin #1" and "Cousin #2" nodes as indicated by the edges connecting them.

Root

The **root** of a tree is the single node that doesn't have a parent. It is the top of the tree. By definition, each tree can only have a single root. In the example above, Grandfather is the root.

Leaf

A tree **leaf** is a node that doesn't have any child nodes. Thus, "Uncle" and "Sister" above are both leaves (even though "Uncle" is at a higher level), because neither has any TreeNodes directly under them. For that matter, "Cousin #1," "Cousin #2," and "You" are also leaves.

Traverse

To **traverse** a tree means to look at each node in the tree. This can be done for the purpose of finding a specific value or for printing out all of the values in a tree. Note that although this term is often used with trees, it does not apply exclusively to trees. It is possible to traverse other data structures. For example, when you use a for loop to look at each element of an array, you are "traversing" the array.

Subtree

A **subtree** can be thought of as a tree within a tree. So in our example above, the following would be a subtree of the main tree:

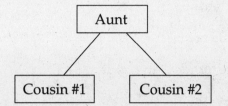

And since a tree can consist of a single node, the following would be a subtree of the subtree above:

In fact, a tree can consist of no nodes. We call this the empty tree.

Binary Tree

A **binary tree** is a type of tree in which each node can have at most two children. You can expect most of the tree-related questions on the AP exam to involve binary trees. You will need to be aware of the recursive nature of binary trees for the exam. A binary tree can be thought of as a node that has a value, a left tree, and a right tree. Note that either the left tree, the right tree, or both can be empty.

THE TREENODE CLASS

On the exam, nodes are represented by the TreeNode class provided by The College Board. Every element in a tree is a TreeNode. A TreeNode is somewhat like the ListNode discussed earlier in this chapter, except that a TreeNode has two member variables which can point to other TreeNodes. An implementation will be shown shortly.

Here is the TreeNode class that will be provided by The College Board on the exam.

```
public class TreeNode
{
    private Object value;
    private TreeNode left;
    private TreeNode right;

    public TreeNode(Object intValue)
    {
      value = initValue;
      left = null;
      right = null;
    }
    public TreeNode(Object initValue,
                        TreeNode initLeft,
                        TreeNode initRight)
    {
      value = initValue;
      left = initLeft;
      right = initRight;
    }

    public Object getValue()
    {
      return value;
    }

    public TreeNode getLeft()
    {
      return left;
    }

    public TreeNode getRight()
    {
      return right;
    }

    public void setValue(Object newValue)
    {
      value = newValue;
    }

    public void setLeft(TreeNode newLeft)
    {
      left = newLeft;
    }

    public void setRight(TreeNode newRight)
    {
        right = newRight;
    }
}
```

The TreeNode class stores a value as an Object and also contains references to up to two child nodes.

A few things to note

- A TreeNode instance can contain references to at most two other nodes. This means that TreeNodes can only be used to represent binary trees.

- A TreeNode instance stores references to its child nodes if it has children, but it does not store a reference to its parent.

BINARY SEARCH TREES

As we saw above, a binary tree is a type of tree in which each node can have two children at most. A binary **search** tree is a type of binary tree in which the value in each node is larger than the value of every node in its left subtree, and smaller or equal to the value of every node in its right subtree.

Based on the definition above, which of the following trees is/are binary search trees?

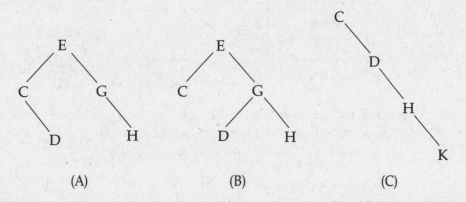

(A)   (B)   (C)

Both (A) and (C) are binary search trees, since the value in each node is larger than the value of every node in its left subtree, and smaller than or equal to the value of every node in its right subtree.

(B) is *not* a binary search tree, since the root node, which contains the value "E" has a node in its right subtree that contains a smaller value, namely "D".

The advantage of a binary search tree is easy to understand. It's the principle of organization. That is, if we're willing to take a little time to organize items when we first insert them, then they are much easier to find later. Of course, you're already familiar with this principle. If you organize your CDs when you first buy them, then it's easy to find them later. If you don't, then it's harder.

Specifically, this means that inserting items into and removing items from a binary search tree takes, on average, $O(\log n)$ time. Contrast this with performing these same operations using another data structure, like an array, which takes $O(n)$ time per operation.

However, in the worst case, insertion into, deletion from, and searching a binary search tree will take $O(n)$ time. This occurs when all nodes fall to the right or all fall to the left of their parent. Choice (C) in the question above is an example of where this has happened. In this case, the binary search tree is in effect a linked list, and its search performance will be reduced to that of a linked list: $O(n)$.

INSERTING ITEMS INTO A BINARY SEARCH TREE

Let's look at an example of how we would organize CDs alphabetically by artist using a binary search tree. We will add the following artists to the tree in the order given:

Elvis, Pixies, Cure, Public Enemy, Beatles, Difranco (Ani)

We start by making the first element the root node.

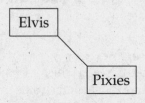

The next artist is Pixies. Since Pixies comes after Elvis alphabetically and is thus greater, we'll place Pixies to the right.

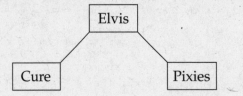

The Cure is next. Since Cure comes before Elvis alphabetically, it goes to the left.

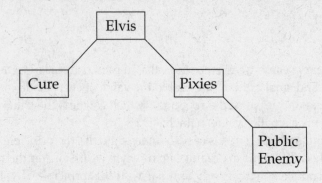

We now need to fit in Public Enemy. Alphabetically, Public Enemy is greater than Elvis, so it goes to the right of Elvis. It's also greater than Pixies so it goes to the right again.

Continuing this pattern, our final tree looks like the following:

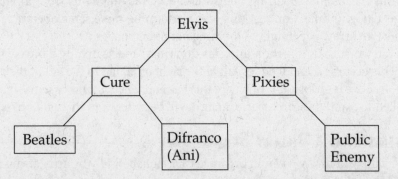

The order in which we insert items into a binary search tree determines what the tree looks like. Consider, for example, if we were to insert the artists above into a binary search tree in the following order:

Pixies, Elvis, Difranco (Ani), Public Enemy, Beatles, Cure

The binary search tree would look like the following after all the items were inserted:

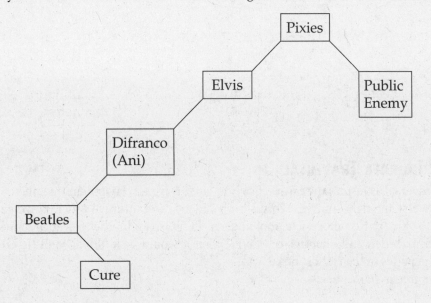

INSERTING (CODE SAMPLE)

```
public TreeNode insert(TreeNode theRoot, Comparable newValue)
{
  if (theRoot == null)
        return new TreeNode(newValue);

  Comparable currentValue = (Comparable) theRoot.getValue();

  if (newValue.compareTo(currentValue) < 0)
  {
        theRoot.setLeft(insert(theRoot.getLeft(), newValue));
        return theRoot;
  }
  else
  {
        theRoot.setRight(insert(theRoot.getRight(), newValue));
        return theRoot;
  }
}
}
```

TRAVERSING A BINARY TREE

The process of stepping through the nodes in a tree is referred to as a traversal. Most often, this traversal process is recursive. Thus, you would write code that stepped through each child node of a given node, unless the node itself were a leaf. Those nodes, in turn, would execute the same code. Eventually, you would reach a leaf, and the process would stop. But that raises a question: Which order should you traverse in? For binary trees, there are three choices: inorder, preorder, and postorder. We will use the binary search tree below to illustrate these traversals.

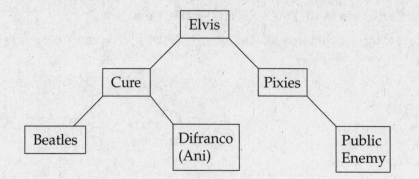

CHOICE 1: INORDER TRAVERSAL

An **inorder traversal** is just a fancy way of saying "first traverse the left subtree, then visit the root node, then traverse the right subtree." This is probably the most intuitive way to traverse a tree. Let's apply this to the binary tree above. The root node is "Elvis" so an inorder traversal of the binary tree would first visit the left child subtree of "Elvis", then it would visit "Elvis" and then the traversal would visit the nodes of the right subtree.

The left subtree is shown below.

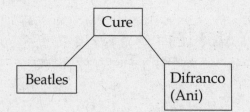

So how do we traverse this subtree? We recursively do an inorder traversal. This means that we first visit the left subtree of the "Cure" node, then we visit the "Cure" node itself, then we visit the right subtree. So the traversal of the subtree above would be

Beatles, Cure, Difranco (Ani)

So now we have traversed the left subtree of "Elvis". The next step is to visit the "Elvis" node itself. Now our traversal looks like this

Beatles, Cure, Difranco (Ani), Elvis

Finally, we conduct an inorder traversal of the right subtree of "Elvis".

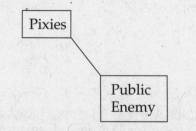

Since we visit the root element before the right subtree in an inorder traversal, the inorder traversal of the subtree above would be

Pixies, Public Enemy

Putting everything together, the inorder traversal of the binary search tree would be

Beatles, Cure, Difranco (Ani), Elvis, Pixies, Public Enemy

Note that the inorder traversal of a binary search tree returns the elements of the tree in order. In our example, the elements of each node in the tree were strings so the elements were returned in alphabetical order.

IMPLEMENTING AN INORDER TRAVERSAL

Here is a method that implements an inorder traversal. The method simply prints out the value of each node as it is visited.

```
public void inOrderTraversal(TreeNode theRoot)
{
  if (theRoot != null)
  {
    inOrderTraversal(theRoot.getLeft());
    System.out.println(theRoot.getValue());
    inOrderTraversal(theRoot.getRight());
  }
}
```

CHOICE 2: PREORDER TRAVERSAL

Preorder traversal is just a fancy way of saying "first visit the root node, then traverse the left subtree, then traverse the right subtree." Thus, for our example binary search tree.

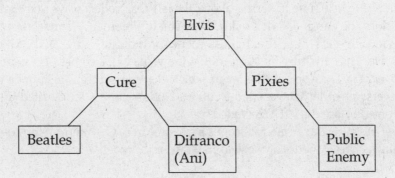

To perform a preorder traversal on the binary search tree above, we first visit the root node ("Elvis"), then we perform a preorder traversal of the left subtree, and then we perform a preorder traversal of the right subtree.

And how do we perform a preorder traversal of the left subtree? First, we visit the root node ("Cure") and then we visit the left subtree followed by the right subtree. Since the left and right subtrees are leaves, our traversal looks like

Elvis, Cure, Beatles, Difranco (Ani)

We then perform a preorder traversal of the right subtree of the "Elvis" node, which gives us

Elvis, Cure, Beatles, Difranco (Ani), Pixies, Public Enemy

An interesting side note: If we were to take the list above and create a binary search tree from it, the new tree would look exactly like the original tree from which the list was constructed. So, for example, a preorder traversal is useful if you want to take a tree and write its contents to a file and then later reconstruct the tree from the contents of the file.

IMPLEMENTING A PREORDER TRAVERSAL

Here is a method that implements a preorder traversal. The method simply prints out the value of each node as it is visited.

```
public void  preOrderTraversal(TreeNode theRoot)
{
  if (theRoot != null)
  {
    System.out.println(theRoot.getValue());
    preOrderTraversal(theRoot.getLeft());
    preOrderTraversal(theRoot.getRight());
  }
}
```

CHOICE 3: POSTORDER TRAVERSAL

Postorder traversal is just a fancy way of saying "first traverse the left subtree, then traverse the left subtree, and *then* visit the root node."

The postorder traversal for our example binary search tree would thus be

Beatles, Difranco (Ani), Cure, Public Enemy, Pixies, Elvis

A little memory hint: In all tree traversals above, the left TreeNode always precedes the right TreeNode. So where does the current Node's value come in? In Preorder (*pre* indicates "previous"), the value comes previous to everything else. In Postorder (*post* indicates "after"), the value Node comes after everything else. Thus, InOrder must mean that the value Node comes between Left and Right.

Three related traversals reverse the order in which the two subtrees of a node are visited. For instance, in a "reverse preorder" traversal, the current Node's value is still visited first, but the right TreeNode is traversed before the left TreeNode.

Finally, a "level-by-level" traversal visits nodes in the tree in each level from top-to-bottom starting at the root. Within each level, nodes are visited in left-to-right order.

To summarize

Traversal	Description
Inorder	Left subtree, Node value, Right subtree
Preorder	Node value, Left subtree, Right subtree
Postorder	Left subtree, Right subtree, Node value
Reverse inorder	Right subtree, Node value, Left subtree
Reverse preorder	Node value, Right subtree, Left subtree
Reverse postorder	Right subtree, Left subtree, Node value
Level-by-level	Start at the root and return values on each level of the tree in left-to-right order

As stated earlier, the time it takes to search a binary search tree is generally $O(\log n)$. However, there is one scenario in which the time is $O(n)$. Consider the diagram below.

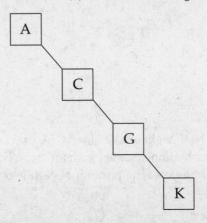

The example above is a binary search tree. However, this is the worst-case scenario because if you lay the structure on its side, you'll see that it looks like a list. To find an element in general, you would have to step through n elements. This makes the performance $O(n)$.

HEAPS

Just as a binary tree is a specialized tree, a **heap** is a specialized binary tree. This specialization manifests itself in two ways:

1. In a max-heap the value of each node is greater than or equal to the values of its children. A node is less than or equal to its children in a min-heap.

2. The tree is complete. That is, each level in the tree is fully populated before the next level is started. Nodes are filled from left to right.

The following is an example of a heap of integers:

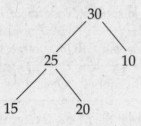

The following, however, is not a heap, since it violates the second condition above:

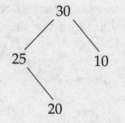

IMPLEMENTING A HEAP

As we've seen above, a heap can be thought of as a binary tree and can, in fact, be implemented with the TreeNode class. A heap is usually implemented with an array, however.

Consider the following heap of letters. The position of each letter in the heap is noted in parentheses.

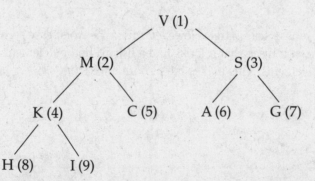

For any node in the heap above, the position of its left child will be double its own position and the position of its right child will be double its own position plus 1. For example, the position of "K" is 4, so the position of its left child is 2 * 4 or 8, and the position of its right child is 2 * 4 + 1 or 9.

Because of this pattern, we can store the values of the heap in an array, where value in the heap is put in its corresponding position in the array. For example, the heap above would be stored as

0	1	2	3	4	5	6	7	8	9
	V	M	S	K	C	A	G	H	I

HASHTABLE

HASHING FUNCTIONS

A **hashing function** is simply a mapping from an object to an integer. For example, you decide that for every number you're given, you're going to add the first two digits together. That's a hashing function. Thus, the hashcode for 13 is $1 + 3 = 4$, and the hashcode for 16 is $1 + 6 = 7$.

What is a **hashtable**? A hashtable associates a hashcode with a given object, based on a hashcode defined for that object. For example, the hashcode of a name might be the ASCII code of the first two letters added together. Thus, for "Smith", the hashcode might be the ASCII code for "S" added to the ASCII code for "m", which is $83 + 109 = 192$. This can make for extremely efficient searches and inserts because the object tells you where to place it.

In concept, this is similar to how a phone book works: The key tells you where to look for the value. However, there is a crucial difference. A phone book can be as large as it needs to be to accommodate all of its information. A hashtable cannot: It has a limited amount of space.

Correspondingly, a hashtable needs to deal with collisions. *A collision occurs when two keys map to the same location.* For example, in the example above, when the ASCII values of the first two letters are added together both "Smith" and "Smithson" map to the same location. How do we know which one to put there? For that matter, how do we find the other one?

Generally, there are two solutions to the problem of collision. The first is to use a really good hashing function: one that will generate a unique hash for each value. The problem here is that it's impossible to prove that a hashing function will ever be completely unique. Also, no matter how unique your hashing function is, you are eventually going to run out of memory space.

The second solution is to use chaining, which is a mechanism by which a key points to a list of all values for that hash code. In the case of the Smith/Smithson collision, the hashtable might look like the following:

192	Smith, Smithson

REVIEW QUESTIONS

Answers to review questions can be found in Chapter 11.

1. Consider the following code segment:

```
Queue que = new ListQueue();
   // ListQueue implements Queue
que.enqueue(new Integer(3));
que.enqueue(new Integer(12));
que.enqueue(new Integer(7));
Integer i = (Integer) que.peekFront();
que.enqueue(new Integer(i.intValue() + 6));
que.enqueue(i);
while (!que.isEmpty())
{
   System.out.print(que.dequeue() + " ");
}
```

What is printed as a result of executing the code segment?

(A) 3 12 7 9 3
(B) 3 12 7 3 3
(C) 12 7 9 3
(D) 12 7 6 3
(E) 3 12 7 6 3

2. Consider the following declarations:

```
Queue myQueue = new ListQueue();
      //ListQueue implements Queue
Stack myStack = new ListStack();
  //ListStack implements Stack
```

Assume that myQueue is initially empty and that myStack initially contains Integer objects with the following values:

```
top  -->       4
               9
               6
               2
bottom  -->    3
```

Consider the following code segment:

```
while (!myStack.isEmpty())
  myQueue.enqueue(myStack.pop());

while (!myQueue.isEmpty())
  myStack.push(myQueue.dequeue());
```

Which of the following best describes myStack and myQueue after the code segment has executed?

(A) Both myStack and myQueue are empty.

(B) myStack is empty, and myQueue contains 4 9 6 2 3, in that order, with 4 at the front of the queue.

(C) myStack is empty, and myQueue contains 3 2 6 9 4, in that order, with 3 at the front of the queue.

(D) myQueue is empty, and myStack contains 4 9 6 2 3, in that order, with 4 at the top of the stack.

(E) myQueue is empty, and myStack contains 3 2 6 9 4, in that order, with 3 at the top of the stack.

3. The following integers are inserted into a binary search tree in the following order:

20   10   28   17   3   15   32

Which of the following represents the tree after the numbers above are inserted?

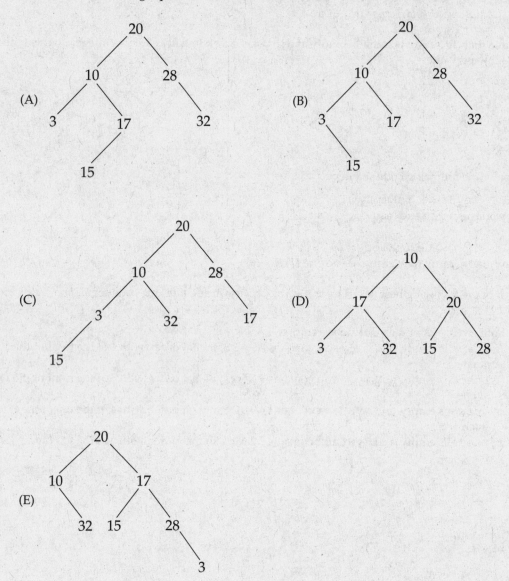

4. Consider the following binary tree:

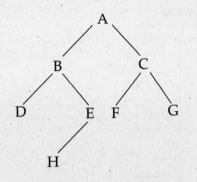

What will be the output of a preorder traversal of the tree?

(A) A B C D E F G H
(B) A B D E H C F G
(C) D H E B F G C A
(D) D B H E A F C G
(E) A B D E C H F G

5. What will be the result of executing a preorder, inorder, and postorder traversal of the following binary tree?

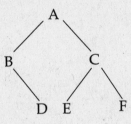

	preorder	inorder	postorder
(A)	"A B D C E F"	"B D A E C F"	"D B E F C A"
(B)	"A B D C E F"	"A B C D E F"	"B D A E C F"
(C)	"B D A E C F"	"D B E F C A"	"F E D C B A"
(D)	"B D A E C F"	"A B C D E F"	"D B E F C A"
(E)	"A B C D E F"	"B D A E C F"	"F E D C B A"

6. The hash table below results from inserting the values 21, 13, 22, 21, 28, 4, 11, 18 in that order. The hash table is an array indexed from 0 to 5 in which collisions are resolved by chaining. In the diagram below, / indicates a null reference.

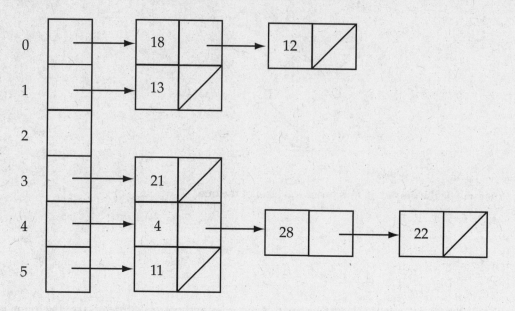

Which of the following could be the hashing function?

(A) theValue – 3
(B) theValue / 6
(C) theValue % 6
(D) (theValue – 2) / 6
(E) (theValue – 2) % 6

Searching and Sorting Algorithms

INTRODUCTION

In this section, we'll review algorithms that are used for searching and sorting arrays and other collections. You do not need to memorize the code for any of the algorithms in this section. You will not be asked to regurgitate the algorithms for the exam. What *is* important is that you can recognize the algorithms when you see them on the exam, and that you understand how each algorithm works as well as the strengths and weaknesses of each.

Please note that the last two algorithms in this chapter, quicksort and heapsort, are *not* covered on the A version of the exam.

SEQUENTIAL SEARCH

SEQUENTIAL SEARCH OVERVIEW

Take a look at the following unordered array of integers:

10	5	7	3	2	1	9	4

Suppose you would like to see if the array contains a certain integer and, if so, at what position in the array the integer is located. For example, perhaps you would like to see if the array contains the integer 2. How could you do this?

One way is to start at the first element in the array and see if it equals 2. If it does, you're done with your search. If the first element is not 2, then look at the second element to see if it is equal to 2. Continue searching through the array one element after the other until you either find what you are looking for or reach the end of the array.

This is a **sequential search**. A sequential search searches an array item-by-item (i.e., in sequence) for an element.

A SEQUENTIAL SEARCH IMPLEMENTATION

Here's how a sequential search can be implemented in Java.

```
// precondition: myNums is an array of ints with length
//                  >=0, searchFor is the int to find in
//                  the array
// postcondition: returns the position of searchFor in the
//                  array myNums, or -1 if searchFor is not
//                  in the array
01: public static int sequentialSearch(int[] myNums,
02:                                              int searchFor)
03: {
04:    for (int i = 0; i < myNums.length; i++)
05:    {
06:       if (myNums[i] == searchFor)
07:       {
08:          return i;
09:       }
10:    }
11:    return -1;
12: }
```

The method sequentialSearch() contains a for loop that looks through each element in the array. The code on line 6 checks if the value of the element at position *i* matches searchFor; if it does, the position of that element is returned on line 8.

What if the element we are searching for does not exist in the array? In this case, the for loop will cycle through the entire array without returning a value on line 8. After the for loop exists, the method will return –1 on line 11. This indicates that searchFor was not in the array.

RECURSIVE IMPLEMENTATION OF SEQUENTIAL SEARCH

Let's take another look at the description of a sequential search. As we'll see, a sequential search can also be described recursively.

When we perform a sequential search on an array, we look at the first item and see if it's what we are looking for. For example, if we wanted to find 6 in the array below, we would start by looking at the first element.

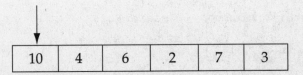

Because the value of the first element doesn't match what we are looking for, we need to search the rest of the array to the right. We can think of this subarray from the second element to the end as an array itself. And how do we see if 6 is in this subarray? We look at the first element in the subarray and see if it matches what we are looking for.

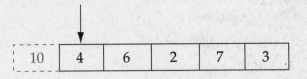

Once again, the value of the element is not 6. So what do we do next? Let's look at the first element of the subarray that begins at the 3rd cell. Aha! We've finally found 6. Now we know it is the 3rd element of the array (position 2, Because arrays are zero-indexed).

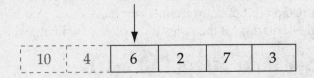

The explanation above may have seemed a bit repetitive but that's the point. If you can describe an algorithm in terms of the same operation on a smaller piece of your data set, and if a base case exists, you have a recursive algorithm.

So what could this algorithm look like? Recall from Chapter 6 that a recursive algorithm needs to have a base case in which the action terminates. What is the base case? It's going to be the simplest array that we could have. This would be an empty array, an array with a length of 0. If we have an empty subarray, then we know that what we are searching for is not in the array and can return –1 from our method.

```
//precondition: x refers to a non-null array,
               currentIndex is >= 0
               searchFor is the element that we are searching
               for in the array
//postcondition:returns the position of searchFor in the
//              array, or -1 if searchFor is not in the
//              array
```

```
01: public int recursiveSequentialSearch (int[] x,
                                            int currentIndex,
                                            int searchFor)
02:   {
03:     if (currentIndex == x.length)
04:     {
05:       return -1;
06:     }
07:     if (x[currentIndex] == searchFor)
08:     {
09:       return currentIndex;
10:     }
11:     return recursiveSequentialSearch(x,
                                          currentIndex + 1,
                                          searchFor);
12:   }
```

The method above accepts 3 arguments.

- *x*, an array that we are searching

- currentIndex, the position in the array that we are going to search

- searchFor, the value that we are going to search for in the array

Line 3 tests our base case. Recall that the largest index in an array is 1 less than the length of the array. Therefore, if currentIndex equals the length of the array, we know that we have reached the end of the array without finding searchFor, so we can return –1.

If currentIndex does not equal the size of the array, we check to see if the value of the element at currentIndex equals searchFor. If it does, we return currentIndex. If it doesn't, we make a recursive call to the method on line 11 starting at the index immediately to the right of currentIndex.

PERFORMANCE OF SEQUENTIAL SEARCH (AB ONLY)

In the **best case**, the element that we are looking for will be the first item in the array. In this case, the time to conduct the search will be constant; it will be independent of the number of items in the array. In Big-Oh notation, this is $O(1)$ time.

In the **worst case**, the sequential search will need to look at every element in the array. The worst case will occur if the element that we are looking for is the last element in the array or if the array does not contain the element we are looking for.

In the worst case, if we double the number of elements in the array, we'll end up doing twice as many comparisons. Because the number of comparisons is proportional to the number of elements in the array, the search time is $O(n)$ in the worst case.

If the array does contain the element that we are looking for, then it is possible that the element could be anywhere in the array (at the beginning, in the middle, or at the end).

On average, the element will be somewhere in the middle, so we will need to look at half of the n elements $\left(\dfrac{n}{2}\right)$ to find what we are looking for. So the **average case** is also $O(n)$.

BINARY SEARCH

BINARY SEARCH OVERVIEW

To illustrate a binary search, let's look at a segment of a popular television game show. *The Price Is Right* used to have a game called the "Clock Game." The show's host, Bob Barker, would ask a contestant to price a particular prize such as a big-screen television, assuming that the price was between, say, $1,000 and $2,000. If the contestant could guess the price within a fixed amount of time, he or she would win the prize. The contestant was allowed to take as many guesses as were needed within the allocated time.

When the contestant guessed a price, Bob Barker would not simply say whether the guess was right or wrong; rather, if the guess was wrong, he would tell the contestant that the guess needed to be higher or lower.

If you were a contestant, what strategy would you use to guess the price? You could start at $1,000 and keep guessing incrementally higher numbers ($1,001; $1,002; $1,003 and so on) until you arrived at the correct price. If you employed this strategy, you would be conducting a sequential search. Most likely though, you would run out of time before you came to the right price and would end up going home with some consolation Turtle Wax instead of a television.

A better strategy would be to make your first guess $1,500. If your guess is correct, you win. But if it's not, Bob will tell you if the price should be higher or lower. If Bob says "higher" you know that the correct price is between $1,501 and $2,000, inclusive. If he says "lower," you know that the price is between $1,000 and $1,499 inclusive. Either way, you will have reduced the number of choices by half with one guess.

Let's say that Bob tells you the price is higher. Now you know that the price is between $1,501 dollars and $2,000. What should your guess next?

Once again, the best strategy is to split the range in half; try a guess of $1,750. If Bob tells you that the price needs to be lower, you know that the correct price is between $1,501 and $1,749. Once again, you've gotten rid of half of the available choices. Keep splitting the range. If you follow this strategy and keep splitting the possible range in half, it will take you at most 10 guesses if the price range is from $1,000 to $2,000.

This strategy takes advantage of the fact that prices have a natural order: They increase from least to greatest. We use a similar strategy when we look up a person in a phone book. If you would like to find the name in a phone book, you wouldn't start with the first name and read each name sequentially until you found it. Instead, you would take advantage of the fact that the names in a phone book are ordered alphabetically.

Say for example that you were given the name "Smith, Joe" to find. A smart way to conduct your search would be to open the phone book approximately in the middle and see if the name is there. Say you open the book in the "M"s. Right away, you know that "Smith, Joe" has to be in the second half of the book; You have eliminated the first half of the elements from your search. You could then continue flipping back and forth in the phone book until you found Joe Smith's name.

The strategy outlined above is called a **binary search**. It is called a binary search because it splits the domain that we are searching into two separate parts (binary means "two").

> **Important:** A binary search should only be used on sorted data. If it is used to search unsorted data, there's a good chance it will give an incorrect answer. In the practice problems at the end of this chapter, we'll explore what happens if a binary search is used on an unordered set of data.

How to Conduct a Binary Search

The array below contains 11 integers in numerical order. For reference, the positions of each cell in the array are printed above the array. Let's see how we would search for the number 13 in the array using a binary search.

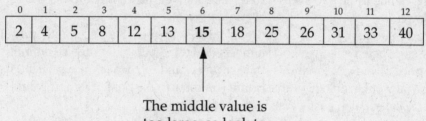

We start by looking at the middle element in the array. The middle element is at the 6th position in the array. The value of this element is 15. Because 15 is larger than what we are looking for, we know that we can eliminate the right half of the array from our search.

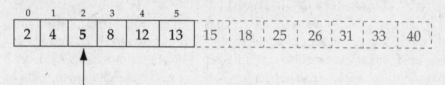

The middle value is too large, so look to the left.

Now we'll look at the middle value of cells 0 through 5 in the array. Note that Because we have an even number of cells, the middle will be between the second and third cell. When this happens, look at the value to the left of the middle. In this case, that returns the value 5.

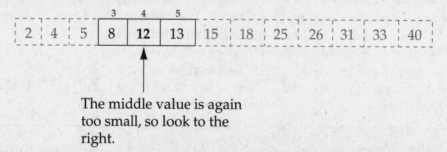

The middle value is now too small, so look to the right.

Five is too small. We've now narrowed our search down to the elements at positions 3, 4, and 5. The element at position 4 is in the middle of these three, so we'll look there to see if its value is 13.

The middle value is again too small, so look to the right.

Once again, the value is smaller than we are looking for. We only have one cell left, though. That's all we need to check.

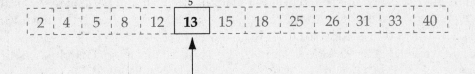

The last cell is 13, so we've found what we're looking for.

ITERATIVE IMPLEMENTATION OF BINARY SEARCH

Here is a common iterative implementation of a binary search. For variety, we will search through a list of Strings instead of a list of numbers.

```
// precondition: letters.length >= 0 and letters is
//                  sorted.
// postcondition: returns the position of searchFor in
//                  letters, or -1 if letters does
//                  not contain searchFor
01: public static int binarySearch(String[] letters,
02:                                       String searchFor)
03: {
04:    int min = 0;
05:    int max = letters.length - 1;

06:       while (min <= max)
07:    {
08:       int mid = (min + max) / 2;
09:       if ((letters[mid]).equals(searchFor))
10:       {
11:          return mid;
12:       }
13:       else if ((myNums[mid]).compareTo(searchFor) < 0)
14:       {
15:          min = mid + 1;
16:       }
17:       else
18:       {
19:          max = mid - 1;
20:       }
21:    }
22:    return -1;
23: }
```

Let's trace through the code using the array below. We'll search for "C", a letter that is not in the array.

searchFor = "C"

A	B	D	F	H

On line 4, min is initially set to 0 and max is initially 4, the maximum position in the array. On the first pass through the while loop, mid will be set to (0 + 4) / 2, which equals 2. On line 8, we check if the letters[2], which is "D", is equal to "C". It isn't, so control passes to Line 12.

On line 12 we see if letters[2] is less than "C". This also is untrue, so control passes to the else block that follows. We now know that "C" is less than the value at letters[2]. On line 18, we set max equal to 2 – 1 or 1, Because we now know that the maximum position that "C" could be in is position 1. Control passes back to line 5.

Because max is 1 and min is 0, mid will be set to 0 on line 7. This means that in the body of the while loop, we will be comparing letters[0], which is "A", to "C". Because "A" is less than "C", we will end up setting min to 1 on line 14; the value of max remains 1. Control will once again pass to the top of the while loop.

Once in the while loop, mid will become 1, and we will compare the value at letters[1], which is "B", to the value we are searching for, "C". Because "B" is less than "C", min gets set to 2 on line 14, and control once again passes to line 5. This time, however, the condition in the while loop is false, Because min is 2 and max is 1, so control passes to line 21, where the method returns –1.

RECURSIVE IMPLEMENTATION OF BINARY SEARCH

In the section, "How to Conduct a Binary Search," you should have noticed that our method had a recursive structure to it. First we look at the middle element of the array to see if it is what we are looking for. If it isn't, we look at the middle elements of either the left or right subarray. We are done with our search when we find what we are looking for or get to the point where our subarray only contains one element.

Here is a recursive implementation of a binary search.

```
// precondition: letters.length >= 0,
//                 0 <= min < letters.length
//                 0 <= max < letters.length
//                 letters is sorted
// postcondition: returns the position of searchFor in
//                 letters, or -1 if letters does
//                 not contain searchFor
01: public int binarySearch(String[] letters,
                                    int min, int max,
                                    String searchFor)
02: {
03:    if (min > max)
04:    {
05:       return -1;
06:    }
07:    else
08:    {
09:       int mid = (min + max) / 2;
10:       if (letters[mid].equals(searchFor))
11:       {
12:          return mid;
13:       }
14:       else if ((letters[mid]).compareTo(searchFor) < 0)
15:       {
16:          return search(letters, mid + 1, max,searchFor);
```

```
17:        }
18:     else
19:     {
20:         return search(letters, min, mid - 1, searchFor);
21:     }
22:   }
23: }
```

We can see that the recursive implementation of binarySearch has the same basic structure as the iterative implementation, with a few notable differences. For example, the condition in the while loop of the iterative implementation that checks if min >= max has been replaced by the base case that returns –1 if min is greater than max. In the iterative implementation, if searchFor was not found, control passed back to the top of the while loop. In the recursive implementation, the binarySearch() method is called again.

Performance of Binary Search (AB only)

In the **best case**, the element that we are looking for will be the middle item in the array. In this case, the time to conduct the search will be constant; it will be independent of the number of items in the array. In Big-Oh notation, this is $O(1)$ time.

The example that we walked through in the "How to Conduct a Binary Search" section shows a worst-case scenario. We didn't find the element until we had reduced the original array down to a subarray of length 1. Even though this was the worst case, we only needed to look at 4 cells in an array of length 13. Contrast this with a sequential search, which, in the worst case, would need to look at all 13 cells to search an array of length 13.

In the **worst case**, the binary search is $O(\log n)$.

In the **average case**, the binary search is also $O(\log n)$.

Finding the Number of Steps in the Worst Case for a Binary Search

If an ordered array has 10 elements, and you use a binary search algorithm to search for a value in the array, what is the maximum number of elements you will need to look at in the array?

We'll come back to this problem in a second, but let's first look at a simpler problem. If we have an array of 2 integers and would like to search for an integer in the array, how many comparisons will we need to make in the worst case?

Recall that the worst case will occur if the element that we are looking for is not in the array. In an array with two elements, we will need to compare our search value to both elements. In other words, we will need to make 2 comparisons:

2 elements → 2 comparisons in worst case

What if we double the number of elements in the array to 4? Because a binary search cuts the number of elements that we need to look at in half, we will need to search an array of length 2 (at most) after the first comparison. We just saw that it takes 2 comparisons to search an array with 2 elements, so we end up with a total of 3 comparisons.

4 elements → 3 comparisons in worst case

What if we have an array with 8 elements? Once again, one comparison will cut this array down to 4 elements. We've seen that it takes 3 comparisons, at most, to search an array with 4 elements, so 8 elements will take 3 + 1, or 4, comparisons.

8 elements → 4 comparisons in worst case

Do you see the pattern? Every time we double the number of elements in the ordered array, we add one to the number of comparisons we need to make in the worst case for a binary search.

In the table below, we compare the maximum number of comparisons needed for a binary search to the maximum number of comparisons needed for a sequential search for ordered arrays of various sizes.

Number of elements in ordered array	Maximum number of comparisons needed for a binary search	Maximum number of comparisons needed for a sequential search
1	1	1
2	2	2
4	3	4
8	4	8
16	5	16
32	6	32
64	7	64
128	8	128
256	9	256
512	10	512

If you look at the second-to-last row, you can see that it will take 9 comparisons at most to search an ordered array of 256 elements using a binary search algorithm. It turns out that 256 is the smallest array that requires 9 comparisons in the worst-case situation.

On the exam, you may be asked to find the maximum number of comparisons required to search an ordered array of a given size.

Example

Given an array of size 300, what is the maximum number of comparisons that you will need to make if you use a binary search algorithm to search for an element in the array?

(A) 5
(B) 9
(C) 10
(D) 150
(E) 300

Here's How to Crack It: The answer is (B). Simply find the smallest number that you need to raise 2 to the power of to get a number larger than 300.

So

$2^1 = 2$ (too small)
$2^2 = 4$ (too small)
$2^3 = 8$ (too small)
$2^4 = 16$ (too small)
$2^5 = 32$ (too small)
$2^6 = 64$ (too small)
$2^7 = 128$ (too small)
$2^8 = 256$ (close, but still too small)
$2^9 = 512$ (this works)

SORTING

In the two sections above (sequential search and binary search), we **searched** arrays for a particular value. On the AP exam, you will also be expected to understand how to **sort** the elements of an un-ordered array into order. The first sorting algorithm that we'll look at is the selection sort.

SELECTION SORT

Consider the array below. We would like to sort this array from least to greatest.

| 8 | 6 | 10 | 2 | 4 |

Our strategy will be to first find the smallest element in the array, and put it in the first position. We will then find the smallest of the remaining elements and put that in the second position. We will continue to do this until the array is ordered.

We can start by looking at every element in the array (starting with the first element) and find the smallest element. It's easy for a person to quickly glance through the array and see which element is smallest, but the sorting algorithm that we will implement can only compare two elements at once. So here's how we can find the smallest element: Take the number in the first cell in the array and assign it to a variable called smallestSoFar. We'll also assign the position of that value to a variable called position. In this case, smallestSoFar will equal 8 and position will be 0. Note that even though we are assigning 8 to smallestSoFar, the first cell of the array still contains 8; we didn't actually remove it.

Now we'll walk through the array and compare the next value to smallestSoFar. The next value is 6, which is less than 8, so smallestSoFar becomes 6 and position becomes 1.

```
smallestSoFar = 6;
position = 1;
```

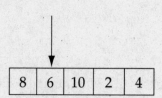

Now let's look at the next value in the array. 10 is larger than 6, so smallestSoFar remains 6.

```
smallestSoFar = 6;
position = 1;
```

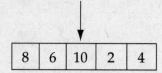

The next value in the array is 2. Two is smaller than 6.

```
smallestSoFar = 2;
position = 3;
```

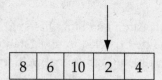

And finally we look at the last element, 4. Because 4 is greater than 2 and we are at the end of the array, we know that 2 is the smallest element.

```
smallestSoFar = 2;
position = 3;
```

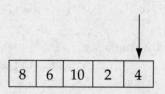

Now we know that 2 is the smallest element in the array. Because we want to order the array from least to greatest, we need to put 2 in the first cell in the array. We don't simply want to overwrite the 8 that is in the first cell, though. What we'll do is swap the 2 with the 8 to get

2	6	10	8	4

Now we have the smallest element in place. Next we'll need to find the second smallest element in the array. We can do this using the same approach we employed to find the smallest element. Because we know that 2 is the smallest element, we only have to look at the elements in positions 1 to 4 for the second smallest element.

Start by assigning 6 to smallestSoFar and 1 to position and then compare 6 to 10. Six is the smaller. Next, compare 6 to 8; 6 is still the smaller. Finally, compare 6 with 4. Four is smaller and because we have no more elements in the array, 4 must be the second smallest element in the array.

Swap 4 with the second element in the array to get

2	4	**10**	8	6

Now do another pass through the array to find the third smallest element, and swap it into the third cell. The third smallest element is 6.

2	4	6	8	**10**

Now we look at the last two elements. Eight is smaller than 10, so we don't need to do anything. Our array is now sorted from least to greatest.

IMPLEMENTATION OF SELECTION SORT

Here is how a selection sort can be implemented in Java. The following implementation will sort the elements from least to greatest and will begin by sorting the smallest elements first.

```
//precondition: numbers is an array of ints
//postcondition: numbers is sorted in ascending order
01: public static void selectionSort1(int[] numbers)
02: {
03:    for (int i = 0; i < numbers.length - 1; i++)
04:    {
05:       int position = i;
06:       for (int k = i + 1; k < numbers.length; k++)
07:       {
08:          if (numbers[k] < numbers[position])
09:          {
10:             position = k;
11:          }
12:       }
13:       int temp = numbers[i];
14:       numbers[i] = numbers[position];
15:       numbers[position] = temp;
16:    }
17: }
```

PERFORMANCE OF SELECTION SORT (AB ONLY)

The selection sort contains two nested for loops. If n is the length of the array, the outer loop will run n times. The number of times that the inner loop runs changes depending on the value of i, the current step of the outer loop. Adding up all of the times that the body of the inner loop will be executed gives $n + (n-1) + (n-2) + (n-3) \ldots + 1$ times which equals $\dfrac{n(n+1)}{2}$ or $\dfrac{n^2+n}{2}$. In Big-Oh notation, this means that selection sort runs in $O(n^2)$ in the best, worst, and average cases.

The selection sort is the slowest of the sorts that we will look at in this chapter. So why bother to use it? Take another look at the array we sorted at the beginning of this section. After one pass through the array, the select sort placed the smallest element in its proper place. After two passes, it placed the second smallest element in its proper place. In other words, we don't have to run through the entire algorithm to achieve partial sorting.

How could this be useful? Consider a case in which you have an unsorted array of 1,000 Student objects, and each Student object has a method that returns a grade-point average for that Student. What if you would like to find the five students with highest grade-point average? In this case, it would be a waste of time to sort the entire array. Instead, we can just run through five cycles of the second implementation of the selection sort shown above, and the top five students will be sorted.

INSERTION SORT

Below is an array with 9 elements. This array is sorted from least to greatest except for the last element.

2	3	5	8	11	14	17	22	**15**

We would like to move 15 so that the entire array is in order. First, we'll temporarily assign 15 to a variable. This will give us room to shift the other elements to the right if needed.

    temp = 15

2	3	5	8	11	14	17	22	

We then compare 15 to the first element to its left: 22. Because 22 is larger than 15, we shift 22 to the right.

    temp = 15

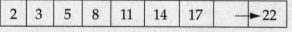

We then compare 15 to the next element: 17. Because 17 is larger, we shift that to the right also.

    temp = 15

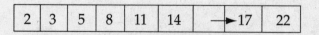

Next we compare 15 to 14. Because 15 is larger, we don't want to shift 14 to the right. Instead, we insert 15 into the empty cell in the array. Now the array is correctly sorted.

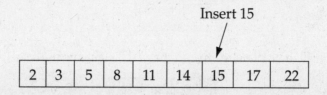

Insert 15

| 2 | 3 | 5 | 8 | 11 | 14 | 15 | 17 | 22 |

Now we'll look at how we can use the idea illustrated above to sort an entire array. This example will start at the beginning of the sorting process.

Here is the array that we are going to sort.

| 8 | 6 | 7 | 10 |

First, we'll look at just the first two elements of the array and make sure that they are sorted relative to each other.

| 8 | 6 | 7 | 10 |

To do this, we'll pull 6 (the number that is farthest to the right in our subarray) out of the array and temporarily assign it to a variable. We'll then compare 6 to 8. Because 8 is larger, shift 8 to the right and then put 6 in the cell where 8 was.

```
temp = 6
```

Here's what the array looks like.

| 6 | 8 | 7 | 10 |

Now we need to put 7 in the proper place relative to 6 and 8. We start by assigning 7 temporarily to a variable.

```
temp = 7
```

| 6 | 8 | | 10 |

We then compare 7 to the first number to its left: 8. Because 7 is less than 8, we shift 8 one place to the right.

```
temp = 7
```

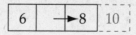

Next, we'll compare 7 to the next number in the array: 6. Because 6 is less than 7, we don't want to shift 6 to the right. Instead, we will put 7 in the second cell. Our array now looks like the following:

6	7	8	10

Now we need to put 10 in its place relative to the first 3 elements in the array.

6	7	8	10

```
temp = 10
```

6	7	8	

First we compare 10 to 8; because 8 is smaller than 10, we don't need to shift 8 to the right. In fact, we can put 10 right back into the cell from which it came.

6	7	8	10

ITERATIVE IMPLEMENTATION OF INSERTION SORT

Here is how an insertion sort can be implemented in Java.

```
// precondition: x is an array of integers; x.length >=0
// postcondition: x is sorted from least to greatest.
01: public static void insertionSort(int[] x)
02: {
03:    for (int i = 1; i < x.length; i++)
04:    {
05:       int temp = x[i];
06:       int j = i - 1;
07:       while (j >= 0 && x[j] > temp)
08:       {
09:          x[j + 1] = x[j];
10:          j--;
11:       }
12:       x[j + 1]  = temp;
13:    }
14: }
```

Note that like the selection sort, the insertion sort contains nested loops. In this case, we have a while loop nested within a for loop.

The for loop, beginning on line 3, proceeds from index 1 to the end of the array. The while loop goes through the array from i to 0 and shifts elements that are larger than temp to the right on line 9. On line 12, we put the value in temp into its proper place in the array.

PERFORMANCE OF INSERTION SORT (AB ONLY)

In the **worst case**, the insertion sort will run in $O(n^2)$ time because of the two nested loops. The worst case will occur with arrays that are sorted in reverse order, such as the following:

15	11	10	8	4	3

Why will this array result in the worst-case performance? Consider a few iterations of the insertion sort on this array. The sort would start by putting 11 in its place. To do this, it needs to compare 11 to 15 and then shift 15 to the right to get

11	15	10	8	4	3

On the next pass, we need to put 10 in its place. We will end up comparing it to both 15 and 11, and shifting those numbers up. To put 8 in its place, we'll end up comparing it to 15, 11, and 10.

So for each element in the array, we need to compare it to all the elements on its left.

For an array with 6 elements, we will need to make $1 + 2 + 3 + 4 + 5$ comparisons if the array is sorted in reverse order. In general, the worst case for an array with n elements will require $\dfrac{n(n-1)}{2}$ comparisons. This is $O(n^2)$.

The best case will occur when the array is already sorted in ascending order. Consider the following array:

2	4	7	11	15	18

To put 4 in its proper place, we will just need to compare it to 2. As for 7, we will just end up comparing it to 4. With 11, a comparison to 7 is all that is needed to see that it is in its proper place. So for each element, we will just need to make 1 comparison. If we double the number of elements, we will need to just double the number of comparisons in the best case. Because the number of comparisons is proportional to the number of elements in the array, the insertion sort is $O(n)$ in the best case.

The average case will occur if the array is randomly sorted. In the average case, we will expect the number of comparisons to be half the number we would get in the worst case. So the average case will require $\dfrac{n(n-1)}{4}$ comparisons, which, while faster than the worst case, is still $O(n^2)$.

MERGESORT

The two sorting algorithms we've looked at so far, selection sort and insertion sort, run in $O(n^2)$ in the worst and average case. **Mergesort** is faster in the worst and average case: It runs in $O(n \log n)$ time.

Here are the steps that the mergesort algorithm follows to sort an array

1. Break the array into two halves.

2. Sort each half.

3. Merge the two sorted halves back together into one sorted array.

You're probably asking, "But how does the algorithm sort each half in step 2?" Here's what it does for each half:

1. It breaks it into two more halves.

2. It sorts the two halves.

3. It merges the two sorted halves into one sorted array.

In other words, mergesort acts recursively. It uses the mergesort algorithm to sort each half of the array.

Mergesort uses what is known as a "divide and conquer" strategy. Mergesort divides an array into two parts and conquers each part separately.

In order to avoid infinite recursive calls, we know that we need a base case. Otherwise, we would keep breaking each subarray into halves. The base case in mergesort is an array with just one element. An array with one element is already sorted.

Mergesort has two different parts: a "sorting" part that sorts pieces of an array and a "merging" part that merges the sorted parts together. Let's take a look at the merging part.

Below are two sorted arrays: a1 and b1. We are going to merge them together into one array.

`array a1:`

2	6	10

`array b1:`

3	5

The first array has 3 elements, the second has 2 elements. Our goal is to merge these two arrays into one ordered array with length 5 that looks like the following:

`array c1:`

2	3	5	6	10

Here's how we'll merge arrays a1 and b1.

We start by comparing the first element in a1 and b1. Because a1 and b1 are ordered, we know that the first element in a1 is the smallest in a1, and the first element in b1 is the smallest in b1. Because 2 is less than 3, we know that 2 is the smallest element in either array; so we put 2 in the first position of c1.

We next compare the second element in a1 (6) with the first element in b1 (3). Because 3 is smaller, we put it in the second position of array c1.

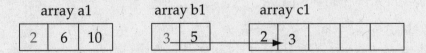

Now we compare the second element of a1 (6) with the second element of b1 (5). Because 5 is smaller, we add it to c1.

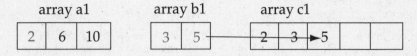

At this point, we have added all of the elements in array b1 to array c1; we still have 2 elements left in array a1. Because these elements are in order, we can add them in the same order to array c1.

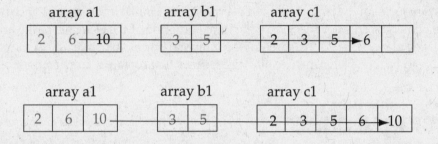

Recursive Implementation of Mergesort

```
//precondition: x.length >= 0,
//               temp.length = x.length
//postcondition: the elements of x are sorted from least
//               to greatest.
01: public static void mergeSort(int[] x,
02:                              int lowPosition,
03:                              int highPosition)
04: {
05:   if (lowPosition == highPosition)
06:   {
07:     return;
08:   }
9:   else
10:   {
11:     int mid = (lowPosition + highPosition) / 2;
12:     mergeSort(x, lowPosition, mid);
13:     mergeSort(x, mid + 1, highPostion);
14:     merge(x, lowPosition, mid + 1, highPosition);
15:   }
16: }
```

In the method call, x is the array that we would like to sort, and temp is an empty array with the same length as x that is used for the merging process. Each time the method is called, lowPosition and highPosition change to indicate which part of the array is being sorted. When the method is initially called, lowPosition will be 0 and highPosition will be x.length − 1.

Note that the base case is defined on line 6. Because lowPosition and highPosition indicate the endpoints of the section of the array that we are currently sorting, if they are the same, it means we are sorting a piece of the array with only 1 element. There is no need to do anything in this case, because a single element is already sorted relative to itself.

If the part of the array that we are sorting has more than 1 element, we split it in half on line 12, and then recursively sort the two halves on lines 13 and 14. After the two halves are sorted, they are merged together by a call to the merge() method on line 15.

The implementation of the merge() method is not shown because you will not be expected to know it for the exam. Instead, just understand the basic structure of the mergeSort() method: An array is broken into two halves, a recursive call to mergeSort is made for each half, and then the two halves are merged back together.

PERFORMANCE OF MERGESORT (AB ONLY)

Mergesort is $O(n \log n)$ in the best, worst, and average cases. Unlike insertion sort and quicksort, the performance of mergesort is not affected by the initial ordering of the elements of the array.

The downside of mergesort is that it requires a temporary array to merge into, so it requires more memory. This can be a problem when dealing with arrays that contain a large amount of data.

QUICKSORT (AB ONLY)

Like mergesort, **quicksort** has two separate parts. One part partitions data into two separate groups, while another part sorts the two groups. Let's take a look at how quicksort would work on an array of integers.

PARTITIONING AN ARRAY

To partition an array in quicksort, we must first choose a pivot value. The goal of partitioning is to get the values that are smaller than the pivot value to the left side of the array and get the values that are larger than the pivot to the right side.

The first thing we need to do is pick a partition value. This value can be any element in the array (and, in fact, doesn't even need to be an element in the array, although it usually is). We'll pick the value of the last element in the array: 7. Our goal is to get all of the elements that are larger than 7 to the right side of the array and get the elements that are smaller than 7 to the left side of the array.

We'll also have two pointers; that points to the first element in the array, and one that points to the second-to-last element in the array. Let's call these pointers left and right.

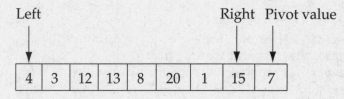

Starting at the left of the array, we want to find the first element that is larger than our pivot value (7). The first element is 4, so this doesn't work. The second value, 3, is also smaller than 7. The value in the third position is larger than 7. We'll move the "left" handle to the third cell so we can keep track of the location the larger value.

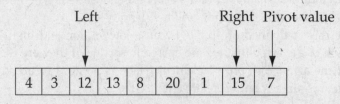

Now let's take a look at the right pointer. Keep in mind that our goal is to get the values that are smaller than the pivot to the left side of the array. The first value that the right pointer points to is bigger than 7, so there is no need to move it. Let's keep looking to the left. The next value, 1, is smaller than the pivot, so we need to move it to the left side of the array.

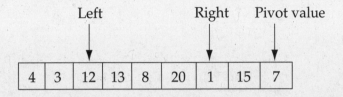

Take a look at where we are. We have one value (12) that we want to move to the right side of the array, and another value (1) that we want to move to the left side. What's the easiest way to do this? Just swap the values. This is what we end up with.

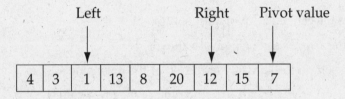

We're not done yet, though. Let's start at the left pointer and keep moving to the right until we find another value that is greater than 7. We don't have to look far: the next value, 13, fits the bill. Now let's move the right pointer to the left until we find a value less than 7. Neither 20 nor 8 works. We'll go ahead and move one more space to the left.

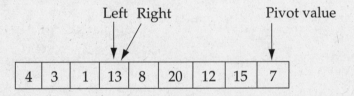

At this point, we know that all the values to the left of the two pointers are less than the pivot (7) and all the values to the right of the pointers are greater than the pivot. What remains to be done? We just need to put the pivot in the proper place. We can do this simply by swapping the pivot value with the value to which left points.

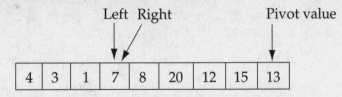

Our array is not sorted, but it's closer to being sorted than it was before. What remains to be done? We need to sort the subarray to the left of our pivot and sort the subarray to the right of the pivot. The pivot is in the correct place.

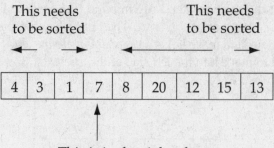

This is in the right place

So how do we sort the left subarray? By quicksorting it! We'll pick a pivot value and move the values that are greater than the pivot to the right and move the values that are less than the pivot to the left. This process continues until we reach subarrays with a length of 1. A subarray with only 1 element is already sorted.

Here, therefore, is the general form of quicksort:

1. Partition the array based on a pivot value.

2. Do a quicksort on the subarray to the left of the pivot value.

3. Do a quicksort on the subarray to the right of the pivot value.

Once again, we have a recursive sorting algorithm.

RECURSIVE IMPLEMENTATION OF QUICKSORT

Here is an implementation of quicksort.

```
01: public static void quicksort(int[] x,
                                  int start,
                                  int end)
02: {
03:   if (end >= start)
04:   {
05:     return;
06:   }
07:   else
08:   {
09:     int pivotValue = partition(x, left, right);
10:     quickSort(x, start, pivotValue - 1);
11:     quickSort(x, pivotValue + 1, end);
12:   }
13: }
```

In the method call, *x* is the array that we are going to sort, and start and end delimit the section of the array that we are going to sort. When the method is first called, start will be 0 and end will be the position of the last cell in the array (x.length – 1). As the method is called recursively, though, start and end will change to indicate the subarray that is being sorted.

The base case is defined on line 3. On line 9, we make a call to partition(). This method partitions the array as described in the section above and then returns the location of the pivotValue in the partitioned array. We then make two recursive calls on lines 10 and 11; the first sorts the subarray to the left of the pivotValue, and the second sorts the subarray to the right of the pivotValue.

PERFORMANCE OF QUICKSORT

For arrays that are initially randomly sorted, quicksort will run in $O(n \log n)$ time. For quicksort to live up to its name and run quickly, however, the pivot values that are chosen m ust be near the median for each subarray. If this is not the case, quicksort will approach $O(n^2)$ performance time.

Consider the following array:

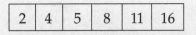

As you can see, this array is already sorted from least to greatest. What would happen if we used the quicksort algorithm to sort the array, and always picked the last value in each subarray as the pivot value?

In this case, we would end up with a subarray that contained 0 elements and another subarray that contained all of the other elements. We are no longer splitting our sorting problem into two smaller problems with half the number of elements to sort. The efficiency of the algorithm is reduced to $O(n^2)$.

What would happen, though, if we used a different approach to pick the pivot value, rather than merely picking the last value in each subarray? What if we picked a random value in each subarray as the pivot value?

Unfortunately, we still could be extremely unlucky with the random value we picked. If the pivot value picked is always the smallest or largest value in the subarray being sorted, we still only reduce our problem by one element during each pass and the runtime of quicksort in the worst case is still $O(n^2)$.

HEAPSORT (AB ONLY)

As we discussed in Chapter 9, a heap is a special type of binary tree that is complete and that satisfies the heap condition. The heap condition (sometimes referred to as the max-heap condition) states that the value of every node is larger than the value of its child nodes. This condition implies that the largest node in the heap is the root node. On the test, you may also run across a min-heap. In a min-heap, the value of every node is smaller than the value of its child nodes.

INSERTING A NODE INTO A HEAP

Consider the following heap of integers. Our goal is to insert the number 35 into this heap.

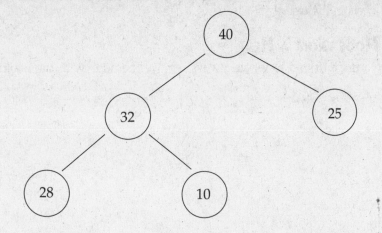

We start by inserting 35 into the first empty location in the heap. At this point, the heap condition is violated because the value of the node with 35 is larger than the value of its parent. The value that we have just inserted is indicated in the darker circle.

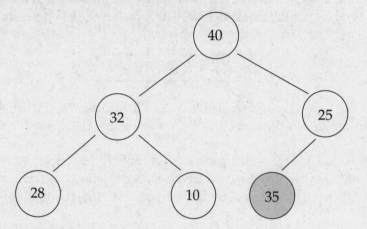

We can fix this by swapping 35 with its parent node.

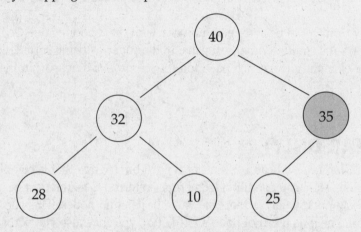

Note that the parent of the node with 35 now contains 40. Because the parent is larger, the heap condition is satisfied and we do not need to swap the node containing 35 with its parent.

Inserting a value into a heap takes $O(\log n)$ time. We will make, at most, one swap per level as we restore the heap condition and, because the heap is complete (and therefore balanced), there are at most $O(\log n)$ levels in the tree.

REMOVING A NODE FROM A HEAP

When we remove a node from a heap, we always remove the node with the maximum key; this is the root node.

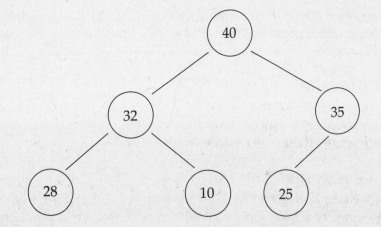

So in our example, we are going to remove the node with a key of 40. Once we remove the node, however, we will have a hole at the root of our heap. We will temporarily fill this hole by moving the node in the last location of the heap to the root. The last node in a heap is the rightmost node in the lowest level of the heap.

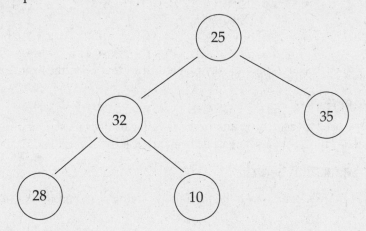

At this point, we have a problem. The root node is no longer the largest node in the heap. We will fix this problem by swapping it with its **largest** child: 35.

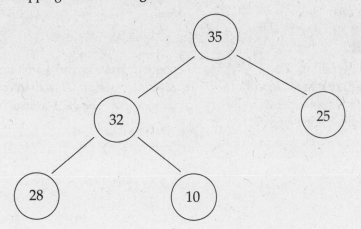

Now the heap condition has been restored.

Deleting the maximum value from the heap also takes $O(\log n)$ time. We will make, at most, one swap per level as we restore the heap condition after moving the last node in the heap to the root and, because the heap is complete (and therefore balanced), there are, at most, $O(\log n)$ levels in the tree.

THE HEAPSORT ALGORITHM

The **heapsort algorithm** works by first inserting values into a heap and then removing the items one by one from the heap. Because the root of a heap always contains the largest key, as we remove nodes from a heap, we will remove those with the largest values first.

PERFORMANCE OF HEAPSORT

As we saw above, the time to insert an item into the heap is $O(\log n)$. Therefore, inserting n items will be $O(n \log n)$. Similarly, it takes $O(\log n)$ time to remove the largest item from a heap. Hence, removing all n elements from a heap is also $O(n \log n)$. Adding these runtimes together, we find that heapsort runs in $O(n \log n)$ time. It is slightly slower than quicksort in the best and average case. Recall, however, that in the worst case, quicksort will run in $O(n^2)$ time. Heapsort does not have this problem. It runs in $O(n \log n)$ time even in the worst case.

SUMMARY

Here is a summary of each searching and sorting algorithm that is on the exam.

SEQUENTIAL SEARCH

A sequential search is used for searching unordered lists. It can also be used for ordered lists; however, the binary search algorithm provides better performance for an ordered list.

Performance of Sequential Search

- **Best case:** $O(1)$—Occurs when the item that is being searched for is the first item in the list

- **Worst case:** $O(n)$—Occurs when the item that is being searched for is the last item in the list or is not in the list at all

- **Average case:** $O(n)$

BINARY SEARCH

The binary search algorithm uses a "divide-and-conquer" strategy for searching **ordered** lists. For ordered lists, the binary search algorithm will provide better performance than the sequential search algorithm, particularly for large lists. A binary search should not be used to search an unordered list. If it is, it will most likely give an incorrect result.

Performance of Binary Search

- **Best case:** $O(1)$—Occurs when the item that is being searched for is the middle item in the list

- **Worst case:** $O(\log n)$—Occurs when the item that is being searched for is not in the list or is in the list, but is not found until the list has been divided down to a sublist of length 1

- **Average case:** $O(\log n)$

HASHTABLE (AB ONLY)

A hashtable provides for very quick insertion and searching. For example, if a program needs a dictionary that it can use to look up the definition of words, a hashtable is probably the data structure you should use. The only disadvantage is that a hashtable cannot be used for accessing data in sequential order.

Performance of Hashtable

- **Best and average case:** $O(1)$—Assumes that the hashing function that is used results in few collisions

- **Worst case:** $O(n)$—If many collisions, then performance will be reduced to that of a sequential search

SELECTION SORT

Selection sort is one of the simplest of the sorting algorithms; however, it is also the slowest because it consists of two nested loops, each of which runs in $O(n)$ time. One advantage to selection sort is that it can be used to partially sort a list. For example, if you have a list of one thousand numbers and just need to find the five largest, then selection sort can just be run through five iterations.

Performance of Selection Sort

- **Best, worst, and average case:** $O(n^2)$

INSERTION SORT

Like selection sort, insertion sort is slow because it is implemented with two nested loops that each run in $O(n)$ time, which leads to $O(n^2)$ performance. Insertion sort performs better than selection sort, however, if the list that is being sorted is almost in order. Insertion sort also provides good performance for inserting new values into a list that is already sorted.

Performance of Insertion Sort

- **Best case:** $O(n)$—Occurs when the list is already sorted

- **Worst case:** $O(n^2)$—Occurs when the list to be sorted is already sorted in reverse order

- **Average case:** $O(n^2)$—Note that even though insertion sort and selection sort are both $O(n^2)$ in the average case, insertion sort will provide better performance

MERGESORT

Mergesort uses a divide-and-conquer strategy to sort data. An advantage is that it provides consistent performance regardless of how the data is initially ordered. A disadvantage is that it uses more memory than other sorting algorithms because it uses a temporary array.

Performance of Mergesort Search

- **Best, worst, and average case:** $O(n \log n)$

QUICKSORT (AB ONLY)

Like mergesort, quicksort is a fast sorting algorithm that uses a recursive divide-and-conquer strategy. The only disadvantage to quicksort is that in certain cases its performance will degenerate to that of selection sort. Poor performance will occur if the pivot value that is selected each time the method is called is far from the median.

Performance of Quicksort

- **Best and average case:** $O(n \log n)$
- **Worst case:** $O(n^2)$

HEAPSORT (AB ONLY)

Heapsort uses a heap to sort data.

Performance of Heapsort Search

- **Best, worst, and average case:** $O(n \log n)$

REVIEW QUESTIONS

Answers to review questions can be found in Chapter 11.

1. Suppose the following values are inserted sequentially into an empty heap in the following order:

   30, 26, 15, 63, 35, 10

   What will the heap look like after the values are inserted?

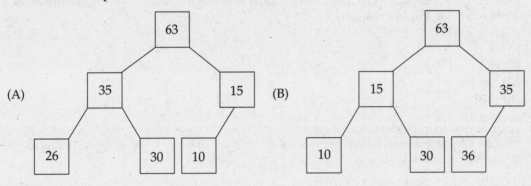

(A)

(B)

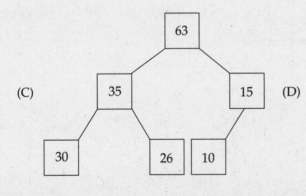

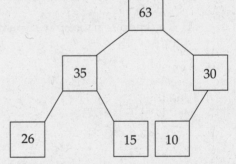

(C)

(D)

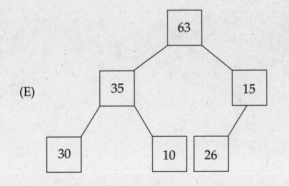

(E)

2. Array num contains 100 integers in ascending order. Assume that you would like to see if num contains the integer 123. If a **sequential search** is used to search for 123, what is the maximum number of elements that must be examined?

(A) 1
(B) 5
(C) 7
(D) 50
(E) 100

3. Array num contains 100 integers in ascending order. Assume that you would like to see if num contains the integer 123. If a **binary search** is used to search for 123, what is the maximum number of elements that must be examined?

(A) 1
(B) 5
(C) 7
(D) 50
(E) 100

4. Assume that an implementation of quicksort that is used to sort an array of integers always uses the first integer in a partition as the pivot value. In which of the following cases will this implementation run the fastest?

   I.   Before the quicksort algorithm is run on the array, the array is already sorted from least to greatest.
   II. Before the quicksort algorithm is run on the array, the array is already sorted from greatest to least.
   III. The integers in the array are in random order.

(A) I only
(B) II only
(C) III only
(D) I and II
(E) I and III

Solutions to Chapter
Review Questions

ANSWER KEY

Chapter 2 (Page 35)
1. E
2. E
3. D
4. D
5. B
6. C
7. A
8. E
9. A
10. C
11. B
12. E
13. D
14. D
15. E
16. E

Chapter 3 (Page 54)
1. B
2. A
3. B
4. D
5. A
6. C

Chapter 4 (Page 72)
1. E
2. D
3. C
4. D
5. C
6. C
7. A
8. B
9. A
10. B
11. See explanations
12. See explanations
13. B
14. D
15. D
16. A
17. D
18. C
19. A
20. B
21. D
22. B
23. C
24. C
25. D
26. D
27. E
28. A

Chapter 5 (Page 110)

1. B
2. E
3. A
4. D
5. A
6. E

Chapter 6 (Page 124)

1. B
2. D
3. D
4. A
5. B
6. B

Chapter 7 (Page 145)

1. C
2. D
3. C
4. B
5. C
6. C
7. D
8. D
9. C
10. A
11. A

Chapter 8 (Page 165)

1. C
2. A
3. C

Chapter 9 (Page 194)

1. A
2. E
3. A
4. B
5. A
6. C

Chapter 10 (Page 227)

1. A
2. E
3. C
4. C

CHAPTER 2

1. **E** Let's start by examining line 3 in the code segment above: double `c = a + b`. `a` is an integer variable and `b` is a double variable. When a double variable is added to an integer variable, the integer is automatically cast to a double before the addition takes place. Therefore, `a + b` will be 20.7; this value will be assigned to `c`.

   Now look at line 4: int `d = a + c`. Because `c` is a double, `a` will once again be cast to a double and `a + c` will be 30.7. This value, which is a double, is then assigned to an integer variable. Because there is a loss of precision when a double value is assigned to an integer variable, the compiler will alert us.

2. **E** The key to this question is remembering that the cast operator `(int)` has precedence over the addition operator. Let's first take a look at expression I. In that case, `a` will first be cast to an `int` (which has no effect because it is already an `int`) and then it will be added to `b`, which is still a `double`: The result of the addition will be a `double`, so we haven't fixed the problem. You can therefore eliminate answer choices (A) and (D).

   In Expression II, `a + b` is enclosed in parenthesis, so the addition will take place first. The result of adding `a` and `b` results in a double (20.7). This `double` is then cast to an `int` (20) and assigned to `d`. This is a legal assignment, so keep answers (B) and (E) and eliminate (C).

   Now let's look at III. Here the `double b` (10.7) is first cast to an `int` (10). This `int` is added to `a`, which is also an `int`. When two `int`s are added, the result is also an `int`, so this expression is also valid.

3. **D** In line 5 of the code segment, we divide `a` by `b`. Because both of the operands are integers, the result will be truncated to an `int`. 11 divided by 4 is 2.75, which is then truncated to 2. We now know that the first number printed will be 2 (assuming we don't run into a compilation error later in the code), so we can get rid of answers (A) and (B).

   In line 7, we once again divide 11 by 4. This time, however, the variables that hold these values are doubles. Therefore the result of dividing 11 by 4 will also be a double: 2.75. We can get rid of answer choice (C).

   In line 9, we yet again divide 11 by 4. The variable that holds 11 is an integer, while the variable that holds 4 is a double. With arithmetic operators, if one of the operands is a double and the other an integer, the integer is automatically cast to a double and the result of the operation is a double. Therefore, we get 2.75 again.

4. **D** This question tests your understanding of short-circuit evaluation. In each code segment, pay attention to the conditional in the `if` statement.

   In the first code segment, the conditional statement is `x < y && 10 < y / z`. First `x < y` is evaluated. Because `x` is 10 and `y` is 20, `x < y` evaluates to `true`. We then need to check `10 < y / z`. Because we divide by zero here, a run-time exception occurs. You can eliminate answers (A) and (E).

Now let's look at the second code segment. The conditional statement is x > y && 10 < y / z. Once again, we first evaluate the operand to the left of the && operator. Because x is *not* greater than y, x > y evaluates to false. There's no need to evaluate the right-hand operand. With the && operator, if the left operand is false, the whole condition is false. Because the right-hand operand is not evaluated, y is never divided by z and a run-time exception does not occur. This means answer choices (B) and (D) are still possible.

In the third code segment, the conditional statement is x < y || 10 < y / z. The left-hand side, x < y evaluates to true. Notice that this time we have the or operator (||) in the middle of the conditional. With an or statement, if the left-hand side is true, the condition is true regardless of the value of the right side. Because the left side is true, there is no need to evaluate the right-hand side, and the division by 0 error never occurs.

5. **B** The first time through the for loop, the value of i will be 1. The value of i is then doubled on each pass through the loop until i is greater than 100. So as we iterate through the loop, the values of i will be: 1 2 4 8 16 32 64.

Inside the loop, the value of i is printed if i / 50 equals 1. When integers are divided, the result is truncated, so i / 50 will equal 0 whenever i is less than 50. Therefore, 2, 4, 8, 16, and 32 will be printed; 64 won't be printed.

6. **C** This question is very similar to the previous one. This time, though, i starts at 200 and is divided by 3 after each pass through the for loop. Note that i /= 3 is equivalent to i = i / 3, and integer division truncates the results. As we iterate through the loop, the values of i will be: 200, 66, 22, 7, 2.

In the body of the loop, i is printed if i % 2 equals 0. i % 2 gives the remainder when i is divided by 2; i will give a remainder of 0 when divided by 2 whenever i is even. Therefore, 200, 66, 22, and 2 will be printed; 7 will not be printed.

7. **A** This question tests your ability to reason through a nested loop. The first thing you should note is that the output is triangular. The first row has two elements, the second has three elements, and so on. Generally, the output of a nested loop will be triangular if the conditional statement of the inner loop is dependent upon the value of the outer loop. If the two loops are independent, the output is usually rectangular.

Let's trace through each answer choice and see which one will give us the first row: 0 1.

The first time we go through the inner loop in answer choice (A), x will be 1, because z starts at 0 and the loop continues while z is less than or **equal to** 1, the inner loop will print out 0 1. So let's keep this choice. For choice (B), the condition of the inner loop is that z is strictly less than x, so this will only print out 0. We can get rid of choice (B). Answer choice (C) will print out 0 1 2 3 4, so we can get rid of that too. Answer choice (D) will print 0 2 4 for the first line. Get rid of it. Answer (E) prints 0 1 for the first line, so we will keep it for now.

We are now down to (A) and (E). Rather than tracing through each segment in its entirety, let's see what the differences are between each segment.

The only difference is the outer for loop. In answer choice (A) it is

```
for (int x = 1; x < 5; x++)
```

and in answer choice (E) it is

```
for (int x = 1; x <= 5; x++) (note the extra equal sign)
```

In answer choice (E), because the body of the outer loop is evaluated 5 times, it will print out 5 rows of number. Because the answer we are looking for only prints out 4 rows, the correct answer must be (A).

8. **E** In this question, we are trying to find the answer choice that *doesn't* work. If the answer to this question is not obvious to you, the best approach is to try each answer choice and see if it could be the value of i. If it can, then get rid of it.

Let's start with (A). Could i be equal to 0? Because x % 50 gives the remainder when x is divided by 50, for i to equal 0, x would have to be evenly divisible by 50. There are plenty of integers that would work for x (50, 100, 150…). In fact, any multiple of 50 would work.

How about (B)? Is there a positive integer we can pick for x that leaves a remainder of 10 when divided by 50? Well, because 50 is evenly divisible by 50, 50 + 10, or 60, would leave a remainder of 10 when divided by 50. Other numbers that would work include 110 and 160. In fact, if you add 10 to any positive multiple of 50, you will get a number that leaves a remainder of 10 when divided by 50.

Following the same logic, we find numbers that leave a remainder of 25 and 40 when divided by 50. For example, 75 and 90 would work. Therefore, we can get rid of (C) and (D).

The only choice left is (E). So why is it that we can't get a remainder of 50 if we divide a positive integer by 50? Consider what happens if we divide 98 by 50. We get a remainder of 48. What if we divide 99 by 50? Now the remainder is 49. It seems if we increase 99 to 100, our remainder will increase to 50! But wait—100 divided by 50 actually leaves a remainder of 0.

The upshot of this example is that the value returned by the modulus operator will always be less than the operand to the right of the modulus operator.

9. **A** Segment 1 works correctly, so we can get rid of our second and third possible answers.

Segment 2 is incorrect, because the conditional 65 <= speed < 75 is illegal. A variable can't be compared to two numbers at once. This code will therefore cause a compile-time error. We can get rid of choice (D).

Segment 3 will compile and run, but it contains a logical error. Assume, for example, that a driver's speed is 85 mph. The driver should receive a fine of 300. If we trace through the code in segment 3, we see that the value of the variable fine is, in fact, set to 300 in the body of the first if loop because the driver's speed is greater than or equal to 75. The problem is that the condition in the second if loop is *also* true: The driver's speed is greater than 65. The body of the second loop is executed and the fine is set to 150. Finally, the condition in the third loop is also true, so the fine is then set to 100. Because Segment 3 is incorrect, we can get rid of our final possible answer. Note that segment 3 would have been correct if we had put "else" in front of the second and third loops.

10. **C** This question tests your ability to trace through a convoluted piece of code. A few things to note

The body of the `if` loop is executed only if `b` is `false`.

The variable `i` is incremented by 5, not by 1, in the `for` loop.

The variable `i` is also incremented by 5 in the body of the `if` loop. This is something you would not normally do in your own code, but it is something you may see on the exam. Don't assume the variable in the conditional of the `for` loop is only modified in the `for` loop.

11. **B** Keep in mind that `&&` returns `true` if both operands are true, `||` returns `true` if one or more of its operands are true, and `!` reverses a boolean value.

The best way to crack questions involving booleans is often to just assign `true` or `false` to the variables and evaluate the expression.

We can break `(a && b) || !(a || b)` into two pieces: `(a && b)` and `!(a || b)`. The variable `c` will be assigned `true` if either of these pieces are true. `(a && b)` is `true` when both `a` and `b` are true. Therefore we can get rid of choice (A) and choice (D).

Let's see what happens if both `a` and `b` are `false`. Clearly `(a && b)` evaluates to `false` in this case, but what about `!(a || b)`? `(a || b)` is `false` if both `a` - and `b` are `false`, but the `!` operator inverts the value to `true`. So because `!(a || b)` is `true`, `(a && b) || !(a || b)` evaluates to `true`. Therefore `c` will be assigned `true` when both `a` and `b` are `false`. We can therefore get rid of answer choice (C).

We are left with answer choices (B) and (E). Let's see what happens when `a` is `false` and `b` is `true`. `(a && b)` evaluates to `false`. `(a || b)` is `true`, so `!(a || b)` is `false`. Therefore, `(a && b) || !(a || b)` is `false` and we can get rid of choice (E).

12. **E** The code will finish executing when the conditional in the `while` loop is false. In other words, when `!( x > y || y >= z)` is `true`. So we need to figure out which of the answer choices is equivalent to `!( x > y || y >= z)`.

Here's how to solve it step by step.

- Recall that `!(a || b)` is equivalent to `!a && !b`. So `!( x > y || y >= z)` becomes `!(x > y) && !(y >= z)`

- `!(x > y)` is equivalent to `x <= y`, so we now have `x <= y && !(y >= z)`

- `!( y >= z)` is equivalent to `y < z`, so we have `x <= y && y < z`

13. **D** Each time the incremental statement (`a++`) is evaluated, the value of `a` is increased by one. So to answer this question, we need to figure out how many times `a` is incremented.

The outer loop will be evaluated 10 times. The inner loop will be evaluated 6 times for each time that the outer loop is evaluated. The code in the body of the second loop will therefore execute 6 * 10 or 60 times. Note that the condition `k <= 5` evaluates to `true` when `k` equals 5. In the third loop, the value of `z` starts at 1 and is doubled after each pass through the loop. So the body of the innermost loop will execute when `i` equals 1, 2, 4 , 8, and 16—or 5 times for each time the middle loop executes. Because 60 * 5 is 300, `a` will be incremented 300 times.

14. **D** The trick to this question is that arithmetic operators don't modify their operands. So if x is 10 when we divide x by 3, the result is 3 but x remains the same. Likewise, taking the modulus of a number does not change the number itself. On the other hand, the post-increment operator (++) *does* change the value of the number it operates on, so x++ will increase the value of x by 1.

15. **E** On the fourth line, a + b will be 13.7, but this result is cast to an int, so x will be 13. On the next line, a is first cast to a double and then divided by c. Because a is a double, c is automatically promoted to a double and the result of dividing the two is also a double. Therefore, y is 2.5.

    On the next line, the parentheses cause the division to take place before the cast. Because a and c are ints, the result of dividing the two is truncated to an int, 2 in this case. The fact that we then cast the result to a double does not bring back the truncated decimal. z is equal to 2, so w = 13 + 2 .5 + 2.

16. **E** Before the while loop is entered, i is equal to 1. The while loop will continue to execute as long as i is less than 5. Because the value of i is never changed in the code, i will always be less than 1 and an infinite loop will occur.

CHAPTER 3

1. **B** Big-Oh notation characterizes how the runtime of a task changes as the amount of data we are dealing with changes. In this case, the data is the number of books that are in the stack of books.

    If there are 100 books in the stack, on average how many steps would it take to find the book that we are looking for? Maybe we would get lucky and the book we seek would be on top of the stack, so we would find it right away. Or we might get very unlucky, and the book that we are looking for would be at the bottom of the stack. Assuming the books are randomly ordered, on average we would expect to have to look through half the books to find the one we seek. So with a stack of 100 books, we would need to look through 50.

    What if we double the number of books to 200? Once again, we would have to look through half of them on average (100 in this case) to find our book.

    So if the number of books doubles, the number of steps it would take to find our book also doubles. In other words, the number of steps is directly proportional to the number of books. This is $O(n)$.

2. **A** Again, consider what happens as the number of books in the stack changes. If there are 100 books in the stack, it only takes us one step to grab the book that is on top. If we double the number of books, it still only takes us one step to get the book on top. In other words, the number of steps is constant; it is independent of the number of books in the stack. This is $O(1)$.

3. **B** Note that the value of x is increased by 2, not just 1, each time through the for loop. If the value of n that is used in the code segment is 10, the body of the for loop will be executed 5 times. What happens if we double the value of n to 20? The body of the for loop will then execute 10 times. So doubling the value of n doubles the time for the code segment to run. In other words, the runtime of the segment is directly proportional to n.

4. **D** Suppose that n is 3. The outer `for` loop will execute 3 times. For each time the outer loop executes, the inner loop will execute 3 times, so the method call in the body of the inner `for` loop will be executed 9 times in total. Now let's look at what happens if we double n to 6. This time the outer loop will execute 6 times and the inner loop will execute 6 times for each time the outer loop executes. The method in the body of the inner loop will therefore be called 36 times.

In this case, we double the value of the input n from 3 to 6 and the time the code segments took to execute increased by a factor of 4 from 9 to 36. So the time increased as a function of the *square* of the input.

5. **A** Notice that x is doubled each time the `for` loop executes. Let's pick 8 for our value of n. As we iterate through the loop, x will be 1, then 2, 4, and 8. So the body of the `for` loop will execute 4 times. Let's see what happens if we double n to 16. This time, x will first be 1, then 2, 4, 8, and 16. The body of the `for` loop will therefore execute 5 times.

Note what happened here. We double the value of n from 8 to 16, but the number of calls to the method only increased by 1. This is an example of logarithmic growth.

6. **C** This time, the counter in the outer loop increases by 1 each time. So the number of times the outer loop executes is directly proportional to n or $O(n)$. The inner loop is the same as the `for` loop from question 3, so it will be $O(\log n)$. Multiplying the two together, we get a total runtime of $O(n \log n)$.

CHAPTER 4

1. **E** Because the database code can, in fact, be developed separately, tested separately, and possibly reused, all of the answers are correct. With questions like these, the easiest approach is to consider each candidate statement suspect, and look for ways in which they could be incorrect. If you find an incorrect one, cross it off, and cross any other answer that might "and" with that answer, because a combination of a true statement and a false statement is a false statement. Alternatively, when a candidate answer is true, put a star next to it. When you're done reading the questions, the one with the most stars wins.

In the above, because all three answers are true statements, we can cross off answers (A), (B), and (C), because they each say that only one statement is correct. Similarly, we can cross off choice (D), because it dismisses the third statement.

2. **D** While the Java language makes it possible to make data fields public, one of the golden rules on the AP Computer Science Exam is that data fields should always be designated *private*. Note that constants that are declared as static and final can be public, however static constants apply to the class as a whole (because of the keyword static) and thus, aren't data fields.

Because data fields must be private, we can get rid of any answer choice that states it can be public. So we can get rid of choices (A), (B), and (E).

Now let's look at answer (C). What would happen if all methods in a class were private? Instances of the class would be useless, because clients couldn't ask the class to do anything for them. Classes need public methods to be useful.

What about answer (D)? The first part is good, because data fields should be private. What about the second sentence? We just saw above that methods can be public. They can also be private. A private method is used internally by a class to help out a public method, but is not directly accessible by client programs.

3. **C** We know that statement I is incorrect, because it violates encapsulation. Thus, any answer that includes statement I can be dismissed out of hand. Thus, we dismiss answer (A), (D), and (E). The implementation of a method can be changed without changing its client programs, so III is correct. We can therefore eliminate answer (B), which dismisses III. Thus, the answer must be (C).

4. **D** Both writeMe methods completely ignore the input that's passed into them, so there's no opportunity for "hi" to be printed. So choice (B) cannot be the answer. The code is syntactically correct, so choice (A) cannot be the answer. Along the same lines, we're not doing anything that requires casting, or dealing with null, or dividing by a number that could potentially be 0, so choice (E) is not the answer. That leaves choices (C) and (D). Because we're creating a String object and passing to a method that takes a String as a parameter, the existence of the writeMe(Object obj) method is inconsequential. Thus, the only valid answer choice is (D).

5. **C** Both writeMe methods completely ignore the input that's passed into them, so there's no opportunity for "hi" to be printed. So choice (D) cannot be the answer. The code is syntactically correct, so choice (A) cannot be the answer. Along the same lines, we're not doing anything that requires casting, or dealing with null, or dividing by a number that could potentially be 0, so choice (E) is not the answer. That leaves choices (B) and (C). Because we're creating an Object and passing to a method that takes an Object as a parameter, the existence of the writeMe(String s) method is inconsequential. Thus, the only valid choice is (C).

6. **C** Both writeMe methods completely ignore the input that's passed into them, so there's no opportunity for "hi" to be printed. So choice (B) cannot be the answer. We can use an Object reference to refer to a String instance, because a String IS-A Object. Thus, the code is not syntactically incorrect, so choice (A) is not the answer. That leaves choices (C), (D), and (E). Because we're not doing any sort of casting, (E) is also an unlikely candidate. That leaves choices (C) and (D). Now the question becomes, when making overloaded calls, does Java pay attention to the type of the reference (which in this case is Object) or the type of the variable (which in this case is String)? It turns out that Java always pays attention to the type of the object, so answer choice (C) is correct.

7. **A** tmp is an Object, *not* a String, thus the code snippet "String tmp = new Object" is illegal. This code will generate a compile-time error.

8. **B** This class is not declaring any methods at all, so choice (C) cannot possibly be correct. The code does not have any syntactical errors, so choice (A) cannot be correct. Answer choice (D) is nonsense, because nothing can be both an attribute and a method, and choice (E), while true, is irrelevant: Being a primitive does not imply that val cannot be an attribute, so the "neither" part of the question is a red herring.

9. **A** Both `writeMe` methods have the same name and same parameter list, but they return different types. This is illegal. Thus, (A) is the right answer.

10. **B** In this question, the `Child` class extends the `Parent` class. In both classes, the writeMe method has the same signature. Therefore, the `writeMe` method of the `Child` class overrides the `writeMe` method of the `Parent` class. Choice (A) is incorrect because an inherited method is one that would not be implemented in the `Child` class. Choice (C) is incorrect because an overloaded method is one in which the method name is the same but the signatures are different. Choices (D) and (E) are incorrect because the `Child` class is neither an interface nor an abstract class. Choice (B) is the correct answer.

11. In these sorts of scenarios, we always start with the parent, or super, class, and we always give it the bare minimal functionality.

    Thus

    ```
    public class Car
    {
    }
    ```

    Because a Car has a wheel, and we know that a wheel is a String, we amend our definition to

    ```
    public class Car
    {
        public String wheel;
    }
    ```

    Finally, we know that a Jaguar IS-A a car, so

    ```
    public class Jaguar extends Car
    {
    }
    ```

12. An interface defines what a class can do. In this case, the class `SampleImpl` only does one thing: It offers the `writeMe(String s)` method. Therefore, the interface would be of the form

    ```
    public interface Sample
    {
        public String writeMe(String s);
    }
    ```

13. **B** A class can, at most, directly extend one other class.

14. **D** A class can implement as many interfaces as it needs to.

15. **D** A given interface can extend as many other interfaces as it needs to.

16. **A** This is a trick question. An interface can *never* implement a class.

17. **D** Choice (A) is not relevant, because `writeMe` is a static method, and thus doesn't need an instance variable. The only print statement in the code explicitly writes out the hard-coded string "hellostring", so choice (B) can't possibly be correct. And because we are not casting, dealing with elements that could be null, or dividing anything, choice (E) is very unlikely. Choice (C) is a possibility, but we're not using a null, nor are we doing anything that could result in a null value. Thus, the answer must be (D).

18. **C** Choice (A) is not relevant, because `writeMe` is a static method, and thus doesn't need an instance variable. The variable var is never initialized to –1, so choice (B) can't possibly be correct. Choice (D) can't be correct because Java doesn't allow values to be unknowable. They are always equal to their initialization value, or 0, if left uninitialized. And choice (E) is partially true, but irrelevant. Variables that are final can be displayed, but not changed. Thus, the answer must be (C).

19. **A** Because we've provided our own constructor for the `Sample` class, we must therefore provide all constructors that our code might use. This code will not compile, because we are attempting to create a Sample object by using the default constructor when we write `Sample s = new Sample();` .

20. **B** This is a tricky question. The only messages that are ever written are the hard-coded strings "me" and "you", so neither choice (A) nor choice (D) can be the answer. That leaves choices (B), (C), or (E). If we trace through the logic of the code into the `writeMe` method, we can see that "hi" is not equal to null, so choice (B) and (E) are left. Now comes the tricky part. The variable "var" is initialized to null, yet the code attempts to call methods on it. This will cause a run-time exception to be thrown because you cannot call methods on a null object. Therefore, (B) is the correct answer.

21. **D** The key to this question is that the attributes `width` and `height` in the `Rectangle` class are private. This means that the values of `width` and `height` can only be directly accessed from within the `Rectangle` class itself. Other classes, including classes like `FilledRectangle` that extend `Rectangle`, can't access private data. Therefore, option III won't work, and we can eliminate answers (C) and (E).

    Option I and II are both legal declarations. Option II explicitly calls the constructor of the `Rectangle` super class that takes two arguments. Keep in mind that if you have a call to `super()` in a constructor, it must be the first statement in the constructor. Because option I does not have an explicit call to a constructor in the super class, the default constructor of `Rectangle` is called.

22. **B** The first statement of choice I will cause a compile-time error. In this statement, we create a `Rectangle` object, but then refer to it using a variable that is of type `FilledRectangle`. This is illegal because the type of the variable must be the same as the type of the object that we create, or a super type.

    In the first statement of choice II, we create a `FilledRectangle` object and then assign it to variable of type `Rectangle`. This is perfectly legal. Think of it this way: The `FilledRectangle` class extends the `Rectangle` class, so we can say that a `FilledRectangle` IS-A `Rectangle`, and can refer to any `FilledRectangle` as a `Rectangle`. Notice that this doesn't work in reverse. It's NOT necessarily true that a `Rectangle` IS-A `FilledRectangle`, so we can't refer to an ordinary `Rectangle` as a `FilledRectangle`. This is the problem we encountered in I.

    The second statement in II is also legal because the `Rectangle` class has a `getHeight()` method.

    What about answer choice III? The first statement is legal for the reasons outlined above. There's a problem with the second statement, however. Even though the variable r3 refers to a `FilledRectangle` object, the variable itself is of type `Rectangle`. Because of this, we can only call methods on the object that are defined in the `Rectangle` class. Because `getColor()` is not defined in `Rectangle`, we will get a compile-time error.

In order to call `getColor()` on r3, we would need to explicitly cast it to a `FilledRectangle`. The following statement could be used to replace the second statement in answer choice III:

```
((FilledRectangle) r3).getColor();
```

The correct answer is (B).

23. **C** This is a good question on which to use Process of Elimination. Don't try to find the best design right away. Instead, first get rid of the answer choices that you know are flawed.

The use of the word *unrelated* is a tip-off that answer choice (A) is incorrect. In general, classes and data fields in a program will be related to each other, otherwise there would really be no point in writing the program in the first place.

Now let's look at answer choice (B). Whenever you are trying to decide if one class is a subclass of the other, ask yourself if an instance of the proposed subclass IS-A instance of the proposed super class. For example, in this case you could ask if a `Pet` IS-A `Apartment`. Obviously not, so get rid of choice (B).

Answer choice (C) looks good. Using primitive data fields allows us to store information about the `Apartment` within an instance of the class. Let's check the rest of the answer choices though.

Like answer choice (B), choice (D) refers to subclasses. The difference this time is that `Apartment` is a subclass of the other classes. There are two problems here. First of all, the IS-A relationship doesn't hold. It would be incorrect to say that an `Apartment` IS-A `Pet`, `Room`, or `Dishwasher`. Here's the other problem: If `Apartment` is a subclass of all three of the other classes, then that means that `Apartment` has three immediate super classes; in other words, `Apartment` extends three other classes. However, in Java, a class can only extend one other class.

Finally, answer choice (E) uses a HAS-A relationship (this is also called *composition*). This design is similar to that of choice (C), except we are using objects instead of primitives, as we did in (C). In this case, using objects will be overkill. For example, the specification from the rental company only states that they want to know if the apartment has a dishwasher. A `boolean` can be used to store this information, so there's really no point in building a `Dishwasher` class. On the other hand, if the rental company had specified that they needed to store a lot of information about the type of dishwasher in each apartment, such as its color, manufacturer, and year of installation, then a `Dishwasher` class would be appropriate.

The correct answer, therefore, is (C).

24. **C** When a class implements an interface, the implemented methods in the class must be declared as `public`. Because the `inter1()` method is private in class A, the class won't compile.

Class B declares that it implements `Inter`, yet it doesn't have an `inter1()` method. This won't cause a problem because B is declared `abstract`. What this means though is that any nonabstract class that extends B will need to implement `inter1()`.

Class C has an `inter1()` method, but the return type is `double`, not `int` as defined in the `Inter` interface. Because of this difference, the class will not compile.

25. **D** (A) is incorrect because the `Motorcycle` class does not define a constructor that takes one argument. Note that unlike other methods, constructors are not inherited, so even though `Motorcycle` extends `Vehicle`, and `Vehicle` defines a constructor that takes one argument, `Motorcycle` will not inherit this constructor.

Choice (B) is incorrect for the same reason that choice (A) is incorrect. Even though our reference type is `Vehicle`, we are still constructing a `Motorcycle`, and the `Motorcycle` class does not define a constructor that takes one argument.

In choice (C), we are creating a `Vehicle` and assigning it to a reference of type `Motorcycle`. This is incorrect because a `Vehicle` is not necessarily a `Motorcycle`. The reference type of a variable must be the same class or a super class of the object that we are trying to assign to it. It cannot be a subclass.

Choice (D) is correct. Because the `Motorcycle` class extends the `Vehicle` class, a `Motorcycle` IS-A `Vehicle` and we can assign a `Motorcycle` instance to a `Vehicle` reference.

The first line in choice (E) is correct, however in the second line we are trying to access a `private` date member. To fix this, we would need to call the `public` method `maxPassengers()` instead. This would look like the following:

```
int max = v3.maxPassengers();
```

Always bear in mind that all data members on the exam will be `private`; only methods are `public`. Therefore, when you use dot notation on an instance of a class, the part that follows the dot should end in parenthesis. The only exception to this that you will see on the test is the `length` attribute of an array.

26. **D** In this case, we create an instance of the class `SubClass` and refer to it as the type of its parent `SuperClass`. When we call `x.B()`, the `B()` method that is defined in `SubClass` will execute (this is polymorphism at work). In `SubClass`, `B()` calls `SuperClass`'s `A()` method, which in turn calls `A()` in the subclass, which then calls `B()` in `SuperClass`. This last method simply returns 7, so no more methods are called. The 7 is added to 2, which is then added to 3 and 5 to give 17.

27. **E** This time, the object that we create is an instance of the `SuperClass` class. Therefore, when we call `y.A()`, the `A()` method of `SuperClass` will execute. When `A()` in `SuperClass` executes, it will call itself, not the `A()` method defined in `SubClass`. Because there is no base case, the method will keep recursively calling itself until a `StackOverFlowError` occurs.

28. **A** Any method that overloads `method1()` must have the same name but differ in its parameter type(s). The only answer choice that does this is (A). A method that overloads another can also differ in the number of parameters it has. So, for example, the following is a signature of a method that would overload `method1()`:

```
public int method1(int x, int y)
```

CHAPTER 5

1. **B** The string is made up, in order, of the following six characters: a, b, \n, \\, \", and c. Note that three of these are escape sequences.

2. **E** The substring "science" begins at position 9 in the string "computer science." Because the `sub-string()` method that takes one argument returns the substring from that argument to the end of the string, answer choice I will return "science", so that eliminates answer choices (B) and (C). Note that the "e" at the end of "computer science" is at position 15. When we use the `substring()` method that takes two arguments, the position of the last letter in the substring will be one less than the number that is passed to the second argument, so s.substring(9, 15) will return "scienc," without an "e". Answer choice III, on the other hand, will include the "e".

3. **A** Because s is a String, `i` and `j` will always be concatenated with s as strings in the expression `s = s + i + j`. Because i and j are always less than a, which is 2, we can eliminate answer choices (B), (D), and (E). We can also see that the first time `s = s + i + j` is evaluated, both i and j will be 0, so the final string must begin with 2 zeros. Therefore, we can eliminate choice (C).

4. **D** Option II is incorrect because it uses single quotes to surround the string. A string must always be surrounded by double quotes. That eliminates answer choice (B), (C), and (E). Both I and III are correct. III uses the shorthand for creating a String object.

5. **A** After the first line executes, we have a variable called s1 that holds a reference to a `String` object with the value "One". After the second line executes we will have a variable called s2 that refers to a `String` object with the value "Two".

   The third line causes s2 to refer to the same object as s1. Because the object with the value "Two" is no longer referenced, it will be garbage-collected.

   The last statement causes s1 to refer to a String object with the value "Three". This doesn't change s2, though; it still refers to the object with the value "One".

6. **E** In I, `"Catch " + 11 + 11;` is evaluated from left to right. Because `"Catch "` is a string, 11 will be appended and we will get `"Catch11 "`. The next 11 is also appended as a string, which results in `"Catch 1111"`. Because I doesn't give us what we are looking for, get rid of answers (A) and (D).

   Using the same reasoning as above, we can see that III does indeed give us `"Catch 22"`. So the answer choices are now down to (C) and (E).

   In II, `(11 + 11)` will be evaluated first due to the parenthesis. Because both operands are integers, the result is an integer: 22. This is then appended to `"Catch "` to give us `"Catch 22"`.

CHAPTER 6

1. **B** In the method above, the base case occurs when x is equal to 0. Because the value that is initially passed to the method is 3543, the base case does not yet apply. Let's see what happens on the line `return ((x % 10) + mystery(x / 10))`.

Make sure that you understand what (x % 10) and (x / 10) do. If x is a base 10 integer, x % 10 will return the units digit. For example, 348 % 10 returns 8. If x is an int variable, then x / 10 will remove the units digit. For example, 348 / 10 returns 34.

The expression within the return statement has two parts (x % 10) and mystery(x / 10).

Let's take a look at (x % 10). This returns the remainder when x is divided by 10. In our case, x is 3543, so 3543 % 10 is 3.

Now what about (x / 10)? 3543 / 10 is 354; integer division truncates the result.

So we now have

```
mystery(3543) = 3 + mystery(354).
```

Following the same logic as above, mystery(354) will be (354 % 10) + mystery(354 / 10) or mystery(354) = 4 + mystery(35).

So what is mystery(35)?

```
mystery(35) = (35 % 10) + mystery(35 / 10)
```

or simplified

```
mystery(35) = 5 + mystery(3);
```

And mystery(3)?

```
mystery(3) = (3 % 10) + mystery( 3 / 10)
```

or simplified

```
mystery(3) = 3 + mystery(0);
```

But mystery(0) equals 0 (this is the base case), so

```
mystery(3)    = 3 + 0 = 3
mystery(35)   = 5 + 3 = 8
mystery(354)  = 4 + 8 = 12
mystery(3543) = 3 + 12 = 15.
```

The correct answer is (B).

2. **D**

```
mystery(6) = 2 * mystery(5)
    mystery(5) = 2 * mystery(4)
        mystery(4) = 2 * mystery(3)
            mystery(3) = 2 * mystery(2)
                mystery(2) = 2 * mystery(1)
                    mystery(1) = 2;
```

So mystery(6) = 2 * 2 * 2 * 2 * 2 * 2 = 64.

3. **D**

On the first pass through the method we get

```
10 + mystery(10 / 2) + mystery(10 / 4)
```

which can be simplified to

```
10 + mystery(5) + mystery(2)
```

So now we need to figure out what `mystery(5)` and `mystery(2)` are and add the results to 10.

First, we'll solve `mystery(5)`

```
mystery(5) = 5 + mystery(5 / 2) + mystery(5 / 4)
                 = 5 + mystery(2) + mystery(1)
mystery(2) = 2 + mystery( 2 / 2) + mystery(2 / 4)
                 = 2 + mystery(1) + mystery(0)
mystery(1) = 1 + mystery(1 / 2) + mystery(1 / 4)
               = 1 + mystery(0) + mystery(0)
```

Note that `mystery(0)` is our base case and returns 0. Working our way back up the recursive calls, we find that `mystery(1) = 1`, `mystery(2) = 3`, and `mystery(5) = 9`. Note that in solving `mystery(5)` we ended up needing to solve `mystery(2)`.

So in our original equation: `10 + mystery(5) + mystery(2)`, we can replace `mystery(5)` with 9 and `mystery(2)` with 3 to get: `10 + 9 + 2`, which equals 22.

4. **A** For any value non-negative number *n* that is passed as an argument to the non-recursive method `mystery()`, the method will return the $0 + 1 + 2 + 3 + \ldots + n$. For example, a call to `mystery(5)` will return 15 $(1 + 2 + 3 + 4 + 5)$. Note that the border case for `mystery()` occurs when 0 is passed to the method. In this case the method returns 0.

Method I (method `mystery2()`) is equivalent to `mystery()`.

Method II (`mystery3()`) is not equivalent. Notice that `mystery2()` does not modify what is returned by the recursive call, whereas `mystery2()` adds x to the results of each recursive call. The method `mystery2()` will return 0 regardless of the value that is passed to the method.

Method III (`mystery4()`) is equivalent to `mystery()` except when x equals 0. If 0 is passed to the method, the loop will infinitely recurse. Because `mystery4()` doesn't handle the border case correctly, so III is incorrect.

Only Method I is equivalent to the `mystery()` method, so answer choice (A) is correct.

5. **B** We originally pass 30 and 18 to the method as *x* and *y* respectively. Each time the method is recursively called, 10 is added to *x* and 3 is subtracted from *y*, therefore *x* will eventually become larger than 100 and *y* will become smaller than 0, so we know that the condition of the base case will eventually be met and infinite recursion won't occur.

Note that the base case returns 1. What about the non–base case? The method return `mystery(x + 10, y - 3)` simply returns whatever was returned by the call to `mystery()`; it doesn't modify it in any way. Because there's no modification of the return value, 1 is the only thing that is ever returned, no matter how many recursive calls occur.

6. **B** The best way to solve this problem is to trace through each answer choice. But don't necessarily start with choice (A). Start with the answer choice that you think you can solve most quickly. In this case, choice (A) will probably take longer to check because it has two recursive calls. Instead, let's start with choice (D). Why (D)? Because each recursive call reduces the integer that we pass as an argument by 4, there won't be as many recursive calls as there will be with the other choices.

With choice (D), the first time through the method, we have `mystery(10) = 4 * mystery(6)`.

We find that mystery(6) = 4 * mystery(2) and mystery(2) = 4 * mystery(-2). Finally, mystery(-2) equals 1 (the base case). Working our way back up the call stack, we get: mystery(2) = 4, mystery(6) = 16 and mystery(10) = 64. So choice (D) is incorrect.

The choice with the next fewest recursive calls is choice (B). For this choice, mystery(10) = 2 * mystery(8); mystery(8) = 2 * mystery(6); mystery(6) = 2 * mystery(4); mystery(4) = 2 * mystery(2); mystery(2) = 2 * mystery(0); and mystery(0) = 1. Therefore, mystery(2) = 2; mystery(4) = 4; mystery(6) = 8; mystery(8) = 16; and mystery(10) = 32.

CHAPTER 7

1. **C** On line 1, an array of Strings is created and assigned to reference s. Note that the array to which s refers can only hold two Strings. This does not prevent us, however, from pointing s to another array that is not of length 2. This is exactly what happens on line 3; s is reassigned to the same array that t references. This array has a length of 3.

Here is what this looks like.

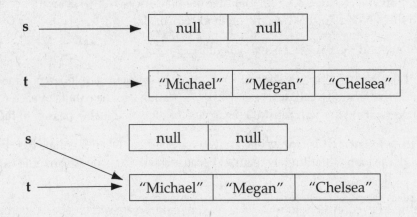

2. **D** In the code segment, the variable a1 is declared as final. This means that once we assign an array to it, a1 must always point to that array. A compile-time error will occur when we try to assign the array referenced by b1 to a1.

3. **C** In the code segment, an array containing two integers is constructed and assigned to a variable named myArray. Because this reference is final, it cannot be assigned to another array. This does not prevent us, however, from changing the contents of the array that the variable myArray points to, as we do in the second line. The key here is that even though we change the contents of the array, it is still the same array.

4. **B** In the for loop in the method Mod3, the variable i keeps track of the position of the array that we are inspecting for each iteration of the loop. a[i], on the other hand, is the value that is located at position i in the array. Segment I will check to see if the position i is divisible by 3; this is not what we are looking for, so answer choices (A) and (D) are incorrect. Segment II will check if the number that is stored in the array at position i is divisible by 3, which is what we are looking for. Segment III will go into an infinite loop the first time it encounters an element

in the array that is divisible by 3, so answer choices (C) and (E) can be eliminated. Only Segment II will get the program to work as intended.

5. **C** Let's walk through this step by step. Remember that the add() method that takes just one argument adds the argument to the end of the list. The following two lines of code add "A" and "B" to the ArrayList one after another:

```
list.add("A")
list.add("B")
```

After the code above executes, the list looks like

[A, B]

The next statement, list.add(0, "C"), adds "C" to the beginning of the list. Now the list looks like

[C, A, B]

After list.add("D") executes, the list looks like

[C, A, B, D]

The set() method replaces the value at the position indicated by the first argument. After list.set(2, "E") executes, the list looks like

[C, A, E, D]

After list.remove(1) executes, the list looks like

[C, E, D]

The correct answer is therefore (C).

6. **C** The key to this question is that as elements are removed from an ArrayList, the elements to the right of the removed element are shifted to the left and their indices are reduced by 1.

On the first pass through the while loop, i will be 0. Because the String in position 0 of letters equals "A", it will be removed and letters will look like

[B, A, A, C, D, B]

The next time through the while loop, i will be 1. The letter in position 1 is equal to "A", so it is removed. Now letters looks like

[B, A, C, D, B]

On the next pass through the ArrayList, i is 2. The letter in position 2 is a C, so it is not removed. The while loop will continue to iterate through the ArrayList, but because none of the Strings in indices higher than 2 are equal to A, nothing else will be removed.

The correct answer is therefore (C).

7. **D** The first time through the `for` loop, the letter in position 0 is removed and `myList` looks like

[B, C, D, E]

The letter that is in position 0, which is now B, is printed.

The next time through the `for` loop, i is 1, so C, the letter in position 1 is removed. Now `myList` looks like

[B, D, E]

The letter that is in position 1, which is now D, is printed.

At this point, i is incremented to 2. The size of `myList` is also 2, so i is no longer less than `myList.size()`. The `for` loop does not execute again.

The correct answer is therefore (D).

8. **D** The variable `numbers.length` is the number of rows in the two-dimensional array `numbers`. The variable `numbers[0].length` is the number of columns. Both the number of rows and the number of columns are 4.

On the first pass through the `for` loop, z is 0 and `numbers[0].length - 1 - z` is 3. So the value of `numbers[0][3]` is added to the total. So, `numbers[0][3]` is 3.

On the next pass, z is 1, `numbers[0].length - 1 - z` is 2, so the value of `numbers[1][2]` (which is 4) is added to the total.

On the next pass, we add the value at `numbers[2][1]`, which is 3, and on the final pass we add the value at `numbers[4][0]`, which is 4.

As you can see, the `for` loop simply finds the sum of one of the diagonals of the array.

9. **C** Note that k is incremented by 2 in the inner `for` loop. The code segment will find the sum of all the integers in columns with an even index.

numbers[0][0] + numbers[0][2] + numbers[0][4] +
numbers[1][0] + numbers[1][2] + numbers[1][4] +
numbers[2][0] + numbers[2][2] + numbers[2][4]

10. **A** The first `for` loop initializes the `ArrayList` list so that it looks like

[1, 2, 3, 4, 5, 6, 7, 8]

Now let's take a look at the second `for` loop. Note that the highest value that j will reach is 7, one less than the size of the list. In the body of the `for` loop, the index of the position that we are setting is j divided by 2; the index can therefore never be greater than 3. In other words, we won't be modifying any values other than those in the first 4 positions of the `ArrayList`. Knowing this, we can eliminate answer choices (D) and (E).

On the first pass through the loop, j is 1 and we call list.set(1 / 2, list.get(1)). Because the result of integer division is truncated, this call is equivalent to list.set(0, list,get(1)), so the value of the element at position 0 is the same as that at position 1 and the ArrayList is

[2, 2, 3, 4, 5, 6, 7, 8]

On the next pass through the for loop, i is 2 and we call list.set(1, list.get(2)). The ArrayList looks like this

[2, 3, 3, 4, 5, 6, 7, 8]

On the next pass we call, list.get(1, list.get(3)). The ArrayList now looks like

[2, 4, 3, 4, 5, 6, 7, 8]

If we continue to iterate through the second for loop, the ArrayList will end up looking like this

[2, 4, 6, 8, 5, 6, 7, 8]

11. **A** For each cell in the two-dimensional array, the code sets the value to the product of the indices for that cell. For example, num[2][3] is set to 2 * 3 or 6.

CHAPTER 8

1. **C** The trick to this question is that p1 and p2 are *not* duplicates, even though they were constructed with the same data. To determine whether two elements are duplicates, Sets use the equals() methods of the elements. Because the Person class does not override the equals() method, the default equals() method provided by the Object class is used, which only returns true if the two object references refer to the same object.

2. **A** The first call to iter.next() on the fifth line above will return "A". "E" is then added to myList after "A", but the call to iter.next() that follows on the next line will return "B", not "E". The call to remove() that then follows will remove "B" from myList. The call to remove() always removes the last item that was returned by a call to next(). The call to iter.next() on the last line will return "C". The correct answer is (A).

3. **C** Because we want to be able to look up the names of students using an object (the name of the club), a Map would be appropriate in this situation, and because we want to look up students based on the name of a club, the club names should be the keys of the map. Therefore, we can eliminate answer choices (A) and (D).

   What type of Map should we use, a TreeMap or a HashMap? The program requirements state that we only need to be able to search by club name; we don't need to print out the names of clubs in order. In this case a HashMap is appropriate, because it provides faster search capabilities. Remember that TreeMaps should be used if you need to keep data sorted. Because we are going to use a HashMap, we can get rid of answer choice (B).

The final decision is whether to use a TreeSet or a HashSet to store the names of the students. Because we want to be able to print the names of the students in sorted order, a TreeSet is appropriate.

CHAPTER 9

1. **A** You can use the Process of Elimination here to narrow down the possible answers. We know that a queue is a line, like you would see at a grocery store. The first person in line is also the first person out. We also know that peeking at the first element in a queue doesn't remove that element: hence the term *peek*. Because the first element in this queue was a 3, and the 3 wasn't removed until we started the while loop, the first output cannot be 12. So, answers (C) and (D) can't be right. That leaves answer choices (A), (B), and (E), which are all the same until you reach the fourth element. We also know that the fourth is 6 plus the first element, which is 9. Therefore, the correct answer is (A).

2. **E** Note that in the second while loop, objects are removed from myQueue until myQueue is empty and these objects are added to myStack. Therefore, only choices (D) and (E) could possibly be the correct answer.

   In the first while loop, objects are popped from myStack and then enqueued in myQueue. Keep in mind that the pop() method removes objects from the top of the stack. After the first while loop has finished executing, myStack is empty and myQueue looks like this

   ```
   front --->   4 9 6 2 3 <---back
   ```

   The next while loop removes each object one by one from the front of myQueue and pushes it onto myStack. After the second while loop has finished executing, myQueue is empty and myStack looks like

   ```
   top -->       3
                 2
                 6
                 9
   bottom -->    4
   ```

   The correct answer is (E).

3. **A** The defining characteristic of a binary search tree is that for any node, the value of the node's left child must be less than the value of the node, and the value of the node's right child must be greater. We can therefore eliminate answer choice (E) because this rule is broken; the node with a value of 28 has a right child with a smaller value.

   When values are inserted into a binary search tree, the first value inserted will always be the root node, no matter how many other values are later inserted into the tree. Because the first value inserted is 20, we can get rid of answer choice (D).

Here is what our binary search tree looks like after we have inserted 20.

And here are the values that we have left to insert.

    10   28   17   3   15   32

Next, we insert 10. Because it is less than 20, it becomes the left child of 20.

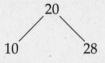

We then insert 28 into the tree. We start by comparing 28 to the root node, 20. Because 28 is larger, it goes to the right.

Now, we need to insert 17. Because 17 is smaller than 20, we look to the left branch of the tree. And 17 is larger than 10, so it becomes the right child of 10.

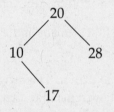

The next number in our list is 3. 3 is smaller than 20, so we go to the left of the tree. 3 is also smaller than 10, so it becomes the left child of 10.

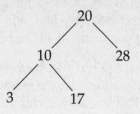

Adding 15 makes the tree look like this

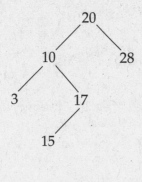

And finally, 32 gives us

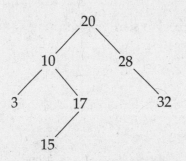

4. **B** A preorder traversal visits the root of a tree first. Next it conducts a preorder traversal on the left child, and then a preorder traversal on the right child.

Because the root is visited first, the first element in the output must be A. We can therefore get rid of answer choices (C) and (D).

Thus, we start at the top, get the A, and go left. Here, we get B, and go left. Here, we get D, and go back up (because there is no left or right child after D). So far, we have ABD, so we can get rid of answer choice (A). Now we go back up to B, and visit its right child, E. Next we get E's left child, which is H. At this point, we can stop, because only one choice starts out with ABDEH, and that's answer choice (B).

5. **A** Chapter 9 reviewed how to find preorder, inorder, and postorder traversals in depth. However, the quickest way to solve this problem is *not* to first write out all of the traversals and then look for the answer. Instead, use what you know about traversals.

The root node is always visited first in a preorder traversal. In the pictured binary tree, the root node is "A", so in this case any answer in which the reorder traversal doesn't start with "A" will be incorrect. Therefore, we can eliminate answer choices (C) and (D).

Next let's take a look at the postorder traversal. In a postorder traversal, the root node, "A", will always be last. Therefore, we can eliminate answer choice (B).

Now we're down to answer choices (A) and (E). Note that the answer choices for preorder and inorder traversals for (A) and (E) are the same, so we shouldn't bother to figure them out. Instead take a look at the postorder traversal. The postorder traversal always starts with the left subtree, so there's no way that the first element could be "F", because "F" is in the right subtree in this case. So get rid of answer choice (E), which leaves (A) as the only answer remaining.

6. **C** Recall from Chapter 8 that a hashing function takes a large range of values and attempts to condense them into a smaller range.

Let's start by looking at answer choice (A) and use the values from the question to test if this could be the hashing function. We'll start by using 12, which is assigned to index 0 of the array. If we subtract 3 from 12 we get 9, not 0, so we can eliminate (A).

If we use 12 with answer choice (B), we get 2, not 0. So get rid of choice (B).

Let's try answer choice (C). 12 % 6 is 0, so this works. But don't put choice (C) as your answer just yet! Just because the hashing function worked for 12, doesn't mean it is the correct answer, it has to work for *all* of the values to be correct. Rather than try all of the values with (C)'s hash function, let's see if we can eliminate choices (D) and (E).

For choice (D), a value of 12 gives us 1. (Remember that integer division truncates the answer.) So (D) is gone.

Finally, choice (E) gives us 4, so that is eliminated too. The answer must be (C).

CHAPTER 10

1. **A** Note that the trees in choices (B) and (E) violate the heap condition, so we can get rid of them right away.

We start by putting 30 in the empty heap. 30 becomes the root.

We then put the next number in the list in the first empty space in the heap. Note that the heap condition is met, because the child node, 26, is less than its parent, 30.

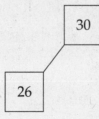

We then add 15 to the next empty spot in the heap. 15 is less than its parent, so once again, the heap condition is met.

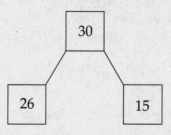

Now we add 63 to the next empty position in the tree. This time, the heap condition is violated. We will need to trickle 63 up the heap.

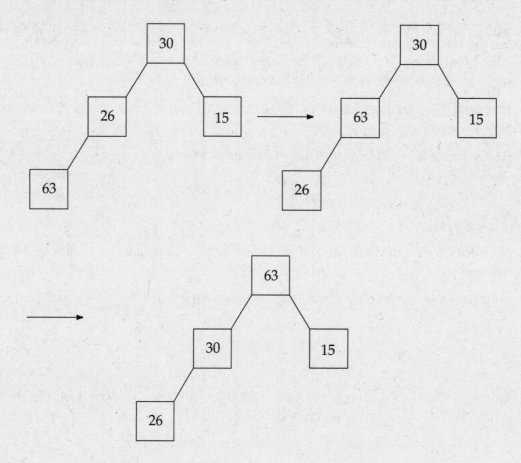

Now we'll insert 35 into the next empty position in the tree.

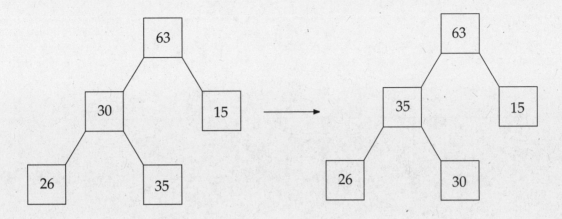

And finally, we insert 10.

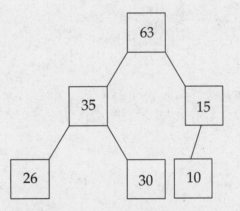

2. **E** A question like this, which asks for the maximum number of comparisons, is asking about the worst-case scenario for the search. The worst case will occur if 123 is not in the array, or is located in the last cell of the array. In this case, we will need to examine all 100 elements in the array. The fact that an array is sorted does not change performance of a sequential search.

3. **C** When a binary search algorithm is used to search an ordered array, the number of elements that need to be searched is cut in half for each element that is examined.

   The way to solve this is to find the smallest number that we need to raise 2 to, in order to get a number larger than 100.

   Using the answers, we see that

   (A) $2^1 = 2$ (This is too small.)
   (B) $2^5 = 32$ (This is also too small.)
   (C) $2^7 = 128$ (This works!)

4. **C** The quicksort algorithm normally runs in $O(n \log n)$ time, but it will run in $O(n^2)$ time if the pivot value is always the smallest or largest value in a partition.

The Marine Biology
Simulation Case Study

INTRODUCTION

A case study is one way to apply the principles learned throughout the AP Computer Science course to a real-world programming problem. The College Board has written the Marine Biology Simulation (MBS) as one example of such a case study. The MBS attempts to model fish interacting in a marine environment. The problem statement, Java source code, documentation, and a narrative that describes the case study and explains the design decisions made throughout are all part of the case study.

    Approximately 20 percent of the AP Computer Science Exam (at least five out of forty multiple-choice questions and one out of four free-response questions) requires knowledge of the MBS.

Questions on the exam will involve analysis of the code, explanation of design decisions, understanding the results of running the program, developing test cases, and making modifications and enhancements to the source code.

Many students avoid the Case Study because it appears too complex. This chapter will review the Marine Biology Simulation Case Study in detail and demonstrate its straightforward, logical structure.

By allowing you to focus on the essential aspects of the Case Study, this chapter will prepare you for the MBS questions and give you that added edge when you take the exam.

OVERVIEW

The premise of the Marine Biology Simulation Case Study is that you are a programmer hired to modify a simulation program created by marine biologists to study fish movement in an environment. The marine biologists would like you to accomplish three goals:

1. Analyze and understand the existing functionality of the program.

2. Understand how the existing code implements the functionality.

3. Be able to modify and extend the existing code in a manner consistent with good object-oriented design principles.

The program itself consists of two major groups of classes and interfaces: the group that provides the core functionality specific to the Marine Biology Simulation and the group that provides the utilities that are useful and necessary to the program, but which are not directly related to marine biology.

The core classes and interfaces include

- the Environment interface and the BoundedEnv and UnboundedEnv classes that implement this interface

- the Fish class and its derived SlowFish and DarterFish classes

- the Simulation class

The utility classes and interfaces include

- the Location and Direction classes and the Locatable interface

- the EnvDisplay and Debug classes

- the Java library classes and associated RandNumGenerator class

Any other source code for the case study is provided as black boxes; in other words, you should be aware of its existence, but you will not be tested on it during the AP exam.

Note that during your analysis of the case study, you may find that you disagree with some of the design decisions made by the authors of the program. This is not only common, but to be expected when you are studying a complex program. In the real-world, you will often not have the luxury of rewriting a program from scratch; you will need to maintain code with a structure or design that is different from what you are used to or from what you would have designed. The case study is a good way to practice this skill.

Finally, while learning the case study you should actually run the code and experiment with modifications to it. It is through this "hands-on" experience that you will be able to understand the interactions among the classes.

UTILITY CLASSES AND INTERFACES

The utility classes and interfaces listed below can stand alone and can be used outside of the case study. They provide the "glue" that helps link together the core functionality of the program.

Consider each of the utility classes and interfaces separately. Understanding their functionality and code will make it easier to understand the functionality of the core classes of the case study:

1. The Location class. This class encapsulates the concept of a position in a rectangular grid as represented by its row number and column number.

2. The Locatable interface. Not to be confused with the Location class, this interface is implemented by objects that have a location associated with them.

3. The Direction class. This class encapsulates the concept of a compass direction on a map as represented by the number of degrees (between 0 and 359 inclusive) clockwise from north.

4. The EnvDisplay interface. This interface defines how the simulation displays the environment.

5. The RandNumGenerator and java.util.Random classes. These classes provide a way to obtain random numbers for use in the case study.

6. The Debug class. This class is used to help verify the correct operation of a program.

7. The java.util.ArrayList class. This is a standard collection class used to manipulate an arbitrarily sized list of objects.

8. The java.awt.Color class. This class encapsulates a color as an ordered triplet representing the amounts of red, green, and blue in the color.

LOCATION CLASS

The Location class encapsulates the concept of a position in a rectangular grid as represented by its row number and column number. The class consists of a constructor and various methods that allow you to manipulate locations.

The Location class is independent of the other classes in the case study. In accordance with good object-oriented design principles, this class could be used with any program that wishes to abstract the idea of a position in a rectangular grid; it is not tied to the Marine Biology Simulation Case Study.

Be sure not to confuse the Location class with the Locatable interface described in the next section. While the two are related, they represent significantly different functionality in the case study.

Constructing a Location

A Location is created with a row number and a column number. For example

```
Location loc = new Location(4, 5);
```

Note that there is no default constructor for the Location class.

int row()

This accessor method returns the row number of this Location. For instance, executing the code segment

```
int r;
r = loc.row();
System.out.print("The row is " + r);
```

results in the output

```
The row is 4
```

int col()

This accessor method returns the column number of this Location. For instance, executing the code segment

```
int c;
c = loc.col();
System.out.print("The column is " + c);
```

results in the output

```
The column is 5
```

boolean equals(Object other)

Two Locations are equal if they both have the same row number and the same column number. Be sure to use the equals method rather than the == operator to compare locations.

int compareTo(Object other)

Because the Location class implements the Comparable interface, the compareTo method is defined. Recall that the compareTo method returns one of three values:

1. Zero if this Location is equal to other; that is, they have the same row number and the same column number.

2. A negative integer if this Location is "less" than other.

3. A positive integer if this Location is "greater" than other.

Locations are ordered by first comparing their rows. The Location with the smaller row number comes before the Location with the larger row number. If the Locations have the same row number, then the Location with the smaller column number comes before the Location with the larger column number.

For example, consider the Locations

```
Location loc1 = new Location(3, 6);
Location loc2 = new Location(4, 2);
Location loc3 = new Location(4, 2);
Location loc4 = new Location(4, 7);
```

The results of comparing the locations would be

```
int result1 = loc1.compareTo(loc2);
        // result1 is negative
int result2 = loc2.compareTo(loc3);
        // result2 is zero
int result3 = loc4.compareTo(loc2);
        // result3 is positive
```

Note that if locA.equals(locB) is true, then locA.compareTo(locB) == 0 and vice versa.

String toString()

This method returns a String that is a human-readable representation of a Location object. The String represents the Location as an ordered pair of integers enclosed in parentheses and separated by a comma. For example, executing the code segment

```
System.out.println(loc.toString());
```

results in the output

```
(4, 5)
```

LOCATABLE INTERFACE

A "locatable" object is an object that keeps track of its own location in its environment. Fish, DarterFish, and SlowFish are all examples of locatable objects because they know their own location.

To determine if an object is locatable, check its class declaration to see if it implements the Locatable interface. Its class signature line must indicate that it "implements Locatable" and the class must provide a location() method that returns the object's location. In addition, a private data field will often be used to store the object's location internally.

For instance, a Fish is locatable

```
public class Fish implements Locatable
{
        private Location myLoc; // stores this fish's
                                     // location
        // postcondition: returns this fish's location
        public Location location()
        {
               return myLoc;
        }
        // ... other constructors, methods, and
        //       private data not shown
}
```

Any "marine object" in the case study must implement the Locatable interface.

DIRECTION CLASS

The Direction class encapsulates the concept of a compass direction on a map as represented by the number of degrees (between 0 and 359 inclusive) clockwise from north. The class consists of direction constants and various methods that allow you to easily work with directions.

As with the Location class, the Direction class is independent of the other classes in the case study. In other words, the Direction class can stand on its own outside of the case study.

Constants

Eight standard directions are predefined constants, which correspond to the eight standard directions on a compass: NORTH, EAST, SOUTH, WEST, NORTHEAST, NORTHWEST, SOUTHEAST, and SOUTHWEST. Each of these directions is referred to by prefixing "Direction." to the name of the direction; for instance

```
Direction forwardDirection = Direction.SOUTH;
```

would set the object forwardDirection to be SOUTH.

Constructing a Direction

Directions can be constructed in one of three ways:

1. Using the default constructor. This creates an object whose direction is north (or 0 degrees).

    ```
    Direction dir1 = new Direction()
    ```

    creates the object dir1 that represents north.

2. Using the Direction(int degrees) constructor. The integer passed to the constructor represents the number of degrees clockwise from north. For instance

    ```
    Direction dir2 = new Direction(90);
    ```

    constructs the object dir2 that represents east

    ```
    Direction dir3 = new Direction(225);
    ```

    constructs the object dir3 that represents southwest, and

    ```
    Direction dir4 = new Direction(300);
    ```

    constructs the object dir4 that represents the direction 300 degrees clockwise from north, or somewhere between northeast and east.

    Note that the number of degrees is always adjusted to be between 0 and 359. The object dir4 above could also have been constructed by the code

    ```
    Direction dir4 = new Direction(660);
    ```

3. Using the Direction(String str) constructor. The string str represents one of the eight standard compass directions: north, south, east, west, northeast, northwest, southeast, and southwest. For example

    ```
    Direction dir5 = new Direction("southwest");
    ```

    constructs the object dir5 that represents southwest.

    Note that the case of str is ignored. Passing "southwest", "Southwest", "SOUTH-WEST", or even "SoUtHwEsT" to the constructor all create the same direction.

int inDegrees()

This method returns the number of degrees clockwise from north for this direction. Using the dir4 object constructed above, executing the code segment

```
System.out.print(dir4.inDegrees());
```

would output 300. The value returned by the inDegrees method is always between 0 and 359 inclusive.

boolean equals(Object other)

Two Directions are equal if they are the same number of degrees clockwise from north. Be sure to use the equals method rather than the == operator to compare directions. Note that because the Direction class does not implement the Comparable interface, you cannot compare Directions using the compareTo method.

Direction toRight()

This method returns a Direction object that represents the direction 90 degrees to the right of, or clockwise from, this Direction. For instance,

```
Direction dir6 = dir1.toRight();
      // dir6 represents east (90 degrees)
Direction dir7 = dir4.toRight();
      // dir7 represents 30 degrees
      // clockwise from north
```

Note that although dir4 represents a direction 300 degrees clockwise from north, and adding 90 degrees gives a direction of 390 degrees, the result is adjusted to 30 degrees so that it ends up between 0 and 359 degrees inclusive while still representing the same compass direction.

Direction toLeft()

This method returns a Direction object that represents the direction 90 degrees to the left of, or counterclockwise from, this Direction. For instance,

```
Direction dir8 = dir1.toLeft();
      // dir8 represents west (270 degrees)
Direction dir9 = dir4.toLeft();
      // dir9 represents 210 degrees
      // clockwise from north
```

Note that although dir1 represents due north (0 degrees), and subtracting 90 degrees gives a direction of –90 degrees, the result is adjusted to 270 degrees so that it ends up between 0 and 359 degrees inclusive while still representing the same compass direction.

Direction toRight(int degrees)

This method returns a Direction object that represents the direction the given number of degrees to the right of, or clockwise from, this Direction. For instance

```
Direction dir10 = dir1.toRight(180);
        // dir10 represents south (180 degrees clockwise
        // from north)
Direction dir11 = dir4.toRight(1000);
        // dir11 represents 220 degrees
        // clockwise from north (1000 degrees clockwise
        // from 300 degrees)
```

Note that although dir4 represents a direction 300 degrees clockwise from north, and adding 1,000 degrees gives a direction of 1,300 degrees, the result is adjusted to 220 degrees so that it ends up between 0 and 359 degrees inclusive while still representing the same compass direction.

Direction toLeft(int degrees)

This method returns a Direction object that represents the direction the given number of degrees to the left of, or counterclockwise from, this Direction. For instance

```
Direction dir12 = dir2.toLeft(45);
        // dir12 represents northeast (45 degrees
        // counterclockwise from east)
Direction dir13 = dir4.toLeft(1000);
        // dir13 represents 20 degrees
        // clockwise from north (1000 degrees
        // counterclockwise from 300 degrees)
```

Note that although dir13 represents a direction 300 degrees clockwise from north, and subtracting 1,000 degrees gives a direction of –700 degrees, the result is adjusted to 20 degrees so that it ends up between 0 and 359 degrees inclusive while still representing the same compass direction.

Direction reverse()

This method returns a Direction object that represents the direction directly opposite—that is, 180 degrees from—this Direction. For instance

```
Direction dir14 = dir2.reverse();
        // dir14 represents west (180 degrees
        // from east)
Direction dir15 = dir4.reverse();
        // dir15 represents 120 degrees
        // clockwise from north (180 degrees
        // from 300 degrees)
```

As with all Direction methods, the Direction returned will be adjusted so that its number of degrees falls between 0 and 359 inclusive.

String toString()

This method returns a String that is a human-readable representation of a Direction object. If this Direction is one of the eight standard compass directions, then the String will be the name of the direction. Otherwise, the String will be the number of degrees clockwise from north followed by the word "degrees". For instance, executing the code segment

```
System.out.println(dir1.toString());
        // dir1 represents north
System.out.println(dir13.toString());
        // dir13 represents 20 degrees
        // clockwise from north
```

results in the output

```
North
20 degrees
```

static Direction randomDirection()

This method creates and returns a new random Direction object. For instance

```
Direction dir16 = Direction.randomDirection();
        // dir16 represents a random direction
        // between 0 and 359 degrees inclusive
```

Note that because randomDirection is a static method, it is called using the ClassName.method() rather than the objectName.method() paradigm.

EnvDisplay Interface

The EnvDisplay interface defines how the simulation displays the environment. Note that because it is an interface, it neither provides code nor defines how the environment should be displayed. It only requires that a class implementing the EnvDisplay interface provide the showEnv method, which does the work of displaying the environment

```
public interface EnvDisplay
{
    void showEnv();
}
```

The display class provided with the case study is the SimpleMBSDisplay. It implements the EnvDisplay interface and draws a very rudimentary graphics representation of the environment when the showEnv method is called.

Note that you do not need to know how the environment is displayed, only that it is displayed when showEnv is called.

RandNumGenerator Class

The RandNumGenerator class works hand in hand with the Random class in the Java library and is explained in the java.util.Random section below.

Debug Class

The Debug class is used to help verify the correct operation of a program. While the Debug class is a useful tool for learning the Case Study and you should know how to call the methods in the class, you do not need to know how the Debug class is implemented and you will not be asked to write Debug statements on the AP exam.

Note that all of the methods of the Debug class are static, which means that they are called using the ClassName.method() rather than the objectName.method() paradigm. For instance

```
Debug.turnOn();
...
Debug.println("This is a debugging message.");
...
Debug.turnOff();
```

static boolean isOn()

This method returns true if debugging is turned on. Otherwise it returns false.

static boolean isOff()

This method returns true if debugging is turned off. Otherwise it returns false.

static void turnOn()

Turns on debugging. Until turned off, it calls to Debug.print and Debug.println will be displayed.

static void turnOff()

Turns off debugging. Until turned on, it calls to Debug.print and Debug.println will not be displayed.

static void restoreState()

This method restores the debugging state (on or off) to what it was immediately before the last call to Debug.turnOn or Debug.turnOff. This is often used in the following situation:

```
public void someMethod()
{
        Debug.turnOn();      // Turns on debugging
        // The body of the method including several
        // Debug.print statements
        Debug.restoreState();     // Restores the previous
                                  // debugging state
}
```

The call to Debug.restoreState sets the debugging state to whatever it was when someMethod was called. Thus, if it was off, debugging will be turned on for someMethod and then turned off when someMethod completes execution. If debugging was on, then it will remain on when someMethod completes execution.

static void print(String message)

If debugging is turned on, the print method outputs the given message using System.out.print. Otherwise the print method does nothing.

static void println(String message)

If debugging is turned on, the println method outputs the given message using System.out.println. Otherwise the println method does nothing.

JAVA LIBRARY CLASSES

In addition to the String class, three classes from the Java library are used in the case study. Be sure to know the core methods and constants for each class as listed below.

java.util.ArrayList Class

The ArrayList class in the Java library is a collection class that provides methods that manipulate an arbitrarily sized list of objects. You are responsible for knowing the following methods:

boolean add(Object obj)

Adds the given object to the end of this list. Returns true.

void add(int index, Object obj)

Adds the given object at the specified position in this list. Objects in this list (if any) that are at or after the specified position are shifted one position further down in the list. Note that index is a zero-based position; the first element of this list is at position 0.

Object get(int index)

Returns the object at the given position in this list. Note that index is a zero-based position; the first element of this list is at position 0.

Object remove(int index)

Removes and returns the object at the specified position in this list. Note that index is a zero-based position; the first element of this list is at position 0.

boolean remove(Object obj)

Removes the given object from this list. Returns true if the object was actually in the list; otherwise returns false.

Object set(int index, Object obj)

Replaces the object at the specified position in this list with the given object. Returns the object that was replaced. Note that index is a zero-based position; the first element of this list is at position 0.

int size()

Returns the number of objects in this list.

java.awt.Color Class

The Color class in the Java library encapsulates a color as an ordered triplet representing the amounts of red, green, and blue in the color. You can either use the eleven predefined constant colors: Color.black, Color.blue, Color.cyan, Color.gray, Color.green, Color.magenta, Color.orange, Color.pink, Color.red, Color.white, and Color.yellow, or you can create your own colors by using the Color constructor: Color(int r, int g, int b).

For example, to create a color that is a shade of deep purple, you would write

```
Color purple = new Color(100, 0, 100);
```

The parameters *r*, *g*, and *b* can range between 0 and 255 with 0 representing the absence of red, green, or blue.

java.util.Random Class

The Random class in the Java library provides methods that return either a random integer value or a random double value. While there are many methods in the Random class, you are responsible for knowing only two of them: nextInt and nextDouble.

int nextInt(int n)

Returns a random integer between 0 and *n* – 1. This method is most often used to pick a random index for selection from an array or ArrayList. See the Fish class for an example of using the nextInt method.

double nextDouble()

Returns a random double value between 0.0 and 1.0. This method is most often used to pick a random probability between 0 and 1. See the SlowFish class for an example of using the nextDouble method.

These two methods work closely with the RandNumGenerator class. This class provides a static method, getInstance, that returns a reference to the same Random object each time. This provides a better (i.e., more random) source of random numbers.

The following code illustrates how the RandNumGenerator method getInstance and the Random methods nextInt and nextDouble should be used:

```
Random randNumGen = RandNumGenerator.getInstance();
// get a random integer between 0 and 3
int randomInteger = randNumGen.nextInt(4);
// get a random value between 0.0 and 1.0
double randomDouble = randNumGen.nextDouble();
```

CORE CLASSES AND INTERFACES

While the utility classes and interfaces listed above can stand alone and can be used outside of the case study, the core classes and interfaces below are deeply intertwined and represent the heart of the program. They provide the abstractions for fish, the environment that the fish live in, and the simulation itself.

Because each core class refers to each of the other classes many times, you should adopt the following strategy for studying this part of the case study:

1. Read through this entire section once to get an overview of the core classes. Don't worry if everything is not clear; your goal is to get a feel for classes, their data and methods, and how the classes call each other.

2. Work through the Case Study starting with the main program. Each time a constructor or method is called, jump to the relevant section of the code and continue working through the program. Execute one, two, or as many steps of the simulation as necessary until you feel comfortable with the program.

3. Read through this entire section one more time for a final overview of the core classes. Now that you have done the detail work, your perspective will have changed and you should find that you understand how each class, constructor, and method fits in to the entire case study.

By following this strategy, you will find that what looks to be a very long and complex program is actually quite well-organized and logical.

Note that when the source code for the core classes is presented below, any comments and debugging statements have been removed from the code to allow you to focus on the heart of the code. You may, however, also wish to review the source code available in this book.

Main Program

There are several different main programs provided by The College Board for the Marine Biology Simulation Case Study. While you do not need to know the detail of *any* of the main programs, you should have an overview of what a typical main program contains.

In general, the main program for the case study is responsible for the following actions:

1. Constructing an environment. Typically this is either a BoundedEnv or an UnboundedEnv, but could be a new environment class that implements the Environment interface.

2. Constructing the fish that live in the environment. These will be standard Fish, DarterFish, or SlowFish objects, or other instances of a class derived from one of these three types of fish.

3. Constructing the display that shows the state of the environment. This will be an instance of a class that implements the EnvDisplay interface.

4. Constructing an instance of the Simulation class and stepping through the simulation.

In other words, the main program sets up the objects needed in the case study and runs the simulation.

Simulation Class

The `Simulation` class controls the simulation by interacting with the environment and the display. The simulation is made up of a series of "timesteps". In each timestep, the simulation asks every fish in the environment to act and then displays the results.

Note that while the simulation controls "the big picture," it does *not* know about the details of how fish act, how the environment stores the fish, or how the environment is displayed.

Private Data

There are two pieces of private data stored by a Simulation object: the environment and the display.

```
private Environment theEnv;
private EnvDisplay theDisplay;
```

The environment is needed by the step method to get all of the fish in the environment so that the simulation can tell them to act. The display is needed so that the simulation can show the results after each step of the simulation.

Note that both the environment and the display are used only by the Simulation class and are not available to other classes via accessor methods.

Simulation Constructor

The constructor for the Simulation class is passed an environment and a display, stores them in its private data, and then asks the display to show the environment.

```
public Simulation(Environment env, EnvDisplay display)
{
    theEnv = env;
    theDisplay = display;
    theDisplay.showEnv();
}
```

void step()

The step method of the Simulation class asks the environment for an array of fish, loops through them asking each one to act, and then asks the display to show the environment.

```
Locatable[] theFishes = theEnv.allObjects();
for (int index = 0; index < theFishes.length; index++)
{
    ((Fish) theFishes[index]).act();
}
theDisplay.showEnv();
```

It is important to note that the fish in the environment are returned in an array of Locatable objects rather than Fish objects. Therefore, each Locatable object in the array must be cast to a Fish object before being asked to act.

ENVIRONMENT INTERFACE

An environment represents the marine setting in which fish live in the simulation. The environment stores the fish and provides methods that allow other classes to add and remove fish from the environment, get a list of all fish in the environment, find out about the various locations in the environment, and retrieve information about the environment itself.

The Environment interface provides the method signatures for a generic environment in the case study. Different types of environments such as the BoundedEnv and UnboundedEnv classes implement this interface.

If you are taking the A exam, you need only know the functionality of the generic Environment interface. If you are taking the AB exam, you also need to understand how the BoundedEnv and UnboundedEnv classes are implemented.

Note that the Environment interface does not specify constructors or private data; these are part of the classes that implement the Environment interface.

int numRows()

Returns the number of rows in this environment. (Returns –1 if the environment is unbounded.)

int numCols()

Returns the number of columns in this environment. (Returns –1 if the environment is unbounded.)

boolean isValid(Location loc)

Returns true if loc is a valid location in this environment; returns false otherwise.

int numCellSides()

Returns the number of sides around each cell. In the environments used in the Case Study, the method numCellSides always returns 4. It is possible, however, that a free-response question may ask you to consider an environment that contains something other than square (four-sided) cells. If the environment contained, for instance, hexagonal cells, numCellSides would return 6.

int numAdjacentNeighbors()

Returns the number of potential neighboring locations for any location in this environment. Typically, this method returns either 4 or 8. Note the difference between numCellSides and numAdjacentNeighbors.

Direction randomDirection()

If numAdjacentNeighbors() is 4, randomDirection returns, at random, one of four directions: Direction.NORTH, Direction.SOUTH, Direction.EAST, or Direction.WEST.

If numAdjacentNeighbors() is 8, randomDirection returns, at random, one of eight directions: Direction.NORTH, Direction.SOUTH, Direction.EAST, Direction.WEST, Direction.NORTHEAST, Direction.NORTHWEST, Direction.SOUTHEAST, or Direction.SOUTHWEST.

Direction getDirection(Location fromLoc, Location toLoc)

Returns the direction from fromLoc to toLoc. For instance

```
Direction dir = getDirection(new Location(3, 4),
                             new Location(3, 3));
```

After executing the code segment, dir will represent the direction west.

Location getNeighbor(Location fromLoc, Direction compassDir)

Returns the location that is in the given direction from the given location. For example

```
Location neighborLoc = getNeighbor(new Location(3, 4),
                                   Direction.WEST);
```

After executing the code segment, neighborLoc will hold the location (3, 3).

ArrayList neighborsOf(Location ofLoc)

Returns an ArrayList of valid Locations that are next to the given location. For example

```
ArrayList theList = neighborsOf(new Location(0, 5));
```

If numAdjacentNeighbors() equals 4, then theList will contain the Locations: (0, 4), (0, 6), and (1, 5). Note that there are only three locations because the location to the west of (0, 5) is not valid.

If numAdjacentNeighbors() equals 8, then theList will contain the Locations: (0, 4), (0, 6), (1, 4), (1, 5), and (1, 6). Note that there are only five locations because the locations to the northwest, west, and southwest of (0, 5) are not valid.

int numObjects()

Returns the number objects (fish) in this environment.

Locatable[] allObjects()

Returns an array of the objects (fish) in this environment. The length of the array is equal to numObjects(). The order in which the objects are returned depends on the implementation of the Environment interface.

boolean isEmpty(Location loc)

Returns true if the given location in this environment is both valid and empty. Returns false otherwise. A location is empty if it does not contain a fish.

Locatable objectAt(Location loc)

Returns the object (fish) at the given location in this environment. Returns null if loc is either not valid or is empty.

void add(Locatable obj)

Adds the given object (fish) to this environment at its location. The location where the fish is added is determined by asking the fish! A precondition of this method is that the location where the fish is to be added must be valid and empty.

void remove(Locatable obj)

Removes the given object (fish) from this environment. A precondition of this method is that the fish actually exists in this environment.

void recordMove(Locatable obj, Location oldLoc)

Updates this environment to show that the given object (fish) has moved to a new location. Note that the old location of the fish is passed to the recordMove method; the new location is determined by asking the fish for its location.

BOUNDEDENV CLASS (AB ONLY)

One way to implement the Environment interface is to store the fish in a two-dimensional array. The BoundedEnv class is such an implementation.

Note that the BoundedEnv class actually extends the SquareEnvironment abstract class; SquareEnvironment actually implements the Environment interface. The SquareEnvironment class provides the code for methods that do not depend on how the fish are stored in the environment—such as the getDirection method. Because it is an abstract class, SquareEnvironment objects cannot be constructed; you must derive another class such as the BoundedEnv or UnboundedEnv classes from the SquareEnvironment class.

While you do need to know how to use all of the methods in the Environment interface, you do not need to know how the methods in the SquareEnvironment abstract class are implemented. You do, however, need to know and understand the implementation of the methods in the BoundedEnv class.

Private Data

Each BoundedEnv object stores two items in its private data: a two-dimensional array of locatable objects (fish), and the number of objects in this environment.

```
private Locatable[][] theGrid;
private int objectCount;
```

Note that because theGrid contains Locatable objects rather than Fish, the BoundedEnv does not need to know the type of the Locatable objects. While these objects are typically fish, they could be objects of any class that implements the Locatable interface. Thus, if the Case Study were extended by designing a new type of marine animal—for example, an octopus—the BoundedEnv class would not need to be modified.

BoundedEnv Constructor

The constructor for the BoundedEnv class is passed two parameters: the number of rows and the number of columns in the environment. It calls its superclass's constructor (the constructor for the SquareEnvironment class) and initializes the array of Locatable objects and the number of objects in this environment.

```
public BoundedEnv(int rows, int cols)
{
        super();
        theGrid = new Locatable[rows][cols];
        objectCount = 0;
}
```

int numRows()

Returns the number of rows in this environment. In a BoundedEnv, the number of rows is the length of the two-dimensional array.

```
public int numRows()
{
        return theGrid.length;
}
```

int numCols()

Returns the number of columns in this environment. In a BoundedEnv, the number of columns is the length of the first row of the two-dimensional array.

```
public int numCols()
{
        return theGrid[0].length;
}
```

boolean isValid(Location loc)

Returns true if loc is a valid location in this environment; returns false otherwise. In a BoundedEnv, a valid location is one in which the row number is between zero and the number of rows minus one inclusive and the column number is between zero and the number of columns minus one inclusive.

```
public boolean isValid(Location loc)
{
        if (loc == null)
                return false;
        return (0 <= loc.row() && loc.row() < numRows())
                &&
                (0 <= loc.col() && loc.col() < numCols());
}
```

int numObjects()

Returns the number of objects in this environment. Note that numObjects is an accessor method for the private data objectCount.

```
public int numObjects()
{
        return objectCount;
}
```

Locatable[] allObjects()

Returns an array of the Locatable objects (fish) in this environment. The length of the array is equal to numObjects(). In a BoundedEnv, the objects are returned in left-to-right, top-to-bottom order (in other words, the objects in the first row are returned in left-to-right order followed by the objects in the second row in left-to-right order, and so on).

```
public Locatable[] allObjects()
{
        Locatable[] theObjects =
                new Locatable[numObjects()];
        int tempObjectCount = 0;
        for (int r = 0; r < numRows(); r++)
        {
                for (int c = 0; c < numCols(); c++)
                {
                        Locatable obj = theGrid[r][c];
                        if (obj != null)
                        {
                                theObjects[tempObjectCount] = obj;
                                tempObjectCount++;
                        }
                }
        }
        return theObjects;
}
```

boolean isEmpty(Location loc)

Returns true if the given location in this environment is both valid and empty. Returns false otherwise.

A location is empty if it does not contain a fish. In a BoundedEnv, an empty location is represented by null in the corresponding element of theGrid.

```
public boolean isEmpty(Location loc)
{
        return isValid(loc) && objectAt(loc) == null;
}
```

Locatable objectAt(Location loc)

Returns the object (fish) at the given location in this environment. Returns null if loc is either not valid or is empty. Remember that empty elements in theGrid are represented by null.

```
public Locatable objectAt(Location loc)
{
        if (!isValid(loc))
                return null;
        return theGrid[loc.row()][loc.col()];
}
```

String toString()

The toString method returns a String that contains a human-readable representation of all of the objects in this environment.

It gets a list of all of the objects by calling its own allObjects method. It then builds a String by starting with the number of objects in this environment and the results of asking each object for its human-readable representation.

Note that the call to toString below is not a recursive call; it is a call to a Locatable object's (fish's) toString method.

```java
public String toString()
{
    Locatable[] theObjects = allObjects();
    String s = "Environment contains " +
                numObjects() + "objects: ";
    for (int index = 0;
            index < theObjects.length; index++)
    {
        s += theObjects[index].toString() + " ";
    }
    return s;
}
```

void add(Locatable obj)

Adds the given object (fish) to this environment at its location. The location where the fish is added is determined by calling the location method of the Fish class. A precondition of this method is that the location where the fish is to be added must be valid and empty.

The add method first checks its precondition and throws an IllegalArgumentException if the given object's location is not valid and empty. It then adds the given fish to the two-dimensional array, theGrid, and increments the private data field, objectCount, representing the number of objects in this environment.

```java
public void add(Locatable obj)
{
    Location loc = obj.location();
    if (! isEmpty(loc))
        throw new IllegalArgumentException(
            "Location " + loc +
            " is not a valid empty location");
    theGrid[loc.row()][loc.col()] = obj;
    objectCount++;
}
```

void remove(Locatable obj)

Removes the given object (fish) from this environment. A precondition of this method is that the fish actually exists in this environment.

The remove method first checks its precondition and throws an IllegalArgumentException if the given fish doesn't exist in this environment. If it does exist, it sets the fish's location in the two-dimensional array, theGrid, to null and decrements the private data field, objectCount, representing the number of objects in this environment.

```
public void remove(Locatable obj)
{
        Location loc = obj.location();
        if (objectAt(loc) != obj)
                throw new IllegalArgumentException(
                        "Cannot remove " + obj +
                        "; not there");
        theGrid[loc.row()][loc.col()] = null;
        objectCount--;
}
```

void recordMove(Locatable obj, Location oldLoc)

Updates this environment to show that the given object (fish) has moved to a new location. Note that the old location of the fish is passed to the recordMove method; the new location is determined by asking the fish for its location. A precondition of this method is that the given object's new location is valid and empty.

The recordMove method first checks its precondition and throws an IllegalArgumentException if the given fish's new location is not valid and empty in this environment. If it is valid and empty, the recordMove method sets the fish's old location in the two-dimensional array, theGrid, to null and stores the fish in its new location in the array.

```
public void recordMove(Locatable obj, Location oldLoc)
{
        Location newLoc = obj.location();
        if (newLoc.equals(oldLoc))
                return;
        Locatable foundObject = objectAt(oldLoc);
        if (! (foundObject == obj && isEmpty(newLoc)))
                throw new IllegalArgumentException(
                        "Precondition violation moving " +
                        obj + " from " + oldLoc);
        theGrid[newLoc.row()][newLoc.col()] = obj;
        theGrid[oldLoc.row()][oldLoc.col()] = null;
}
```

UNBOUNDEDENV CLASS (AB ONLY)

A second way to implement the Environment interface is to store the fish in an ArrayList. In this implementation, there is no predetermined size for the environment (as there is in the BoundedEnv class). The UnboundedEnv class is such an implementation.

Note that the BoundedEnv class actually extends the SquareEnvironment abstract class; SquareEnvironment actually implements the Environment interface. The SquareEnvironment class provides the code for methods that do not depend on how the fish are stored in the environment—such as the getDirection method. Because it is an abstract class, SquareEnvironment objects cannot be constructed; you must derive another class such as the BoundedEnv or UnboundedEnv classes from the SquareEnvironment class.

While you do need to know how to use all of the methods in the Environment interface, you do not need to know how the methods in the SquareEnvironment abstract class are implemented. You do, however, need to know and understand the implementation of the methods in the UnboundedEnv class.

Private Data

Each UnboundedEnv object stores only one item in its private data: an ArrayList containing all of the Locatable objects (fish) in this environment.

```
private ArrayList objectList;
```

As with theGrid in the BoundedEnv environment, because objectList contains Locatable objects rather than Fish, the UnboundedEnv does not need to know anything about what type of Locatable objects they are. While these objects are typically fish, they could be objects of any class that implements the Locatable interface. Thus, if the Case Study were extended by designing a new type of marine animal—for example, an octopus—the UnboundedEnv class would not need to be modified.

UnboundedEnv Constructor

The constructor for the UnboundedEnv class is not passed any parameters. It calls its super class's constructor (the constructor for the SquareEnvironment class) and initializes its private data.

```
public UnboundedEnv()
{
    super();
    objectList = new ArrayList();
    objectCount = 0;
}
```

int numRows()

Returns –1 because unbounded environments do not have a fixed number of rows.

```
public int numRows()
{
    return -1;
}
```

int numCols()

Returns –1 because unbounded environments do not have a fixed number of columns.

```
public int numCols()
{
    return -1;
}
```

boolean isValid(Location loc)

In an unbounded environment, any non-null location is valid.

```
public boolean isValid(Location loc)
{
    return loc != null;
}
```

int numObjects()

Returns the number of objects in this environment. The size of the ArrayList objectList is the number of objects.

```
public int numObjects()
{
        return objectList.size();
}
```

Locatable[] allObjects()

Returns an array of the Locatable objects (fish) in this environment. The length of the array is equal to numObjects(). Note that in an UnboundedEnv, the objects are not returned in any particular order.

```
public Locatable[] allObjects()
{
        Locatable[] objectArray =
                new Locatable[objectList.size()];
        for (int index = 0;
                index < objectList.size(); index++)
        {
                objectArray[index] =
                        (Locatable) objectList.get(index);
        }
        return objectArray;
}
```

boolean isEmpty(Location loc)

Returns true if the given location in this environment is empty. Returns false otherwise.

A location is empty if it does not contain a fish. In an UnboundedEnv, an empty location doesn't appear in objectList.

```
public boolean isEmpty(Location loc)
{
        return (objectAt(loc) == null);
}
```

Locatable objectAt(Location loc)

Returns the object (fish) at the given location in this environment. Returns null if loc is either not valid or is empty.

The method objectAt first gets the index of the given location in objectList by calling the private method indexOf of the UnboundedEnv class. If the location exists, then the resulting index is used to get and return the actual object from objectList; if not, objectAt returns null.

```
public Locatable objectAt(Location loc)
{
        int index = indexOf(loc);
        if (index == -1)
                return null;
        return (Locatable) objectList.get(index);
}
```

String toString()

The toString method returns a String that contains a human-readable representation of all of the objects in this environment.

The UnboundedEnv version of toString is exactly the same as the BoundedEnv version. It gets a list of all of the objects by calling its own allObjects method. It then builds a String by starting with the number of objects in this environment and the results of asking each object for its human-readable representation.

Note that the call to toString below is not a recursive call; it is a call to a Locatable object's (fish's) toString method.

```
public String toString()
{
    Locatable[] theObjects = allObjects();
    String s = "Environment contains " +
               numObjects() + "objects: ";
    for (int index = 0;
         index < theObjects.length; index++)
    {
        s += theObjects[index].toString() + " ";
    }
    return s;
}
```

void add(Locatable obj)

Adds the given object (fish) to this environment at its location. The location where the fish is added is determined by calling the location method of the Fish class. A precondition of this method is that the location where the fish is to be added must be valid and empty.

The add method first checks its precondition and throws an IllegalArgumentException if the given object's location is not valid and empty. If it is valid and empty, the add method adds the fish to this environment's list of objects, objectList.

```
public void add(Locatable obj)
{
    Location loc = obj.location();
    if (! isEmpty(loc))
        throw new IllegalArgumentException(
            "Location " + loc +
            " is not a valid empty location");
    objectList.add(obj);
}
```

void remove(Locatable obj)

Removes the given object (fish) from this environment. A precondition of this method is that the fish actually exists in this environment.

The remove method first checks its precondition and throws an IllegalArgumentException if the given fish doesn't exist in this environment. If it does exist, the remove method removes the fish from this environment's list of objects, objectList.

```
        public void remove(Locatable obj)
        {
                int index = indexOf(obj.location());
                if (index == -1)
                        throw new IllegalArgumentException(
                                "Cannot remove " + obj +
                                "; not there");
                objectList.remove(index);
        }
```

void recordMove(Locatable obj, Location oldLoc)

Updates this environment to show that the given object (fish) has moved to a new location. Note that the old location of the fish is passed to the recordMove method; the new location is determined by asking the fish for its location. This method succeeds if there is only one fish at the new location in this environment and either the fish did not move or there are no fish at the old location in this environment.

The recordMove method first walks through this environment's ArrayList of objects, objectList, to count how many objects are at the fish's old location, oldLoc, and how many objects are at the fish's new location, obj.location(). It then throws an IllegalArgumentException if there is not exactly one object at the new location or if fish's location has changed and there are any objects at the fish's old location.

```
        public void recordMove(Locatable obj, Location oldLoc)
        {
                int objectsAtOldLoc = 0;
                int objectsAtNewLoc = 0;
                Locatable newLoc = obj.location();
                for (int index = 0;
                        index < objectList.size(); index++)
                {
                        Locatable thisObj =
                                (Locatable) objectList.get(index);
                        if (thisObj.location().equals(oldLoc))
                                objectsAtOldLoc++;
                        if (thisObj.location().equals(newLoc))
                                objectsAtNewLoc++;
                }
                if (! (objectsAtNewLoc == 1 &&
                        (oldLoc.equals(newLoc) ||
                         objectsAtOldLoc == 0)))
                {
                        throw new IllegalArgumentException(
                                "Precondition violation moving " +
                                obj + " from " + oldLoc);
                }
        }
```

int indexOf(Location loc)

The indexOf method is a helper method for an UnboundedEnv that returns the index in this environment's private data field objectList of the object with the given location.

It loops through the list of all of the objects in this environment. If the location of the current object in the list is equal to the given location, the indexOf method returns the index of that object. If no object in the list has the same location as the given object, the indexOf method returns –1.

Note that indexOf is a protected method, which means it can only be called by an UnboundedEnv or an object whose class is derived from an UnboundedEnv.

```
protected int indexOf(Location loc)
{
    for (int index = 0;
         index < objectList.size(); index++)
    {
        Locatable obj =
            (Locatable) objectList.get(index);
        if (obj.location().equals(loc))
            return index;
    }
    return -1;
}
```

FISH CLASS

The Fish class encapsulates the data and functionality of a standard fish in the Marine Biology Simulation. There are two versions of the Fish class: the original version and the version in which fish breed and die.

In the simple version, a Fish moves in every timestep of the simulation. A Fish moves by randomly picking an empty neighboring location in its environment and moving there. Note, however, that a Fish is not allowed to move backward.

In the version in which fish breed and die, a Fish first tries to breed. If it is not successful (based on a set probability and whether there are neighboring locations in which to add child fish), it tries to move as in the simple version.

After the Fish breeds or moves, the Fish may die according to a set probability.

Like any marine object in an environment, the Fish class implements the Locatable interface.

The Fish class is also the base class for the SlowFish and DarterFish classes.

Private Data

A Fish contains five standard private data fields and two additional private data fields if breeding and dying are implemented. The variable theEnv holds the environment in which a Fish lives. The variable myId holds the unique ID number for each Fish, which remains constant throughout the life of a Fish. The private data fields myLoc, myDir, and myColor store the location, direction, and color of the Fish respectively.

```
private Environment theEnv;
private int myId;
private Location myLoc;
private Direction myDir;
private Color myColor;
```

If breeding and dying are implemented for Fish, two additional private data fields are available. The variables probOfBreeding and probOfDying hold the percentage likelihood that this Fish will breed or die in each timestep.

```
private double probOfBreeding;
private double probOfDying;
```

Note, however, that probOfBreeding and probOfDying are not constants. Thus, one type of question involving the case study might be to modify the Fish class so that the probability of breeding or dying changes based on some parameter, such as a fish's age or its proximity to a certain location in the environment.

Finally, there is also one class data variable that is shared among all Fish objects that are constructed.

```
private static int nextAvailableID = 1;
```

This variable is the unique identifier that is assigned to the private data field myId when a Fish is constructed. Once myId has been given the value nextAvailableID in the initialize method, nextAvailableID is incremented so that it will have the correct value for the next Fish to be constructed.

Fish Constructors

There are three different Fish constructors. All three of the constructors call the initialize method of the Fish class to set the private data methods of the fish and to add this Fish to its environment.

The first constructor takes only two parameters: the environment and the location where the Fish is constructed. It initializes its private data fields with the environment, the location, a random direction, and a random color.

```
public Fish(Environment env, Location loc)
{
        initialize(env, loc,
                    env.randomDirection(), randomColor());
}
```

The second constructor takes three parameters: the environment, the location where the Fish is constructed, and the initial direction of the fish. It initializes its private data fields with the environment, the location, the direction, and a random color.

```
public Fish(Environment env, Location loc,
            Direction dir)
{
        initialize(env, loc, dir, randomColor());
}
```

The third constructor takes four parameters: the environment, the location where the Fish is constructed, the initial direction, and the initial color. It initializes the private data fields of the Fish appropriately.

```
public Fish(Environment env, Location loc,
            Direction dir, Color col)
{
        initialize(env, loc, dir, col);
}
```

void initialize(Environment env, Location loc, Direction dir, Color col)

The initialize method performs four functions for each of the constructors of the Fish class:

1. It sets the private data fields theEnv, myLoc, myDir, and myColor to the values of its parameters; env, loc, dir, and col respectively.

2. It sets myId to the class variable nextAvailableID and increments nextAvailableID.

3. It adds this Fish to its environment. Note that it does this by passing "this", representing this Fish, to the add method of theEnv.

4. It optionally sets the private data fields probOfBreeding and probOfDying appropriately.

```
private void initialize(Environment env, Location loc,
                                 Direction dir, Color col)
{
    theEnv = env;
    myId = nextAvailableID;
    nextAvailableID++;
    myLoc = loc;
    myDir = dir;
    myColor = col;
    theEnv.add(this);
    probOfBreeding = 1.0 / 7.0;
    probOfDying = 1.0 / 5.0;
}
```

Note that the initialize method is designated private so that it can only be called from a method or constructor of the Fish class. In fact, initialize is only called from the three Fish constructors.

Color randomColor()

A Fish that is constructed without specifying a color (called with the first or second constructor) is given a color at random. Recall from earlier in this section that a Color object is constructed by passing three integers between 0 and 255 inclusive. These parameters represent the amounts of red, green, and blue that make up the color.

To form a random color, the randomColor method generates three random integers between 0 and 255 inclusive and returns the Color constructed from those parameters.

```
protected Color randomColor()
{
    Random randNumGen =
         RandNumGenerator.getInstance();
    return new Color(randNumGen.nextInt(256),
                      randNumGen.nextInt(256),
                      randNumGen.nextInt(256));
}
```

Note that randomColor is a protected method, which means it can only be called by a Fish or an object whose class is derived from a Fish.

int id()

This accessor method returns the unique ID number for this fish.

```
public int id()
{
    return myId;
}
```

Environment environment()

Returns the environment of this fish.

```
public Environment environment()
{
    return theEnv;
}
```

Color color()

Returns the color of this fish.

```
public Color color()
{
    return myColor;
}
```

Location location()

Returns the current location of this fish.

```
public Location location()
{
    return myLoc;
}
```

Direction direction()

Returns the direction that this fish is facing.

```
public Direction direction()
{
    return myDir;
}
```

boolean isInEnv()

Returns true if this fish is still in its environment. Returns false otherwise.

A fish is in its environment if the fish is equal to the object at this fish's location in the environment. Note that == is used for comparing Fish because the objects and the private data of the objects need to be equivalent.

```
public boolean isInEnv()
{
    return environment().objectAt(location()) ==
            this;
}
```

String toString()

Returns a String containing a human-readable representation of a Fish consisting of its ID number, its location, and its direction.

```
public String toString()
{
    return id() +
            location().toString() +
            direction().toString();
}
```

void act()

The act method of the Fish class is called once during each timestep by the step method of the Simulation class to ask this Fish to act. A Fish acts as follows:

1. If this Fish is not in its environment—for instance, if it already has been removed from the environment—the act method returns without doing anything.

2. This Fish tries to breed by calling its breed method. If it does not breed successfully, this Fish tries to move by calling its move method.

3. This Fish finally decides whether it should die by getting a random number between 0.0 and 1.0. If that number is less than its probability of dying (as defined by its private data field probOfDying), then the Fish removes itself from its environment by calling its die method.

```
public void act()
{
    if (! isInEnv())
        return;
    if (! breed())
        move();
    Random randNumGen =
        RandNumGenerator.getInstance();
    if (randNumGen.nextDouble() < probOfDying)
        die();
}
```

boolean breed()

The breed method of the Fish class is called once during each timestep by the act method of the Fish class. A Fish breeds as follows:

1. This Fish first decides whether it should breed by getting a random number between 0.0 and 1.0. If that number is greater than or equal to its probability of breeding (as defined by its private data field probOfBreeding), then this Fish does not breed and the breed method returns false to indicate that this Fish did not successfully breed.

2. Otherwise this Fish tries to breed. A Fish breeds by first getting a list of its empty neighboring cells by calling its method emptyNeighbors. If this Fish has no empty neighboring cells, then the breed method returns false to indicate that this Fish did not successfully breed.

3. If there is at least one empty neighboring cell, then this Fish loops through the list of empty neighboring cells and constructs a new Fish at each location by calling the Fish method generateChild. The breed method then returns true to indicate that this Fish did breed successfully.

Note that breed is a protected method, which means it can only be called by a Fish or an object whose class is derived from a Fish.

```
protected boolean breed()
{
        Random randNumGen =
                RandNumGenerator.getInstance();
        if (randNumGen.nextDouble() >= probOfBreeding)
            return false;

        ArrayList emptyNbrs = emptyNeighbors();
        if (emptyNbrs.size() == 0)
            return false;
        for (int index = 0;
                index < emptyNbrs.size(); index++)
        {
            Location loc =
                    (Location) emptyNbrs.get(index);
            generateChild(loc);
        }
        return true;
}
```

void generateChild(Location loc)

The generateChild method of the Fish class creates a new Fish at the given location. The new Fish is constructed in the same environment and with the same color as this Fish and given a random direction.

Note that generateChild is a protected method, which means it can only be called by a Fish or an object whose class is derived from a Fish.

```
protected void generateChild(Location loc)
{
        Fish child =
            new Fish(environment(), loc,
                        environment().randomDirection(),
                        color());
}
```

void move()

The move method of the Fish class first calls its own nextLocation method. If the location returned is different from the current location of the Fish, then the Fish calls its own changeLocation method to change its location and changes its direction using its own changeDirection method if it turned in order to move. Otherwise, the Fish does not move.

Note that move is a protected method, which means it can only be called by a Fish or an object whose class is derived from a Fish.

```
protected void move()
{
        Location nextLoc = nextLocation();
        if (! nextLoc.equals(location()))
        {
                Location oldLoc = location();
                changeLocation(nextLoc);
                Direction newDir =
                        environment().getDirection(oldLoc,
                                                        nextLoc);
                changeDirection(newDir);
        }
}
```

Location nextLocation()

The nextLocation method of the Fish class first gets a list of empty cells (neighbors) around the current location of the Fish by calling its method emptyNeighbors. It then checks the cell immediately behind itself and removes it from the list of empty cells. If the list of empty cells is empty, then this Fish can't move and the nextLocation method returns the current location of this Fish. Otherwise, it returns a random cell in the list of empty cells.

Note that nextLocation is a protected method, which means it can only be called by a Fish or an object whose class is derived from a Fish.

```
protected Location nextLocation()
{
        ArrayList emptyNbrs = emptyNeighbors();
        Direction oppositeDir = direction().reverse();
        Location locationBehind =
                environment().getNeighbor(location(),
                                                oppositeDir);
        emptyNbrs.remove(locationBehind);
        if (emptyNbrs.size() == 0)
                return location();
        Random randNumGen =
                RandNumGenerator.getInstance();

        int randNum =
                randNumGen.nextInt(emptyNbrs.size());

        return (Location) emptyNbrs.get(randNum);
}
```

ArrayList emptyNeighbors()

In order to return an ArrayList containing empty locations (neighbors) of the current location of this Fish, the emptyNeighbors method of the Fish class first gets a list of all locations around its current location by calling the neighborsOf method of the Environment class. It then checks each of the locations in this list using the Environment method isEmpty and adds only the empty locations to a new ArrayList, which is then returned.

Note that emptyNeighbors is a protected method, which means it can only be called by a Fish or an object whose class is derived from a Fish.

```
protected ArrayList emptyNeighbors()
{
        ArrayList nbrs =
                environment().neighborsOf(location());
        ArrayList emptyNbrs = new ArrayList();
        for (int index = 0;
                index < nbrs.size(); index++)
        {
                Location loc = (Location) nbrs.get(index);
                if (environment().isEmpty(loc))
                        emptyNbrs.add(loc);
        }
        return emptyNbrs;
}
```

void changeLocation(Location newLoc)

The changeLocation method of the Fish class changes the location of this Fish by setting the private data field myLoc to the given location newLoc and then recording the change with the environment. Note that only changes of location need to be recorded with the environment; changing any other attribute of a Fish does not.

Note that changeLocation is a protected method, which means it can only be called by a Fish or an object whose class is derived from a Fish.

```
protected void changeLocation(Location newLoc)
{
        Location oldLoc = location();
        myLoc = newLoc;
        environment().recordMove(this, oldLoc);
}
```

void changeDirection(Direction newDir)

The changeDirection method of the Fish class changes the direction of this Fish by setting the private data field myDir to the given direction newDir.

Note that changeDirection is a protected method, which means it can only be called by a Fish or an object whose class is derived from a Fish.

```
protected void changeDirection(Direction newDir)
{
        myDir = newDir;
}
```

void die()

In order for a Fish to die it needs only to be removed from its environment. The die method of the Fish class does exactly that by asking the environment to remove this Fish. Note that the variable this, which is passed to the remove method of the environment, represents this Fish.

Once the die method is called by a Fish, that Fish should not attempt to change its location.

Note that die is a protected method, which means it can only be called by a Fish or an object whose class is derived from a Fish.

```
protected void die()
{
        environment().remove(this);
}
```

DarterFish Class

The DarterFish class extends the Fish class to simulate a new type of fish. In any given timestep, a DarterFish tries to move forward two cells if it can. If it can't move forward two cells, it tries to move forward one cell. If it can't move forward one cell, then it reverses direction but does not move.

Note that in order to move forward one or two cells, both the cell the DarterFish is moving to and any intervening cells must be empty.

In extending the Fish class, the DarterFish overrides the Fish constructors, the generateChild method, the move method, and the nextLocation method. It has no new private data fields.

DarterFish Constructors

Because there are three Fish constructors, there are also three DarterFish constructors.

The first constructor takes only two parameters: the environment and the location where the DarterFish is constructed, and calls the Fish constructor to create a Fish with the environment, the location, a random direction, and yellow as the color. Note that while Fish are given a random color if the color is not specified in the constructor, DarterFish are colored yellow if the color is not specified.

```
public DarterFish(Environment env, Location loc)
{
        super(env, loc,
                env.randomDirection(), Color.yellow);
}
```

The second constructor takes three parameters: the environment, the location where the DarterFish is constructed, and the initial direction, and calls the Fish constructor to create a Fish with the environment, the location, the direction, and yellow as the color.

```
public DarterFish(Environment env, Location loc,
                  Direction dir)
{
        super(env, loc, dir, Color.yellow);
}
```

The third constructor takes four parameters: the environment, the location where the DarterFish is constructed, the initial direction, and the initial color, and calls the Fish constructor to create the appropriate Fish.

```
public DarterFish(Environment env, Location loc,
                  Direction dir, Color col)
{
        super(env, loc, dir, col);
}
```

void generateChild(Location loc)

Like its counterpart in the Fish class, the generateChild method of the DarterFish class creates a new DarterFish at the given location. The new DarterFish is constructed in the same environment and with the same color as this DarterFish and given a random direction.

Note that generateChild is a protected method, which means it can only be called by a DarterFish or an object whose class is derived from a DarterFish.

```
protected void generateChild(Location loc)
{
        DarterFish child =
          new DarterFish(environment(), loc,
                          environment().randomDirection(),
                          color());
}
```

void move()

The move method of the DarterFish class first calls its own nextLocation method. If the location returned is the same as the current location of the DarterFish, then the DarterFish reverses its direction. Otherwise, the DarterFish changes its location to the location returned by the nextLocation method.

Note that move is a protected method, which means it can only be called by a DarterFish or an object whose class is derived from a DarterFish.

```
protected void move()
{
        Location nextLoc = nextLocation();
        if (! nextLoc.equals(location()))
                changeLocation(nextLoc);
        else
                changeDirection(direction().reverse());
}
```

Location nextLocation()

The nextLocation method of the DarterFish class first calculates the locations of the first and second cells in front of the current location of the DarterFish. If both are empty, it returns the second cell's location. If only the cell directly in front of the DarterFish is empty, the nextLocation method returns the location of that cell. Otherwise the nextLocation method returns the current location of the DarterFish.

Note that nextLocation is a protected method, which means it can only be called by a DarterFish or an object whose class is derived from a DarterFish.

```
protected Location nextLocation()
{
        Environment env = environment();
        Location oneInFront =
                env.getNeighbor(location(), direction());
        Location twoInFront =
                env.getNeighbor(oneInFront, direction());
        if (env.isEmpty(oneInFront))
        {
                if (env.isEmpty(twoInFront))
                        return twoInFront;
                else
                        return oneInFront;
        }
        return location();
}
```

SlowFish Class

The SlowFish class also extends the Fish class to simulate a new type of fish. A SlowFish moves like a standard Fish except that in any given timestep, it has only a 20 percent (1 in 5) chance of moving.

In extending the Fish class, the SlowFish overrides the Fish constructors, the generateChild method, and the nextLocation method. It has one new private data field, which stores the probability of moving in a given timestep.

Private Data

A SlowFish contains a new private data field, probOfMoving, which represents the likelihood that a SlowFish moves in a given timestep of the simulation. The value is set by the SlowFish constructors and is not changed during the Case Study.

```
private double probOfMoving;
```

Note, however, that probOfMoving is not a constant. Thus, one type of question involving the case study might be to modify the SlowFish class so that the probability of moving changes based on some parameter, such as a fish's age or its proximity to a certain location in the environment.

SlowFish Constructors

Because there are three Fish constructors, there are also three SlowFish constructors.

The first constructor takes only two parameters: the environment and the location where the Slow-Fish is constructed, and calls the Fish constructor to create a Fish with the environment, the location, a random direction, and red as the color. Note that while Fish are given a random color, if the color is not specified in the constructor, SlowFish are colored red if the color is not specified. In this constructor, the probability of moving is set to 20 percent.

```
public SlowFish(Environment env, Location loc)
{
        super(env, loc,
                env.randomDirection(), Color.red);
        probOfMoving = 1.0 / 5.0;
}
```

The second constructor takes three parameters: the environment, the location where the SlowFish is constructed, and the initial direction, and calls the Fish constructor to create a Fish with the environment, the location, the direction, and red as the color. The probability of moving is set to 20 percent.

```
public SlowFish(Environment env, Location loc,
                Direction dir)
{
    super(env, loc, dir, Color.red);
    probOfMoving = 1.0/5.0;
}
```

The third constructor takes four parameters: the environment, the location where the SlowFish is constructed, the initial direction, and the initial color, and calls the Fish constructor to create the appropriate Fish. The probability of moving is set to 20 percent.

```
public SlowFish(Environment env, Location loc,
                Direction dir, Color col)
{
    super(env, loc, dir, col);
    probOfMoving = 1.0/5.0;
}
```

void generateChild(Location loc)

Like its counterparts in the Fish and DarterFish classes, the generateChild method of the SlowFish class creates a new SlowFish at the given location. The new SlowFish is constructed in the same environment and with the same color as this SlowFish and given a random direction.

Note that generateChild is a protected method, which means it can only be called by a SlowFish or an object whose class is derived from a SlowFish.

```
protected void generateChild(Location loc)
{
    SlowFish child =
        new SlowFish(environment(), loc;
                     environment().randomDirection(),
                     color());
}
```

Location nextLocation()

The nextLocation method of the SlowFish class first decides whether this fish should move during this timestep. If it should move, it gets and returns its next location by calling the nextLocation of the Fish class. If it decides not to move, it returns its current location.

The SlowFish decides whether it should move by getting a random number between 0.0 and 1.0. If that number is less than its probability of moving (as defined by its private data field probOfMoving), then the SlowFish moves.

Note that nextLocation is a protected method which means it can only be called by a SlowFish or an object whose class is derived from a SlowFish.

```
protected Location nextLocation()
{
    Random randNumGen =
        RandNumGenerator.getInstance();
    if (randNumGen.nextDouble() < probOfMoving)
        return super.nextLocation();
    else
        return location();
}
```

DATA FILES

The College Board provides a working example of the Marine Biology Simulation Case Study program that displays the environment in a graphical user interface. The main method for this program is in the MBSGUI (Marine Biology Simulation Graphical User Interface) class.

Note that while the MBSGUI class is not tested on the AP exam, it is useful to understand the structure of the data files so that you can experiment with the case study.

A data file is a text-based configuration file that provides information about the environment and the fish in the environment.

The first line of the file specifies the type of environment (bounded or unbounded) and, if bounded, the number of rows and columns in the environment. For instance

```
bounded 4 7
```

specifies a bounded environment with four rows and seven columns, while

```
unbounded
```

specifies an unbounded environment. Subsequent lines in the file define the type, location, and direction of fish in the environment. For example, the lines

```
Fish 6 5 North
SlowFish 3 4 South
DarterFish 10 10 East
```

define three fish:

1. A standard Fish at location (5, 5) facing north.

2. A SlowFish at location (3, 4) facing south.

3. A DarterFish at location (10, 10) facing east.

To use a data file with the MBSGUI class, run the program and then choose "Open environment file…" from the "File" menu and select the data file to open.

TYPES OF QUESTIONS

There will be at least five multiple-choice questions and one free-response question on the AP exam concerning the Marine Biology Simulation Case Study. Questions will cover topics such as:

1. Modifying the case study according to a change in the program specification. For instance, you may be asked to change the behavior of a Fish.

2. Extending the case study to provide new functionality. For example, you may be asked to extend the Fish class by creating a DiagonalFish that moves only diagonally.

3. Choosing the best design among several alternatives. For instance, you may be asked to decide the best data structure to store Fish in an Environment.

4. Choosing among different strategies for extending the case study. For example, you may be asked to create a new marine animal that is not a fish, but behaves in a manner similar to a DarterFish, and asked whether it would be better to extend the Fish class, extend the DarterFish class, or create a new class.

5. Understanding how the case study program works. For instance, you may be asked to determine how many possible configurations can occur in one or two steps of the simulation given an initial configuration of fish.

6. Creating test data. For example, you may be given a section of code and asked which set of test data will best show that the code works as specified.

Work through the practice problems in The College Board's overview of the Marine Biology Simulation Case Study and do the questions on the practice exams in this book. Because almost 20 percent of the AP exam concerns the case study, a thorough knowledge and understanding of the case study can easily make a one- or even two-point difference in your final AP score.

SOURCE CODE

SIMULATION.JAVA

```
// AP(r) Computer Science Marine Biology Simulation:
// The Simulation class is copyright(c) 2002 College Entrance
// Examination Board (www.collegeboard.com).
//
// This class is free software; you can redistribute it and/or modify
// it under the terms of the GNU General Public License as published by
// the Free Software Foundation.
//
// This class is distributed in the hope that it will be useful,
// but WITHOUT ANY WARRANTY; without even the implied warranty of
// MERCHANTABILITY or FITNESS FOR A PARTICULAR PURPOSE.  See the
// GNU General Public License for more details.
```

```java
/**
 *   AP&reg; Computer Science Marine Biology Simulation:<br>
 *   A <code>Simulation</code> object controls a simulation of fish
 *   movement in an <code>Environment</code>.
 *
 *   <p>
 *   The <code>Simulation</code> class is
 *   copyright&copy; 2002 College Entrance Examination Board
 *   (www.collegeboard.com).
 *
 *   @author Alyce Brady
 *   @version 1 July 2002
 *   @see Environment
 *   @see EnvDisplay
 *   @see Fish
 **/
public class Simulation
{

    // Instance Variables: Encapsulated data for each simulation object
    private Environment theEnv;
    private EnvDisplay  theDisplay;
    /** Constructs a <code>Simulation</code> object for a particular
     *   environment.
     *   @param env      the environment on which the simulation will run
     *   @param display an object that knows how to display the environment
     **/
    public Simulation(Environment env, EnvDisplay display)
    {
        theEnv = env;
        theDisplay = display;
        // Display the initial state of the simulation.
        theDisplay.showEnv();
        Debug.println("-------- Initial Configuration --------");
        Debug.println(theEnv.toString());
        Debug.println("---------------------------------------");
    }
    /** Runs through a single step of this simulation. **/
    public void step()
    {
        // Get all the fish in the environment and ask each
        // one to perform the actions it does in a timestep.
        Locatable[] theFishes = theEnv.allObjects();
        for ( int index = 0; index < theFishes.length; index++ )
        {
            ((Fish)theFishes[index]).act();
        }
        // Display the state of the simulation after this timestep.
        theDisplay.showEnv();
        Debug.println(theEnv.toString());
        Debug.println("-------- End of Timestep --------");
    }
}
```

ENVIRONMENT.JAVA

```
// AP(r) Computer Science Marine Biology Simulation:
// The Environment interface is copyright(c) 2002 College Entrance
// Examination Board (www.collegeboard.com).
//
// This class is free software; you can redistribute it and/or modify
// it under the terms of the GNU General Public License as published by
// the Free Software Foundation.
//
// This class is distributed in the hope that it will be useful,
// but WITHOUT ANY WARRANTY; without even the implied warranty of
// MERCHANTABILITY or FITNESS FOR A PARTICULAR PURPOSE.  See the
// GNU General Public License for more details.
import java.util.ArrayList;
/**
 *   AP&reg; Computer Science Marine Biology Simulation:<br>
 *   <code>Environment</code> provides an interface for a two-dimensional,
 *   grid-like environment containing locatable objects.  For example,
 *   it could be an environment of fish for a marine biology simulation.
 *
 *   <p>
 *   The <code>Environment</code> interface is
 *   copyright&copy; 2002 College Entrance Examination Board
 *   (www.collegeboard.com).
 *
 *   @author Alyce Brady
 *   @author APCS Development Committee
 *   @version 1 July 2002
 *   @see Direction
 *   @see Locatable
 *   @see Location
 **/
public interface Environment
{
    // accessor methods for determining environment dimensions
        /** Returns number of rows in this environment.
         *   @return    the number of rows, or -1 if the environment is unbounded
         **/
        int numRows();
        /** Returns number of columns in this environment.
         *   @return    the number of columns, or -1 if the environment is unbounded
         **/
        int numCols();
    // accessor methods for navigating around this environment
        /** Verifies whether a location is valid in this environment.
         *   @param  loc     location to check
         *   @return <code>true</code> if <code>loc</code> is valid;
         *           <code>false</code> otherwise
         **/
        boolean isValid(Location loc);
        /** Returns the number of sides around each cell.
         *   @return    the number of cell sides in this environment
         **/
        int numCellSides();
        /** Returns the number of adjacent neighbors around each cell.
         *   @return    the number of adjacent neighbors
         **/
```

```
    int numAdjacentNeighbors();
    /** Generates a random direction.  The direction returned by
     *  <code>randomDirection</code> reflects the direction from
     *  a cell in the environment to one of its adjacent neighbors.
     *  @return a direction
     **/
    Direction randomDirection();
    /** Returns the direction from one location to another.
     *  @param  fromLoc         starting location for search
     *  @param  toLoc           destination location
     *  @return direction from <code>fromLoc</code> to <code>toLoc</code>
     **/
    Direction getDirection(Location fromLoc, Location toLoc);
    /** Returns the adjacent neighbor (whether valid or invalid) of a location
     *  in the specified direction.
     *  @param  fromLoc         starting location for search
     *  @param  compassDir      direction in which to look for adjacent neighbor
     *  @return neighbor of <code>fromLoc</code> in given direction
     **/
    Location getNeighbor(Location fromLoc, Direction compassDir);
    /** Returns the adjacent neighbors of a specified location.
     *  Only neighbors that are valid locations in the environment will be
     *  included.
     *  @param  ofLoc           location whose neighbors to get
     *  @return a list of locations that are neighbors of <code>ofLoc</code>
     **/
    ArrayList neighborsOf(Location ofLoc);
// accessor methods that deal with objects in this environment
    /** Returns the number of objects in this environment.
     *  @return    the number of objects
     **/
    int numObjects();
    /** Returns all the objects in this environment.
     *  @return .  an array of all the environment objects
     **/
    Locatable[] allObjects();
    /** Determines whether a specific location in this environment is
     *  empty.
     *  @param loc  the location to test
     *  @return        <code>true</code> if <code>loc</code> is a
     *                 valid location in the context of this environment
     *                 and is empty; <code>false</code> otherwise
     **/
    boolean isEmpty(Location loc);
    /** Returns the object at a specific location in this environment.
     *  @param loc    the location in which to look
     *  @return         the object at location <code>loc</code>;
     *                  <code>null</code> if <code>loc</code> is not
     *                  in the environment or is empty
     **/
    Locatable objectAt(Location loc);
// modifier methods
    /** Adds a new object to this environment at the location it specifies.
     *  (Precondition: <code>obj.location()</code> is a valid empty location.)
     *  @param obj the new object to be added
     *  @throws      IllegalArgumentException if the precondition is not met
     **/
```

```
    void add(Locatable obj);
    /** Removes the object from this environment.
     *   (Precondition: <code>obj</code> is in this environment.)
     *   @param obj       the object to be removed
     *   @throws          IllegalArgumentException if the precondition is not met
     **/
    void remove(Locatable obj);
    /** Updates this environment to reflect the fact that an object moved.
     *   (Precondition: <code>obj.location()</code> is a valid location
     *   and there is no other object there.
     *   Postcondition: <code>obj</code> is at the appropriate location
     *   (<code>obj.location()</code>), and either <code>oldLoc</code> is
     *   equal to <code>obj.location()</code> (there was no movement) or
     *   <code>oldLoc</code> is empty.)
     *   @param obj        the object that moved
     *   @param oldLoc     the previous location of <code>obj</code>
     *   @throws           IllegalArgumentException if the precondition is not met
     **/
    void recordMove(Locatable obj, Location oldLoc);
}
```

BOUNDENDENV.JAVA

```java
// AP(r) Computer Science Marine Biology Simulation:
// The BoundedEnv class is copyright(c) 2002 College Entrance
// Examination Board (www.collegeboard.com).
//
// This class is free software; you can redistribute it and/or modify
// it under the terms of the GNU General Public License as published by
// the Free Software Foundation.
//
// This class is distributed in the hope that it will be useful,
// but WITHOUT ANY WARRANTY; without even the implied warranty of
// MERCHANTABILITY or FITNESS FOR A PARTICULAR PURPOSE.  See the
// GNU General Public License for more details.
/**
 *   AP&reg; Computer Science Marine Biology Simulation:<br>
 *   The <code>BoundedEnv</code> class models a bounded, two-dimensional,
 *   grid-like  environment containing locatable objects.  For example,
 *   it could be an environment of fish for a marine biology simulation.
 *
 *   <p>
 *   The <code>BoundedEnv</code> class is
 *   copyright&copy; 2002 College Entrance Examination Board
 *   (www.collegeboard.com).
 *
 *   @author Alyce Brady
 *   @author APCS Development Committee
 *   @version 1 July 2002
 *   @see Locatable
 *   @see Location
 **/
public class BoundedEnv extends SquareEnvironment
{
    // Instance Variables: Encapsulated data for each BoundedEnv object
    private Locatable[][] theGrid;  // grid representing the environment
    private int objectCount;        // # of objects in current environment
  // constructors
    /** Constructs an empty BoundedEnv object with the given dimensions.
     *   (Precondition: <code>rows > 0</code> and <code>cols > 0</code>.)
     *   @param rows         number of rows in BoundedEnv
     *   @param cols         number of columns in BoundedEnv
     **/
    public BoundedEnv(int rows, int cols)
    {
        // Construct and initialize inherited attributes.
        super();
        theGrid = new Locatable[rows][cols];
        objectCount = 0;
    }
  // accessor methods
    /** Returns number of rows in the environment.
     *   @return   the number of rows, or -1 if this environment is unbounded
     **/
    public int numRows()
    {
        return theGrid.length;
    }
```

```java
/** Returns number of columns in the environment.
 *   @return    the number of columns, or -1 if this environment is unbounded
 **/
public int numCols()
{
    // Note: according to the constructor precondition, numRows() > 0, so
    // theGrid[0] is non-null.
    return theGrid[0].length;
}
/** Verifies whether a location is valid in this environment.
 *   @param  loc     location to check
 *   @return <code>true</code> if <code>loc</code> is valid;
 *           <code>false</code> otherwise
 **/
public boolean isValid(Location loc)
{
    if ( loc == null )
        return false;
    return (0 <= loc.row() && loc.row() < numRows()) &&
           (0 <= loc.col() && loc.col() < numCols());
}
/** Returns the number of objects in this environment.
 *   @return    the number of objects
 **/
public int numObjects()
{
    return objectCount;
}
/** Returns all the objects in this environment.
 *   @return     an array of all the environment objects
 **/
public Locatable[] allObjects()
{
    Locatable[] theObjects = new Locatable[numObjects()];
    int tempObjectCount = 0;
    // Look at all grid locations.
    for ( int r = 0; r < numRows(); r++ )
    {
        for ( int c = 0; c < numCols(); c++ )
        {
            // If there's an object at this location, put it in the array.
            Locatable obj = theGrid[r][c];
            if ( obj != null )
            {
                theObjects[tempObjectCount] = obj;
                tempObjectCount++;
            }
        }
    }
    return theObjects;
}
/** Determines whether a specific location in this environment is
 *   empty.
 *   @param loc  the location to test
 *   @return        <code>true</code> if <code>loc</code> is a
 *                  valid location in the context of this environment
 *                  and is empty; <code>false</code> otherwise
 **/
```

```java
public boolean isEmpty(Location loc)
{
    return isValid(loc) && objectAt(loc) == null;
}
/** Returns the object at a specific location in this environment.
 *   @param loc    the location in which to look
 *   @return        the object at location <code>loc</code>;
 *                  <code>null</code> if <code>loc</code> is not
 *                  in the environment or is empty
 **/
public Locatable objectAt(Location loc)
{
    if ( ! isValid(loc) )
        return null;
    return theGrid[loc.row()][loc.col()];
}
/** Creates a single string representing all the objects in this
 *   environment (not necessarily in any particular order).
 *   @return      a string indicating all the objects in this environment
 **/
public String toString()
{
    Locatable[] theObjects = allObjects();
    String s = "Environment contains " + numObjects() + " objects: ";
    for ( int index = 0; index < theObjects.length; index++ )
        s += theObjects[index].toString() + " ";
    return s;
}

// modifier methods
/** Adds a new object to this environment at the location it specifies.
 *   (Precondition: <code>obj.location()</code> is a valid empty location.)
 *   @param obj the new object to be added
 *   @throws      IllegalArgumentException if the precondition is not met
 **/
public void add(Locatable obj)
{
    // Check precondition.   Location should be empty.
    Location loc = obj.location();
    if ( ! isEmpty(loc) )
        throw new IllegalArgumentException("Location " + loc +
                                " is not a valid empty location");
    // Add object to the environment.
    theGrid[loc.row()][loc.col()] = obj;
    objectCount++;
}
/** Removes the object from this environment.
 *   (Precondition: <code>obj</code> is in this environment.)
 *   @param obj       the object to be removed
 *   @throws      IllegalArgumentException if the precondition is not met
 **/
public void remove(Locatable obj)
{
    // Make sure that the object is there to remove.
    Location loc = obj.location();
    if ( objectAt(loc) != obj )
        throw new IllegalArgumentException("Cannot remove " +
                                obj + "; not there");
```

```
        // Remove the object from the grid.
        theGrid[loc.row()][loc.col()] = null;
        objectCount--;
    }
    /** Updates this environment to reflect the fact that an object moved.
     *    (Precondition: <code>obj.location()</code> is a valid location
     *    and there is no other object there.
     *    Postcondition: <code>obj</code> is at the appropriate location
     *    (<code>obj.location()</code>), and either <code>oldLoc</code> is
     *    equal to <code>obj.location()</code> (there was no movement) or
     *    <code>oldLoc</code> is empty.)
     *    @param obj        the object that moved
     *    @param oldLoc     the previous location of <code>obj</code>
     *    @throws    IllegalArgumentException if the precondition is not met
     **/
    public void recordMove(Locatable obj, Location oldLoc)
    {
        // Simplest case: There was no movement.
        Location newLoc = obj.location();
        if ( newLoc.equals(oldLoc) )
            return;
        // Otherwise, oldLoc should contain the object that is
        //    moving and the new location should be empty.
        Locatable foundObject = objectAt(oldLoc);
        if ( ! (foundObject == obj && isEmpty(newLoc)) )
            throw new IllegalArgumentException("Precondition violation moving "
                    + obj + " from " + oldLoc);
        // Move the object to the proper location in the grid.
        theGrid[newLoc.row()][newLoc.col()] = obj;
        theGrid[oldLoc.row()][oldLoc.col()] = null;
    }
}
```

UNBOUNDEDENV.JAVA

```java
// AP(r) Computer Science Marine Biology Simulation:
// The UnboundedEnv class is copyright(c) 2002 College Entrance
// Examination Board (www.collegeboard.com).
//
// This class is free software; you can redistribute it and/or modify
// it under the terms of the GNU General Public License as published by
// the Free Software Foundation.
//
// This class is distributed in the hope that it will be useful,
// but WITHOUT ANY WARRANTY; without even the implied warranty of
// MERCHANTABILITY or FITNESS FOR A PARTICULAR PURPOSE.  See the
// GNU General Public License for more details.
import java.util.ArrayList;
/**
 *  AP&reg; Computer Science Marine Biology Simulation:<br>
 *  The <code>UnboundedEnv</code> class models an unbounded, two-dimensional,
 *  grid-like environment containing locatable objects.  For example, it
 *  could be an environment of fish for a marine biology simulation.
 *
 *  <p>
 *  Modification History:
 *  - Created to support multiple environment representations:
 *    this class represents a second implementation of the
 *    <code>Environment</code> interface.
 *
 *  <p>
 *  The <code>UnboundedEnv</code> class is
 *  copyright&copy; 2002 College Entrance Examination Board
 *  (www.collegeboard.com).
 *
 *  @author Alyce Brady
 *  @author APCS Development Committee
 *  @version 1 July 2002
 *  @see Locatable
 *  @see Location
 **/
public class UnboundedEnv extends SquareEnvironment
{
    // Instance Variables: Encapsulated data for each UnboundedEnv object
    private ArrayList objectList;    // list of Locatable objects in environment
    // constructors
    /** Constructs an empty UnboundedEnv object.
     **/
    public UnboundedEnv()
    {
        // Construct and initialize inherited attributes.
        super();
        objectList = new ArrayList();
    }
    // accessor methods
    /** Returns number of rows in this environment.
     * @return   the number of rows, or -1 if the environment is unbounded
     **/
    public int numRows()
```

```
{
    return -1;
}
/** Returns number of columns in this environment.
 *   @return    the number of columns, or -1 if the environment is unbounded
 **/
public int numCols()
{
    return -1;
}
/** Verifies whether a location is valid in this environment.
 *   @param  loc    location to check
 *   @return <code>true</code> if <code>loc</code> is valid;
 *           <code>false</code> otherwise
 **/
public boolean isValid(Location loc)
{
    // All non-null locations are valid in an unbounded environment.
    return loc != null;
}
/** Returns the number of objects in this environment.
 *   @return    the number of objects
 **/
public int numObjects()
{
    return objectList.size();
}
/** Returns all the objects in this environment.
 *   @return    an array of all the environment objects
 **/
public Locatable[] allObjects()
{
    Locatable[] objectArray = new Locatable[objectList.size()];
    // Put all the environment objects in the list.
    for ( int index = 0; index < objectList.size(); index++ )
    {
        objectArray[index] = (Locatable) objectList.get(index);
    }
    return objectArray;
}
/** Determines whether a specific location in this environment is
 *   empty.
 *   @param loc  the location to test
 *   @return       <code>true</code> if <code>loc</code> is a
 *                 valid location in the context of this environment
 *                 and is empty; <code>false</code> otherwise
 **/
public boolean isEmpty(Location loc)
{
    return (objectAt(loc) == null);
}
/** Returns the object at a specific location in this environment.
 *   @param loc     the location in which to look
 *   @return         the object at location <code>loc</code>;
 *                   <code>null</code> if <code>loc</code> is empty
 **/
public Locatable objectAt(Location loc)
```

```
{
    int index = indexOf(loc);
    if ( index == -1 )
        return null;
    return (Locatable) objectList.get(index);
}
/** Creates a single string representing all the objects in this
 *  environment (not necessarily in any particular order).
 *  @return    a string indicating all the objects in this environment
 **/
public String toString()
{
    Locatable[] theObjects = allObjects();
    String s = "Environment contains " + numObjects() + " objects: ";
    for ( int index = 0; index < theObjects.length; index++ )
        s += theObjects[index].toString() + " ";
    return s;
}

// modifier methods
/** Adds a new object to this environment at the location it specifies.
 *  (Precondition: <code>obj.location()</code> is a valid empty location.)
 *  @param obj the new object to be added
 *  @throws    IllegalArgumentException if the precondition is not met
 **/
public void add(Locatable obj)
{
    // Check precondition.  Location should be empty.
    Location loc = obj.location();
    if ( ! isEmpty(loc) )
        throw new IllegalArgumentException("Location " + loc +
                                        " is not a valid empty location");
    // Add object to the environment.
    objectList.add(obj);
}
/** Removes the object from this environment.
 *  (Precondition: <code>obj</code> is in this environment.)
 *  @param obj       the object to be removed
 *  @throws    IllegalArgumentException if the precondition is not met
 **/
public void remove(Locatable obj)
{
    // Find the index of the object to remove.
    int index = indexOf(obj.location());
    if ( index == -1 )
        throw new IllegalArgumentException("Cannot remove " +
                                        obj + "; not there");
    // Remove the object.
    objectList.remove(index);
}
/** Updates this environment to reflect the fact that an object moved.
 *  (Precondition: <code>obj.location()</code> is a valid location
 *  and there is no other object there.
 *  Postcondition: <code>obj</code> is at the appropriate location
 *  (<code>obj.location()</code>), and either <code>oldLoc</code> is
 *  equal to <code>obj.location()</code> (there was no movement) or
 *  <code>oldLoc</code> is empty.)
 *  @param obj          the object that moved
 *  @param oldLoc     the previous location of <code>obj</code>
 *  @throws    IllegalArgumentException if the precondition is not met
 **/
```

```
        public void recordMove(Locatable obj, Location oldLoc)
        {
            int objectsAtOldLoc = 0;
            int objectsAtNewLoc = 0;
            // Look through the list to find how many objects are at old
            // and new locations.
            Location newLoc = obj.location();
            for ( int index = 0; index < objectList.size(); index++ )
            {
                Locatable thisObj = (Locatable) objectList.get(index);
                if ( thisObj.location().equals(oldLoc) )
                    objectsAtOldLoc++;
                if ( thisObj.location().equals(newLoc) )
                    objectsAtNewLoc++;
            }
            // There should be one object at newLoc.  If oldLoc equals
            // newLoc, there should be one at oldLoc; otherwise, there
            // should be none.
            if ( ! ( objectsAtNewLoc == 1 &&
                     ( oldLoc.equals(newLoc) || objectsAtOldLoc == 0 ) ) )
            {
                throw new IllegalArgumentException("Precondition violation moving "
                    + obj + " from " + oldLoc);
            }
        }
    }
    // internal helper method
    /** Get the index of the object at the specified location.
     *  @param loc     the location in which to look
     *  @return        the index of the object at location <code>loc</code>
     *                     if there is one; -1 otherwise
     **/
    protected int indexOf(Location loc)
    {
        // Look through the list to find the object at the given location.
        for ( int index = 0; index < objectList.size(); index++ )
        {
            Locatable obj = (Locatable) objectList.get(index);
            if ( obj.location().equals(loc) )
            {
                // Found the object -- return its index.
                return index;
            }
        }
        // No such object found.
        return -1;
    }
}
```

Fish.java

```
// AP(r) Computer Science Marine Biology Simulation:
// The Fish class is copyright(c) 2002 College Entrance
// Examination Board (www.collegeboard.com).
//
// This class is free software; you can redistribute it and/or modify
// it under the terms of the GNU General Public License as published by
// the Free Software Foundation.
//
// This class is distributed in the hope that it will be useful,
// but WITHOUT ANY WARRANTY; without even the implied warranty of
// MERCHANTABILITY or FITNESS FOR A PARTICULAR PURPOSE.  See the
// GNU General Public License for more details.
import java.awt.Color;
import java.util.ArrayList;
import java.util.Random;
/**
 *   AP&reg; Computer Science Marine Biology Simulation:<br>
 *   A <code>Fish</code> object represents a fish in the Marine Biology
 *   Simulation. Each fish has a unique ID, which remains constant
 *   throughout its life.  A fish also maintains information about its
 *   location and direction in the environment.
 *
 *   <p>
 *   Modification History:
 *   - Modified to support a dynamic population in the environment:
 *     fish can now breed and die.
 *
 *   <p>
 *   The <code>Fish</code> class is
 *   copyright&copy; 2002 College Entrance Examination Board
 *   (www.collegeboard.com).
 *
 *   @author Alyce Brady
 *   @author APCS Development Committee
 *   @version 1 July 2002
 *   @see Environment
 *   @see Direction
 *   @see Location
 **/
public class Fish implements Locatable
{
    // Class Variable: Shared among ALL fish
    private static int nextAvailableID = 1;    // next avail unique identifier
    // Instance Variables: Encapsulated data for EACH fish
    private Environment theEnv;                 // environment in which the fish lives
    private int myId;                          // unique ID for this fish
    private Location myLoc;                     // fish's location
    private Direction myDir;                    // fish's direction
    private Color myColor;                      // fish's color
// THE FOLLOWING TWO INSTANCE VARIABLES ARE NEW IN CHAPTER 3 !!!
    private double probOfBreeding;        // defines likelihood in each timestep
    private double probOfDying;           // defines likelihood in each timestep
  // constructors and related helper methods
    /** Constructs a fish at the specified location in a given environment.
     *   The Fish is assigned a random direction and random color.
     *   (Precondition: parameters are non-null; <code>loc</code> is valid
```

```
 *    for <code>env</code>.)
 *    @param env      environment in which fish will live
 *    @param loc      location of the new fish in <code>env</code>
 **/
public Fish(Environment env, Location loc)
{
    initialize(env, loc, env.randomDirection(), randomColor());
}
/** Constructs a fish at the specified location and direction in a
 *    given environment.  The Fish is assigned a random color.
 *    (Precondition: parameters are non-null; <code>loc</code> is valid
 *    for <code>env</code>.)
 *    @param env      environment in which fish will live
 *    @param loc      location of the new fish in <code>env</code>
 *    @param dir      direction the new fish is facing
 **/
public Fish(Environment env, Location loc, Direction dir)
{
    initialize(env, loc, dir, randomColor());
}
/** Constructs a fish of the specified color at the specified location
 *    and direction.
 *    (Precondition: parameters are non-null; <code>loc</code> is valid
 *    for <code>env</code>.)
 *    @param env      environment in which fish will live
 *    @param loc      location of the new fish in <code>env</code>
 *    @param dir      direction the new fish is facing
 *    @param col      color of the new fish
 **/
public Fish(Environment env, Location loc, Direction dir, Color col)
{
    initialize(env, loc, dir, col);
}
/** Initializes the state of this fish.
 *    (Precondition: parameters are non-null; <code>loc</code> is valid
 *    for <code>env</code>.)
 *    @param env      environment in which this fish will live
 *    @param loc      location of this fish in <code>env</code>
 *    @param dir      direction this fish is facing
 *    @param col      color of this fish
 **/
private void initialize(Environment env, Location loc, Direction dir,
                        Color col)
{
    theEnv = env;
    myId = nextAvailableID;
    nextAvailableID++;
    myLoc = loc;
    myDir = dir;
    myColor = col;
    theEnv.add(this);
    // object is at location myLoc in environment
// THE FOLLOWING CODE IS NEW IN CHAPTER 3 !!!
    // For now, every fish is equally likely to breed or die in any given
    // timestep, although this could be individualized for each fish.
    probOfBreeding = 1.0/7.0;    // 1 in 7 chance in each timestep
    probOfDying = 1.0/5.0;       // 1 in 5 chance in each timestep
}
```

```java
/** Generates a random color.
 *   @return        the new random color
 **/
protected Color randomColor()
{
    // There are 256 possibilities for the red, green, and blue attributes
    // of a color.  Generate random values for each color attribute.
    Random randNumGen = RandNumGenerator.getInstance();
    return new Color(randNumGen.nextInt(256),      // amount of red
                     randNumGen.nextInt(256),      // amount of green
                     randNumGen.nextInt(256));     // amount of blue
}

// accessor methods
/** Returns this fish's ID.
 *   @return         the unique ID for this fish
 **/
public int id()
{
    return myId;
}
/** Returns this fish's environment.
 *   @return         the environment in which this fish lives
 **/
public Environment environment()
{
    return theEnv;
}
/** Returns this fish's color.
 *   @return         the color of this fish
 **/
public Color color()
{
    return myColor;
}
/** Returns this fish's location.
 *   @return          the location of this fish in the environment
 **/
public Location location()
{
    return myLoc;
}
/** Returns this fish's direction.
 *   @return          the direction in which this fish is facing
 **/
public Direction direction()
{
    return myDir;
}
/** Checks whether this fish is in an environment.
 *   @return   <code>true</code> if the fish is in the environment
 *             (and at the correct location); <code>false</code> otherwise
 **/
public boolean isInEnv()
{
    return environment().objectAt(location()) == this;
}
```

```
    /** Returns a string representing key information about this fish.
     *  @return  a string indicating the fish's ID, location, and direction
     **/
    public String toString()
    {
        return id() + location().toString() + direction().toString();
    }

  // modifier method
// THE FOLLOWING METHOD IS MODIFIED FOR CHAPTER 3 !!!
//         (was originally a check for aliveness and a simple call to move)
    /** Acts for one step in the simulation.
     **/
    public void act()
    {
        // Make sure fish is alive and well in the environment -- fish
        // that have been removed from the environment shouldn't act.
        if ( ! isInEnv() )
            return;
        // Try to breed.
        if ( ! breed() )
            // Did not breed, so try to move.
            move();
        // Determine whether this fish will die in this timestep.
        Random randNumGen = RandNumGenerator.getInstance();
        if ( randNumGen.nextDouble() < probOfDying )
            die();
    }

  // internal helper methods
// THE FOLLOWING METHOD IS NEW FOR CHAPTER 3 !!!
    /** Attempts to breed into neighboring locations.
     *  @return      <code>true</code> if fish successfully breeds;
     *               <code>false</code> otherwise
     **/
    protected boolean breed()
    {
        // Determine whether this fish will try to breed in this
        // timestep.  If not, return immediately.
        Random randNumGen = RandNumGenerator.getInstance();
        if ( randNumGen.nextDouble() >= probOfBreeding )
            return false;
        // Get list of neighboring empty locations.
        ArrayList emptyNbrs = emptyNeighbors();
        Debug.print("Fish " + toString() + " attempting to breed.   ");
        Debug.println("Has neighboring locations: " + emptyNbrs.toString());
        // If there is nowhere to breed, then we're done.
        if ( emptyNbrs.size() == 0 )
        {
            Debug.println("  Did not breed.");
            return false;
        }
        // Breed to all of the empty neighboring locations.
        for ( int index = 0; index < emptyNbrs.size(); index++ )
        {
            Location loc = (Location) emptyNbrs.get(index);
            generateChild(loc);
        }
        return true;
    }
```

```
// THE FOLLOWING METHOD IS NEW FOR CHAPTER 3 !!!
    /** Creates a new fish with the color of its parent.
     *  @param loc     location of the new fish
     **/
    protected void generateChild(Location loc)
    {
        // Create new fish, which adds itself to the environment.
        Fish child = new Fish(environment(), loc,
                                environment().randomDirection(), color());
        Debug.println("  New Fish created: " + child.toString());
    }
    /** Moves this fish in its environment.
     **/
    protected void move()
    {
        // Find a location to move to.
        Debug.print("Fish " + toString() + " attempting to move.   ");
        Location nextLoc = nextLocation();
        // If the next location is different, move there.
        if ( ! nextLoc.equals(location()) )
        {
            // Move to new location.
            Location oldLoc = location();
            changeLocation(nextLoc);
            // Update direction in case fish had to turn to move.
            Direction newDir = environment().getDirection(oldLoc, nextLoc);
            changeDirection(newDir);
            Debug.println("  Moves to " + location() + direction());
        }
        else
            Debug.println("  Does not move.");
    }
    /** Finds this fish's next location.
     *  A fish may move to any empty adjacent locations except the one
     *  behind it (fish do not move backwards).  If this fish cannot
     *  move, <code>nextLocation</code> returns its current location.
     *  @return    the next location for this fish
     **/
    protected Location nextLocation()
    {
        // Get list of neighboring empty locations.
        ArrayList emptyNbrs = emptyNeighbors();
        // Remove the location behind, since fish do not move backwards.
        Direction oppositeDir = direction().reverse();
        Location locationBehind = environment().getNeighbor(location(),
                                                             oppositeDir);
        emptyNbrs.remove(locationBehind);
        Debug.print("Possible new locations are: " + emptyNbrs.toString());
        // If there are no valid empty neighboring locations, then we're done.
        if ( emptyNbrs.size() == 0 )
            return location();
        // Return a randomly chosen neighboring empty location.
        Random randNumGen = RandNumGenerator.getInstance();
        int randNum = randNumGen.nextInt(emptyNbrs.size());
        return (Location) emptyNbrs.get(randNum);
    }
```

```
      /** Finds empty locations adjacent to this fish.
       *  @return     an ArrayList containing neighboring empty locations
       **/
      protected ArrayList emptyNeighbors()
      {
          // Get all the neighbors of this fish, empty or not.
          ArrayList nbrs = environment().neighborsOf(location());
          // Figure out which neighbors are empty and add those to a new list.
          ArrayList emptyNbrs = new ArrayList();
          for ( int index = 0; index < nbrs.size(); index++ )
          {
              Location loc = (Location) nbrs.get(index);
              if ( environment().isEmpty(loc) )
                  emptyNbrs.add(loc);
          }
          return emptyNbrs;
      }
      /** Modifies this fish's location and notifies the environment.
       *  @param  newLoc     new location value
       **/
      protected void changeLocation(Location newLoc)
      {
          // Change location and notify the environment.
          Location oldLoc = location();
          myLoc = newLoc;
          environment().recordMove(this, oldLoc);
          // object is again at location myLoc in environment
      }
      /** Modifies this fish's direction.
       *  @param  newDir     new direction value
       **/
      protected void changeDirection(Direction newDir)
      {
          // Change direction.
          myDir = newDir;
      }
// THE FOLLOWING METHOD IS NEW FOR CHAPTER 3 !!!
      /** Removes this fish from the environment.
       **/
      protected void die()
      {
          Debug.println(toString() + " about to die.");
          environment().remove(this);
      }
}
```

DARTERFISH.JAVA

```java
// AP(r) Computer Science Marine Biology Simulation:
// The DarterFish class is copyright(c) 2002 College Entrance
// Examination Board (www.collegeboard.com).
//
// This class is free software; you can redistribute it and/or modify
// it under the terms of the GNU General Public License as published by
// the Free Software Foundation.
//
// This class is distributed in the hope that it will be useful,
// but WITHOUT ANY WARRANTY; without even the implied warranty of
// MERCHANTABILITY or FITNESS FOR A PARTICULAR PURPOSE.  See the
// GNU General Public License for more details.
import java.awt.Color;
/**
 *  AP&reg; Computer Science Marine Biology Simulation:<br>
 *  The <code>DarterFish</code> class represents a fish in the Marine
 *  Biology Simulation that darts forward two spaces if it can, moves
 *  forward one space if it can't move two, and reverses direction
 *  (without moving) if it cannot  move forward.  It can only "see" an
 *  empty location two cells away if the cell in between is empty also.
 *  In other words, if both the cell in front of the darter and the cell
 *  in front of that cell are empty, the darter fish will move forward
 *  two spaces.  If only the cell in front of the darter is empty, it
 *  will move there.  If neither forward cell is empty, the fish will turn
 *  around, changing its direction but not its location.
 *
 *  <p>
 *  <code>DarterFish</code> objects inherit instance variables and much
 *  of their behavior from the <code>Fish</code> class.
 *
 *  <p>
 *  The <code>DarterFish</code> class is
 *  copyright&copy; 2002 College Entrance Examination Board
 *  (www.collegeboard.com).
 *
 *  @author APCS Development Committee
 *  @author Alyce Brady
 *  @version 1 July 2002
 **/
public class DarterFish extends Fish
{
  // constructors
    /** Constructs a darter fish at the specified location in a
     *  given environment.   This darter is colored yellow.
     *   (Precondition: parameters are non-null; <code>loc</code> is valid
     *   for <code>env</code>.)
     *  @param env     environment in which fish will live
     *  @param loc     location of the new fish in <code>env</code>
     **/
    public DarterFish(Environment env, Location loc)
    {
        // Construct and initialize the attributes inherited from Fish.
        super(env, loc, env.randomDirection(), Color.yellow);
    }
```

```
    /** Constructs a darter fish at the specified location and direction in a
     *  given environment.   This darter is colored yellow.
     *  (Precondition: parameters are non-null; <code>loc</code>
     *  is valid for <code>env</code>.)
     *  @param env      environment in which fish will live
     *  @param loc      location of the new fish in <code>env</code>
     *  @param dir      direction the new fish is facing
     **/
    public DarterFish(Environment env, Location loc, Direction dir)
    {
        // Construct and initialize the attributes inherited from Fish.
        super(env, loc, dir, Color.yellow);
    }


    /** Constructs a darter fish of the specified color at the specified
     *  location and direction.
     *  (Precondition: parameters are non-null; <code>loc</code> is valid
     *  for <code>env</code>.)
     *  @param env      environment in which fish will live
     *  @param loc      location of the new fish in <code>env</code>
     *  @param dir      direction the new fish is facing
     *  @param col      color of the new fish
     **/
    public DarterFish(Environment env, Location loc, Direction dir, Color col)
    {
        // Construct and initialize the attributes inherited from Fish.
        super(env, loc, dir, col);
    }
// redefined methods
    /** Creates a new darter fish.
     *  @param loc      location of the new fish
     **/
    protected void generateChild(Location loc)
    {
        // Create new fish, which adds itself to the environment.
        DarterFish child = new DarterFish(environment(), loc,
                                          environment().randomDirection(),
                                          color());
        Debug.println("  New DarterFish created: " + child.toString());
    }
    /** Moves this fish in its environment.
     *  A darter fish darts forward (as specified in <code>nextLocation</code>)
     *  if possible, or reverses direction (without moving) if it cannot move
     *  forward.
     **/
    protected void move()
    {
        // Find a location to move to.
        Debug.print("DarterFish " + toString() + " attempting to move.   ");
        Location nextLoc = nextLocation();
        // If the next location is different, move there.
        if ( ! nextLoc.equals(location()) )
        {
            changeLocation(nextLoc);
            Debug.println("  Moves to " + location());
        }
```

```
        else
        {
            // Otherwise, reverse direction.
            changeDirection(direction().reverse());
            Debug.println("   Now facing " + direction());
        }
    }
    /** Finds this fish's next location.
     *  A darter fish darts forward two spaces if it can, otherwise it
     *  tries to move forward one space.  A darter fish can only move
     *  to empty locations, and it can only move two spaces forward if
     *  the intervening space is empty.  If the darter fish cannot move
     *  forward, <code>nextLocation</code> returns the fish's current
     *  location.
     *  @return    the next location for this fish
     **/
    protected Location nextLocation()
    {
        Environment env = environment();
        Location oneInFront = env.getNeighbor(location(), direction());
        Location twoInFront = env.getNeighbor(oneInFront, direction());
        Debug.println("   Location in front is empty? " +
                            env.isEmpty(oneInFront));
        Debug.println("   Location in front of that is empty? " +
                            env.isEmpty(twoInFront));
        if ( env.isEmpty(oneInFront) )
        {
            if ( env.isEmpty(twoInFront) )
                return twoInFront;
            else
                return oneInFront;
        }
        // Only get here if there isn't a valid location to move to.
        Debug.println("   Darter is blocked.");
        return location();
    }
}
```

SLOWFISH.JAVA

```
// AP(r) Computer Science Marine Biology Simulation:
// The SlowFish class is copyright(c) 2002 College Entrance
// Examination Board (www.collegeboard.com).
//
// This class is free software; you can redistribute it and/or modify
// it under the terms of the GNU General Public License as published by
// the Free Software Foundation.
//
// This class is distributed in the hope that it will be useful,
// but WITHOUT ANY WARRANTY; without even the implied warranty of
// MERCHANTABILITY or FITNESS FOR A PARTICULAR PURPOSE.  See the
// GNU General Public License for more details.
import java.awt.Color;
import java.util.ArrayList;
import java.util.Random;
/**
 *  AP&reg; Computer Science Marine Biology Simulation:<br>
 *  The <code>SlowFish</code> class represents a fish in the Marine Biology
 *  Simulation that moves very slowly.  It moves so slowly that it only has
 *  a 1 in 5 chance of moving out of its current cell into an adjacent cell
 *  in any given timestep in the simulation.  When it does move beyond its
 *  own cell, its movement behavior is the same as for objects of the
 *  <code>Fish</code> class.
 *
 *  <p>
 *  <code>SlowFish</code> objects inherit instance variables and much of
 *  their behavior from the <code>Fish</code> class.
 *
 *  <p>
 *  The <code>SlowFish</code> class is
 *  copyright&copy; 2002 College Entrance Examination Board
 *  (www.collegeboard.com).
 *
 *  @author Alyce Brady
 *  @version 1 July 2002
 **/
public class SlowFish extends Fish
{
    // Instance Variables: Encapsulated data for EACH slow fish
    private double probOfMoving;      // defines likelihood in each timestep
  // constructors
    /** Constructs a slow fish at the specified location in a
     *  given environment.   This slow fish is colored red.
     *   (Precondition: parameters are non-null; <code>loc</code> is valid
     *   for <code>env</code>.)
     *   @param env     environment in which fish will live
     *   @param loc     location of the new fish in <code>env</code>
     **/
    public SlowFish(Environment env, Location loc)
    {
        // Construct and initialize the attributes inherited from Fish.
        super(env, loc, env.randomDirection(), Color.red);
        // Define the likelihood that a slow fish will move in any given
        // timestep.  For now this is the same value for all slow fish.
        probOfMoving = 1.0/5.0;          // 1 in 5 chance in each timestep
    }
```

```java
/** Constructs a slow fish at the specified location and direction in a
 *  given environment.   This slow fish is colored red.
 *  (Precondition: parameters are non-null; <code>loc</code> is valid
 *  for <code>env</code>.)
 *  @param env      environment in which fish will live
 *  @param loc      location of the new fish in <code>env</code>
 *  @param dir      direction the new fish is facing
 **/
public SlowFish(Environment env, Location loc, Direction dir)
{
    // Construct and initialize the attributes inherited from Fish.
    super(env, loc, dir, Color.red);
    // Define the likelihood that a slow fish will move in any given
    // timestep.  For now this is the same value for all slow fish.
    probOfMoving = 1.0/5.0;          // 1 in 5 chance in each timestep
}


/** Constructs a slow fish of the specified color at the specified
 *  location and direction.
 *  (Precondition: parameters are non-null; <code>loc</code> is valid
 *  for <code>env</code>.)
 *  @param env      environment in which fish will live
 *  @param loc      location of the new fish in <code>env</code>
 *  @param dir      direction the new fish is facing
 *  @param col      color of the new fish
 **/
public SlowFish(Environment env, Location loc, Direction dir, Color col)
{
    // Construct and initialize the attributes inherited from Fish.
    super(env, loc, dir, col);
    // Define the likelihood that a slow fish will move in any given
    // timestep.  For now this is the same value for all slow fish.
    probOfMoving = 1.0/5.0;          // 1 in 5 chance in each timestep
}
// redefined methods
/** Creates a new slow fish.
 *  @param loc      location of the new fish
 **/
protected void generateChild(Location loc)
{
    // Create new fish, which adds itself to the environment.
    SlowFish child = new SlowFish(environment(), loc,
                                  environment().randomDirection(),
                                  color());
    Debug.println("  New SlowFish created: " + child.toString());
}
/** Finds this fish's next location.  A slow fish moves so
 *  slowly that it might not move out of its current cell in
 *  the environment.
 **/
protected Location nextLocation()
{
    // There's only a small chance that a slow fish will actually
    // move in any given timestep, defined by probOfMoving.
    Random randNumGen = RandNumGenerator.getInstance();
    if ( randNumGen.nextDouble() < probOfMoving )
        return super.nextLocation();
```

```
        else
        {
            Debug.println("SlowFish " + toString() +
                          " not attempting to move.");
            return location();
        }
    }
}
```

The Princeton Review
AP Computer Science A
Practice Test

COMPUTER SCIENCE A

SECTION I

Time—1 hour and 15 minutes

Number of Questions—40

Percent of Total Grade—50

Directions: Determine the answer to each of the following questions or incomplete statements, using the available space for any necessary scratchwork. Then decide which is the best of the choices given and fill in the corresponding oval on the answer sheet. No credit will be given for anything written in the examination booklet. Do not spend too much time on any one problem.

Notes:

- Assume that the classes listed in the Quick Reference sheet have been imported where appropriate. A Quick Reference to the AP Java classes is included as part of the exam.

- Assume that declarations of variables and methods appear within the context of an enclosing class.

- Assume that method calls that are not prefixed with an object or class name appear within the context of the class in which the method is declared.

- Unless otherwise noted in the question, assume that parameters in method calls are not null.

MULTIPLE-CHOICE QUESTIONS

USE THIS SPACE FOR SCRATCHWORK.

1. Consider the following code segment:

```
int a;
int b;
a = 10;
b = 0;
if (a > 0)
        if (a > 15)
                if (a > 20)
                        b = 1;
        else
                        b = 2;
    else
        b = 3;
```

After executing this code segment, what is the value of b?

(A) 0
(B) 1
(C) 2
(D) 3
(E) 10

GO ON TO THE NEXT PAGE

2. Assume that `A` is an integer variable. Which of the following lines of code are equivalent?

     I. `A++;`
    II. `A + 1;`
   III. `A += 1;`

(A) I and II
(B) I and III
(C) II and III
(D) I, II, and III
(E) None of the above

3. Consider the following function:

```
public void mystery(int n)
{
        int k;

        for (k = 0 ; k < n ; k++)
                mystery(k);
        System.out.print(n);
}
```

What value is returned by the call `mystery(3)`?

(A) `0123`
(B) `3210`
(C) `00123`
(D) `00100123`
(E) `001001120011223`

GO ON TO THE NEXT PAGE

4. Consider an array of integers.

4	10	1	2	6	7	3	5

If selection sort is used to order the array from smallest to largest values, which of the following represents a possible state of the array at some point during the selection sort process?

(A)	1	4	10	2	3	6	7	5
(B)	1	2	4	6	10	7	3	5
(C)	1	2	3	10	6	7	4	5
(D)	4	3	1	2	6	7	10	5
(E)	5	3	7	6	2	1	10	4

5. Consider the following definitions and code segment:

```
int k;
int A[];
A = new int[7];
for (k = 0; k < A.length; k++)
    A[k] = A.length - k;
for (k = 0; k < A.length - 1; k++)
    A[k+1] = A[k];
```

What values will A contain after the code segment is executed?

(A)	1	1	2	3	4	5	6
(B)	1	2	3	4	5	6	7
(C)	6	6	5	4	3	2	1
(D)	7	7	6	5	4	3	2
(E)	7	7	7	7	7	7	7

GO ON TO THE NEXT PAGE

```
public class PostOffice
{
    // constructor initializes boxes
    // to length 100
    public PostOffice()
    { /* implementation not shown */ }

    // returns the given p.o. box
    // 0 <= theBox < getNumBoxes()
    public Box getBox(int theBox)
    { /* implementation not shown */ }

    // returns the number of p.o. boxes
    public int getNumBoxes()
    { /* implementation not shown */ }

    // private data members and
    // other methods not shown
}

public class Box
{
    // constructor
    public Box()
    { /* implementation not shown */ }

    // returns the number of this box
    public int getBoxNumber()
    { /* implementation not shown */ }

    // returns the number of pieces
    // of mail in this box
    public int getMailCount()
    { /* implementation not shown */ }

    // returns the given piece of mail
    // 0 <= thePiece < getMailCount()
    public Mail getMail(int thePiece)
    { /* implementation not shown */ }

    // true if the box has been assigned
    // to a customer
    public boolean isAssigned()
    { /* implementation not shown */ }

    // true if the box contains mail
    public boolean hasMail()
    { /* implementation not shown */ }
```

```
    // private data members and
    // other methods not shown
}

public class Mail
{
    // private members, constructors, and
    // other methods not shown
}
```

6. Consider the following code segment:

```
    PostOffice p[];
    p = new PostOffice[10];
```

Assuming that the box has been assigned and that it has at least four pieces of mail waiting in it, what is the correct way of getting the fourth piece of mail from the 57th box of the tenth post office of p?

(A) `Mail m = p[10].getBox(57).getMail(4);`
(B) `Mail m = p[9].getBox(56).getMail(3);`
(C) `Mail m = p.getBox(57).getMail(4)[10];`
(D) `Mail m = getMail(getBox(p[9], 56), 3);`
(E) `Mail m = new Mail(10, 57, 4);`

GO ON TO THE NEXT PAGE

7. Consider the incomplete function `printBoxesWithout-Mail` given below. `printBoxesWithoutMail` should print the box numbers of all of the boxes that do not contain mail.

```java
public void printBoxesWithoutMail(
PostOffice p[])
{
        for (int k = 0; k < p.length ; k++)
        {
                for (int x = 0;
                        x < p[k].getNumBoxes();
                        x++)
                {
                        // loop body
                }
        }
}
```

Which of the following could be used to replace `// loop body` so that `printBoxesWithoutMail` works as intended?

(A)
```java
if (p[k].getBox(x).isAssigned() &&
    !p[k].getBox(x).hasMail())
{
  System.out.println(
    p[k].getBox(x).getBoxNumber());
}
```

(B)
```java
if (p[x].getBox(k).isAssigned() &&
    !p[x].getBox(k).hasMail())
{
  System.out.println(
    p[x].getBox(k).getBoxNumber());
}
```

(C)
```java
if (p[k].getBox(x).isAssigned() &&
    !p[k].getBox(x).hasMail())
{
  System.out.println(
      p[k].getBoxNumber(x));
}
```

(D)
```java
if (p[x].getBox(k).isAssigned() &&
    !p[x].getBox(k).hasMail())
{
  System.out.println(
      p[x].getBoxNumber(k));
}
```

(E)
```java
if (p[x].getBox(k).isAssigned() &&
    p[x].getBox(k).getMail() == 0)
{
  System.out.println(k);
}
```

GO ON TO THE NEXT PAGE

8. Assume that a and b are `boolean` variables that have been initialized. Consider the following code segment:

```
a = a && b;
b = a || b;
```

Which of the following statements is/are true?

   I.   The final value of a is the same as the initial value of a.
   II. The final value of b is the same as the initial value of b.
   III. The final value of a is the same as the initial value of b.

(A) I only
(B) II only
(C) III only
(D) I and II only
(E) II and III only

9. Consider the following code segment:

```
int x;
x = 53;
if (x > 10)
        System.out.print("A");
if (x > 30)
        System.out.print("B");
else if (x > 40)
        System.out.print("C");
if (x > 50)
        System.out.print("D");
if (x > 70)
        System.out.print("E");
```

What is output when the code is executed?

(A) A
(B) D
(C) ABD
(D) ABCD
(E) ABCDE

GO ON TO THE NEXT PAGE

10. Consider the following code segment:

```
int j;
int k;
for (j = -2; j <= 2; j = j + 2)
{
      for (k = j; k < j + 3; k++)
      {
            System.out.print(k + " ");
      }
}
```

What is output when the code is executed?

(A) -2 -1 0
(B) -2 -1 0 1 2
(C) 0 1 2 0 1 2 0 1 2
(D) -2 0 2
(E) -2 -1 0 0 1 2 2 3 4

11. Consider the following method mystery:

```
public void mystery(int count, String s)
{
      if (count <= 0)
            return;
      if (count % 3 == 0)
            System.out.print(s + "--" + s);
      else if (count % 3 == 1)
            System.out.print(s + "-" + s);
      else
            System.out.print(s);
      mystery(count - 1, s);
}
```

What is output by the call mystery(5, "X")?

(A) XX-XX--XXX-X
(B) XX-XX-XX-XX
(C) XXX--XX-X-XX--XXX
(D) XX-XXX--XXX-XX
(E) XXXXX

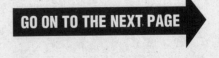
GO ON TO THE NEXT PAGE

Questions 12–13 refer to the following class and method descriptions.

Class `Table` has a method, `getPrice`, which takes no parameters and returns the price of the table.

Class `Chair` also has a method, `getPrice`, which takes no parameters and returns the price of the chair.

Class `DiningRoomSet` has a constructor which is passed a `Table` object and an `ArrayList` of `Chair` objects. It stores these parameters in its private data fields `myTable` and `myChairs`.

Class `DiningRoomSet` has a method, `getPrice`, which takes no parameters and returns the price of the dining room set. The price of a dining room set is calculated as the sum of the price of its table and all of its chairs.

12. What is the correct way to define the signature of the constructor for the `DiningRoomSet` class?

(A) `public void DiningRoomSet(Table t, ArrayList chairs)`
(B) `public DiningRoomSet(Table t, ArrayList chairs)`
(C) `public void DiningRoomSet(Table t, ArrayList Chair chairs)`
(D) `public DiningRoomSet(Table t, ArrayList Chair chairs)`
(E) `public DiningRoomSet(Table t, Chair chairs)`

GO ON TO THE NEXT PAGE

13. What is the correct way to implement the `getPrice` method of the `DiningRoomSet` class?

(A)
```
public double getPrice(Table t, ArrayList
    chairs)
{
  return t.getPrice() +
       chairs.getPrice();
}
```

(B)
```
public double getPrice(Table t, ArrayList
    chairs)
{
  return myTable.getPrice() +
       myChairs.getPrice();
}
```

(C)
```
public double getPrice()
{
  return myTable.getPrice() +
       myChairs.getPrice();
}
```

(D)
```
public double getPrice()
{
  double result = myTable.getPrice();
  for (int k = 0;
      k < myChairs.size(); k++)
  {
    result += ((Chair)
      myChairs.get(k)).getPrice();
  }
  return result;
}
```

(E)
```
public double getPrice()
{
  double result = myTable.getPrice();
  for (int k = 0;
      k < myChairs.length; k++)
  {
    result += ((Chair)
      myChairs[k]).getPrice();
  }
  return result;
}
```

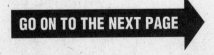

14. Consider the following output:

```
6 5 4 3 2 1
5 4 3 2 1
4 3 2 1
3 2 1
2 1
1
```

Which of the following code segments produces the above output when executed?

(A)
```java
for (int j = 6; j < 0; j--)
{
    for (int k = j; k > 0; k--)
    {
        System.out.print(k + " ");
    }
    System.out.println("");
}
```

(B)
```java
for (int j = 6; j >= 0; j--)
{
    for (int k = j; k >= 0; k--)
    {
        System.out.print(k + " ");
    }
    System.out.println("");
}
```

(C)
```java
for (int j = 0; j < 6; j++)
{
    for (int k = 6 - j; k > 0; k--)
    {
        System.out.print(k + " ");
    }
    System.out.println("");
}
```

(D)
```java
for (int j = 0; j < 6; j++)
{
    for (int k = 7 - j; k > 0; k--)
    {
        System.out.print(k + " ");
    }
    System.out.println("");
}
```

(E)
```java
for (int j = 0; j < 6; j++)
{
    for (int k = 6 - j; k >= 0; k--)
    {
        System.out.print(k + " ");
    }
    System.out.println("");
}
```

GO ON TO THE NEXT PAGE

15. Consider the following code segment:

```
ArrayList list = new ArrayList();
list.add(new Integer(7));
list.add(new Integer(6));
list.add(1, new Integer(5));
list.add(1, new Integer(4));
list.add(new Integer(3));
list.set(2, new Integer(2));
list.add(1, new Integer(1));
System.out.println(list);
```

What is printed as a result of executing this code segment?

(A) [1, 4, 2, 7, 6, 3]
(B) [7, 1, 4, 2, 6, 3]
(C) [7, 2, 5, 4, 3, 1]
(D) [7, 6, 2, 4, 3, 1]
(E) [7, 1, 2]

Questions 16–20 refer to the code from the Marine Biology Simulation Case Study. A copy of the code is available from The College Board's website or in Chapter 12 of this book.

16. Consider the following bounded environment containing three fish:

After one step of the simulation, how many different configurations of fish are possible?

(A) 1
(B) 2
(C) 3
(D) 4
(E) 5

17. Consider the original version and two proposed modifications to the nextLocation method of the DarterFish class.

Original version

```
protected Location nextLocation()
{
        Environment env = environment();
        Location oneInFront =
           env.getNeighbor(location(),
           direction());
        Location twoInFront =
           env.getNeighbor(oneInFront,
           direction());
        if (env.isEmpty(oneInFront))
        {
                if (env.isEmpty(twoInFront))
                        return twoInFront;
                else
                        return oneInFront;
        }
        return location();
}
```

Modification 1

```
protected Location nextLocation()
{
        Environment env = environment();
        Location oneInFront =
           env.getNeighbor(location(),
           direction());
        Location twoInFront =
           env.getNeighbor(oneInFront,
           direction());
        if (env.isEmpty(oneInFront))
                return oneInFront;
        else if (env.isEmpty(twoInFront))
                return twoInFront;
        else
                return location();
}
```

Modification 2

```
protected Location nextLocation()
{
        Environment env = environment();
        Location oneInFront =
           env.getNeighbor(location(),
           direction());
        Location twoInFront =
           env.getNeighbor(oneInFront,
           direction());
        if (env.isEmpty(twoInFront))
               return twoInFront;
        else if (env.isEmpty(oneInFront))
               return oneInFront;
        else
               return location();
}
```

Which of the following statements is true?

(A) The original version always returns the same location as Modification 1 except when location oneInFront is not empty and location twoInFront is empty.
(B) The original version always returns the same location as Modification 2 except when location oneInFront is not empty and location twoInFront is empty.
(C) Modification 1 always returns the same location as Modification 2.
(D) Modification 1 only returns the same location as Modification 2 when location oneInFront is not empty.
(E) Modification 1 only returns the same location as Modification 2 when location twoInFront is not empty.

GO ON TO THE NEXT PAGE

18. Consider a new class of fish derived from the `Fish` class.

```
public class MysteryFish extends Fish
{
        protected Location nextLocation()
        {
                Location result;
                result = super.nextLocation();
                if (location().equals(environment().
                  getNeighbor(result, direction().toRight())))
                {
                        return result;
                }
                else
                {
                        return location();
                }
        }
        // ... constructors and other methods
        //      not shown
}
```

What is the best description of the movement of a `Mystery-Fish`?

(A) It moves right in each timestep of the simulation.

(B) It moves left in each timestep of the simulation unless the location to its left is not empty. Otherwise it does not move.

(C) It moves right in each timestep of the simulation unless the location to its right is not empty. Otherwise it does not move.

(D) It moves left in a given timestep of the simulation either if the location to its left is empty and the locations to its front and right are not empty or if a randomly chosen neighboring empty location is the location to its left. Otherwise it does not move.

(E) It moves right in a given timestep of the simulation either if the location to its right is empty and the locations to its front and left are not empty or if a randomly chosen neighboring empty location is the location to its right. Otherwise it does not move.

GO ON TO THE NEXT PAGE

19. Consider changing the Marine Biology Simulation to keep track of how many times a standard fish does not move. If a standard fish has not moved for five timesteps in a row, it dies.

    In order to implement this change using good object-oriented design principles, which class(es) would need to be modified?

    I.   The Fish class.
    II. The BoundedEnv class.
    III. The Simulation class.

    (A) I only
    (B) III only
    (C) I and II
    (D) I and III
    (E) I, II, and III

20. A method is *deterministic* if, given its parameters, it is possible to predict exactly what it will return. A method is *probabilistic* if, given its parameters, each possible result has a known probability of occurring.

    Which of the following is the correct way to classify the next-Location methods in the Fish, DarterFish, and Slow-Fish classes?

	Fish	DarterFish	SlowFish
(A)	probabilistic	deterministic	probabilistic
(B)	probabilistic	probabilistic	deterministic
(C)	deterministic	probabilistic	deterministic
(D)	deterministic	deterministic	deterministic
(E)	probabilistic	probabilistic	probabilistic

Questions 21–23 refer to the following incomplete class declaration used to represent fractions with integral numerators and denominators.

```
public class Fraction
{
      private int numerator;
      private int denominator;
      public Fraction()
      {
            numerator = 0;
            denominator = 1;
      }
      public Fraction(int n, int d)
      {
            numerator = n;
            denominator = d;
      }
      // postcondition: returns the
      //    numerator
      public int getNumerator()
      { /* implementation not shown */ }
      // postcondition: returns the
      //    denominator
      public int getDenominator()
      { /* implementation not shown */ }
      // postcondition: returns the greatest
      // common divisor of x and y
      public int gcd(int x, int y)
      { /* implementation not shown */ }
      // postcondition: returns the Fraction
      //    that is the result of multiplying
      //    this Fraction and f
      public Fraction multiply(Fraction f)
      { /* implementation not shown */ }
      // ... other methods not shown
}
```

GO ON TO THE NEXT PAGE

21. Consider the method `multiply` of the `Fraction` class.

```
// postcondition: returns the Fraction
//    that is the result of multiplying
//    this Fraction and f
public Fraction multiply(Fraction f)
{ /* missing code */ }
```

Which of the following statements can be used to replace `/* missing code */` so that the multiply method is correctly implemented?

```
I.  return Fraction(
        numerator * f.getNumerator(),
        denominator * f.getDenominator();
```

```
II. return new Fraction(
        numerator * f.numerator,
        denominator * f.denominator);
```

```
III. return new Fraction(
        numerator * f.getNumerator(),
        denominator * f.getDenominator());
```

(A) I only
(B) II only
(C) III only
(D) I and III
(E) II and III

22. Consider the use of the Fraction class to multiply the fractions $\frac{3}{4}$ and $\frac{7}{19}$. Consider the following code:

```
Fraction fractionOne;
Fraction fractionTwo;
Fraction answer;
fractionOne = new Fraction(3, 4);
fractionTwo = new Fraction(7, 19);
/* missing code */
```

Which of the following could be used to replace `/* missing code */` so that answer contains the result of multiplying `fractionOne` by `fractionTwo`?

```
(A) answer = fractionOne * fractionTwo;
(B) answer = multiply(fractionOne,
                 fractionTwo);
(C) answer = fractionOne.multiply(fractionTwo);
(D) answer = new Fraction(fractionOne,
                 fractionTwo);
(E) answer = (fractionOne.getNumerator() *
              fractionTwo.getNumerator()) /
             (fractionOne.getDenominator() *
              fractionTwo.getDenominator());
```

GO ON TO THE NEXT PAGE

23. The following incomplete class declaration is intended to extend the `Fraction` class so that fractions can be manipulated in reduced form (lowest terms).

Note that a fraction can be reduced to lowest terms by dividing both the numerator and denominator by the greatest common divisor (gcd) of the numerator and denominator.

```
public class ReducedFraction
     extends Fraction
{
     private int reducedNumerator;
     private int reducedDenominator;
     // ... constructors and other methods
     //      not shown
}
```

Consider the following proposed constructors for the `ReducedFraction` class:

```
I.  public ReducedFraction()
    {
        reducedNumerator = 0;
        reducedDenominator = 1;
    }

II. public ReducedFraction(int n, int d)
    {
        numerator = n;
        denominator = d;
        reducedNumerator = n / gcd(n, d);
        reducedDenominator = d / gcd(n, d);
    }

III. public ReducedFraction(int n, int d)
     {
         super(n, d);
         reducedNumerator = n / gcd(n, d);
         reducedDenominator = d / gcd(n, d);
     }
```

Which of these constructor(s) would be legal for the `ReducedFraction` class?

(A) I only
(B) II only
(C) III only
(D) I and III
(E) II and III

GO ON TO THE NEXT PAGE

24. Consider s1 and s2 defined as follows:

```
String s1 = new String("hello");
String s2 = new String("hello");
```

Which of the following is/are correct ways to see if s1 and s2 hold identical strings?

```
  I. if (s1 == s2)
          /* s1 and s2 are identical */

 II. if (s1.compareTo(s2) == 0)
          /* s1 and s2 are identical */

III. if (s1.equals(s2))
          /* s1 and s2 are identical */
```

(A) I only
(B) III only
(C) I and III only
(D) II and III only
(E) I, II, and III

25. Consider the following variable and method declarations:

```
String s;
String t;
public void mystery(String a, String b)
{
    a = a + b;
    b = b + a;
}
```

Assume that s has the value "Elizabeth" and t has the value "Andrew" and mystery(s, t) is called. What are the values of s and t after the call to mystery?

	<u>a</u>	<u>b</u>
(A)	Elizabeth	Andrew
(B)	ElizabethAndrew	AndrewElizabeth
(C)	ElizabethAndrew	AndrewElizabethAndrew
(D)	ElizabethAndrew	ElizabethAndrewAndrew
(E)	ElizabethAndrewElizabeth	AndrewElizabethAndrew

GO ON TO THE NEXT PAGE

26. Consider the following incomplete and *incorrect* class declaration:

```
public class Point implements Comparable
{
        private int x;
        private int y;
        public boolean compareTo(Point other)
        {
                return (x == other.x &&
                            y == other.y);
        }
        // ... constructors and other methods
        //      not shown
}
```

For which of the following reasons is the above class declaration incorrect?

    I. Objects may not access private data fields of other objects in the same class.

    II. The Comparable interface requires that compareTo be passed an Object rather than a Point.

    III. The Comparable interface requires that compareTo return an int rather than a boolean.

(A) I only
(B) III only
(C) I and III
(D) II and III
(E) I, II, and III

GO ON TO THE NEXT PAGE

27. Consider the following abstraction of a `for` loop where `<1>`, `<2>`, `<3>`, and `<4>` represent legal code in the indicated locations:

```
for (<1>; <2>; <3>)
{
        <4>
}
```

Which of the following `while` loops has the same functionality as the above `for` loop?

(A)
```
<1>;
while (<2>)
{
  <3>;
  <4>
}
```

(B)
```
<1>;
while (<2>)
{
  <4>
  <3>;
}
```

(C)
```
<1>;
while (!<2>)
{
  <3>;
  <4>
}
```

(D)
```
<1>;
while (!<2>)
{
  <4>
  <3>;
}
```

(E)
```
<1>;
<3>;
while (<2>)
{
  <4>
  <3>;
}
```

28. Consider the following expression:

```
a / b + c - d % e * f
```

Which of the expressions given below is equivalent to the one given above?

(A) ((a / b) + (c - d)) % (e * f)
(B) ((((a / b) + c) - d) % e) * f
(C) ((a / b) + c) - (d % (e * f))
(D) (a / ((b + c) - d) % e) * f
(E) ((a / b) + c) - ((d % e) * f)

29. Assume that a program declares and initializes x as follows:

```
String[] x;
x = new String[10];
initialize(x);      // Fills the array x with
                    // valid strings each of
                    // length 5
```

Which of the following code segments correctly traverses the array and prints out the first character of all ten strings followed by the second character of all ten strings, and so on?

```
 I.  int i;
     int j;
     for (i = 0 ; i < 10 ; i++)
       for (j = 0 ; j < 5 ; j++)
            System.out.print(
              x[i].substring(j, j+1));

 II. int i;
     int j;
     for (i = 0 ; i < 5 ; i++)
       for (j = 0 ; j < 10 ; j++)
            System.out.print(
              x[j].substring(i, i+1));

III. int i;
     int j;
     for (i = 0 ; i < 5 ; i++)
       for (j = 0 ; j < 10 ; j++)
            System.out.print(
              x[i].substring(j, j+1));
```

(A) I only
(B) II only
(C) I and II
(D) II and III
(E) I, II, and III

GO ON TO THE NEXT PAGE

30. Consider the following declaration and assignment statements:

```
int a = 7;
int b = 4;
double c;
c = a / b;
```

After the assignment statement is executed, what is the value of c?

(A) 1.0
(B) 1.75
(C) 2.0
(D) An error occurs because c was not initialized.
(E) An error occurs because a and b are integers and c is a double.

31. Consider the following code segment:

```
int x;
x = /* initialized to an integer */;
if (x % 2 == 0 && x / 3 == 1)
        System.out.print("Yes");
```

For what values of x will the word "Yes" be printed when the code segment is executed?

(A) 0
(B) 4
(C) Whenever x is even and x is not divisible by 3
(D) Whenever x is odd and x is divisible by 3
(E) Whenever x is even and x is divisible by 3

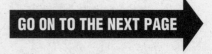

32. Consider the following incomplete class definition:

```
public class SomeClass
{
        private String myName;
        // postcondition: returns myName
        public String getName()
        { /* implmentation not shown */ }
        // postcondition: myName == name
        public void setName(String name)
        { /* implmentation not shown */ }
        // ... constructors, other methods
        //      and private data not shown
}
```

Now consider the method swap, not part of the SomeClass class.

```
// precondition: x and y are correctly
//    constructed
// postcondition: the names of objects
//    x and y are swapped
public void swap(SomeClass x, SomeClass y)
{
        <missing code>
}
```

Which of the following code segments can replace <missing code> so that the method swap works as intended?

I.
```
SomeClass temp;

temp = x;
x = y;
y = temp;
```

II.
```
String temp;

temp = x.myName;
x.myName = y.myName;
y.myName = temp;
```

III.
```
String temp;

temp = x.getName();
x.setName(y.getName());
y.setName(temp);
```

(A) I only
(B) III only
(C) I and III
(D) II and III
(E) I, II, and III

33. A bookstore wants to store information about the different types of books it sells.

For each book, it wants to keep track of the title of the book, the author of the book, and whether the book is a work of fiction or nonfiction.

If the book is a work of fiction, then the bookstore wants to keep track of whether it is a romance novel, a mystery, or science fiction.

If the book is a work of nonfiction, then the bookstore wants to keep track of whether it is a biography, a cookbook, or a self-help book.

Which of the following is the best design?

(A) Use one class, Book, which has three data fields: String title, String author, and int bookType.
(B) Use four unrelated classes: Book, Title, Author, and BookType.
(C) Use a class Book which has two data fields: String title, String author, and a subclass: BookType.
(D) Use a class Book which has two data fields: String title, String author, and six subclasses: RomanceNovel, Mystery, ScienceFiction, Biography, Cookbook, and SelfHelpBook.
(E) Use a class Book which has two data fields: String title, String author, and two subclasses: FictionWork and NonFictionWork. The class FictionWork has three subclasses, RomanceNovel, Mystery, and ScienceFiction. The class NonFictionWork has three subclasses: Biography, Cookbook, and SelfHelpBook.

34. Consider the following code:

```
public int mystery(int x)
{
        if (x == 1)
                return <missing value>;
        else
                return (2 * mystery(x-1)) + x;
}
```

Which of the following can be used to replace *<missing value>* so that mystery(4) returns 34?

(A) 0
(B) 1
(C) 2
(D) 3
(E) 4

GO ON TO THE NEXT PAGE

35. Consider the following code segment:

```
int[] X;
int[] Y;
X = initializeX(); // returns a valid
                   // initialized int[]
Y = initializeY(); // returns a valid
                   // initialized int[]
for (int k = 0;
     k < X.length && X[k] == Y[k];
     k++)
{
     /* some code */
}
```

Assuming that after X and Y are initialized, X.length == Y.length, which of the following must be true after executing this code segment?

(A) k < X.length
(B) k < X.length && X[k] == Y[k]
(C) k < X.length && X[k] != Y[k]
(D) k >= X.length || X[k] == Y[k]
(E) k >= X.length || X[k] != Y[k]

36. Which of the following would *not* cause a run-time exception?

(A) Dividing an integer by zero
(B) Using an object that has been declared but not instantiated
(C) Accessing an array element with an array index that is equal to the length of the array
(D) Attempting to cast an object to a subclass of which it is not an instance
(E) Attempting to call a method with the wrong number of arguments

37. Assume that a and b are properly initialized variables of type Double.

Which of the following is an equivalent expression to:

```
a.doubleValue() != b.doubleValue()
```

(A) a != b
(B) a.notEquals(b)
(C) !(a.doubleValue().equals(b.doubleValue()))
(D) !(a.compareTo(b))
(E) a.compareTo(b) != 0

38. Which of the following would be the least effective way of ensuring reliability in a program?

(A) Encapsulating functionality in a class by declaring all data fields to be public
(B) Defining and following preconditions and postconditions for every method
(C) Including assertions at key places in the code
(D) Using descriptive variable names
(E) Indenting code in a consistent and logical manner

GO ON TO THE NEXT PAGE

39. Consider a dictionary that has 1,000 pages with 50 words on each page.

In order to look up a given target word, a student is considering using one of the following three methods:

Method 1

Use a binary search technique to find the correct page (comparing the target word with the first word on a given page). When the correct page is found, use a sequential search technique to find the target word on the page.

Method 2

Use a sequential search technique to find the correct page (comparing the target word with the first word on a given page). When the correct page is found, use another sequential search technique to find the target word on the page.

Method 3

Use a sequential search technique on all of the words in the dictionary to find the target word.

Which of the following best characterizes the greatest number of words that will be examined using each method?

	Method 1	Method 2	Method 3
(A)	10	50	1,000
(B)	55	500	2,500
(C)	55	525	25,000
(D)	60	1,050	1,050
(E)	60	1,050	50,000

40. Which of the following is *not* a peripheral?

(A) A color laser printer
(B) A monitor
(C) A word processing application
(D) A mouse
(E) An external CD-ROM drive

END OF SECTION I

IF YOU FINISH BEFORE TIME IS CALLED, YOU MAY
CHECK YOUR WORK ON THIS SECTION.

DO NOT GO ON TO SECTION II UNTIL YOU ARE TOLD TO DO SO.

COMPUTER SCIENCE A
SECTION II
Time—1 hour and 45 minutes
Number of Questions—4
Percent of Total Grade—50

Directions: SHOW ALL YOUR WORK. REMEMBER THAT PROGRAM SEGMENTS ARE TO BE WRITTEN IN JAVA™.

Notes:

- Assume that the classes listed in the Quick Reference sheet have been imported where appropriate. A Quick Reference to the AP Java classes is included as part of the exam.

- Assume that declarations of variables and methods appear within the context of an enclosing class.

- Assume that method calls that are not prefixed with an object or class name appear within the context of the class in which the method is declared.

- Unless otherwise noted in the question, assume that parameters in method calls are not null.

- Unless otherwise noted, assume that methods are called only when their preconditions are satisfied.

FREE-RESPONSE QUESTIONS

1. In a certain school, students are permitted to enroll in one elective class from a list of electives offered. Because there are a limited number of spaces in each class for students, and because some electives are more popular than others, a lottery system was devised by the school to assign students to electives.

   Each student lists three choices for electives. The school orders the students randomly and assigns each student to the first available elective in the student's list of three choices. If none of the three choices is available (because those electives are fully enrolled), the school does not assign the student to an elective.

   After the school attempts to assign all of the students to electives, it produces a list of students it was unable to assign.

   For example, suppose there are six electives available to students: Astronomy, Ballroom Dance, Basketweaving, Constitutional Law, Marine Biology, and Programming.

   The following table shows the name, maximum enrollment, and current enrollment for six electives after 64 students have been successfully assigned to electives:

GO ON TO THE NEXT PAGE

Elective Name	Maximum Enrollment	Current Enrollment
Astronomy	12	12
Ballroom Dance	20	3
Basketweaving	15	14
Constitutional Law	10	7
Marine Biology	10	10
Programming	30	30

Note that three electives, Astronomy, Programming, and Marine Biology, are fully enrolled and are no longer options for students.

Now suppose that the following students need to be assigned to electives:

Student	First Choice getChoice(0)	Second Choice getChoice(1)	Third Choice getChoice(2)
Andrew	Programming	Marine Biology	Ballroom Dance
David	Constitutional Law	Basketweaving	Programming
Elizabeth	Marine Biology	Programming	Astronomy
Ethan	Basketweaving	Marine Biology	Astronomy
Katharine	Programming	Basketweaving	Marine Biology

Andrew's first and second choices are fully enrolled, but his third choice has openings. Andrew will be enrolled in Ballroom Dance.

David's first choice has openings. David will be enrolled in Constitutional Law.

All three of Elizabeth's choices are fully enrolled. Elizabeth will remain unassigned to an elective.

Ethan's first choice has one opening left. Ethan will be enrolled in Basketweaving. Note that Basketweaving is now fully enrolled.

GO ON TO THE NEXT PAGE ➤

All three of Katharine's choices are now fully enrolled. Katharine will remain unassigned to an elective.

In this problem, the school is modeled by the class School. Students and electives are modeled by the classes Student and Elective respectively.

The School class includes the following methods and private data:

- studentList—This ArrayList holds the list of students in the order in which the students should be scheduled.

- electiveList—This ArrayList holds the electives that students may choose.

- getElectiveByName—This method returns the Elective in electiveList with the given name.

- assignElectivesToStudents—This method encapsulates the functionality of assigning students (if possible) their first, second, or third elective choice.

- studentsWithoutElectives—This method returns an ArrayList containing students that have not been assigned an elective.

GO ON TO THE NEXT PAGE ➡

```
public class School
{
        private ArrayList studentList;
        // each entry is an instance of a
        // Student representing one student
        // at the school; students are in
        // the order they should be scheduled
        private ArrayList electiveList;
        // each entry is an instance of an
        // Elective representing one elective
        // offered at the school
        // precondition: name is the name of an
        //    Elective in electiveList
        // postcondition: returns the Elective
        //    in electiveList with the given
        //    name
        private Elective
             getElectiveByName(String name)
        { /* to be implemented in part (a) */ }
        // postcondition: All Students in
        //    studentList have been either
        //    assigned their first available
        //    elective choice or not assigned;
        //    All Electives in electiveList have
        //    been updated appropriately as
        //    Students are assigned to them
        public void assignElectivesToStudents()
        { /* to be implemented in part (b) */ }
        // postcondition: returns a list of
        //    those Students who have not been
        //    assigned an Elective
        public ArrayList
             studentsWithoutElectives()
        { /* to be implemented in part (c) */ }
        // ... constructors, other methods,
        //       and other private data not shown
}
```

The Student class includes the following methods and private data:

- getChoice—This method returns the name of the given elective choice of the student. The first elective choice has index 0, the second has index 1, and the third has index 2.

- hasElective—This method returns true if the student has been assigned an elective; it returns false otherwise.

- assignElective—This method assigns the given elective to this student.

```
public class Student
{
        // precondition: 0 <= index < 3
        // postcondition: returns the name
        //    of the given elective choice
        public String getChoice(int index)
        { /* code not shown */ }
        // postcondition: returns true if
        //    an Elective has been assigned
        //    to this Student
        public boolean hasElective()
        { /* code not shown */ }
        // precondition: e is not null
        // postcondition: e has been assigned
        //    to this Student; e has not been
        //    modified
        public void assignElective(Elective e)
        { /* code not shown */ }
        // ... constructors, other methods,
        //       and other private data not shown
}
```

The Elective class includes the following methods:

- getName—This method returns the name of this elective.

- getMaxClassSize—This method returns the maximum number of students that can be assigned to this elective.

- getClassSize—This method returns the number of students that have been assigned to this elective.

- addStudent—This method assigns the given student to this elective.

GO ON TO THE NEXT PAGE

```
public class Elective
{
        // postcondition: returns the name
        //    of this Elective
        public String getName()
        { /* code not shown */ }
        // postcondition: returns the
        //    maximum number of Students
        //    that can be added to this
        //    Elective
        public int getMaxClassSize()
        { /* code not shown */ }
        // postcondition: returns the
        //    number of Students that have
        //    been added to this Elective;
        //    0 <= getClassSize() <=
        //    getMaxClassSize()
        public int getClassSize()
        { /* code not shown */ }
        // precondition: getClassSize() <
        //    getMaxClassSize(); s is not null
        // postcondition: s has been added to
        //    this Elective; getClassSize() has
        //    been increased by 1
        public void addStudent(Student s)
        { /* code not shown */ }
        // ... constructors, other methods,
        //       and other private data not shown
}
```

(a) Write the `School` method `getElectiveByName`. Method `getElectiveByName` should return the Elective in `electiveList` that has the given name.

Complete method `getElectiveByName` below.

```
// precondition: name is the name of an
//    Elective in electiveList
// postcondition: returns the Elective in
//    electiveList with the given name
private Elective
        getElectiveByName(String name)
```

(b) Write the `School` method `assignElectivesToStudents`. Method `assignElectivesToStudents` should assign electives to students as described at the beginning of this question.

In writing method `assignElectivesToStudents` you may use the `private` helper method `getElectiveByName` specified in part (a). Assume that `getElectiveByName` works as specified, regardless of what you wrote in part (a). Solutions that reimplement functionality provided by this method, rather than invoking it, will not receive full credit.

Complete method `assignElectivesToStudents` below.

```
// postcondition: All Students in
//    studentList have been either
//    assigned their first available
//    elective choice or not assigned;
//    All Electives in electiveList have
//    been updated appropriately as
//    Students are assigned to them
public void assignElectivesToStudents()
```

(c) Write the `School` method `studentsWithoutElectives`. Method `studentsWithoutElectives` should return `ArrayList` of all `Students` in `studentList` who do not have an `Elective` assigned to them.

Complete method `studentsWithoutElectives` below.

```
// postcondition: returns a list of those
//    Students who have not been assigned
//    an Elective
public ArrayList studentsWithoutElectives()
```

2. Consider a deck of *n* cards where *n* is even and each card is uniquely labeled from 1 to *n*.

A *shuffle* is performed when the deck is divided into two stacks and the stacks are interlaced so that a new stack is formed by alternately taking cards from each stack.

For instance, a deck of ten cards is in order when the card labeled 0 is on the top of the deck and the card labeled 9 is on the bottom of the deck.

Dividing the deck in half produces two stacks of cards—one stack with cards 0 through 4, the other with cards 5 through 9. Interlacing the stacks produces a deck in the following order:

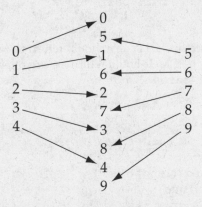

The number of times needed to shuffle the deck until it returns to its original order is called the *reorder count*. Note that the reorder count for a deck of ten cards is six:

Shuffle number

Original	1	2	3	4	5	6
0	0	0	0	0	0	0
1	5	7	8	4	2	1
2	1	5	7	8	4	2
3	6	3	6	3	6	3
4	2	1	5	7	8	4
5	7	8	4	2	1	5
6	3	6	3	6	3	6
7	8	4	2	1	5	7
8	4	2	1	5	7	8
9	9	9	9	9	9	9

A deck is modeled by the following incomplete declaration of the **Deck** class:

```
public class Deck
{
        private int[] cards;

        public Deck(int numCards)
        { /* code not shown */ }
        public boolean inOrder()
        { /* to be implemented in part (a) */ }
        public void shuffle()
        { /* to be implemented in part (b) */ }
        public int reorderingCount()
        { /* to be implemented in part (c) */ }
}
```

(a) Write the Deck method inOrder. Method inOrder should return true if the cards in the deck are in numerical order from 0 to cards.length - 1 and should return false otherwise. Cards are in numerical order if cards[k] == k for all 0 <= k < cards.length.

Complete method inOrder below.

```
// precondition: For all k such that
//     0 <= k < cards.length,
//     0 <= cards[k] < cards.length and
//     each cards[k] is unique
// postcondition: returns true if
//     cards[k] == k for all
//     0 <= k < cards.length; returns
//     false otherwise
public boolean inOrder()
```

GO ON TO THE NEXT PAGE →

(b) Write the Deck method shuffle. Method shuffle should divide the deck into two equal stacks and interlace them evenly as described at the beginning of this question.

Complete method shuffle below.

```
// postcondition: the deck is shuffled by
//    dividing the deck into two equal stacks
//    that are evenly interlaced
public void shuffle()
```

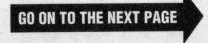
GO ON TO THE NEXT PAGE

(c) Write the `Deck` method `reorderCount`. Method `reorderCount` should return the number of shuffles necessary to return the deck to its original order.

In writing method `reorderCount` you may use the methods `inOrder` and `shuffle` as specified in parts (a) and (b). Assume that `inOrder` and `shuffle` work as specified, regardless of what you wrote in parts (a) and (b). Solutions that reimplement functionality provided by these methods, rather than invoking them, will not receive full credit.

Complete method `reorderCount` below.

```
// postcondition: returns the number of
//    shuffles necessary to return the cards
//    in the deck to their original numerical
//    order such that inOrder() == true; the
//    cards in the deck are in their original
//    numerical order
public int reorderCount()
```

GO ON TO THE NEXT PAGE

3. Consider the design of an electronic cookbook modeled with the following class declarations:

```
public class Cookbook
{
        private ArrayList recipeList;
        // each entry is an instance of a
        // Recipe representing one recipe
        // in the cookbook
        // precondition: numPeople > 0
        // postcondition: All recipes in
        //    recipeList have been converted to
        //    serve numPeople number of people
        public void standardize(int numPeople)
        { /* code not shown */ }
        // ... constructors, other methods,
        //       and other private data not shown
}
public class Ingredient
{
        private String name;
        // the name of this ingredient
        private double amount;
        // the amount of this ingredient needed
        // in the recipe
        // postcondition: returns the amount of
        //    this ingredient needed in the
        //    recipe
        public double getAmount()
        { /* code not shown */ }
        // precondition: amt > 0.0
        // postcondition: amount has been set
        //    to amt
        public void setAmount(double amt)
        { /* code not shown */ }
        // ... constructors and other methods
        //       not shown
}
```

GO ON TO THE NEXT PAGE

(a) A recipe in the cookbook is modeled by the class `Recipe` with the following data and operations:

Data

- the name of the recipe
- the list of ingredients used in the recipe
- the description of the preparation process for the recipe
- the number of people served by the recipe

Operations

- create a recipe with a given name and number of people served
- add an ingredient to the recipe
- set the description of the preparation process for the recipe
- return the name of the recipe
- return the number of people served by the recipe
- scale the recipe to serve a given new number of people by changing the amount of each ingredient appropriately

Write the definition of the class `Recipe`, showing the appropriate data definitions and constructor and method signatures. You should *not* write the implementations of the constructor or methods for the `Recipe` class.

GO ON TO THE NEXT PAGE

(b) Using the signature you wrote in part (a), write the implementation for the method that scales the recipe to serve a given new number of people.

In writing this method, you may call any of the methods in the Recipe class (as you defined it in part (a)) or in the Ingredient class. Assume that these methods work as specified.

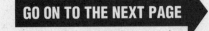
GO ON TO THE NEXT PAGE

(c) Write the Cookbook method standardize as described at the beginning of the question.

In writing this method, you may call any of the methods in the Recipe class (as you defined it in part (a)). Assume that these methods work as specified.

Complete method standardize below.

```
// precondition: numPeople > 0
// postcondition: All recipes in
//    recipeList have been scaled to
//    serve numPeople number of people
public void standardize(int numPeople)
```

4. This question involves reasoning about the code from the Marine Biology Simulation Case Study. A copy of the code is available from The College Board website or in Chapter 12 of this book.

Consider that the Environment class has been modified so that each location in the environment has eight neighbors instead of four neighbors. Specifically, a given location now has neighbors to the north, south, east, west, northeast, northwest, southeast, and southwest. Accordingly, the neighborsOf method of the Environment class has been modified so that it returns as many as eight neighbors of a given location.

Consider also that the Fish class has been modified so that each fish has an integer size associated with it. The new method, size, returns the size of the fish.

Now consider a new type of fish called a shark. A shark has all of the characteristics of a fish with the following exceptions:

- A shark may only move straight ahead or diagonally to the left or right. In other words, a shark may only move to the location directly in front of its current location or to one of the two locations next to the location directly in front of its current location

- A shark may move either to an empty location in the environment or to a location containing a smaller fish

- When a shark moves to a location containing a smaller fish, it eats that fish and that fish is removed from the environment

- A shark *must* move during each timestep. If it cannot move—either because it is blocked from doing so by larger fish or by the edge of the environment—it dies

The modifications that have been made to the Environment class are shown below.

```
public class Environment
{
        // ...constructors, methods, and
        //     private data as in the original
        //     version
        // postcondition: Returns an ArrayList
        // of up to eight adjacent neighbors of
        // the given location; only neighbors
        // that are valid locations in the
        // environment will be included
        public ArrayList
          neighborsOf(Location ofLoc)
        { /* code not shown */ }
}
```

GO ON TO THE NEXT PAGE

The modifications that have been made to the Fish class are shown below.

```
public class Fish
{
        // ...constructors, methods, and other
        //     private data as in the original
        //     version
        private int mySize;              // fish's size
        // postcondition: returns the size
        //     of this fish
        public int size()
        { /* code not shown */ }
}
```

Sharks are modeled by the Shark class which inherits functionality from the Fish class.

```
public class Shark extends Fish
{
        // postcondition: Returns true if loc
        //     is a valid location in the
        //     environment and is either
        //     directly in front of or diagonally
        //     left or right in front of this
        //     shark; returns false otherwise
        protected boolean isValid(Location loc)
        { /* code not shown */ }
        // precondition: loc is a neighbor of
        //     this shark's location
        // postcondition: Returns true if loc
        //     is a valid location and is either
        //     empty or contains an object
        //     smaller than this shark; returns
        //     false otherwise
        protected boolean isLegal(Location loc)
        { /* to be implemented in part (a) */ }
        // postcondition: Returns a list of
        //     locations that this shark can
        //     legally move to
        protected ArrayList movableNeighbors()
        { /* to be implemented in part (b) */ }
        // postcondition: The shark has been
        //     moved in its environment according
        //     to its rules
        protected void move()
        { /* to be implemented in part (c) */ }
        // ... constructors, other methods,
        //     and other private data not shown
}
```

(a) Write the `Shark` helper method `isLegal` which returns **true** if the shark can legally move to the given location.

Complete method `isLegal` below.

```
// precondition: loc is a neighbor of
//    this shark's location
// postcondition: Returns true if loc is a
//    valid location and is either empty or
//    contains an object smaller than this
//    shark; returns false otherwise
protected boolean isLegal(Location loc)
```

GO ON TO THE NEXT PAGE ➡

(b) Write the `Shark` helper method `movableNeighbors` which returns an `ArrayList` of neighbors that this shark can legally move to.

In writing this method, you may call any of the methods in the Marine Biology Simulation that are accessible to a `Shark`. Assume that these methods work as specified. You may also use the method `isLegal` as specified in part (a). Assume that `isLegal` works as specified, regardless of what you wrote in part (a). Solutions that reimplement functionality provided by this method, rather than invoking it, will not receive full credit.

Complete method `movableNeighbors` below.

```
// postcondition: Returns a list of
//    locations that this shark can
//    legally move to
protected ArrayList movableNeighbors()
```

(c) Write the `Shark` method `move` as described at the beginning of the question.

In writing this method, you may call any of the methods in the Marine Biology Simulation that are accessible to a `Shark`. Assume that these methods work as specified.

Complete method `move` below.

```
// postcondition: The shark has been moved
//    in its environment according to its
//    rules
protected void move()
```

END OF EXAMINATION

Answers and Explanations to the AP Computer Science A Practice Test

MULTIPLE-CHOICE QUESTIONS

1. **D** This code tests your knowledge of how nested `if-else` statements work and your knowledge of the `dangling-else` problem.

   The `dangling-else` problem occurs when there are fewer `else` clauses than `if` clauses and most often results in a difficult-to-find logical error in the program when the code is not indented correctly.

   In this problem, despite the misleading indentation, each `else` clause should be associated with the most recent `if` clause.

   Re-indenting this code segment correctly gives the following:

   ```
   int a;
   int b;
   a = 10;
   b = 0;
   if (a > 0)
        if (a > 15)
             if (a > 20)
                 b = 1;
             else
                 b = 2;
        else
             b = 3;
   ```

   Now it is easy to see what the code does. The value of a is 10—it is greater than 0 yet not greater than 15. Therefore, the `else b = 3` clause is executed and b is set to 3.

   Note that with the exception of problems that specifically test logical errors introduced by mis-indenting code, code segments will always be presented on the AP exam with correct indentation.

2. **B** Statement I uses the post-increment operator to add 1 to the variable A and store the result back in the variable A.

   Statement II adds 1 to the variable A but does not store the result. This statement effectively does nothing and A is unchanged.

   Statement III adds 1 to the variable A and stores the result back in the variable A.

   Statements I and III are equivalent.

3. **D** In questions involving recursion, it is often best to start with either the base case or the smallest value used as an argument to the recursive function.

   In this problem, the function `mystery` is called with values 0, 1, 2, and 3.

   `mystery(0)` does not execute the recursive call in the `for` loop and prints the value 0.

`mystery(1)` calls `mystery(0)` and then prints the value 1. Since `mystery(0)` prints the value 0, `mystery(1)` prints 01.

`mystery(2)` calls `mystery(0)` and `mystery(1)`, and then prints the value 2. Using the output from `mystery(0)` and `mystery(1)` as calculated above, `mystery(2)` prints 0012.

Finally, `mystery(3)` calls, in order, `mystery(0)`, `mystery(1)`, and `mystery(2)`, and then prints 3 to result in 00100123.

In other words, the calling sequence looks like this

Function Call	Prints
`mystery(3)`	
`mystery(0)`	
`System.out.print(0)`	0
`mystery(1)`	
`mystery(0)`	
`System.out.print(0)`	0
`System.out.print(1)`	1
`mystery(2)`	
`mystery(0)`	
`System.out.print(0)`	0
`mystery(1)`	
`mystery(0)`	
`System.out.print(0)`	0
`System.out.print(1)`	1
`System.out.print(2)`	2
`System.out.print(3)`	3

4. **C** Selection sort walks through the array finding the smallest element in the part of the array not yet sorted. It then swaps that smallest element with the first unsorted element.

Start with the original array of values.

4	10	1	2	6	7	3	5

The smallest element is 1. We swap that with the first unsorted element, 4. The array now looks like this.

1	10	4	2	6	7	3	5

The smallest element in the unsorted part of the array (from 10 to 5) is 2. We swap that with the first unsorted element, 10.

1	2	4	10	6	7	3	5

Continuing the process, the smallest element in the unsorted part of the array (from 4 to 5) is 3. We swap that with the first unsorted element, 4.

1	2	3	10	6	7	4	5

At this point, we match answer (C) and are finished.

For good measure, we'll complete the moves for SelectionSort, giving us

1	2	3	4	6	7	10	5
1	2	3	4	5.	7	10	6
1	2	3	4	5	6	10	7
1	2	3	4	5	6	7	10

5. **E** The array, A, has seven elements with indices from 0 to 6. The first for loop sets each element in the array to the length of the array, 7, minus the index value.

7	6	5	4	3	2	1

The second for loop puts the value of the kth element of the array into the $(k + 1)^{st}$ element. Be careful! A quick glance might lead you to believe that each value is shifted in the array one spot to the right giving an answer of (D).

However, a step-by-step analysis demonstrates that the first value in the array is copied into every array element.

k	Assignment	A[]						
0	A[1] = A[0]	7	7	5	4	3	2	1
1	A[2] = A[1]	7	7	7	4	3	2	1
2	A[3] = A[2]	7	7	7	7	3	2	1
3	A[4] = A[3]	7	7	7	7	7	2	1
4	A[5] = A[4]	7	7	7	7	7	7	1
5	A[6] = A[5]	7	7	7	7	7	7	7

6. **B** Choices (C), (D), and (E) are syntactically invalid according to the given class definitions.

In choice (C), p is used as a PostOffice object rather than an array of PostOffice objects.

Choice (D) treats getMail and getBox as static methods without invoking them from an object.

Choice (E) creates a new Mail object attempting to use a Mail constructor. Even if such a constructor were available, there would be no way for the constructor to know about p, the array of PostOffices.

Choices (A) and (B) differ only in the indices of the array and methods. There are two clues in the question that indicate that choice (B) is the correct answer.

First, p is declared as an array of ten PostOffices. This means that p[10] would raise an Array-IndexOutOfBoundsException. Remember that p[9] actually refers to the tenth post office.

Second, the comments in the class definitions for the getBox and getMail methods indicate that the parameter they take is zero-based. Therefore, they should be passed an integer one less than the number of the box or piece of mail needed.

7. **A** In the method `printBoxesWithoutMail`, the loop variable `k` refers to the index of the post office and the loop variable `x` refers to the index of the box within the post office.

Choice (A) is correct. It checks to see if the box is assigned and if it does not have mail using the appropriate methods of the `Box` class. It then prints out the box number of the box.

Choice (B) is similar to choice (A) but incorrectly interchanges `x` and `k`.

Choice (C) attempts to print the box number of a post office by omitting the call to the method `getBox`.

Choice (D) is similar to (C) but interchanges `x` and `k`.

Choice (E) prints the index of the post office rather than the index of the box.

8. **B** There are four possibilities for the values of `a` and `b`. Either both `a` and `b` are true, both `a` and `b` are false, `a` is true and `b` is false, or `a` is false and `b` is true.

Analyzing the possibilities in a table, we see that in all four cases, the final value of `b` is the same as the initial value of `b`.

a (initial value)	b (initial value)	a = a && b (final value)	b = a || b (final value)
true	true	true	true
false	false	false	false
true	false	false	false
false	true	false	true

Remember when calculating `b = a || b` that `a` has already been modified. Therefore, use the final, rather than the initial, value of `a` when calculating the final value of `b`.

9. **C** The best way to solve this problem is to look at each if statement individually.

```
if (x > 10)
        System.out.print("A");
```

Because the value of x is 53, it is greater than 10 and the letter "A" is printed.

```
if (x > 30)
        System.out.print("B");
else if (x > 40)
        System.out.print("C");
```

Again, the value of x is greater than 30, so the letter "B" is printed. Note that the second conditional (if x > 40) is not tested because it is part of the *else* clause.

```
if (x > 50)
        System.out.print("D");
```

The letter "D" is printed because the value of x is also greater than 50.

```
if (x > 70)
        System.out.print("E");
```

However, the value of x is not greater than 70, so the letter "E" is not printed.

10. **E** This problem tests your ability to work with nested `for` loops. Although it appears complicated at first glance, it can easily be solved by systematically walking through the code.

Be sure to write the values of the variables j and k down on paper; don't try to keep track of j and k in your head. Use the empty space in the question booklet for this purpose.

Code	j	k	Output
Initialize j to the value -2.	–2		
Test the condition: j <= 2? Yes.	–2		
Initialize k to the value that j has.	–2	–2	
Test the condition: k < j + 3? Yes.	–2	–2	
Output k.	–2	–2	-2
Update k: k++	–2	–1	-2
Test the condition: k < j + 3? Yes.	–2	–1	-2
Output k.	–2	–1	–2 –1
Update k: k++	–2	0	–2 –1
Test the condition: k < j + 3? Yes.	–2	0	–2 –1
Output k.	–2	0	–2 –1 0
Update k: k++	–2	1	–2 –1 0
Test the condition: k < j + 3? No.	–2	1	–2 –1 0
Update j: j = j + 2	0	1	–2 –1 0
Test the condition: j <= 2. Yes.	0	1	–2 –1 0
Initialize k to the value that j has.	0	0	–2 –1 0
Test the condition: k < j + 3? Yes.	0	0	–2 –1 0
Output k.	0	0	–2 –1 0 0

At this point we can stop because choice (E) is the only choice that starts -2 -1 0 0.

11. **A** To solve this problem, first note that `count % 3` is equal to the remainder when `count` is divided by 3.

Because 5 % 3 = 2, calling `mystery(5, "X")` will print X, call `mystery(4, "X")`, and return.

Because 4 % 3 = 1, calling `mystery(4, "X")` will print X-X, call `mystery(3, "X")`, and return. At this point, choices (C) and (E) have been eliminated.

Because 3 % 3 = 0, calling `mystery(3, "X")` will print X--X, call `mystery(2, "X")`, and return. Note that you can stop at this point because choices (B) and (D) have also been eliminated from consideration.

To continue for the sake of completeness, because 2 % 3 = 2, calling `mystery(2, "X")` will print X, call `mystery(1, "X")`, and return.

Because 1 % 3 = 1, calling `mystery(1, "X")` will print X-X, call `mystery(0, "X")`, and return.

Finally, calling `mystery(0, "X")` will simply return because `count` is less than or equal to zero.

Putting it all together, `mystery(5, "X")` prints

XX-XX--XXX-X

12. **B** The only information that we need to solve the problem is the first sentence in the description of the constructor.

Class `DiningRoomSet` has a constructor, which is passed a `Table` object and an `ArrayList` of `Chair` objects.

Because we are writing a constructor, we can immediately eliminate choices (A) and (C), which are void methods. Constructors *never* return anything.

Choice (E) is incorrect because the constructor is passed a `Table` object and a `Chair` object; not a `Table` object and an `ArrayList` of `Chair` objects.

Choice (C) is incorrect because the second parameter has two types associated with it. It should have only one type: `ArrayList`.

Choice (B) is correct.

13. **D** The best way to solve this problem is to eliminate choices.

Choices (A) and (B) are incorrect because the class description states that the `getPrice` method of the `DiningRoomSet` class does not take any parameters.

Choice (C) can be eliminated because the private data field `myChairs` is not a `Chair`; it is an `ArrayList`. Therefore, it does not have a `getPrice` method.

This leaves choices (D) and (E). You need to know that `ArrayLists` are accessed using the `get` method while arrays are accessed using the [] notation.

`MyChairs` is an `ArrayList`, so the correct answer is choice (D).

14. **C** To solve this type of problem, use information about the output and the loops to eliminate incorrect choices. Then, if necessary, work through the code for any remaining choices to determine the correct answer.

There are six lines of output. By examining the outer loop of each of the choices, we can eliminate choice (B) because it will traverse the loop seven times, and during each traversal at least one number will be printed.

We can also eliminate choice (A) because the outer loop will never be executed. The initial value of j is 6, but the condition j < 0 causes the loop to terminate immediately.

Turning our attention to the inner loop, we can eliminate choice (D) because the first time through the loop, a 7 will be printed—clearly not the correct output.

Finally, we can eliminate choice (E) because the condition of the inner loop, k >= 0 will cause a 0 to be printed at the end of each line.

This leaves choice (C), which is indeed the correct answer.

15. **B** This problem tests your knowledge of the methods of the ArrayList class.

The following table shows the contents of list after each line of code.

Code	Contents of list	Explanation
list = new ArrayList();	[ ]	A newly created ArrayList is empty.
list.add(new Integer(7));	[7]	Adds 7 to the end of list.
list.add(new Integer(6));	[7, 6]	Adds 6 to the end of list.
list.add(1, new Integer(5));	[7, 5, 6]	Inserts 5 into list at position 1 shifting elements to the right as necessary.
list.add(1, new Integer(4));	[7, 4, 5, 6]	Inserts 4 into list at position 1 shifting elements to the right as necessary.
list.add(new Integer(3));	[7, 4, 5, 6, 3]	Adds 3 to the end of list.
list.set(2, new Integer(2));	[7, 4, 2, 6, 3]	Replaces the number at position 2 in list with 2.
list.add(1, new Integer(1));	[7, 1, 4, 2, 6, 3]	Inserts 1 into list at position 1 shifting elements to the right as necessary.

16. **D** Fish move in top-to-bottom, left-to-right order (in other words, the order in which we read English words in a paragraph of text). Each fish can move to any of its three neighboring locations (to the front or side of the fish) as long as that location is empty.

In the given configuration, label the fish A, B, and C.

Fish A has only one possible move—to location (0, 1). After moving, fish A now faces east.

Fish B now has two possible moves. It can move to the location that fish A just vacated—(0, 0) and face north—or it can move to location (2, 0) and face east.

Whichever location fish B moves to, fish C has two possible moves. Fish C can either move to location (1, 0) or to location (2, 1).

These moves result in four possible ending configurations.

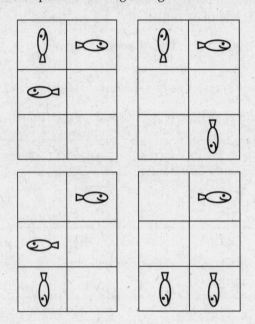

17. **B** Assume that we have a DarterFish moving to the west.

There are only four possible configurations of the environment in the two locations immediately to the west of the DarterFish: both are empty, both are occupied, the closer location is empty and the farther location is occupied, or the closer location is occupied and the farther location is empty.

Now look at the resulting configurations after the DarterFish has been moved according to each of the three nextLocation methods.

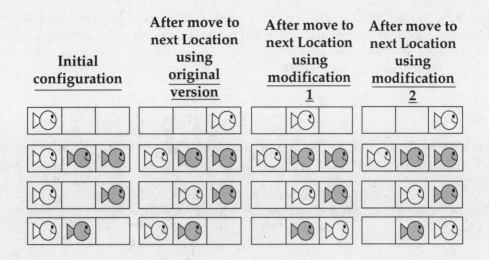

Initial configuration	After move to next Location using original version	After move to next Location using modification 1	After move to next Location using modification 2

Based on this table, evaluate each of the answer choices.

Choice (A) is incorrect because the location returned by the original version is different from the location returned by Modification 1 in two cases.

Choice (C) is incorrect because the location returned by Modification 1 is different from the location returned by Modification 2 when both locations directly in front of the DarterFish are empty.

Choices (D) and (E) are incorrect because Modifications 1 and 2 return the same location in three different cases.

Choice (B) is correct.

18. **D** The two keys to solving this problem are understanding the conditional expression in the nextLocation method of the MysteryFish class and understanding the nextLocation method of the Fish class.

The nextLocation method of the MysteryFish class first calls the nextLocation method of its superclass (Fish) to get a possible location to move to (result).

```
result = super.nextLocation();
```

It then checks to see if turning *right* from result leads to the current location of the fish.

```
if (location().equals(environment().getNeighbor(result,
        direction().toRight())))
```

Note that this is the same as checking to see if turning *left* from the current location of the fish leads to the result location.

If so, it returns the result location; otherwise it returns the current location of the fish.

Based on this analysis, choices (A), (C), and (E) can be eliminated.

Because the nextLocation method of the Fish class returns a randomly chosen neighboring empty location that is *not* the location directly behind the fish, choice (B) is also eliminated and choice (D) is correct.

19. **A** One of the fundamentals of object-oriented design is that each object stores and maintains its own information. In this problem, a fish can keep track of how many timesteps have passed without movement and can remove itself from the environment as required. No other class needs to know about this information.

To implement the change, only the `Fish` class is modified. A private data field, `didNotMove-Count`, is added to the `Fish` class and initialized to 0 in the `initialize` method.

The `move` method is modified to increment `didNotMoveCount` when the fish's new location is the same as its current location and to set `didNotMoveCount` back to 0 if the fish changes location.

The `act` method is modified to remove the fish from the environment if `didNotMoveCount` reaches 5.

20. **A** The `nextLocation` method in both the `Fish` and `SlowFish` class uses a random number to decide which of several locations the fish might move to. Therefore, it is impossible to predict exactly which location will be returned by the `nextLocation` method.

For a `DarterFish`, it is possible to predict exactly where it will move to based on its location, its direction, and the configuration of its environment. See the solution to question 17 for an example.

Choice (A) is correct. `Fish` and `SlowFish` have probabilistic `nextLocation` methods; `Darter-Fish` has a deterministic `nextLocation` method.

21. **E** Although all three responses look very similar, statement I does not actually construct a new `Fraction` because it is missing the keyword `new`.

Note that because `f` is also a `Fraction` object, the current `Fraction` object can also access `f`'s private data. Contrast this with the behavior of derived objects in question 23.

22. **C** Choice (C) correctly multiplies `fractionOne` by `fractionTwo` and returns the result as a `Fraction`. Furthermore, it is the only code that compiles!

Choice (A) is incorrect because the multiplication operator, *, is not defined to work on `Fraction` objects.

Choice (B) is incorrect because the `multiply` method only takes one parameter and it is not correctly invoked by a `Fraction` object.

Choice (D) attempts to create a new `Fraction` object but incorrectly constructs it by passing two `Fraction` objects rather than two integers.

Finally, while choice (E) calculates the value of the result of the multiplication, it incorrectly assigns that value to a `Fraction` object rather than an integer or double variable.

23. **D** Statement II is illegal because derived classes may not access the private data of their super classes. In other words, the constructor for a `ReducedFraction` may not directly access `numerator` and `denominator` in the `Fraction` class.

Statement I is legal. This default constructor of the `ReducedFraction` class will automatically call the default constructor of the `Fraction` class and the private data of both classes will be set appropriately.

Statement III is also legal. The call `super(n, d)` invokes the second constructor of the `Fraction` class which sets the private data of the `Fraction` class appropriately. The private data of the `ReducedFraction` class is then set explicitly in the `ReducedFraction` constructor.

Note that if the call `super(n, d)` were not present, statement III would still be legal. However, it would create a *logical error* in the code as the default constructor of the `Fraction` class would be invoked and the private data of the `Fraction` class would not be set appropriately.

24. **D** Statement I is incorrect. It compares the two objects s1 and s2 rather than their contents. This is an important distinction as two different objects may hold the same data.

Statement II is correct. The `compareTo` method of the `String` class returns 0 if the two `String` objects hold the same strings.

Statement III is also correct. The `equals` method of the `String` class returns `true` if the two `String` objects hold the same strings.

25. **A** The values of *s* and *t* are not changed! In Java, all parameters to methods are passed by value and after a method returns to its caller, the value of the caller's parameters are not modified.

Contrast this with question 32, in which the private data of objects is modified by a function even though the objects themselves are not changed.

26. **D** Statement I is incorrect. An object may access private data of another object of its own class. Accessing `other.x` and `other.y` is legal because `other` is a variable in the `Point` class.

Statements II and III are correct. The signature for the `compareTo` method of the `Comparable` interface is

```
public int compareTo(Object other)
```

It requires that `compareTo` be passed an `Object` and return an `int`.

Statement III is also correct. The `equals` method of the `String` class returns `true` if the two `String` objects hold the same strings.

27. **B** An example will help clarify this question.

Consider the following `for` loop:

```
for (int k = 0; k < 5; k++)
{
        System.out.println(k);
}
```

This prints out the integers 0 to 4; one number per line.

It is equivalent to the `while` loop.

```
int k = 0;
while (k < 5)
{
        System.out.println(k);
        k++;
}
```

Matching "`int k = 0`" to *<1>*; "`k < 5`" to *<2>*; "`k++`" to *<3>* and "`System.out.println(k);`" to *<4>*, we can see that choice (B) is correct.

28. **E** This question tests your knowledge of operator precedence.

In Java, multiplication, division, and modulus are performed before addition and subtraction. If more than one operator in an expression has the same precedence, the operations are performed left-to-right.

Parenthesizing the expression one step at a time

```
        a / b + c - d % e * f
⇒       (a / b) + c - d % e * f
⇒       (a / b) + c - (d % e) * f
⇒       (a / b) + c - ((d % e) * f)
⇒       ((a / b) + c) - ((d % e) * f)
```

29. **B** Only statement II correctly prints out the first character of all ten strings followed by the second character of all ten strings, and so on.

Statement I prints all of the characters of the first string followed by all of the characters of the second string, and so on.

Statement III prints all of the characters of the first string followed by all of the characters of the second string, and so on—but only for the first five strings.

30. **A** It is perfectly legal to assign a value of type int to a variable of type double in an expression. However, certain rules apply when evaluating the expression.

In the expression

```
c = a / b;
```

a and b are both integers. Therefore, the / operator represents integer division. The result of the division is truncated by discarding the fractional component.

In this example, 7 / 4 has the value 1—the result of truncating 1.75.

When assigning an integer to a variable of type double, the integer value is converted to its equivalent double value.

Note that the variable c is, in fact, initialized. Specifically, it is initialized to the value a / b.

31. **B** For the code to print the word "Yes", two conditions must be true.

- The remainder must be zero when x is divided by 2. In other words, x must be even.
- The value after truncating the result when x is divided by 3 must be 1. In other words, $1 \leq x / 3 < 2$.

The second condition is more narrow than the first. The only integers that fulfill the second condition are 3, 4, and 5.

Of those, only 4 is even and therefore also fulfills the first condition.

32. **B** Statement I is incorrect because all parameters in Java are passed by value. After a method returns to its caller, the value of the caller's parameters are not modified. The strings will not be swapped.

Statement II is incorrect because myName is a private data field of the SomeClass class and may not be accessed by the swap method. Note that the question specifically states that the swap method is *not* a method of the SomeClass class. Be sure to watch for statements that narrow the answer possibilities.

Statement III correctly swaps the names of the objects.

Contrast this with question 25, which also concerns parameter passing.

33. **E** The way to approach this type of design problem is to look for HAS-A and IS-A relationships among the distinct pieces of data.

A book HAS-A title and author. The title and author should be data fields of the `Book` class, either as `String`s or as their own unrelated classes.

This information is not enough to answer the question though.

Looking for the IS-A relationships, a mystery IS-A work of fiction which IS-A book. Therefore, it makes good design sense for these three items to be separate classes. Specifically, `Mystery` should be a subclass of `FictionWork`, which should be a subclass of `Book`.

Similarly, `RomanceNovel` and `ScienceFiction` should be subclasses of `FictionWork` and `Biography`, `Cookbook`, and `SelfHelpBook` should be subclasses of `NonFictionWork`, which should be a subclass of `Book`.

Only choice (E) meets all of these design criteria.

34. **C** In order to solve this recursive problem, work backward from the base case to the known value of `mystery(4)`.

Let y represent the *<missing value>*. Note that `mystery(1) = y`.

Now calculate `mystery(2)`, `mystery(3)`, and `mystery(4)` in terms of y.

```
mystery(2) = 2 * mystery(1) + 2
           = 2 * y + 2
mystery(3) = 2 * mystery(2) + 3
           = 2 * (2 * y + 2) + 3
           = 4 * y + 4 + 3
           = 4 * y + 7

mystery(4) = 2 * mystery(3) + 4
           = 2 * (4 * y + 7) + 4
           = 8 * y + 14 + 4
           = 8 * y + 18
```

Because `mystery(4)` also equals 34, set `8*y + 18 = 34` and solve for y.

```
8 * y + 18 = 34
8 * y = 16
y = 2
```

35. **E** The `for` loop terminates when the condition is no longer true. This can happen either because k is no longer less than `X.length` or because `X[k]` does not equal `Y[k]`. Choice (E) states this formally.

Another way to approach the problem is to use DeMorgan's law to negate the condition in the `for` loop.

Recall that DeMorgan's law states that

```
! (p && q) is equivalent to !p || !q
```

Negating the condition in the `for` loop gives us

```
  ! (k < X.length && X[k] == Y[k])
=> !(k < X.length) || !(X[k] == Y[k])
=> k >= X.length || X[k] != Y[k]
```

This method also gives choice (E) as the correct answer.

36. **E** Choices (A), (B), (C), and (D) are examples of an `ArithmeticException`, a `NullPointerException`, an `ArrayIndexOutOfBoundsException`, and a `ClassCastException`.

Be careful! While choice (E) may appear to be an example of an `IllegalArgumentException`, it is actually an example of an error that is caught at compile time rather than at runtime.

An `IllegalArgumentException` occurs when a method is called with an argument that is either illegal or inappropriate—for instance, passing –1 to a method that expects to be passed only positive integers.

37. **E** First note that a and b are of type `Double`, *not* of type `double`. This distinction is important. The type `double` is a primitive type; the type `Double` is a subclass of the `Object` class that implements the `Comparable` interface. A `Double` is an object wrapper for a `double` value.

Choice (A) is incorrect. It compares a and b directly rather than the `double` values inside the objects. Even if a and b held the same value, they might be different objects.

Choice (B) is incorrect. The `Double` class does not have a notEquals method.

Choice (C) is incorrect. `a.doubleValue()` returns a `double`. Because `double` is a primitive type, it does not have any methods. Had this choice been

```
!(a.equals(b))
```

it would have been correct.

The expression `a.compareTo(b)` returns a value less than zero if `a.doubleValue()` is less than `b.doubleValue()`; a value equal to zero if `a.doubleValue()` is equal to `b.doubleValue()`, and a value greater than zero if `a.doubleValue()` is greater than `b.doubleValue()`.

Choice (D) is incorrect because the `compareTo` method does not return a `boolean`.

Choice (E) is correct.

38. **A** While "encapsulating functionality in a class" sounds like (and is) a good thing, "declaring all data fields to be public" is the exact opposite of good programming practice. Data fields in a class should be declared to be private in order to hide the underlying representation of an object. This, in turn, helps increase system reliability.

39. **E** Method 1 examines at most 10 words using a binary search technique on 1,000 pages to find the correct page. It then searches sequentially on the page to find the correct word. If the target word is the last word on the page, this method will examine all 50 words on the page. Therefore, method 1 will examine at most 60 words.

Method 2 first uses a sequential search technique to find the correct page. If the target word is on the last page, this method will examine the first word on all 1,000 pages. Then, as with method 1, it may examine as many as all 50 words on the page to find the target word. Therefore, method 2 will examine at most 1,050 words.

Method 3 sequentially searches through all of the words in the dictionary. Because there are 50,000 words in the dictionary and the target word may be the last word in the dictionary, this method may have to examine all 50,000 words in order to find the target word.

40. **C** A peripheral is a hardware device that you use with your computer. Printers, monitors, keyboards, mice, and external disk drives are all examples of peripherals.

Choice (C) is correct because a word-processing application is software, not hardware.

FREE-RESPONSE QUESTIONS

1. (a)
```
private Elective getElectiveByName(
    String name)
{
        for (int eIndex = 0;
                eIndex < electiveList.size;
                eIndex++)
        {
                Elective e = (Elective)
                    electiveList.get(eIndex);
                String eName = e.getName();
                if (name.equals(eName))
                        return e;
        }
}
```

   (b)
```
public void assignElectivesToStudents()
{
        for (int sIndex = 0;
                sIndex < studentList.size;
                sIndex++)
        {
                Student s = (Student)
                    studentList.get(sIndex);
                int choice = 0;
                while (choice < 3 &&
                        !s.hasElective())
                {
                        String name =
                            s.getChoice(choice);
                        Elective e =
                            getElectiveByName(name);
                        if (e.getClassSize() <
                            e.getMaxClassSize())
                        {
                                e.addStudent(s);
                                s.assignElective(e);
                        }
                        choice += 1;
                }
        }
}
```

```
(c) public ArrayList studentsWithoutElectives()
   {
         ArrayList result = new ArrayList();
         for (int sIndex = 0;
              sIndex < studentList.size;
              sIndex++)
         {
              Student s = (Student)
                 studentList.get(sIndex);
              if (!s.hasElective())
                    result.add(s);
         }
         return result;
   }
```

2. (a)
```
public boolean inOrder()
{
        for (int k = 0;
            k < cards.length; k++)
        {
                if (cards[k] != k)
                        return false;
        }
        return true;
}
```

(b)
```
public void shuffle()
{
        int[] newCards = new int[cards.length];
        for (int k = 0;
            k < cards.length; k++)
        {
                if (k % 2 == 0)
                        newCards[k] = k / 2;
                else
                        newCards[k] =
                            (cards.length / 2) +
                            (k / 2);
        }
        cards = newCards;
}
```

(c)
```
public int reorderCount()
{
        int count = 0;
        while (!inOrder() || count == 0)
        {
                shuffle();
                count += 1;
        }
        return count;
}
```

3. (a)
```
public class Recipe
{
        private String name;
        private ArrayList ingredientList;
        private String preparationProcess;
        private int numberServed;
        public Recipe(String recipeName,
                int numServed)
        { /* implementation not needed */ }
        public void addIngredient(Ingredient
                newIngredient)
        { /* implementation not needed */ }
        public void setPreparationProcess(
                String newPreparationProcess)
        { /* implementation not needed */ }
        public String getName()
        { /* implementation not needed */ }
        public int getNumberServed()
        { /* implementation not needed */ }
        public void scale(int newNumberServed)
        { /* implementation not needed */ }
}
```

```
(b) public void scale(int newNumberServed)
    {
            double oldAmount;
            double newAmount;
            for (int k = 0;
                  k < ingredientList.size; k++)
            {
                    Ingredient ingred = (Ingredient)
                       ingredientList.get(k);
                    oldAmount = ingred.getAmount();
                    newAmount = newNumberServed *
                         (oldAmount / numberServed);
                    ingred.setAmount(newAmount);
            }
            numberServed = newNumberServed;
    }


(c) public void standardize(int numPeople)
    {
            for (int k = 0;
                  k < recipeList.size; k++)
            {
                    Recipe r =
                       (Recipe) recipeList.get(k);
                    r.scale(numPeople);
            }
    }
```

4. (a)
```
protected boolean isLegal(Location loc)
{
        return isValid(loc) &&
           (environment().isEmpty(loc) ||
           size() >
           ((fish)(environment().objectAt(loc)).size());
}
```

(b)
```
protected ArrayList movableNeighbors()
{
        ArrayList nbrs =
          environment().neighborsOf(location());
        ArrayList movableNbrs =
          new ArrayList();
        for (int index = 0;
              index < nbrs.size(); index++)
        {
             Location loc =
                (Location) nbrs.get(index);
             if (isLegal(loc))
                   movableNbrs.add(loc);
        }
        return movableNbrs;
}
```

(c)
```
protected void move()
{
        Location newLoc = nextLocation();
        if (!newLoc.equals(location()))
        {
             if (! environment().
                 isEmpty(newLoc))
             {
                  environment().remove(
                    environment().objectAt(
                    newLoc));
             }
             Location oldLoc = location();
             changeLocation(newLoc);
             Direction newDir =
                environment().getDirection(
                oldLoc, newLoc);
             changeDirection(newDir);
        }
        else
             environment().remove(this);
}
```

The Princeton Review
AP Computer Science
AB Practice Test

COMPUTER SCIENCE AB

SECTION I

Time—1 hour and 15 minutes

Number of Questions—40

Percent of Total Grade—50

Directions: Determine the answer to each of the following questions or incomplete statements, using the available space for any necessary scratchwork. Then decide which is the best of the choices given and fill in the corresponding oval on the answer sheet. No credit will be given for anything written in the examination booklet. Do not spend too much time on any one problem.

Notes:

- Assume that the classes listed in the Quick Reference sheet have been imported where appropriate. A Quick Reference to the AP Java classes is included as part of the exam.

- Assume that the implementation classes are used for any questions referring to linked lists or trees and that the interfaces for stacks, queues, and priority queues behave as specified.

- Assume that declarations of variables and methods appear within the context of an enclosing class.

- Assume that method calls that are not prefixed with an object or class name appear within the context of the class in which the method is declared.

- Unless otherwise noted in the question, assume that parameters in method calls are not null.

MULTIPLE-CHOICE QUESTIONS

USE THIS SPACE FOR SCRATCHWORK.

1. Consider the following method:

```
public static int mystery(int a, int b)
{
    if (a <= 0)
        return b;
    else
        return mystery(a - 2, b);
}
```

What value is returned by the call mystery(12, 5)?

(A) 5
(B) 6
(C) 12
(D) 60
(E) 15625

GO ON TO THE NEXT PAGE

2. Consider the following expression tree:

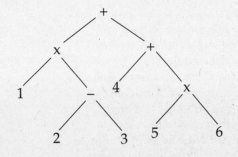

Which of the traversals given below is/are equivalent to the expression tree given above?

    I. preorder: `+ x 1 - 2 3 + 4 x 5 6`
    II. postorder: `1 2 3 - x 4 + 5 6 x +`
    III. inorder: `((1 x (2 - 3)) + (4 + (5 x 6)))`

(A) I only
(B) II only
(C) III only
(D) I and III
(E) II and III

<u>Questions 3–4</u> refer to the following incomplete class declaration for a new data structure called a Quack—a combination of a queue and a stack.

```
public class Quack
{
            // Constructor initializes myData
      public Quack()
      { /* implementation not shown */ }
            // Adds x to the back end of the
            // Quack.
      public void enquack(Object x)
      { /* implementation not shown */ }
            // if front is true, returns
            // the object at the front end of
            // the Quack; otherwise returns
            // the object at the back end of
            // the Quack. Assumes the Quack
            // is not empty.
      public Object dequack(boolean front)
      { /* implementation not shown */ }
            // Returns true if the Quack has
            // no objects; otherwise returns
            // false.
      public boolean isEmpty()
      { /* implementation not shown */ }
      <designation> ArrayList myData;
      // ... other methods and data
      //      not shown
}
```

GO ON TO THE NEXT PAGE

3. Which of the following is the best choice for `<designa-tion>` and the best reason for that choice?

   (A) `<designation>` should be `private` so that programs using a `Quack` will not be able to modify `myData` by using methods `enquack` and `dequack`, thereby preserving the principle of data stability.

   (B) `<designation>` should be `private` so that programs using a `Quack` can only modify `myData` by using methods such as `enquack` and `dequack`, thereby preserving the principle of information hiding.

   (C) `<designation>` should be `private` as an indication to programs using a `Quack` that `myData` can be modified directly but that it is *better* to modify `myData` only by using methods such as `enquack` and `dequack`, thereby preserving the principle of maximum information dissemination.

   (D) `<designation>` should be `public` because programs using a `Quack` need to know how the `Quack` class has been implemented in order to use it.

   (E) `<designation>` should be `public`. Otherwise, only objects constructed from derived subclasses of a `Quack` will be able to modify the contents of a `Quack`.

4. Assume that the `Quack` class is implemented in a way such that the worst case algorithmic runtime of the `enquack` and `dequack` methods is $O(1)$.

   Consider the problem of designing a `Quack` class method, `smallest`, to find the smallest-valued object in a `Quack`. If the `Objects` in the `Quack` implement the `Comparable` interface and their `compareTo` method has an $O(1)$ runtime, what is the best algorithmic runtime of the `smallest` method?

   (A) $O(1)$
   (B) $O(\log n)$
   (C) $O(n)$
   (D) $O(n \log n)$
   (E) $O(n^2)$

GO ON TO THE NEXT PAGE

5. Consider the following method definition:

```
public static int mystery(int n)
{
        if (n <= 1)
                return 2;
        else
                return 1 + mystery(n - 3);
}
```

Which of the following lines of code can replace the line in mystery containing the recursive call so that the functionality of mystery does not change?

(A) return 1 + ((n + 2) / 3);
(B) return 1 + ((n + 3) / 2);
(C) return 2 + ((n + 1) / 3);
(D) return 2 + ((n + 2) / 3);
(E) return 3 + ((n + 1) / 2);

GO ON TO THE NEXT PAGE

Questions 6–7 refer to root, a TreeNode that is represented by the following structure:

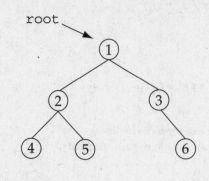

6. What will be output by the following code segment?

```
TreeNode current;
Queue q = new ListQueue();
      // ListQueue implements Queue
if (root == null)
      System.out.println("Tree is empty");
else
{
      q.enqueue(root);

      while (! q.isEmpty())
      {
            current = q.dequeue();
            System.out.print(
                  current.getValue());

            if (current.getLeft() != null)
                  q.enqueue(current.getLeft());

            if (current.getRight() != null)
                  q.enqueue(current.getRight());
      }
}
```

(A) 425136
(B) 132546
(C) 123456
(D) 136254
(E) 124536

GO ON TO THE NEXT PAGE

7. What will be output by the following code segment?

```
TreeNode current;
Stack s = new ListStack();
      // ListStack implements Stack
if (root == null)
      System.out.println("Tree is empty");
else
{
      s.push(root);

      while (! s.isEmpty())
      {
            current = s.pop();
            System.out.print(
                  current.getValue());

            if (current.getLeft() != null)
                  s.push(current.getLeft());

            if (current.getRight() != null)
                  s.push(current.getRight());
      }
}
```

(A) 425136
(B) 132546
(C) 123456
(D) 136254
(E) 124536

8. Consider a binary tree in which each node has either no children (a leaf node) or exactly two children (a parent node). If the tree has n leaf nodes, how many parent nodes will the tree have?

(A) n
(B) $n-1$
(C) $n+1$
(D) $2^n - n$
(E) $2n - 1$

9. Consider the following incomplete method `mystery`:

```
public static boolean mystery(
        boolean a, boolean b, boolean c)
{
        return <expression>;
}
```

What should `<expression>` be replaced with so that `mys-tery` returns `true` when exactly two of its three parameters are `true`; otherwise `mystery` returns `false`?

(A) `(a && b && !c) ||`
    `(a && !b && c) ||`
    `(!a && b && c)`

(B) `(a && b && !c) &&`
    `(a && !b && c) &&`
    `(!a && b && c)`

(C) `(a || b || !c) &&`
    `(a || !b || c) &&`
    `(!a || b || c)`

(D) `(a && b) ||`
    `(a && c) ||`
    `(b && c)`

(E) `(a || b) &&`
    `(a || c) &&`
    `(b || c)`

10. Consider the following code segment:

```
int x;

x = 5 - 4 + 9 * 12 / 3 - 10;
```

What is the value of x after the code segment is executed?

(A) 13
(B) 27
(C) 30
(D) -57
(E) -10

GO ON TO THE NEXT PAGE

11. What is the best way to declare a variable myStrings that will store 50 String values if each String will be no longer than 25 characters?

   (A) `ArrayList myStrings[String[50]];`
   (B) `ArrayList myStrings = new String[50];`
   (C) `ArrayList myStrings = new String[25];`
   (D) `String[] myStrings = new String[50, 25];`
   (E) `String[] myStrings = new String[50];`

12. Consider the functions mystery1 and mystery2.

```
void mystery1(int[] v)
{
        int j;
        int k;

        for (j = 0; j < v.length; j += 2)
                for (k = 1; k < v.length; k *= 2)
                        mystery2(j, k, v);
}
void mystery2(int x, int y, int[] a)
{
        /* implementation not shown */
}
```

If the algorithmic runtime of mystery2 is $O(n)$ (where n is the number of elements in the array), what is the algorithmic runtime of mystery1?

   (A) $O(n \log n)$
   (B) $O(n \log^2 n)$
   (C) $O(n^2)$
   (D) $O(n^2 \log n)$
   (E) $O(n^3)$

GO ON TO THE NEXT PAGE

13. Consider the following precondition, postcondition, and signature for the getDigit method:

```
// precondition: n >= 0
//                   whichDigit >= 0
// postcondition: Returns the digit of n in
//                   the whichDigit position
//                   when the digits of n are
//                   numbered from right to
//                   left starting with zero.
//                   Returns 0 if whichDigit >=
//                   number of digits of n.
int getDigit(int n, int whichDigit)
```

Consider also the following three possible implementations of the getDigit method:

```
I. if (whichDigit == 0)
      return n % 10;
   else
      return getDigit(n / 10, whichDigit-1);

II. return (n / (int) Math.pow(10, whichDigit))
      % 10;

III. for (int k = 0; k < whichDigit; k++)
      n /= 10;
   return n % 10;
```

Which implementation(s) would satisfy the postcondition of the getDigit method?

(A) I and II
(B) I and III
(C) II and III
(D) I, II, and III
(E) None of the above

14. Consider an array of integers.

    4   10   1   2   6   7   3   5

    Assume that QuickSort is used to order the array from smallest to largest values and the first value in the array is chosen as the pivot value.

    Which of the following represents the state of the array immediately before the first recursive calls in the QuickSort process?

(A)	1	4	10	2	3	6	7	5
(B)	1	2	4	6	10	7	3	5
(C)	2	3	1	4	6	7	10	5
(D)	4	3	1	5	6	7	10	2
(E)	5	3	7	6	2	1	10	4

15. Assume that a program declares and initializes v as follows:

```
String[] v;
v = initialize();        // Returns an array of
                         // length 10 containing
                         // ten valid strings
```

    Which of the following code segments correctly traverses the array *backwards* and prints out the elements (one per line)?

    I.
```
for (int k = 9; k >= 0; k--)
System.out.println(v[k]);
```

    II.
```
int k = 0;
while (k < 10)
{
  System.out.println(v[9-k]);
  k++;
}
```

    III.
```
int k = 10;
while (k >= 0)
{
  System.out.println(v[k]);
  k--;
}
```

    (A) I only
    (B) II only
    (C) I and II only
    (D) II and III only
    (E) I, II, and III

GO ON TO THE NEXT PAGE

Questions 16–20 refer to the code from the Marine Biology
Simulation Case Study. A copy of the code is available from
The College Board's website or in Chapter 12 of this book.

16. Consider a bounded 3 × 3 environment containing the following kinds of fish:

Fish	Slowfish	Darterfish
⬭	⬭	⬭

Assuming that fish do not breed or die, which of the following configurations will always remain the same after one complete step of the simulation?

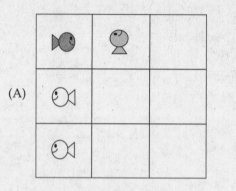

(A)   (B)

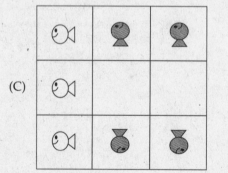

(C)   (D)

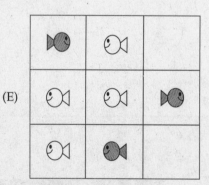

(E)

GO ON TO THE NEXT PAGE

Questions 17–18 refer to the following three proposed designs for storing `Fish` (and other `Locatable` objects) in the `BoundedEnv` class.

Design 1

`BoundedEnv` stores `Fish` (and other `Locatable` objects) in a two-dimensional array of `Locatable` objects.

Design 2

`BoundedEnv` stores `Fish` (and other `Locatable` objects) in a sparse array of `Locatable` objects. Objects in a row are represented by a `LinkedList` of `Locatable` objects ordered by the column number of the object; the rows (the `LinkedLists`) are stored in an `ArrayList` indexed by the row number of the object.

Design 3

`BoundedEnv` stores `Fish` (and other `Locatable` objects) in a `LinkedList` of `Locatable` objects ordered first by row number and then by column number for objects with the same row number.

17. Which of the following statements is false?

(A) The `objectAt` method of the `BoundedEnv` class will have a faster algorithmic runtime with Design 1 than with Design 2 or Design 3.

(B) The `isEmpty` method of the `BoundedEnv` class will have a faster algorithmic runtime with Design 1 than with Design 2 or Design 3.

(C) The `add` method of the `BoundedEnv` class will have a faster algorithmic runtime with Design 1 than with Design 2 or Design 3.

(D) The `remove` method of the `BoundedEnv` class will have a faster algorithmic runtime with Design 1 than with Design 2 or Design 3.

(E) The `allObjects` method of the `BoundedEnv` class will have a faster algorithmic runtime with Design 1 than with Design 2 or Design 3.

GO ON TO THE NEXT PAGE

18. Which of the following statements is true?

(A) With minor modifications to the add, remove, and recordMove methods, Designs 2 and 3 allow multiple objects to exist at any given location in the environment. Design 1 allows only one object at any given location.

(B) With minor modifications to the add, remove, and recordMove methods, Design 3 allows multiple objects to exist at any given location in the environment. Designs 1 and 2 allow only one object at any given location.

(C) With minor modifications to the add, remove, and recordMove methods, Design 2 allows multiple objects to exist at any given location in the environment. Designs 1 and 3 allow only one object at any given location.

(D) Design 1 allows the BoundedEnv class to be subclassed. Designs 2 and 3 do not allow the BoundedEnv class to be subclassed.

(E) Designs 1 and 2 allow the BoundedEnv class to be subclassed. Design 3 does not allow the BoundedEnv class to be subclassed.

19. Consider adding a new environment to the Marine Biology Simulation.

The new environment, CylindricalEnv, is a bounded environment with the property that a fish in column 0 can move west to the same row in column (numCols − 1) and a fish in column (numCols − 1) can move east to the same row in column 0.

In order to design this new environment using good object-oriented principles, which of the following class signatures would be the best way to define this environment?

(A) public class CylindricalEnv
        extends Environment
(B) public class CylindricalEnv
        implements Environment
(C) public class CylindricalEnv
        extends BoundedEnv
(D) public class CylindricalEnv
        implements BoundedEnv
(E) public class CylindricalEnv
        implements BoundedEnv
        implements Environment

GO ON TO THE NEXT PAGE

20. Consider a modification to the `initialize` method of the
    `Fish` class to ensure that the parameters to the method satisfy
    the preconditions of the method—specifically, that the `env`
    parameter is not `null`.

    What is the correct way to raise an exception in the `initial-
    ize` method if the `env` parameter is `null`?

    (A) ```
        if (env == null)
            raise exception("Illegal argument");
        ```
    (B) ```
        if (env == null)
            raise new IllegalArgumentException;
        ```
    (C) ```
        if (env == null)
            catch IllegalArgumentException(
              "env is null");
        ```
    (D) ```
        if (env == null)
            throw IllegalArgumentException(
              "env is null");
        ```
    (E) ```
        if (env == null)
            throw new IllegalArgumentException(
              "env is null");
        ```

        ```

Questions 21–23 refer to the following incomplete class declaration used to represent calendar dates.

```
public class Date implements Comparable
{
        private int month;
                // represents month 0-11
        private int day;
                // represents day of the month
                // 0-31
        private int year;
                // represents the year
        // constructor sets the private data
        public Date(int m, int d, int y)
        { /* implementation not shown */ }
        // postcondition: returns the month
        public int getMonth()
        { /* implementation not shown */ }
        // postcondition: returns the day
        public int getDay()
        { /* implementation not shown */ }
        // postcondition: returns the year
        public int getYear()
        { /* implementation not shown */ }
        // postcondition: returns the number of
        //                days which, when
        //                added to this Date
        //                gives newDate
        public int daysUntil(Date newDate)
        { /* implementation not shown */ }
        // postcondition: returns true if
        //                the month, day, and
        //                year of this Date are
        //                are equal to those of
        //                other; otherwise
        //                returns false
        public boolean equals(Date other)
        { /* implementation not shown */ }
        // ... other methods not shown
}
```

GO ON TO THE NEXT PAGE →

21. Consider the method compareTo of the Comparable inter-
    face as implemented by the Date class.

    Which of the following method signatures is appropriate for
    the compareTo method?

    (A) public int compareTo(Object other)
    (B) public boolean compareTo(Object other)
    (C) public int compareTo(Date other)
    (D) public boolean compareTo(Date other)
    (E) public int compareTo(Date d1, Date d2)

22. Which of the following code segments could be used to
    implement the equals method of the Date class so that the
    equals method works as intended?

```
  I. if (month == other.month)
       if (day == other.day)
             if (year == other.year)
                   return true;
     return false;
```

```
 II. if (month == other.getMonth() &&
         day == other.getDay() &&
         year == other.getYear())
       return true;
     else
       return false;
```

```
III. return !((getMonth() != other.month) ||
             (getDay() != other.day) ||
             (getYear() != other.year));
```

(A) I only
(B) II only
(C) III only
(D) I and II
(E) I, II, and III

23. During the testing of the Date class, it is determined that the class does not correctly handle leap years—although it handles non–leap years correctly.

   In which method of the Date class is the problem most likely to be found?

   (A) the Date constructor
   (B) the getMonth method
   (C) the getDay method
   (D) the daysUntil method
   (E) the equals method

24. Consider the following methods:

```
public static void mystery()
{
        int[] A;
        A = initialize();
                // returns a valid initialized
                // array of integers
        for (int k = 0; k < A.length / 2; k++)
                swap(A[k], A[A.length - k - 1]);
}
public static void swap(int x, int y)
{
        int temp;
        temp = x;
        x = y;
        y = temp;
}
```

   Which of the following best characterizes the effect of the for loop in the method mystery?

   (A) It sorts the elements of A.
   (B) It reverses the elements of A.
   (C) It reverses the order of the first half of A and leaves the second half unchanged.
   (D) It reverses the order of the second half of A and leaves the first half unchanged.
   (E) It leaves all of the elements of A in their original order.

GO ON TO THE NEXT PAGE

25. Consider the following code segment:

```
int[][] A = new int [4][3];
for (int j = 0; j < A[0].length; j++)
    for (int k = 0; k < A.length; k++)
        if (j == 0)
            A[k][j] = 0;
        else if (k % j == 0)
            A[k][j] = 1;
        else
            A[k][j] = 2;
```

What are the contents of A after the code segment has been executed?

(A) 0 0 0 0
     1 1 1 1
     1 2 1 2

(B) 0 1 1 1
     0 2 2 2
     0 1 2 1

(C) 0 0 0
     1 1 2
     1 1 1
     1 1 2

(D) 0 1 1
     0 2 1
     0 2 2
     0 2 1

(E) 0 1 1
     0 1 2
     0 1 1
     0 1 2

26. Consider the following code segment:

```
Stack s = new ListStack();
        // ListStack implements Stack

Object obj;
s.push("A");
s.push("B");
obj = s.peekTop();
s.push(obj + "" + obj);
s.push("C");
s.push("D");
obj = s.peekTop();
obj += "" + s.pop();
s.push(obj + "" + obj);
while (! s.isEmpty())
        System.out.print(s.pop());
```

What is printed as the result of executing this code segment?

(A) ABBBCDDD
(B) ABBBCDDDD
(C) BAACDAAAA
(D) DDDCBBBA
(E) DDDDCBBBA

GO ON TO THE NEXT PAGE

27. Consider the following method:

```
public static int mystery(int x, int y)
{
    if (x > 0)
        return x;
    else if (y > 0)
        return y;
    else
        return x / y;
}
```

In accordance with good design and testing practices, which of the following is the best set of test cases (x, y) for the method mystery?

(A) (3, 4),(-3, 4),(-3, -4)
(B) (3, 4),(-3, 4),(-3, 0)
(C) (3, 4),(3, -4),(-3, -4),(-3, 0)
(D) (3, 4),(3, -4),(-3, -4),(-3, 4),(-3, 0)
(E) (3, 4),(2, 5),(3, -4),(-3, 0),(4, 0),(0, 0)

28. The following integers are inserted into an empty binary search tree in the following order:

    53   12   26   2   3   67   60   99   1

Which traversal of the tree would produce the following output?

    53   12   2   1   3   26   67   60   99

(A) Preorder
(B) Inorder
(C) Postorder
(D) Reverse preorder
(E) Level-by-level

29. Consider a proposed new method, rotateLeft, of the java.util.LinkedList class that takes the first node in the list and puts it at the end of the list, the second node in the list and makes it the first node, the third node in the list and makes it the second node, and so on.

If rotateLeft does not create or delete any nodes in the list, and does not copy any data values, what is the best algorithmic runtime possible (where n is the number of nodes in the linked list) for the function rotateLeft?

(A) $O(1)$
(B) $O(\log n)$
(C) $O(n)$
(D) $O(n^2)$
(E) $O(n^3)$

30. Consider the following method mystery:

```
public static int mystery(TreeNode t)
{
        if (t == null)
                return 0;
        else if (t.getLeft() == null &&
                    t.getRight() == null)
                return 1;
        else if (t.getLeft() == null)
                return mystery(t.getRight());
        else if (t.getRight() == null)
                return mystery(t.getLeft());
        else
                return 1 + mystery(t.getLeft()) +
                        mystery(t.getRight());
}
```

Which of the following is the best description of the functionality of mystery?

(A) mystery returns the total number of nodes in the tree whose root is t.
(B) mystery returns the number of leaf nodes in the tree whose root is t.
(C) mystery returns the number of nodes with exactly one child in the tree whose root is t.
(D) mystery returns the number of nodes with either no children or exactly two children in the tree whose root is t.
(E) mystery returns the number of levels in the tree whose root is t.

GO ON TO THE NEXT PAGE

31. Consider the following code segment:

```
LinkedList theList = new LinkedList();
theList.add("A");
theList.add("B");
theList.add("C");
theList.add("D");
theList.add("E");
Object obj;
Object obj2;
ListIterator itr = theList.listIterator();
while (itr.hasNext())
{
        obj = itr.next();
        if (itr.hasNext())
                obj2 = itr.next();
        itr.set(obj);
}
Iterator itr2 = theList.iterator();
while (itr2.hasNext())
        System.out.print(itr2.next());
```

What is output when the code segment is executed?

(A) ABCDE
(B) ACE
(C) AACCE
(D) BBDD
(E) BBBDDE

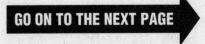

32. Consider the following three proposed implementations of method `reverse`, intended to reverse the order of objects in a Queue:

```
I. public static void reverse(Queue q)
   {
     Stack s = new ListStack();
           // ListStack implements Stack
     while (! q.isEmpty())
           s.push(q.dequeue());
     while (! s.isEmpty())
           q.enqueue(s.pop());
   }

II. public static void reverse(Queue q)
    {
      Object obj;
      if (! q.isEmpty())
      {
            obj = q.dequeue();
            reverse(q);
            q.enqueue(obj);
      }
    }

III. public static void reverse(Queue q)
     {
       Stack s = new ListStack();
             // ListStack implements Stack
       for (int k = 0; k < q.size(); k++)
             s.push(q.dequeue());
       for (int k = 0; k < s.size(); k++)
             q.enqueue(s.pop());
     }
```

Which of the above implementations of method `reverse` work as intended?

(A) I only
(B) III only
(C) I and II
(D) I and III
(E) I, II, and III

33. Consider the data structures represented by
`java.util.HashSet` and `java.util.TreeSet`.

Assuming that n refers to the number of elements in the data set, which of the following statements is true?

(A) If the size of the data set is known when the data structure is created and it is important to add objects to and remove objects from the data set in guaranteed $O(1)$ time, then the data set should be represented by a `TreeSet`.

(B) If the size of the data set is unknown when the data structure is created and it is important to determine if an object is contained in the data set in guaranteed $O(1)$ time, then the data set should be represented by a `TreeSet`.

(C) If the size of the data set is unknown when the data structure is created and it is important to add objects to and remove objects from the data set in guaranteed $O(\log n)$ time, then the data set should be represented by a `TreeSet`.

(D) If it is important that the iterator of the set returns the elements of the set in sorted order, then the data set should be represented by a `HashSet`.

(E) If it is important that iterating over the entire set can be done in guaranteed $O(\log n)$ total time, then the data set should be represented by a `HashSet`.

34. Consider a binary tree. Let n_0 be the number of nodes in the tree with no children, let n_1 be the number of nodes in the tree with exactly one child, and let n_2 be the number of nodes in the tree with exactly two children.

Which of the following statements best describes the relationships among n_0, n_1, and n_2?

(A) $n_0 > n_1 > n_2$
(B) $n_2 > n_1 > n_0$
(C) $n_1 > n_0 > n_2$
(D) $n_0 > n_2$; the relationships between n_1 and n_0 and between n_1 and n_2 cannot be determined from the information given.
(E) The relationships cannot be determined from the information given.

GO ON TO THE NEXT PAGE

35. Consider the following method:

```
public static void quicksort(
      int[] A, int first, int last)
{
      if (first >= last)
            return;
      int pivotValue = A[last];
      int pivotIndex = pivot(
            A, first, last, pivotValue);
      /* assertion */
      quicksort(A, first, pivotIndex-1);
      quicksort(A, pivotIndex+1, last);
}
```

In order for the method `quicksort` to work as intended, what would be a true assertion at the location in the code marked `/* assertion */`?

(A) first < pivotValue < last
(B) first < pivotIndex < last
(C) for all j such that first ≤ j ≤
       pivotValue: A[j] ≤ pivotValue
(D) for all j such that first ≤ j ≤
       pivotIndex: A[j] ≤ pivotIndex
(E) for all j such that first ≤ j ≤
       pivotIndex: A[j] ≤ pivotValue

GO ON TO THE NEXT PAGE

36. Consider the design of two hash functions to be applied to 1,000 objects containing names (sequences of one or more letter) and telephone numbers (sequences of nine digits). The records will be stored in a hash table (an array) of fixed size 1,500.

The first hash function should be applied only to the name of the object. The second hash function should be used to resolve collisions of the first hash function and should be applied only to the telephone number of the object. Collisions of the second hash function should be resolved by linear probing.

Which of the following statements is true?

(A) If `name1` comes before `name2` alphabetically, then the value returned by the first hash function when applied to `name1` should be smaller than the value returned by the first hash function when applied to `name2`.

(B) If `name1` comes before `name2` alphabetically, then the value returned by the second hash function when applied to `telephone1` should be smaller than the value returned by the second hash function when applied to `telephone2`.

(C) If `telephone1` comes before `telephone2` numerically, then the value returned by the second hash function when applied to `telephone1` should be smaller than the value returned by the second hash function when applied to `telephone2`.

(D) Both hash functions should return integer values between 0 and 1,499.

(E) The first hash function should return a valid telephone number; the second hash function should return integer values between 0 and 1,499.

GO ON TO THE NEXT PAGE

37. Assume that a min-heap containing ten integers is stored in an array A such that A[0] represents the minimum value in the heap.

Which of the following arrays represents a valid min-heap?

(A) 1   2   3   5   7   6   9   8   4
(B) 1   2   5   3   7   6   9   8   4
(C) 1   2   7   4   5   9   8   3   6
(D) 1   3   2   5   7   8   9   6   4
(E) 1   9   8   7   6   5   4   3   2

38. Each of the following lists of numbers is inserted in order into its own empty binary search tree. Which list produces the most balanced tree?

(A) 4   3   1   6   2   5   7
(B) 5   3   4   6   2   7   1
(C) 4   5   2   7   3   1   6
(D) 2   4   1   3   6   7   5
(E) 4   6   5   2   1   7   3

GO ON TO THE NEXT PAGE

39. Consider the following incomplete method:

```
// precondition: t is the root of a
// binary search tree
// postcondition: Returns the number of
//                levels (height) of the
//                tree t. The height of an
//                empty (null) tree is 0;
//                the height of a tree with
//                exactly one node is 1.
public static int height(TreeNode t)
{
    /* program segment */
}
```

Which of the following code segments can be used to replace /* program segment */ so that the function height satisfies its postcondition?

```
I.  if (t == null)
       return 0;
    else if (height(t.getLeft()) <
            height(t.getRight()))
       return height(t.getRight());
    else
       return height(t.getLeft());
```

```
II. if (t == null)
       return 0;
    else if (t.getLeft() == null &&
            t.getRight() == null)
       return 1;
    else
       return 1 + height(t.getLeft()) +
                height(t.getRight());
```

```
III. if (t == null)
        return 0;
     else if (height(t.getLeft()) <=
             height(t.getRight()))
        return 1 + height(t.getRight());
     else
        return 1 + height(t.getLeft());
```

(A) I only
(B) II only
(C) III only
(D) I and III only
(E) II and III only

GO ON TO THE NEXT PAGE

40. If X, Y, and Z are integer values, the boolean expression

```
(X > Y) && (Y > Z)
```

can be replaced by which of the following?

(A) X > Z
(B) (X < Y) || (Y < Z)
(C) (X <= Y) || (Y <= Z)
(D) !((X < Y) || (Y < Z))
(E) !((X <= Y) || (Y <= Z))

END OF SECTION I

IF YOU FINISH BEFORE TIME IS CALLED, YOU MAY
CHECK YOUR WORK ON THIS SECTION.

DO NOT GO ON TO SECTION II UNTIL YOU ARE TOLD TO DO SO.

COMPUTER SCIENCE AB
SECTION II
Time—1 hour and 45 minutes
Number of Questions—4
Percent of Total Grade—50

Directions: SHOW ALL YOUR WORK. REMEMBER THAT PROGRAM SEGMENTS ARE TO BE WRITTEN IN JAVA™.

Notes:

- Assume that the classes listed in the Quick Reference sheet have been imported where appropriate. A Quick Reference to the AP Java classes is included as part of the exam.

- Assume that the implementation classes are used for any questions referring to linked lists or trees and that the interfaces for stacks, queues, and priority queues behave as specified.

- Assume that declarations of variables and methods appear within the context of an enclosing class.

- Assume that method calls that are not prefixed with an object or class name appear within the context of the class in which the method is declared.

- Unless otherwise noted in the question, assume that parameters in method calls are not null.

- Unless otherwise noted, assume that methods are called only when their preconditions are satisfied.

FREE-RESPONSE QUESTIONS

1. A monochrome (black-and-white) screen is a rectangular grid of pixels that can be either white or black. A pixel is a location on the screen represented by its row number and column number.

   Consider the following proposal for modeling a screen and its pixels.

   A black pixel on the screen is modeled by an object of type `Pixel`. The `Pixel` class includes the following private data and methods:

   - `row`—this int holds the row number of this pixel

   - `col`—this int holds the column number of this pixel

   - `Pixel` constructor—this constructor creates a `Pixel` based on the given row and column

   - `getRow`—this method returns the row number of this pixel

   - `getCol`—this method returns the column number of this pixel

GO ON TO THE NEXT PAGE

```
public class Pixel
{
      private int row;
      private int col;
      public Pixel(int r, int c)
      { row = r; col = c; }
      public int getRow()
      { return row; }
      public int getCol()
      { return col; }
}
```

A screen is modeled by an object of type Screen. Internally, the screen is represented by an array of linked lists of pixels. The index into the array represents the given row on the screen; the linked list at that element represents the *black* pixels at the various columns in order from smallest to largest column. *White pixels are not stored in the linked list.* A pixel not in the list is assumed to be white.

The Screen class includes the following private data and methods:

- data—The array of linked lists.

- pixelAt—This method returns the Pixel at the given location if it exists (i.e., is black) in this Screen. Otherwise, this method returns null.

- pixelOn—This method creates and stores a black Pixel at the appropriate place in the array of linked lists based on the given row and column number.

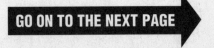

```
public class Screen
{
        private LinkedList[] data;
        private int numCols;
        // postcondition: data is created with
        //                height elements;
        //                numCols is set to
        //                width
        public Screen(int width, int height)
        { /* to be implemented in part (a) */ }
        // precondition: 0 <= row <=
        //                data.length-1;
        //                0 <= col <= numCols-1
        // postcondition: returns the pixel at
        //                the given row and col
        //                if it exists (black)
        //                or null if the pixel
        //                doesn't exist (white)
        public Pixel pixelAt(int row, int col)
        { /* to be implemented in part (b) */ }

        // precondition: 0 <= row <=
        //                data.length-1;
        //                0 <= col <= numCols-1;
        //                the pixel at row,col
        //                does not exist
        //                in this Screen
        // postcondition: adds the pixel at
        //                the given row and col
        //                so that pixels in a
        //                given row of data are
        //                in increasing column
        //                order
        public void pixelOn(int row, int col)
        { /* to be implemented in part (c) */ }

        // ... constructors, other methods,
        //     and other private data not shown
}
```

GO ON TO THE NEXT PAGE →

(a) Write the constructor for the Screen class. The constructor should initialize the private data of the Screen class as appropriate.

Complete the constructor for the Screen class below.

```
// postcondition: data is created with
//                height elements; numCols
//                is set to width
public Screen(int width, int height)
```

(b) Write the `Screen` method `pixelAt`. Method `pixelAt` should return the pixel at the given row and column of the screen if that pixel exists (i.e., is black). Otherwise `pixelAt` should return `null`.

Complete method `pixelAt` below.

```
// precondition: 0 <= row <=
//                   data.length-1;
//                   0 <= col <= numCols-1
// postcondition: returns the pixel at
//                   the given row and col
//                   if it exists (black)
//                   or null if the pixel
//                   doesn't exist (white)
public Pixel pixelAt(int row, int col)
```

GO ON TO THE NEXT PAGE

(c) Write the `Screen` method `pixelOn`. Method `pixelOn` should modify this `Screen` so that a pixel is stored at the given row and column.

Complete method `pixelOn` below.

```
// precondition: 0 <= row <=
//                  data.length-1;
//               0 <= col <= numCols-1;
//               the pixel at row,col
//               does not exist
//               in this Screen
// postcondition: adds the pixel at
//                  the given row and col
//                  so that pixels in a
//                  given row of data are
//                  in increasing column
//                  order
public void pixelOn(int row, int col)
```

GO ON TO THE NEXT PAGE

2. A binary search tree is a data structure that can be represented as a binary tree in which the value of any node in the tree is greater than or equal to the values of the nodes of its left subtree and less than or equal to the values of the nodes of its right subtree.

Insertion and deletion in a binary search tree takes $O(\log n)$ time on average, but can degrade to $O(n)$ time if the tree is extremely unbalanced.

One type of balanced binary search tree is called a **red-black tree**. This data structure ensures that no path in the tree from the root to a leaf is more than twice as long as any other path. As a result, insertion and deletion in a red-black tree is guaranteed to take no more than $O(\log n)$ time.

A red-black tree works by maintaining the following properties:

- every node in the tree is either red or black
- the root is black
- both children of a red node are black
- all paths from a node down to a leaf have the same number of black nodes

A **left rotation** in a red-black tree of a node x involves rearranging nodes in the tree so that the original structure

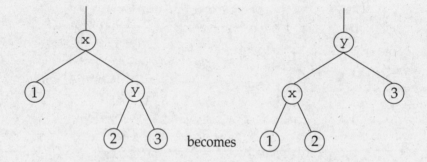

becomes

after the rotation. This maintains the binary search property of the tree, but may affect the red-black property.

A **right rotation** in a red-black tree reverses the effect of a left rotation. For instance, a right rotation of a node y involves rearranging nodes in the tree so that the original structure

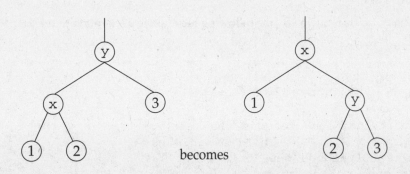

becomes

after the rotation. Like a left rotation, a right rotation maintains the binary search property of the tree, but may affect the red-black property.

Insertion into a red-black tree involves finding the correct location to insert the node in the same manner as inserting into a standard binary search tree, coloring the new node red, and then "fixing up" the colors and performing rotations on certain nodes so that the red-black tree again has the above properties.

Fixing up the tree can be done by starting with the newly inserted node and applying the following algorithm:

- if the node's parent is black, return
- otherwise, one of five cases will occur

1. The node's uncle is red. In this case, color the parent black, the uncle black, the grandparent red, and recursively fix up the tree starting with the node's grandparent.

2. The node's uncle is black, the node is the right child of its parent, and the node's parent is the left child of the node's grandparent. In this case, perform a left rotation on the node's parent and recursively fix up the tree starting with the node's left child (its former parent).

3. The node's uncle is black and the node is the left child of its parent, and the node's parent is the left child of the node's grandparent. In this case, change the node's parent to black, change the node's grandparent to red, perform a right rotation on the node's grandparent, and return.

4. The node's uncle is black, the node is the left child of its parent, and the node's parent is the right child of the node's grandparent. In this case, perform a right rotation on the node's parent and recursively fix up the tree starting with the node's right child (its former parent).

5. The node's uncle is black and the node is the right child of its parent, and the node's parent is the right child of the node's grandparent. In this case, change the node's parent to black, change the node's grandparent to red, perform a left rotation on the node's grandparent, and return.

This question involves the implementation of a red-black tree.

GO ON TO THE NEXT PAGE

A node in a red-black tree is modeled by the following incomplete declaration of the RBTreeNode class:

```
public class RBTreeNode
{
        final int RED = 0;
        final int BLACK = 1;

        // postcondition: returns the left
        //                child of this node
        public RBTreeNode getLeft()
        { /* code not shown */ }
        // postcondition: returns the right
        //                child of this node
        public RBTreeNode getRight()
        { /* code not shown */ }
        // postcondition: returns the parent
        //                of this node
        public RBTreeNode getParent()
        { /* code not shown */ }
        // postcondition: returns the color
        //                of this node
        public int getColor()
        { /* code not shown */ }
        // postcondition: sets the left
        //                child of this node
        //                to the given node
        public void setLeft(RBTreeNode newLeft)
        { /* code not shown */ }
        // postcondition: sets the right
        //                child of this node
        //                to the given node
        public void setRight(
            RBTreeNode newRight)
        { /* code not shown */ }
        // postcondition: sets the parent
        //                of this node
        //                to the given node
        public void setParent(
            RBTreeNode newParent)
        { /* code not shown */ }
        // postcondition: sets the color
        //                of this node
        //                to the given color
        public void setColor(int newColor)
        { /* code not shown */ }
        // precondition: x has an uncle.
        // postcondition: Returns the sibling
        //                of this node's
        //                parent.
        public RBTreeNode getUncle()
        { /* to be implemented in part (a) */ }
        // ... constructors, other methods, and
        //     private data not shown
}
```

GO ON TO THE NEXT PAGE

A red-black tree is modeled by the following incomplete class declaration of the RBTree class:

```
public class RBTree
{
        private RBTreeNode root;
        // precondition: The right child of x
        //                    is not null.
        // postcondition: The tree has been
        //                    rotated so that x is
        //                    now the left child of
        //                    its right child and
        //                    x's right child is
        //                    now its former right
        //                    child's left child.
        private void rotateLeft(RBTreeNode x)
        { /* to be implemented in part (b) */ }
        // precondition: The left child of x
        //                    is not null.
        // postcondition: The tree has been
        //                    rotated so that x is
        //                    now the right child
        //                    of its left child and
        //                    x's left child is
        //                    now its former left
        //                    child's right child.
        private void rotateRight(RBTreeNode x)
        { /* code not shown */ }
        // precondition: x is not the root of
        //                    tree.
        // postcondition: The tree has the red-
        //                    black properties.
        private void fixup(RBTreeNode x)
        { /* to be implemented in part (c) */ }
        // ... constructors, other methods, and
        //        private data not shown
}
```

GO ON TO THE NEXT PAGE

(a) Write the `RBTreeNode` method `getUncle`. Method `getUncle` should return the sibling of a node's parent. For instance, in the tree

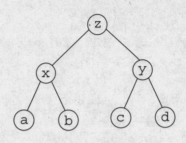

`a.getUncle()` and `b.getUncle()` should return node y while
`c.getUncle()` and `d.getUncle()` should return node x.

Complete method `getUncle` below.

```
// precondition: x has an uncle.
// postcondition: Returns the sibling of
//                this node's parent.
public RBTreeNode getUncle()
```

(b) Write the `RBTree` method `rotateLeft`. Method `rotateLeft` should rotate `RBTreeNode` x so that the original structure

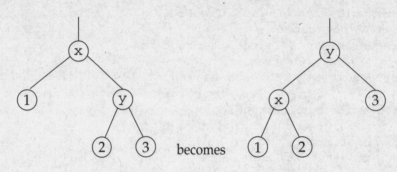

becomes

after the rotation.

Complete method `rotateLeft` below.

```
// precondition: The right child of x is
//               not null.
// postcondition: The tree has been
//                rotated so that x is
//                now the left child of
//                its right child and
//                x's right child is
//                now its former right
//                child's left child.
private void rotateLeft(RBTreeNode x)
```

GO ON TO THE NEXT PAGE

(c) Write the `RBTree` method fixup. Method fixup should fix up the red-black tree according to the following algorithm:

- if the node's parent is black, return
- otherwise, one of five cases will occur

1. The node's uncle is red. In this case, color the parent black, the uncle black, the grandparent red, and recursively fix up the tree starting with the node's grandparent.

2. The node's uncle is black, the node is the right child of its parent, and the node's parent is the left child of the node's grandparent. In this case, perform a left rotation on the node's parent and recursively fix up the tree starting with the node's left child (its former parent).

3. The node's uncle is black and the node is the left child of its parent, and the node's parent is the left child of the node's grandparent. In this case, change the node's parent to black, change the node's grandparent to red, perform a right rotation on the node's grandparent, and return.

4. The node's uncle is black, the node is the left child of its parent, and the node's parent is the right child of the node's grandparent. In this case, perform a right rotation on the node's parent and recursively fix up the tree starting with the node's right child (its former parent).

5. The node's uncle is black and the node is the right child of its parent, and the node's parent is right child of the node's grandparent. In this case, change the node's parent to black, change the node's grandparent to red, perform a left rotation on the node's grandparent, and return.

In writing method fixup you may use the methods `getUncle` and `rotateLeft` as specified in parts (a) and (b). Assume that `getUncle` and `rotateLeft` work as specified, regardless of what you wrote in parts (a) and (b). Solutions that reimplement functionality provided by these methods, rather than invoking them, will not receive full credit.

Complete method fixup below.

```
// precondition: x is not the root of
//                  tree.
// postcondition: The tree has the red-
//                  black properties.
private void fixup(RBTreeNode x)
```

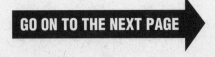
GO ON TO THE NEXT PAGE

3. A binary, or base two, integer is a number consisting of digits that are either 0 or 1. Digits in a binary integer are numbered from right to left starting with 0.

The decimal value of the binary integer is the sum of each digit multiplied by 2^d where d is the number of the digit.

For example, the decimal value of the binary integer 1011010 is

$$(0 * 2^0) + (1 * 2^1) + (0 * 2^2) + (1 * 2^3) + (1 * 2^4) + (0 * 2^5) + (1 * 2^6)$$

$$= \quad 0 + 2 + 0 + 8 + 16 + 0 + 64$$

$$= \quad 90$$

A decimal integer can be converted into its corresponding binary integer according to the following algorithm:

- calculate the remainder when the decimal integer is divided by 2. This is the rightmost digit of the corresponding binary integer

- divide the decimal integer by 2 using integer division. If the result is 0, stop. Otherwise repeat the algorithm using the new value of the decimal integer

GO ON TO THE NEXT PAGE ➤

The digits produced will be in right-to-left order in the binary integer.

For instance, the decimal integer 90 can be converted into its corresponding binary integer as follows:

$$90 \% 2 = 0 \quad \text{(the rightmost digit)}$$

$$90 / 2 = 45 \quad 45 \% 2 = 1 \quad \text{(the second digit from the right)}$$

$$45 / 2 = 22 \quad 22 \% 2 = 0 \quad \text{(the third digit from the right)}$$

$$22 / 2 = 11 \quad 11 \% 2 = 1 \quad \text{(the fourth digit from the right)}$$

$$11 / 2 = 55 \% 2 = 1 \quad \text{(the fifth digit from the right)}$$

$$5 / 2 = 22 \% 2 = 0 \quad \text{(the sixth digit from the right)}$$

$$2 / 2 = 11 \% 2 = 1 \quad \text{(the leftmost digit)}$$

$$1 / 2 = 0$$

Consider the design of a class that represents an arbitrary length non-negative binary integer.

The operations on this class include

- constructing an empty binary integer with value zero
- constructing a binary integer from an arbitrary non-negative decimal integer
- returning a binary integer that represents the result of adding another binary integer to this binary integer
- returning the result of converting this binary integer to a `String`

In addition, the binary integer class should fully implement the `Comparable` interface.

GO ON TO THE NEXT PAGE

(a) Write the definition of a binary integer class, showing the appropriate data definitions, constructors, and method signatures. You should *not* write the implementations of the constructor or any of the methods you define for the binary integer class.

GO ON TO THE NEXT PAGE →

(b) Using the signature you wrote in part (a), write the implementation for the operation that constructs a binary integer from an arbitrary decimal integer.

In writing this method, you may call any of the methods in the binary integer class (as you defined it in part (a)). Assume that these methods work as specified.

GO ON TO THE NEXT PAGE

(c) Using the binary integer class (as you defined it in part (a)), complete the following method, Test, that adds the following pairs of decimal integers in binary and output the larger of the two binary sums. Test is *not* a method of the binary integer class.

Pair 1: 2,314,279,623 and 3,236,550,123. Pair 2: 3,412,579,010 and 2,128,250,735.

In writing this method, you may call any of the methods in the binary integer class (as you defined it in part (a)). Assume that these methods work as specified.

Complete method Test below.

```
public static void Test()
```

GO ON TO THE NEXT PAGE →

4. This question involves reasoning about the code from the Marine Biology Simulation Case Study. A copy of the code is available from The College Board website or in Chapter 12 of this book.

Consider a proposal that the simulation using an unbounded environment be modified as follows:

- a fish keeps track of its age. Its age is set to 0 in the constructor of the Fish class and is incremented by 1 each time the act method of the Fish class is called

- the environment allows multiple objects to exist at the same location

- fish act as before with one exception: Before moving, if a fish is currently the oldest object in the environment, it dies and is replaced by two new fish at the same location. The two new fish are half the age of the fish that dies. The two new fish both immediately move as usual

- the Locatable interface is modified to include an equals method. The Fish class implements the equals method. Two fish are equal if their IDs are the same

- the Locatable interface is modified to extend the Comparable interface. The Fish class now implements the Comparable interface that orders fish by their age

- the environment uses a priority queue to keep track of the oldest object in the environment. If more than one object in the environment has the same age, one of the objects is arbitrarily chosen as the oldest

The class PQueue that implements the PriorityQueue interface has been provided.

```
public class PQueue implements PriorityQueue
{
        { /* implementation not shown */ }
}
```

The modifications that have been made to the Locatable interface are shown below.

```
public interface Locatable
        extends Comparable
{
        Location location();
        boolean equals(Object obj);
}
```

GO ON TO THE NEXT PAGE

The relevant modifications that have been made to the Fish class are shown below.

```
public class Fish implements Locatable
{
    private int myAge;
    // postcondition: constructs a fish in
    //      the specified environment at the
    //      specified location with the
    //      specified direction, color, and
    //      age
    public Fish(Environment env,
                Location loc,
                Direction dir,
                Color col,
                int age)
    { /* implementation not shown */ }
    // postcondition: as in the original
    //      version except that it also
    //      sets myAge to age
    private void initialize(
        Environment env,
        Location loc,
        Direction dir,
        Color col,
        int age)
    { /* implementation not shown */ }
    // postcondition: returns the age
    //      of this fish
    public int age()
    { /* implementation not shown */ }
    // postcondition: returns true if this
    //      fish and other have the same id
    public boolean equals(Object other)
    { /* implementation not shown */ }
    // postcondition: returns -1 if this fish
    //      is younger than other; 0 if this
    //      fish and other are the same age;
    //      and 1 if this fish is older than
    //      other
    public int compareTo(Object other)
    { /* implementation not shown */ }
    // postcondition: The fish has acted
    //      in its environment according to
    //      its rules
    public void act()
    { /* to be implemented in part (c) */ }
    // ...other constructors, methods, and
    //      private data not shown
}
```

GO ON TO THE NEXT PAGE

The relevant modifications that have been made to the UnboundedEnv class are shown below.

```
public class UnboundedEnv
        extends SquareEnvironment
{
        private PQueue pq;
        // postcondition: Returns true if obj
        //     is the oldest object in this
        //     environment; returns false
        //     otherwise
        public boolean isOldest(Locatable obj)
        { /* to be implemented in part (a) */ }
        // postcondition: obj has been added
        //     to this environment; pq has been
        //     updated appropriately
        public void add(Locatable obj)
        { /* to be implemented in part (b) */ }
        // ...other constructors, methods, and
        //     private data not shown
}
```

(a) Write the UnboundedEnv method isOldest that returns true if the given Locatable object is currently the oldest object in the environment.

Complete method isOldest below.

```
// postcondition: Returns true if obj is
//    the oldest object in this environment;
//    returns false otherwise
public boolean isOldest(Locatable obj)
```

(b) Write the UnboundedEnv method add. This method should add the given Locatable object to the environment and update the priority queue appropriately.

In writing this method, you may call any of the methods in the Marine Biology Simulation that are accessible to an UnboundedEnv. Assume that these methods work as specified.

Complete method add below.

```
// postcondition: obj has been added
//    to this environment; pq has been
//    updated appropriately
public void add(Locatable obj)
```

GO ON TO THE NEXT PAGE

(c) Write the `Fish` method `act`. This method should check if this fish is in its environment. If it is not, the method should do nothing.

Otherwise, if this fish is the oldest fish in the environment, it should create two child fish exactly like itself but with half of its age. The children fish should move immediately. This fish should then die.

Otherwise, this fish should age one step and then move.

In writing this method, you may call any of the methods in the Marine Biology Simulation that are accessible to a `Fish`. Assume that these methods work as specified. You may also use the `Environment` methods `isOldest` as specified in part (a) and `add` as specified in part (b). Assume that `isOldest` and `add` work as specified, regardless of what you wrote in parts (a) and (b). Solutions that reimplement functionality provided by these methods, rather than invoking them, will not receive full credit.

Complete method `act` below.

```
// postcondition: The fish has acted
//     in its environment according to its
//     rules
public void act()
```

END OF EXAMINATION

16

Answers and Explanations to the AP Computer Science AB Practice Test

MULTIPLE-CHOICE QUESTIONS

1. **A** This problem is actually quite simple to answer because the value of b never changes. Eventually a will be equal to zero and the value of b will be returned by each call to `mystery`.

2. **D** Recall that a preorder traversal of a binary tree outputs the value of the root, followed by the preorder traversal of the left subtree, followed by the preorder traversal of the right subtree.

    Statement I is correct.

    Walking through the steps of the preorder traversal (the parentheses are used to show the subtrees but are not necessary in a preorder traversal)

    (+ *left right*)
    (+ (x *left right*) (+ *left right*))
    (+ (x 1 (− *left right*)) (+ 4 (x *left right*)))
    (+ (x 1 (− 2 3)) (+ 4 (x 5 6)))

    Statement II is incorrect.

    A postorder traversal of a binary tree outputs a postorder traversal of the left subtree followed by a postorder traversal of the right subtree followed by the value of the root of the tree.

    Walking through the steps of the postorder traversal (again, the parentheses are used to show the subtrees but are not necessary in a postorder traversal)

    (*left right* +)
    ((*left right* x) (*left right* +) +)
    ((1 (*left right* −) x) (4 (*left right* x) +) +)
    ((1 (2 3 −) x) (4 (5 6 x) +) +)

    At this point, you can rule out choices (B), (C), and (E).

    Statement III is correct.

    An inorder traversal of a binary tree outputs an inorder traversal of the left subtree, followed by the value of the root, followed by an inorder traversal of the right subtree.

    Walking through the steps of the inorder traversal

    (*left* + *right*)
    ((*left* x *right*) + (*left* + *right*))
    ((1 x (*left* − *right*)) + (4 + (*left* x *right*)))
    ((1 x (2 − 3)) + (4 + (5 x 6)))

    Because only statements I and III are true, the correct answer is choice (D).

3. **B** In general, data fields of a class are designated private in order to hide the implementation of the class. This ensures that the functionality of the class—as seen by the programmer using the class—does not change if the implementation changes. Choice (B) is correct.

Choice (A) is incorrect. Methods of a class are able to access the private data of their class.

Choice (C) is incorrect. Data fields that are designated as private cannot be modified outside their class.

Choice (D) is incorrect. A program does not need to know how a class is implemented in order to use it.

Choice (E) is incorrect. The methods `enquack` and `dequack` are public and accessible to any program using the `Quack` class. These methods modify the contents of a `Quack`.

4. **C** Because the objects in the `Quack` are not ordered in any way, the best algorithm to find the smallest-valued object is to examine each element—an $O(n)$ proposition.

Note that it might appear that the `enquack` method can be modified to keep track of the smallest-valued object as objects are added to the `Quack`, resulting in a constant time algorithm for `smallest`. Unfortunately, this attempt fails when the smallest-valued object is removed from the `Quack`. It now takes $O(n)$ time to find the new smallest-valued object.

5. **C** The fastest way to solve this problem is to make a table of values for `mystery(n)` and see which gives answers that match those given by the original method.

Note that we can stop filling in answers for a particular choice as soon as one of the answers does not match the answer given by the original method.

n	Original	(A)	(B)	(C)	(D)	(E)
2	3	2	3	3	3	4
3	3	-	4	3	4	-

After checking two values, only choice (C) provides answers that are the same as the original method. Choice (C) is correct.

6. **C** This code describes a breadth-first search or a level-by-level traversal of the binary tree.

Walking through the code step-by-step produces the following table. Note that the nodes in the tree are represented by their value.

Line of code	current	q	Comments	Cumulative Output
while (! q.isEmpty())		1	q.isEmpty() == false	
current = q.dequeue();	1			
System.out.print(current.get-Value());	1			1
if (current.getLeft() != null)	1		current.getLeft() != null	1
q.enqueue(current.getLeft());	1	2		1
if (current.getRight() != null)	1	2	current.getRight() != null	1
q.enqueue(current.getRight());	1	23		1
while (! q.isEmpty())	1	23	q.isEmpty() == false	1
current = q.dequeue();	2	3		1
System.out.print(current.get-Value());	2	3		12
if (current.getLeft() != null)	2	3	current.getLeft() != null	12
q.enqueue(current.getLeft());	2	34		12
if (current.getRight() != null)	2	34	current.getRight() != null	12
q.enqueue(current.getRight());	2	345		12
while (! q.isEmpty())	2	345	q.isEmpty() == false	12
current = q.dequeue();	3	45		12
System.out.print(current.get-Value());	3	45		123

At this point, you can stop because only choice (C) starts with "123".

Contrast this problem with question 7, which uses a stack instead of a queue to traverse the tree.

7. **D** This code describes a rightmost depth-first search or a reverse preorder traversal of the binary tree.

Walking through the code step-by-step produces the following table. Note that the nodes in the tree are represented by their value.

Line of code	current	s	Comments	Cumulative Output
while (! s.isEmpty())		1	s.isEmpty() == false	
current = s.pop();	1			
System.out.print(current.get-Value());	1			1
if (current.getLeft() != null)	1		current.getLeft() != null	1
s.push(current.getLeft());	1	2		1
if (current.getRight() != null)	1	2	current.getRight() != null	1
s.push(current.getRight());	1	32		1
while (! s.isEmpty())	1	32	s.isEmpty() == false	1
current = s.pop();	3	2		1
System.out.print(current.get-Value());	3	2		13
if (current.getLeft() != null)	3	2	current.getLeft() == null	13
if (current.getRight() != null)	3	2	current.getRight() != null	13
s.push(current.getRight());	3	62		13
while (! s.isEmpty())	3	62	s.isEmpty() == false	13
current = s.pop();	6	2		13
System.out.print(current.get-Value());	6	2		136

At this point, you can stop because only choice (D) starts with "136".

Contrast this problem with question 6, which uses a queue instead of a stack to traverse the tree.

8. **B** There are two approaches to solving this problem. Either draw some binary trees and carefully count the nodes, or start with the simplest case and generalize. Because it is very easy to make a mistake when drawing the trees, if you have time you should try both approaches to verify that you have the correct result.

Consider the following binary tree whose nodes have either exactly zero or exactly two children. Each node is labeled as a parent (P) or a leaf (L).

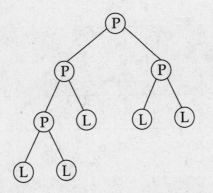

There are 4 parent nodes and 5 leaf nodes in the tree. Because $n = 5$ (the number of leaf nodes), the only choice that corresponds to the number of parent nodes is (B).

See question 34 for a way to generalize this result.

9. **A** There are two ways to solve this problem. The first (and easiest) way is to translate the English description of the return value into a boolean statement. Having exactly two of the three parameters be `true` means that either a and b are `true` and c is `false` OR a and c are `true` and b is `false` OR b and c are `true` and a is `false`. This translates directly into choice (A).

The second way to solve this problem is to create a table of the eight possible combinations of values for a, b, and c. Fill in the result for each of the five choices and determine which choice meets the criteria.

a	b	c	(A)	(B)	(C)	(D)	(E)
false	false	false	false	false	true	false	false
false	false	true	false	false	false	false	false
false	true	false	false	false	false	false	false
true	false	false	false	false	false	false	false
true	true	true	false	false	true	true	true
true	true	false	true	false	true	true	true
true	false	true	true	false	true	true	true
false	true	true	true	false	true	true	true

Choice (A) is the only choice that is `true` when exactly two of a, b, and c are `true`.

10. **B** This problem tests your knowledge of operator precedence in expressions. Multiplication and division are performed before addition and subtraction. Operations that are at the same precedence level are performed in left-to-right order.

Applying these rules to the code segment in the question

```
x     = 5 - 4 + 9 * 12 / 3 - 10
      = 5 - 4 + (9 * 12) / 3 - 10
      = 5 - 4 + 108 / 3 - 10
      = 5 - 4 + (108 / 3) - 10
      = 5 - 4 + 36 - 10
      = (5 - 4) + 36 - 10
      = 1 + 36 - 10
      = (1 + 36) - 10
      = 37 - 10
      = 27
```

Choice (B) is correct.

11. **E** `String` objects are dynamic in the sense that they do not have a maximum length (other than one imposed by a limit of available memory!). Therefore, choices (C) and (D), which appear to refer to a 25-character `String` limit, can be eliminated immediately.

Choice (A) can be eliminated because it is not valid Java code.

Choice (B) can be eliminated because an array of `Strings` is being instantiated and then incorrectly assigned to an `ArrayList` object.

Choice (E) correctly declares and creates an array of 50 `Strings`.

12. **D** The runtime of the outer loop of `mystery1` is linearly dependent on n, the length of the array—specifically, it iterates $n/2$ times.

The runtime of the inner loop of `mystery1` is logarithmically dependent on n—specifically, it iterates $\log_2 n$ times.

As indicated in the question, the runtime of `mystery2` is $O(n)$.

Therefore, the runtime of `mystery1` can be calculated by multiplying the runtime of the outer loop by the runtime of the inner loop by the runtime of `mystery2`: $O(n) \times O(\log n) \times O(n) = O(n^2 \log n)$. Choice (D) is correct.

13. **D** Implementation I is correct. This implementation recursively finds the correct digit by noting that the rightmost digit of n can be found by taking the remainder when n is divided by 10 (the base case). Other digits of n can be found by dividing n by 10 and finding the digit one place to the right (the recursive case).

Implementation II is correct. The `pow` method calculates $10^{whichDigit}$. Dividing n by this number gives a number whose rightmost digit is the target digit. Taking the remainder of this number divided by 10 returns the correct digit.

Implementation III is correct. The loop has the same effect as dividing n by $10^{whichDigit}$. The implementation then returns the correct digit by taking the remainder of this number divided by 10.

14. **C** QuickSort first partitions the array around the pivot value, then recursively sorts the part of the array to the left of the pivot and recursively sorts the part of the array to the right of the pivot.

After a pivot step is completed, the values smaller than the pivot value will occur first in the array, followed by the pivot value, followed by the values larger than the pivot value.

Because 4 is the pivot value, the only valid choice is (C).

15. **C** Statement I is correct. This is the most straightforward way of traversing the array backwards and printing out the values. The `for` loop causes k to take on values from 9 down to 0 and print out the kth element of v.

Statement II is also correct. Although k takes on values from 0 up to 9, the array index `9-k` gives the correct indices of 9 down to 0.

Statement III is incorrect. The first time through the loop, k will have a value of 10, which will raise an `ArrayIndexOutOfBounds` exception.

Choice (C) is the correct answer.

16. **C** A `Fish` can move to any of its three neighboring locations (to the front or side of the fish) as long as that location is empty.

A `SlowFish` moves in the same manner as a `Fish` except it only has a 20 percent chance of moving in any given step of the simulation.

A `DarterFish` moves only forward one or two cells. If the `DarterFish` is blocked from moving, it will reverse its direction.

Choices (A) and (B) are incorrect. Any configuration containing a `DarterFish` will change after a step of the simulation: either the `DarterFish` will move or it will reverse direction.

Choice (D) is incorrect. The fish at (0, 2) can move to its right.

Choice (E) is incorrect. The fish at (1, 2) can either move to its left or to its right.

Choice (C) is correct because none of the fish are able to move.

17. **E** The `objectAt`, `isEmpty`, `add`, and `remove` methods in the `BoundedEnv` class all need to access *one* object in the environment. Only Design 1, using a two-dimensional array, can access an individual object in constant time. Designs 2 and 3 cannot access an object directly; instead they may need to look through all of the objects in a given row (Design 2) or the entire environment (Design 3) to find the object.

On the other hand, the `allObjects` method takes only as long as the number of objects in the environment for Designs 2 and 3, but always takes $O(n)$ time (where n is the number of cells in the environment) for Design 1 because `allObjects` must examine every element of the two-dimensional array to produce a list of objects.

18. **A** Choices (D) and (E) are clearly false. The implementation design for a class has no effect on whether or not other classes can be derived from that class.

Choice (A) is true and choices (B) and (C) are false. Design 1 only allows one object in the array at any given location. Designs 2 and 3 both store the objects in the environment as a list of objects, not based on their location. Two objects with the same location can both be in the list.

19. **C** The `Environment` class is an interface and therefore cannot be extended; it can only be implemented. This eliminates choice (A).

Similarly, the `BoundedEnv` class cannot be implemented; it can only be extended. This eliminates choices (D) and (E).

Choices (B) and (C) are both legal ways to define the `CylindricalEnv`. However, only choice (C) takes advantage of the fact that a `CylindricalEnv` is a special type of `BoundedEnv`. Choice (C) is the correct answer.

20. **E** The only legal way to raise an exception in Java is to use the `throw` command. This eliminates choices (A), (B), and (C).

When throwing an exception, think of the exception as a class name and the exception to be thrown as an object of the class that needs to be constructed. Creating an object requires the use of the `new` keyword; therefore choice (E) is the correct way to throw the exception.

Note that `IllegalArgumentExceptions` are also thrown in the Marine Biology Simulation Case Study in the `add`, `remove`, and `recordMove` methods of the `BoundedEnv` class. You can always look at the case study code provided with the exam to get a reminder of the syntax for throwing exceptions.

21. **A** Choice (A) is correct. The `compareTo` method takes an `Object` as a parameter and returns an integer.

Note that this signature is always the same, no matter what class implements the `Comparable` interface.

22. **E** All three statements are correct.

Statement I returns **true** only if the conditions in all three `if` statements are satisfied.

Statement II combines the three tests into one `if` statement condition and returns **true** if that condition is satisfied.

Statement III returns the opposite of checking if any one of the month, day, or year are not equal. This is an application of DeMorgan's law (see question 40 for another example).

23. **D** The `daysUntil` method is the only method that needs to know about leap years in order to work properly. For example, for the date February 27, the number of days until March 2 is different according to whether or not the year is a leap year.

All of the other methods do not depend on whether the year is a leap year.

24. **E** In Java, parameters to methods are passed by value. Thus, the values of any arguments in the code that calls the method are not changed by calling the method.

In this question, despite its misleading name, the `swap` method does not change the arguments of the code that calls `swap`.

Because `swap` has no effect, choice (E) is correct: The elements of `A` are left in their original order.

25. **E** To solve this problem, first eliminate choices (A) and (B) as they represent two-dimensional arrays that have 3 rows and 4 columns, not 4 rows and 3 columns as indicated in the code segment.

Note that `k` iterates through the rows and `j` iterates through the columns.

Second, examine the value at `A[1][0]`. This value is set when `k = 1` and `j = 0`. Because `j` has the value 0, `A[1][0]` should be set to 0. This eliminates choice (C).

Finally, examine the value at `A[1][1]`. This value is set when `k = 1` and `j = 1`. Because `k % j` has the value 0, `A[1][1]` should be set to 1. This eliminates choice (D).

Choice (E) is correct.

26. E A `stack` is a Last-In-First-Out data structure. To solve this problem keep track of the contents of `s` and of the variable `obj` as each line of code is executed.

Line of Code	Stack s after execution	obj after execution
`s.push("A");`	A	
`s.push("B");`	AB	
`obj = s.peekTop();`	AB	B
`s.push(obj + "" + obj);`	ABBB	B
`s.push("C");`	ABBBC	B
`s.push("D");`	ABBBCD	B
`obj = s.peekTop();`	ABBBCD	D
`obj += "" + s.pop();`	ABBBC	DD
`s.push(obj + "" + obj);`	ABBBCDDDD	DD

When the contents of the stack are popped off and printed, the output is the contents of the stack in reverse order: DDDDCBBBA.

Choice (E) is correct.

27. D A good set of test data exercises every conditional test in the code including cases that generate errors.

In the method `mystery`, a good set of test cases must include, at the minimum, data that allow each of the `return` statements to be executed.

- `x > 0` and `y = <anything>`
- `x <= 0` and `y > 0`
- `x <= 0` and `y < 0`
- `x <= 0` and `y = 0` (the error condition)

Only choice (D) meets all four of these criteria.

28. A A question involving binary search trees is usually not solvable solely by inspection. To answer this type of question correctly, first draw the binary search tree.

Recall that a binary search tree is a binary tree in which for every node, all of the children in the node's left subtree are smaller than the node and all of the children in the node's right subtree are larger than the node.

Form the tree by inserting the given numbers in order. Start at the root and move down the tree to the left or the right based on whether the node to be inserted is smaller or larger than the node currently being examined.

In this question, form the binary search tree as follows:

53 is inserted into the empty tree at the root.

12 is less than 53, so insert it as the left child of 53.

26 is less than 53, move to the left. 26 is greater than 12, so insert it as the right child of 12.

2 is less than 53, move to the left. 2 is less than 12, so insert it as the left child of 12.

3 is less than 53, move to the left. 3 is less than 12, move to the left. 3 is greater than 2, so insert it as the right child of 2.

At this point, the binary search tree should look like this

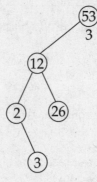

Completing the tree

67 is greater than 53, so insert it as the right child of 53.

60 is greater than 53, so move to the right. 60 is less than 67, so insert it as the left child of 67.

99 is greater than 53, so move to the right. 99 is greater than 67, so insert it as the right child of 67.

1 is less than 53, so move to the left. 1 is less than 12, so move to the left. 1 is less than 2, so insert it as the left child of 2.

The final binary search tree looks like this

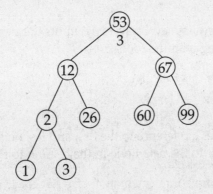

Now examine the tree to see which of the traversals is correct.

Choice (A) is correct. A preorder traversal outputs the value of the root of the tree followed by a preorder traversal of the left subtree followed by a preorder traversal of the right subtree.

In a preorder traversal, the root of the tree is the first element in the list.

A preorder traversal of this tree gives

| 53 | 12 | 2 | 1 | 3 | 26 | 67 | 60 | 99 |

Choice (B) is incorrect. An inorder traversal outputs an inorder traversal of the left subtree followed by the value of the root of the tree followed by an inorder traversal of the right subtree.

More importantly, an inorder traversal of a binary search tree (not just a binary tree, but a binary *search* tree) produces a sorted list of the values in the tree.

An inorder traversal of this tree gives

| 1 | 2 | 3 | 12 | 26 | 53 | 60 | 67 | 99 |

Choice (C) is incorrect. A postorder traversal outputs a postorder traversal of the left subtree followed by a postorder traversal of the right subtree followed by the value of the root of the tree.

In a postorder traversal, the root of the tree is the last element in the list.

A postorder traversal of this tree gives

| 1 | 3 | 2 | 26 | 12 | 60 | 99 | 67 | 53 |

Choice (D) is incorrect. A reverse preorder traversal is similar to a preorder traversal except that it outputs the right side of the tree before the left side of the tree. Specifically, it outputs a reverse preorder traversal of the right subtree followed by a reverse preorder traversal of the left subtree followed by the value of the root of the tree.

Like a preorder traversal, in a reverse preorder traversal, the root of the tree is the first element in the list.

A reverse preorder traversal of this tree gives

53   67   99   60   12   26   2   3   1

Choice (E) is incorrect. A level-by-level traversal outputs the elements of the tree in left-to-right, top-to-bottom order starting with the root.

A level-by-level traversal of this tree gives

53   12   67   2   26   60   99   1   3

29. **A** The `LinkedList` class stores a reference to the first and last nodes in the linked list. Each node in the list stores a reference to the next node in the list and to the previous node in the list.

Pseudocode for a constant time implementation of `rotateLeft` can be written as:

1) Assign the first node in the list to a temporary node.

2) Set the first node in the list to be the second node in the list (the first node's "next" node).

3) Set the new first node's "previous" node to `null`.

4) Set the "next" node of the last node in the list to be the temporary node.

5) Set the "next" node of the temporary node to `null`.

6) Set the "previous" node of the temporary node to be the last node of the list.

7) Set the last node of the list to be the next node of the last node of the list.

Each of these seven steps takes constant time. Therefore, the entire method also takes constant—$O(1)$—time.

30. **D** The way to approach this problem is to determine when a node is counted—that is, when it contributes to the value returned by `mystery`.

In the method, there are two places where a node is counted: when the node has no children and when it has exactly two children. If the node is `null` or has exactly one child, the node is not counted.

It is also important to ensure that all of the nodes below any given node are also handled; the recursive calls to `mystery` accomplish this.

Because all of the nodes are handled and only nodes with no children or exactly two children are counted, choice (D) is correct.

31. C After adding the first five letters of the alphabet to the linked list, walk through each line of the while loop.

Line of code	obj	obj2	theList	Comments
obj = itr.next()	A		ABCDE ⇑	
if (itr.next())	A		ABCDE ⇑	itr.next() returns true
obj2 = itr.next()	A	B	ABCDE ⇑	
itr.set(obj)	A	B	AACDE ⇑	
while (itr.hasNext())	A	B	AACDE ⇑	itr.hasNext() returns true
obj = itr.next()	C	B	AACDE ⇑	
if (itr.next())	C	B	AACDE ⇑	itr.next() returns true
obj2 = itr.next()	C	D	AACDE ⇑	
itr.set(obj)	C	D	AACCE ⇑	
while (itr.hasNext())	C	D	AACCE ⇑	itr.hasNext() returns true
obj = itr.next()	E	D	AACCE ⇑	
if (itr.next())	E	D	AACCE ⇑	itr.next() returns false
itr.set(obj)	E	D	AACCE ⇑	
while (itr.hasNext())	E	D	AACCE ⇑	itr.hasNext() returns false

Creating a new iterator and walking through the linked list prints "AACCE". Choice (C) is correct.

32. **C** Statement I is correct. The first `while` loop takes all of the elements of the queue and pushes them onto a stack. The second `while` loop pops all of the objects off of the stack and adds them back into the queue. The effect is to reverse the elements of the queue.

Statement II is correct. This code recursively reverses the elements of the queue. If the queue is empty, it is already reversed. Otherwise, the code dequeues the first element, recursively reverses the remainder of the queue, and then enqueues that first element to the end of the queue.

Statement III is incorrect. The interfaces for `Stack` and `Queue` do not specify a `size` method. However, even if a `size` method were available that returned the number of elements in the stack or queue, statement III would still be incorrect. In this case, the number of elements in the stack or queue would decrease each time through the loop and the loop would only iterate through half of the elements in the stack or queue. At the end of the `reverse` method of statement III, the queue will only have three-quarters of its original number of elements.

Because statements I and II are correct and statement III is incorrect, choice (C) is the correct answer.

33. **C** Choice (C) is correct and choices (A) and (B) are incorrect because the `java.util.TreeSet` class guarantees $O(\log n)$ runtime for the methods `add`, `remove`, and `contains` with no restrictions on the size of the data set.

Choice (D) is incorrect because the `java.util.HashSet` class makes no guarantees as to the order of the elements returned by its iterator.

Choice (E) is incorrect because the total time needed to iterate for *any* implementation of a `Set` is $O(n)$.

34. **D** To solve this problem, start with a tree with a single node and add nodes, one at a time, keeping track of the relationships among n_0, n_1, and n_2.

For a tree with a single node, the node had no children, so $n_0 = 1$, $n_1 = 0$, and $n_2 = 0$.

Add a node as a left child of the root. Now $n_0 = 1$, $n_1 = 1$, and $n_2 = 0$.

There are now two places to add a new node: either as the right child of the root or as the left or right child of the node added in the previous step. If the new node is added as the right child of the root, $n_0 = 2$, $n_1 = 0$, and $n_2 = 1$. Alternatively, if the new node is added as a child of the other node, $n_0 = 1$, $n_1 = 2$, and $n_2 = 0$.

At this point, it appears that n_0 is always larger than n_2 and that the size of n_1 is not related to either n_0 or n_2. To prove this, generalize by examining the three possibilities that can occur when a node is added to the tree:

1. The node is added as the root of the tree. After adding the node, $n_0 = 1$, $n_1 = 0$, and $n_2 = 0$. Note that this can only happen once.

2. The node is added as the child of an existing node that has no children. In this case, n_0 stays the same (the existing node no longer has no children, but the new node has no children), n_1 increases by one (the existing node now has one child), and n_2 is not affected.

3. The node is added as the child of an existing node that already has one child. In this case, n_0 increases by one (the new node has no children), n_1 decreases by one (the existing node no longer has just one child), and n_2 increases by one (the existing node now has two children).

n_0 starts out larger than n_2 in case 1. This relationship is not affected by cases 2 and 3. Therefore, $n_0 > n_2$.

However, by repeatedly adding nodes that match case 2, n_1 can be made arbitrarily larger than both n_0 and n_2 without changing the relationship between n_0 and n_2. Thus, the relationships between n_1 and n_0 and between n_1 and n_2 cannot be determined.

35. **E** The assertion in this question refers to the information that is returned after the `pivot` method is called.

Choice (A) is incorrect. The variables `first` and `last` refer to the first and last index of the portion of the array being sorted. The value of the last element has no relationship to the array indices.

Choice (B) is incorrect. If the portion of the array being sorted only has two elements, then `last = first + 1` and `pivotIndex` must be equal to either `first` or `last`.

Choice (C) is incorrect. The variable `pivotValue` is not an index into the array.

Choice (D) is incorrect. The variable `pivotIndex` has no relationship to the value of the elements in the array.

Choice (E) is correct. After the pivot, all of the elements of the array to the left of where the pivot value ends up in the array (`pivotIndex`) are less than or equal to the `pivotValue`.

36. **D** Hash functions take an argument and return an index into a hash table. The index returned must be between zero and the table size minus one.

Only choice (D) meets these criteria.

37. **B** Recall that a min-heap is a complete binary tree such that the value of each node is smaller than the value of its children. A min-heap is stored in array A using a level-by-level traversal such that the smallest element of the heap (the root) is stored in A[0].

Choice	Heap	Valid heap?
(A)	Tree: 1; children 2, 3; 2's children 5, 7; 3's children 6, 9; 5's children 8, 4	No. Node 5 is larger than its right child.
(B)	Tree: 1; children 2, 5; 2's children 3, 7; 5's children 6, 9; 3's children 8, 4	Yes.
(C)	Tree: 1; children 2, 7; 2's children 4, 5; 7's children 9, 8; 4's children 3, 6	No. Node 4 is larger than its left child.
(D)	Tree: 1; children 3, 2; 3's children 5, 7; 2's children 8, 9; 5's children 6, 4	No. Node 5 is larger than its right child.
(E)	Tree: 1; children 9, 8; 9's children 7, 6; 8's children 5, 4; 7's children 3, 2	No. Node 9, 8 and 7 are larger than their children.

Choice (B) is the only valid min-heap.

38. E The fastest way to solve this problem is to draw the binary trees formed by each choice. The tree that has the fewest levels is the most balanced tree.

Choice	Binary Tree	Number of Levels
(A)		4
(B)		4
(C)		4
(D)		4
(E)		3

Choice (E) has the fewest levels and produces the most balanced tree.

39. **C** Statement I is not correct. This code will always return zero because it continues to recursively call `height` until `t` is `null`, at which time it returns zero.

Statement II is not correct. This code actually returns the number of nodes in the tree. For each leaf node in the tree, it returns one; for each non-leaf node, it recursively counts the nodes in the left subtree, recursively counts the nodes in the right subtree, adds the two results together, and adds one to count the non-leaf node.

Statement III is correct. The height at any given node in the tree is given by adding one to the larger of the heights of the node's two subtrees.

Because only statement III is correct, choice (C) is the correct answer.

40. **E** The easiest way to solve this problem is to use DeMorgan's law. This states that

`!(p && q)` is equivalent to `!p || !q`

or, negating both sides

`p && q` is equivalent to `!(!p || !q)`.

In this problem, set `p` to `(X > Y)` and `q` to `(Y > Z)`.

`!p` becomes `(X <= Y)` and `!q` becomes `(Y <= Z)`.

Finally, `!(!p || !q)` becomes `!((X <= Y) || (Y <= Z))`.

Therefore, choice (E) is correct.

Note that although choice (A) appears to be correct because it follows the transitive property of inequality, consider the two boolean equations after setting `X` to 6, `Y` to 8, and `Z` to 4.

`(6 > 8) && (8 > 4)` is false, but `6 > 4` is true.

FREE-RESPONSE QUESTIONS

1. (a)
```
public Screen(int width, int height)
{
        numCols = width;
        data = new LinkedList[height];
        for (int k = 0; k < height; k++)
                data[k] = new LinkedList();
}
```

(b)
```
public Pixel pixelAt(int row, int col)
{
        LinkedList theRow = data[row];
        Iterator itr = theRow.iterator();
        Pixel p;
        while (itr.hasNext())
        {
                p = (Pixel) itr.next();
                if (p.getCol() == col)
                        return p;
        }
        return null;
}
```

(c)
```
public void pixelOn(int row, int col)
{
        Pixel newPxl = new Pixel(row, col);
        Pixel p;
        LinkedList theRow = data[row];
        ListIterator itr =
                theRow.listIterator();
        while (itr.hasNext())
        {
                p = (Pixel) itr.next();
                if (newPxl.getCol() > p.getCol())
                {
                        itr.previous();
                        itr.add(newPxl);
                        return;
                }
        }
        itr.previous();
        itr.add(p);
}
```

2. (a)
```
public RBTreeNode getUncle()
{
        RBTreeNode p = getParent();
        RBTreeNode gp = p.getParent();
        if (gp.getLeft() == p)
              return gp.getRight();
        else
              return gp.getLeft();
}
```

(b)
```
private void rotateLeft(RBTreeNode x)
{
        RBTreeNode y = x.getRight();
        RBTreeNode node1 = x.getLeft();
        RBTreeNode node2 = y.getLeft();
        RBTreeNode node3 = y.getRight();
        RBTreeNode xParent = x.getParent();
        x.setRight(node2);
        node2.setParent(x);
        y.setLeft(x);
        x.setParent(y);
        y.setParent(xParent);
        if (xParent == null)
              root = y;
        else if (xParent.getLeft() == x)
              xParent.setLeft(y);
        else
              xParent.setRight(y);
}
```

```
(c) private void fixup(RBTreeNode x)
      {
              RBTreeNode p = x.getParent();
              if (p.getColor() == BLACK)
                  return;

              if (x.getUncle().getColor() == RED)
              {
                  p.setColor(BLACK);
                  x.getUncle().setColor(BLACK);
                  p.getParent().setColor(RED);
                  fixup(p.getParent());
                  return;
              }

              if (x.getUncle().getColor() == BLACK &&
                  x == p.getRight() &&
                  p == p.getParent().getLeft())
              {
                  rotateLeft(p);
                  fixup(p);
                  return;
              }
              if (x.getUncle().getColor() == BLACK &&
                  x == p.getLeft() &&
                  p == p.getParent().getLeft())
              {
                  p.setColor(BLACK);
                  p.getParent().setColor(RED);
                  rotateRight(p.getParent());
                  return;
              }

              if (x.getUncle().getColor() == BLACK &&
                  x == p.getLeft() &&
                  p == p.getParent().getRight())
              {
                  rotateRight(p);
                  fixup(p);
                  return;
              }
              if (x.getUncle().getColor() == BLACK &&
                  x == p.getRight() &&
                  p == p.getParent().getRight())
              {
                  p.setColor(BLACK);
                  p.getParent().setColor(RED);
                  rotateLeft(p.getParent());
                  return;
              }
      }
```

3. (a)
```
public class BinaryInt implements Comparable
{
        private ArrayList digits;
        public BinaryInt()
        { /* implementation not needed */ }
        public BinaryInt(int decimalValue)
        { /* implementation not needed */ }
        public BinaryInt add(BinaryInt other)
        { /* implementation not needed */ }
        public String toString()
        { /* implementation not needed */ }
        public int compareTo(Object other)
        { /* implementation not needed */ }
}
```

(b)
```
public BinaryInt(int decimalValue)
{
        digits = new ArrayList();
        while (decimalValue > 0)
        {
                digits.add(
                    new Integer(decimalValue % 2));
                decimalValue /= 2;
        }
}
```

(c)
```
public static void Test()
{
        BinaryInt a1 =
                new BinaryInt(2314279623);
        BinaryInt a2 =
                new BinaryInt(3236550123);
        BinaryInt aSum = a1.add(a2);
        BinaryInt b1 =
                new BinaryInt(3412579010);
        BinaryInt b2 =
                new BinaryInt(2128250735);
        BinaryInt bSum = b1.add(b2);
        if (aSum.compareTo(bSum) > 0)
                System.out.print(aSum.toString());
        else
                System.out.print(bSum.toString());
}
```

4. (a)
```
public boolean isOldest(Locatable obj)
    {
        Locatable oldest =
                (Locatable) pq.peekMin();
        return obj.equals(oldest);
    }
```

(b)
```
public void add(Locatable obj)
    {
        objectList.add(obj);
        pq.add(obj);
    }
```

(c)
```
public void act()
    {
        if (! isInEnv())
            return;
        if (environment().isOldest(this))
        {
            Fish child1 =
                    new Fish(environment(),
                            location(),
                            direction(),
                            color(),
                            age() / 2);
            Fish child2 =
                    new Fish(environment(),
                            location(),
                            direction(),
                            color(),
                            age() / 2);
            child1.move();
            child2.move();
            environment().remove(this);
        }
        else
        {
            myAge += 1;
            move();
        }
    }
```

APPENDIX

LICENSE

GNU GENERAL PUBLIC LICENSE
Version 2, June 1991

Copyright (C) 1989, 1991 Free Software Foundation, Inc.
59 Temple Place, Suite 330,
Boston, MA   02111-1307   USA
Everyone is permitted to copy and distribute verbatim copies
of this license document, but changing it is not allowed.

Preamble

The licenses for most software are designed to take away your freedom to share and change it. By contrast, the GNU General Public License is intended to guarantee your freedom to share and change free software—to make sure the software is free for all its users. This General Public License applies to most of the Free Software Foundation's software and to any other program whose authors commit to using it. (Some other Free Software Foundation software is covered by the GNU Library General Public License instead.) You can apply it to your programs, too.

When we speak of free software, we are referring to freedom, not price. Our General Public Licenses are designed to make sure that you have the freedom to distribute copies of free software (and charge for this service if you wish), that you receive source code or can get it if you want it, that you can change the software or use pieces of it in new free programs; and that you know you can do these things.

To protect your rights, we need to make restrictions that forbid anyone to deny you these rights or to ask you to surrender the rights. These restrictions translate to certain responsibilities for you if you distribute copies of the software, or if you modify it.

For example, if you distribute copies of such a program, whether gratis or for a fee, you must give the recipients all the rights that you have. You must make sure that they, too, receive or can get the source code. And you must show them these terms so they know their rights.

We protect your rights with two steps: (1) copyright the software, and (2) offer you this license which gives you legal permission to copy, distribute and/or modify the software.

Also, for each author's protection and ours, we want to make certain that everyone understands that there is no warranty for this free software. If the software is modified by someone else and passed on, we want its recipients to know that what they have is not the original, so that any problems introduced by others will not reflect on the original authors' reputations.

Finally, any free program is threatened constantly by software patents. We wish to avoid the danger that redistributors of a free program will individually obtain patent licenses, in effect making the program proprietary. To prevent this, we have made it clear that any patent must be licensed for everyone's free use or not licensed at all.

The precise terms and conditions for copying, distribution and modification follow.   GNU GENERAL PUBLIC LICENSE TERMS AND CONDITIONS FOR COPYING, DISTRIBUTION AND MODIFICATION:

0. This License applies to any program or other work which contains a notice placed by the copyright holder saying it may be distributed under the terms of this General Public License. The "Program", below, refers to any such program or work, and a "work based on the Program" means either the Program or any derivative work under copyright law: that is to say, a work containing the Program or a portion of it, either verbatim or with modifications and/or translated into another language.   (Hereinafter, translation is included without limitation in the term "modification".)   Each licensee is addressed as "you".

Activities other than copying, distribution and modification are not covered by this License; they are outside its scope.   The act of running the Program is not restricted, and the output from the Program is covered only if its contents constitute a work based on the Program (independent of having been made by running the Program). Whether that is true depends on what the Program does.

1. You may copy and distribute verbatim copies of the Program's source code as you receive it, in any medium, provided that you conspicuously and appropriately publish on each copy an appropriate copyright notice and disclaimer of warranty; keep intact all the notices that refer to this License and to the absence of any warranty; and give any other recipients of the Program a copy of this License along with the Program.

You may charge a fee for the physical act of transferring a copy, and you may at your option offer warranty protection in exchange for a fee.

2. You may modify your copy or copies of the Program or any portion of it, thus forming a work based on the Program, and copy and distribute such modifications or work under the terms of Section 1 above, provided that you also meet all of these conditions:

a) You must cause the modified files to carry prominent notices stating that you changed the files and the date of any change.

b) You must cause any work that you distribute or publish, that in whole or in part contains or is derived from the Program or any part thereof, to be licensed as a whole at no charge to all third parties under the terms of this License.

c) If the modified program normally reads commands interactively when run, you must cause it, when started running for such interactive use in the most ordinary way, to print or display an announcement including an appropriate copyright notice and a notice that there is no warranty (or else, saying that you provide a warranty) and that users may redistribute the program under these conditions, and telling the user how to view a copy of this License. (Exception: if the Program itself is interactive but does not normally print such an announcement, your work based on the Program is not required to print an announcement.) These requirements apply to the modified work as a whole. If identifiable sections of that work are not derived from the Program, and can be reasonably considered independent and separate works in themselves, then this License, and its terms, do not apply to those sections when you distribute them as separate works. But when you distribute the same sections as part of a whole which is a work based on the Program, the distribution of the whole must be on the terms of this License, whose permissions for other licensees extend to the entire whole, and thus to each and every part regardless of who wrote it.

Thus, it is not the intent of this section to claim rights or contest your rights to work written entirely by you; rather, the intent is to exercise the right to control the distribution of derivative or collective works based on the Program.

In addition, mere aggregation of another work not based on the Program with the Program (or with a work based on the Program) on a volume of a storage or distribution medium does not bring the other work under the scope of this License.

3. You may copy and distribute the Program (or a work based on it, under Section 2) in object code or executable form under the terms of Sections 1 and 2 above provided that you also do one of the following:

    a) Accompany it with the complete corresponding machine-readable source code, which must be distributed under the terms of Sections 1 and 2 above on a medium customarily used for software interchange; or,

    b) Accompany it with a written offer, valid for at least three years, to give any third party, for a charge no more than your cost of physically performing source distribution, a complete machine-readable copy of the corresponding source code, to be distributed under the terms of Sections 1 and 2 above on a medium customarily used for software interchange; or,

    c) Accompany it with the information you received as to the offer to distribute corresponding source code. (This alternative is allowed only for noncommercial distribution and only if you received the program in object code or executable form with such an offer, in accord with Subsection b above.)

The source code for a work means the preferred form of the work for making modifications to it. For an executable work, complete source code means all the source code for all modules it contains, plus any associated interface definition files, plus the scripts used to control compilation and installation of the executable. However, as a special exception, the source code distributed need not include anything that is normally distributed (in either source or binary form) with the major components (compiler, kernel, and so on) of the operating system on which the executable runs, unless that component itself accompanies the executable.

If distribution of executable or object code is made by offering access to copy from a designated place, then offering equivalent access to copy the source code from the same place counts as distribution of the source code, even though third parties are not compelled to copy the source along with the object code.

4. You may not copy, modify, sublicense, or distribute the Program except as expressly provided under this License. Any attempt otherwise to copy, modify, sublicense or distribute the Program is void, and will automatically terminate your rights under this License. However, parties who have received copies, or rights, from you under this License will not have their licenses terminated so long as such parties remain in full compliance.

5. You are not required to accept this License, since you have not signed it. However, nothing else grants you permission to modify or distribute the Program or its derivative works. These actions are prohibited by law if you do not accept this License. Therefore, by modifying or distributing the Program (or any work based on the Program), you indicate your acceptance of this License to do so, and all its terms and conditions for copying, distributing or modifying the Program or works based on it.

6. Each time you redistribute the Program (or any work based on the Program), the recipient automatically receives a license from the original licensor to copy, distribute or modify the Program subject to these terms and conditions. You may not impose any further restrictions on the recipients' exercise of the rights granted herein. You are not responsible for enforcing compliance by third parties to this License.

7. If, as a consequence of a court judgment or allegation of patent infringement or for any other reason (not limited to patent issues), conditions are imposed on you (whether by court order, agreement or otherwise) that contradict the conditions of this License, they do not excuse you from the conditions of this License. If you cannot distribute so as to satisfy simultaneously your obligations under this License and any other pertinent obligations, then as a consequence you may not distribute the Program at all. For example, if a patent license would not permit royalty-free redistribution of the Program by all those who receive copies directly or indirectly through you, then the only way you could satisfy both it and this License would be to refrain entirely from distribution of the Program.

If any portion of this section is held invalid or unenforceable under any particular circumstance, the balance of the section is intended to apply and the section as a whole is intended to apply in other circumstances.

It is not the purpose of this section to induce you to infringe any patents or other property right claims or to contest validity of any such claims; this section has the sole purpose of protecting the integrity of the free software distribution system, which is implemented by public license practices. Many people have made generous contributions to the wide range of software distributed through that system in reliance on consistent application of that system; it is up to the author/donor to decide if he or she is willing to distribute software through any other system and a licensee cannot impose that choice.

This section is intended to make thoroughly clear what is believed to be a consequence of the rest of this License.

8. If the distribution and/or use of the Program is restricted in certain countries either by patents or by copyrighted interfaces, the original copyright holder who places the Program under this License may add an explicit geographical distribution limitation excluding those countries, so that distribution is permitted only in or among countries not thus excluded. In such case, this License incorporates the limitation as if written in the body of this License.

9. The Free Software Foundation may publish revised and/or new versions of the General Public License from time to time. Such new versions will be similar in spirit to the present version, but may differ in detail to address new problems or concerns.

    Each version is given a distinguishing version number. If the Program specifies a version number of this License which applies to it and "any later version", you have the option of following the terms and conditions either of that version or of any later version published by the Free Software Foundation. If the Program does not specify a version number of this License, you may choose any version ever published by the Free Software Foundation.

10. If you wish to incorporate parts of the Program into other free programs whose distribution conditions are different, write to the author to ask for permission. For software which is copyrighted by the Free Software Foundation, write to the Free Software Foundation; we sometimes make exceptions for this. Our decision will be guided by the two goals of preserving the free status of all derivatives of our free software and of promoting the sharing and reuse of software generally.

11. BECAUSE THE PROGRAM IS LICENSED FREE OF CHARGE, THERE IS NO WARRANTY FOR THE PROGRAM, TO THE EXTENT PERMITTED BY APPLICABLE LAW. EXCEPT WHEN OTHERWISE STATED IN WRITING THE COPYRIGHT HOLDERS AND/OR OTHER PARTIES PROVIDE THE PROGRAM "AS IS" WITHOUT WARRANTY OF ANY KIND, EITHER EXPRESSED OR IMPLIED, INCLUDING, BUT NOT LIMITED TO, THE IMPLIED WARRANTIES OF MERCHANTABILITY AND FITNESS FOR A PARTICULAR PURPOSE. THE ENTIRE RISK AS TO THE QUALITY AND PERFORMANCE OF THE PROGRAM IS WITH YOU. SHOULD THE PROGRAM PROVE DEFECTIVE, YOU ASSUME THE COST OF ALL NECESSARY SERVICING, REPAIR OR CORRECTION.

12. IN NO EVENT UNLESS REQUIRED BY APPLICABLE LAW OR AGREED TO IN WRITING WILL ANY COPYRIGHT HOLDER, OR ANY OTHER PARTY WHO MAY MODIFY AND/OR REDISTRIBUTE THE PROGRAM AS PERMITTED ABOVE, BE LIABLE TO YOU FOR DAMAGES, INCLUDING ANY GENERAL, SPECIAL, INCIDENTAL OR CONSEQUENTIAL DAMAGES ARISING OUT OF THE USE OR INABILITY TO USE THE PROGRAM (INCLUDING BUT NOT LIMITED TO LOSS OF DATA OR DATA BEING RENDERED INACCURATE OR LOSSES SUSTAINED BY YOU OR THIRD PARTIES OR A FAILURE OF THE PROGRAM TO OPERATE WITH ANY OTHER PROGRAMS), EVEN IF SUCH HOLDER OR OTHER PARTY HAS BEEN ADVISED OF THE POSSIBILITY OF SUCH DAMAGES.

END OF TERMS AND CONDITIONS

How to Apply These Terms to Your New Programs

If you develop a new program, and you want it to be of the greatest possible use to the public, the best way to achieve this is to make it free software which everyone can redistribute and change under these terms.

To do so, attach the following notices to the program. It is safest to attach them to the start of each source file to most effectively convey the exclusion of warranty; and each file should have at least the "copyright" line and a pointer to where the full notice is found.

<one line to give the program's name and a brief idea of what it does.> Copyright (C) 19yy <name of author>

This program is free software; you can redistribute it and/or modify it under the terms of the GNU General Public License as published by the Free Software Foundation; either version 2 of the License, or (at your option) any later version.

This program is distributed in the hope that it will be useful, but WITHOUT ANY WARRANTY; without even the implied warranty of MERCHANTABILITY or FITNESS FOR A PARTICULAR PURPOSE. See the GNU General Public License for more details.

You should have received a copy of the GNU General Public License along with this program; if not, write to the Free Software Foundation, Inc., 59 Temple Place, Suite 330, Boston, MA 02111-1307 USA

Also add information on how to contact you by electronic and paper mail.

If the program is interactive, make it output a short notice like this when it starts in an interactive mode:

Gnomovision version 69, Copyright (C) 19yy name of author Gnomovision comes with ABSOLUTELY NO WARRANTY; for details type `show w'. This is free software, and you are welcome to redistribute it under certain conditions; type `show c' for details.

The hypothetical commands `show w' and `show c' should show the appropriate parts of the General Public License. Of course, the commands you use may be called something other than `show w' and `show c'; they could even be mouse-clicks or menu items--whatever suits your program.

You should also get your employer (if you work as a programmer) or your school, if any, to sign a "copyright disclaimer" for the program, if necessary. Here is a sample; alter the names:

Yoyodyne, Inc., hereby disclaims all copyright interest in the program `Gnomovision' (which makes passes at compilers) written by James Hacker.

<signature of Ty Coon>, 1 April 1989   Ty Coon, President of Vice

This General Public License does not permit incorporating your program into proprietary programs. If your program is a subroutine library, you may consider it more useful to permit linking proprietary applications with the library. If this is what you want to do, use the GNU Library General Public License instead of this License.

Index

ABOUT THE AUTHORS

MEHRAN HABIBI

Mehran(Max) Habibi has more than 8 years of software development experience with IBM, MCI/WorldCom, OCLC, NetJets, BankOne, and Influx Consulting, with roles ranging from tester to developer to architect. He has worked with .NET, Java, wireless, and COM technologies, and is the author the best-selling The Sun Certified Java Developer Exam with J2SE 1.4(Apress), and soon to be released Regular Real World Regular Expressions with J2SE(Apress). He can be reached at: coach@influxs.com.

MICHAEL FRITZ

Michael Fritz works as a Web Programmer at Franklin University in Columbus, Ohio, where he helps develop online learning systems. He previously worked for the Princeton Review where he taught hundreds of students how to excel on standardized tests.

ROBB CUTLER

Robb Cutler is the Department Chair of Computer Science at The Harker School, a K-12 college preparatory school in San Jose, California, the heart of Silicon Valley, where he also teaches AP Computer Science and post-AP seminars on various computer science topics.

After graduating from Dartmouth College with a B.A. in computer science and spending more than 15 years as a software engineer, technical manager, and consultant, Robb sold his business in the late 1990s and found a new passion in teaching and working with students.

Extremely concerned about issues of gender equity in computer science, Robb is always looking for new ways to make computer science more accessible to everyone. He can be reached at: robbc@apcomputerscience.net.

The Princeton Review

1. YOUR NAME: _____
(Print)   Last   First   M.I.

SIGNATURE: _____ **DATE:** ___ / ___ / ___

HOME ADDRESS: _____
(Print)   Number and Street

_____
City   State   Zip Code

PHONE NO. : _____
(Print)

IMPORTANT: Please fill in these boxes exactly as shown on the back cover of your test book.

2. TEST FORM
_____

5. YOUR NAME

First 4 letters of last name				FIRST INIT	MID INIT
A	A	A	A	A	A
B	B	B	B	B	B
C	C	C	C	C	C
D	D	D	D	D	D
E	E	E	E	E	E
F	F	F	F	F	F
G	G	G	G	G	G
H	H	H	H	H	H
I	I	I	I	I	I
J	J	J	J	J	J
K	K	K	K	K	K
L	L	L	L	L	L
M	M	M	M	M	M
N	N	N	N	N	N
O	O	O	O	O	O
P	P	P	P	P	P
Q	Q	Q	Q	Q	Q
R	R	R	R	R	R
S	S	S	S	S	S
T	T	T	T	T	T
U	U	U	U	U	U
V	V	V	V	V	V
W	W	W	W	W	W
X	X	X	X	X	X
Y	Y	Y	Y	Y	Y
Z	Z	Z	Z	Z	Z

6. DATE OF BIRTH

Month	Day	Year
JAN		
FEB		
MAR	0 0	0 0
APR	1 1	1 1
MAY	2 2	2 2
JUN	3 3	3 3
JUL	4 4	4
AUG	5 5	5
SEP	7 7	7
OCT	8 8	8
NOV	9 9	9
DEC		

3. TEST CODE   4. REGISTRATION NUMBER

TEST CODE: 0 A 0 0 0 0 0 0 0 0 0
1 B 1 1 1 1 1 1 1 1 1
2 C 2 2 2 2 2 2 2 2 2
3 D 3 3 3 3 3 3 3 3 3
4 E 4 4 4 4 4 4 4 4 4
5 F 5 5 5 5 5 5 5 5 5
7 G 7 7 7 7 7 7 7 7 7
8 8 8 8 8 8 8 8 8
9 9 9 9 9 9 9 9 9

7. SEX
- MALE
- FEMALE

The Princeton Review

Section 1

Start with number 1 for each new section.
If a section has fewer questions than answer spaces, leave the extra answer spaces blank.

1. A B C D E
2. A B C D E
3. A B C D E
4. A B C D E
5. A B C D E
6. A B C D E
7. A B C D E
8. A B C D E
9. A B C D E
10. A B C D E
11. A B C D E
12. A B C D E
13. A B C D E
14. A B C D E
15. A B C D E

16. A B C D E
17. A B C D E
18. A B C D E
19. A B C D E
20. A B C D E
21. A B C D E
22. A B C D E
23. A B C D E
24. A B C D E
25. A B C D E
26. A B C D E
27. A B C D E
28. A B C D E
29. A B C D E
30. A B C D E

31. A B C D E
32. A B C D E
33. A B C D E
34. A B C D E
35. A B C D E
36. A B C D E
37. A B C D E
38. A B C D E
39. A B C D E
40. A B C D E

The Princeton Review

Completely darken bubbles with a No. 2 pencil. If you make a mistake, be sure to erase mark completely. Erase all stray marks.

1. YOUR NAME: _____
(Print)   Last   First   M.I.

SIGNATURE: _____   **DATE:** ___ / ___ / ___

HOME ADDRESS: _____
(Print)   Number and Street

_____
City   State   Zip Code

PHONE NO. : _____
(Print)

IMPORTANT: Please fill in these boxes exactly as shown on the back cover of your test book.

2. TEST FORM

3. TEST CODE

4. REGISTRATION NUMBER

5. YOUR NAME

First 4 letters of last name				FIRST INIT	MID INIT

6. DATE OF BIRTH

Month	Day		Year	
JAN				
FEB				
MAR	0	0	0	0
APR	1	1	1	1
MAY	2	2	2	2
JUN	3	3	3	3
JUL		4	4	4
AUG		5	5	5
SEP		7	7	7
OCT		8	8	8
NOV		9	9	9
DEC				

7. SEX
- MALE
- FEMALE

The Princeton Review
© 2006 The Princeton Review, Inc.
FORM NO. 00001-PR

Section 1

Start with number 1 for each new section.
If a section has fewer questions than answer spaces, leave the extra answer spaces blank.

1. A B C D E
2. A B C D E
3. A B C D E
4. A B C D E
5. A B C D E
6. A B C D E
7. A B C D E
8. A B C D E
9. A B C D E
10. A B C D E
11. A B C D E
12. A B C D E
13. A B C D E
14. A B C D E
15. A B C D E

16. A B C D E
17. A B C D E
18. A B C D E
19. A B C D E
20. A B C D E
21. A B C D E
22. A B C D E
23. A B C D E
24. A B C D E
25. A B C D E
26. A B C D E
27. A B C D E
28. A B C D E
29. A B C D E
30. A B C D E

31. A B C D E
32. A B C D E
33. A B C D E
34. A B C D E
35. A B C D E
36. A B C D E
37. A B C D E
38. A B C D E
39. A B C D E
40. A B C D E

NOTES

NOTES

NOTES

NOTES

AP Exams

Cracking the AP Biology Exam,
2006–2007 Edition
0-375-76525-5 • $17.00/C$24.00

Cracking the AP Calculus AB & BC Exams,
2006–2007 Edition
0-375-76526-3 • $18.00/C$26.00

Cracking the AP Chemistry Exam,
2006–2007 Edition
0-375-76527-1 • $17.00/C$24.00

**Cracking the AP Computer Science
A & AB Exams,** 2006–2007 Edition
0-375-76528-X • $19.00/C$27.00

**Cracking the AP Economics (Macro &
Micro) Exams,** 2006–2007 Edition
0-375-76535-2 • $17.00/C$24.00

**Cracking the AP English Language and
Composition Exam,** 2006–2007 Edition
0-375-76536-0 • $17.00/C$24.00

Cracking the AP English Literature Exam,
2006–2007 Edition
0-375-76537-9 • $17.00/C$24.00

**Cracking the AP Environmental
Science Exam,** 2006–2007 Edition
0-375-76538-7 • $17.00/C$24.00

Cracking the AP European History Exam,
2006–2007 Edition
0-375-76539-5 • $17.00/C$24.00

Cracking the AP Physics B & C Exams,
2006–2007 Edition
0-375-76540-9 • $19.00/C$27.00

Cracking the AP Psychology Exam,
2006–2007 Edition
0-375-76529-8 • $17.00/C$24.00

Cracking the AP Spanish Exam,
2006–2007 Edition
0-375-76530-1 • $17.00/C$24.00

Cracking the AP Statistics Exam,
2006–2007 Edition
0-375-76531-X • $19.00/C$27.00

**Cracking the AP U.S. Government
and Politics Exam,** 2006–2007 Edition
0-375-76532-8 • $17.00/C$24.00

Cracking the AP U.S. History Exam,
2006–2007 Edition
0-375-76533-6 • $17.00/C$24.00

Cracking the AP World History Exam,
2006–2007 Edition
0-375-76534-4 • $17.00/C$24.00

SAT Subject Tests

Cracking the SAT Biology E/M Subject Test,
2005-2006 Edition
0-375-76447-X • $19.00/C$27.00

Cracking the SAT Chemistry Subject Test,
2005-2006 Edition
0-375-76448-8 • $18.00/C$26.00

Cracking the SAT French Subject Test,
2005-2006 Edition
0-375-76449-6 • $18.00/C$26.00

Cracking the SAT Literature Subject Test,
2005-2006 Edition
0-375-76446-1 • $18.00/C$26.00

**Cracking the SAT Math 1 and 2
Subject Tests,** 2005-2006 Edition
0-375-76451-8 • $19.00/C$27.00

Cracking the SAT Physics Subject Test,
2005-2006 Edition
0-375-76452-6 • $19.00/C$27.00

Cracking the SAT Spanish Subject Test,
2005-2006 Edition
0-375-76453-4 • $18.00/C$26.00

**Cracking the SAT U.S. & World History
Subject Tests,** 2005-2006 Edition
0-375-76450-X • $19.00/C$27.00

Available at Bookstores Everywhere
PrincetonReview.com

Need More?

If you're looking to learn more about how to excel on the AP Exams, you're in the right place. The Princeton Review has three great options.

Princeton Review for the AP Exams

Our online review programs for 14 different AP Exams include:
- Content that is fully aligned with the actual exam topics
- Tailored study plan
- Full-length diagnostic exam
- Drills that build skills and develop conceptual understanding
- Loads of practice questions, written in the AP Exam format

Private Tutoring

If you need maximum flexibility and test prep tailored to your particular learning style, then this is your preferred option. Tutoring is best if you:
- Learn better with personal instruction
- Need flexibility with dates and locations
- Only need to focus on specific areas of the test or specific academic areas

Cracking the AP Exams Book Series

If you like our *Cracking the AP Computer Science A & AB Exam*, check out:
- *Cracking the AP U.S. History Exam*
- *Cracking the AP Statistics Exam*
- *Cracking the AP Spanish Exam*
- *Cracking the AP Calculus AB & BC Exam*

To learn more, visit *PrincetonReview.com/AP* or call 800-2Review.